Introduction to
ARCHITECTURAL SCIENCE
The basis of sustainable design

Introduction to

ARCHITECTURAL SCIENCE
The basis of sustainable design

Third edition

Steven V. Szokolay

Routledge
Taylor & Francis Group

LONDON AND NEW YORK

First edition published 2003
by Architectural Press

Second edition published 2008
by Architectural Press

Third edition published 2014
by Routledge
2 Park Square, Milton Park, Abingdon, Oxon OX14 4RN

and by Routledge
711 Third Avenue, New York, NY 10017

Routledge is an imprint of the Taylor & Francis Group, an informa business

© 2014 Steven V. Szokolay   **1006973894**

British Library Cataloguing in Publication Data
A catalogue record for this book is available from the British Library

Library of Congress Cataloging in Publication Data
Szokolay, S. V.
Introduction to architectural science : the basis of sustainable design / Steven V. Szokolay. – Third, extended edition.
pages cm
Includes bibliographical references and index.
1. Buildings–Environmental engineering. 2. Sustainable buildings–Design and construction.
I. Title.
TH6021.S965 2014
720'.47–dc23
2013025354

ISBN: 978-0-415-82498-9 (pbk)
ISBN: 978-1-315-85240-9 (ebk)

Typeset in Univers by
Servis Filmsetting Ltd, Stockport, Cheshire

Printed and bound in Great Britain by TJ International Ltd.

CONTENTS

PREFACE TO THE THIRD EDITION

Some terms used in the title of this work need to be defined and explained at the outset.

Architectural Science

The term 'building science' has been well established since at least 1944, when Geeson published his book of that title (English Universities Press) and D. A. G. Reed's book of the same title was published by Longmans. The subject became important after the 1958 Oxford Conference of the RIBA, when it formally became an important part of architectural education.

The same year, the term 'Architectural Science' was introduced by H. J. Cowan, the first professor of that designation at Sydney University, expressing his intention of providing the scientific basis for architectural design. Initially his main concern was the science of materials, construction and structures. He started the publication of the quarterly *Architectural Science Review* and founded the Architectural Science Association (ANZAScA) as primarily an informal grouping of teachers of the subject. Originally this association was concerned with the building fabric, with the physical science aspects of architectural design, later extending the field to include the science of indoor environments, thermal, acoustic and lighting. During my presidency (1982) we included the relevant areas of social sciences.

Subsequently the use of energy and resources in building became the main concern.

Sustainability

In 1972, the United Nations Conference (in Stockholm) on the Human Environment led to the Brundtland Report, and the 1992 UN Conference on Environment and Development (UNCED), the World Summit, in Rio de Janeiro. This had produced the 'Rio Declaration' and the Agenda 21, a programme for the twenty-first century. The extreme green lobby was vociferous in opposing any development, as they thought this to be harmful for the natural environment. However, the third world lobby demanded development, as their right to 'catch up' with the developed world. Finally the consensus has emerged that development is needed and is acceptable as long as it is sustainable. This was defined by Brundtland as 'development that meets the needs of the present without compromising the ability of future generations to meet their own need.'

This became recognised and adapted by (*inter alia*) the International Union of Architects (IUA) Congress in Chicago (1993) and was subsequently endorsed by most national architectural bodies.

Sustainable design

Since then, unfortunately, some extreme exponents of post-modernism came to consider architecture purely as an art-form, denying Sullivan's tenet: 'form follows function'. This has led to the most extravagant, unorthodox, contorted and crazy buildings. The odd few of these can be tolerated here and there in an existing sober and solid urban context, but heaven forbid this becoming the 'norm'. It is pure formalism, at the expense of function and environmental decency.

These became dominant in the glossies, the current fashion in architecture. Many consider 'architectural science' as an oxymoron, some suggesting that in architectural education it is counter-productive, curbing or even destroying any imaginative talent of students. It also gives fuel to the erroneous but general belief of the broad public, that architecture is a luxury, that it is irrelevant to 'real life', to building.

It is contradictory and almost schizophrenic (if not fraudulent) that at the same time many such professionals claim that what they produce is sustainable architecture, sustainable design. Here it is suggested that without science, architecture cannot be sustainable. Science is not opposed to design, it does not compete with or replace design, but it is part and parcel of it. The designer can only exercise his/her imagination if the physical basis is understood. Scientific understanding should permeate the intuitive, inventive design. Science can give valuable design tools but it can also provide checking tools for use as the design develops.

As far as architecture itself is considered, I rather like the 'cocktail shaker' analogy. I know that *analogia non probat*, that analogy is not a proof, but it is usefully indicative. Science is one of the inputs into the shaker, along with materials, construction and structures studies as well as some social sciences. In a cocktail the individual inputs, such as basil, chilli or bitters, may not be enjoyable, but they are essential ingredients. The design studio (and design practice) are the cocktail shakers. The technique of shaking, the rhythm, the movement, the often associated dance-steps, possibly even some singing are unimportant, as long as all the ingredients are there and are well shaken.

Some years ago, the (then) head of a school of architecture where Architectural Science has been abolished as a subject, in response to my query, explained that there is no one to teach it and there is no textbook to present the relevant knowledge in a rigorous and disciplined manner. This gave me the first impetus some ten years ago to attempt to produce such a book. I made use of many of my lecture notes accumulated over a teaching career of some 30 years, but supplementing and extending these with much new matter, with recent developments. What follows is the result of this attempt.

INTRODUCTION

Four chains of thought led to the idea of this book and to the definition of its content:

1 It can no longer be disputed that the resources of this Earth are finite, that its capacity to absorb our wastes is limited, that if we (as a species) want to survive, we cannot continue our ruthless exploitation of the environment. Where our actions would affect the environment, we must act in a sustainable manner. There are many good books that deal with the need for sustainability (e.g. Vale and Vale, 1991; Farmer, 1999; Roaf *et al.*, 2001; Smith, 2001, Beggs, 2002, Brophy and Lewis, 2011). This book assumes that the reader is in agreement with these tenets and needs no further persuasion.

2 Architecture is the art and science of building. There exists a large literature on architecture as an art, on the cultural and social significance of architecture – there is no need to discuss these issues here.

3 The term 'bioclimatic architecture' was coined by Victor Olgyay in the early 1950s and fully explained in his book, *Design with Climate* (1963). He synthesised elements of human physiology, climatology and building physics, with a strong advocacy of architectural regionalism and of designing in sympathy with the environment. In many ways he can be considered an important progenitor of what we now call 'sustainable architecture'.

4 Architecture, as a profession, is involved in huge investments of money and resources. Our professional responsibility is great, not only to our clients and to society, but also for sustainable development. Many excellent books and other publications deal with sustainable development in qualitative terms. However, professional responsibility demands expertise and competence. It is in this narrow area where this work intends to supplement the existing literature.

This book is intended to give an introduction to architectural science, to provide an understanding of the physical phenomena we are to deal with and to provide the tools for realising the many good intentions. Many projects in recent times claim to constitute sustainable development, to be sustainable architecture. But are they really green or sustainable? Some new terms have started appearing in the literature, such as 'greenwash' – meaning that a conventional building is designed and then claimed to be 'green'. Or 'pure rhetoric – no substance', with the same meaning.

My hope is that after absorbing the contents of this modest work, the reader will be able to answer this question. After all, the main aim of any education is to develop a critical faculty.

Building environments affect us through our sensory organs:

1 the eye, i.e. vision, a condition of which is light and lighting; the aim is to ensure visual comfort but also to facilitate visual performance;
2 the ear, i.e. hearing: appropriate conditions for listening to wanted sound must be ensured, but also the elimination (or control) of unwanted sound: noise;
3 thermal sensors, located over the whole body surface, in the skin; this is not just a sensory channel, as the body itself produces heat and has a number of adjustment mechanisms but it can function only within a fairly narrow range of temperatures and only an even narrower range would be perceived as comfortable. Thermal conditions appropriate for human well-being must be ensured.

What is important for the designer is to be able to control the indoor environmental conditions: heat, light and sound. Reyner Banham (1969) in his *Architecture of the Well-tempered Environment* postulated that comfortable conditions can be provided by a building itself (passive control) or by the use of energy (active control), and that if we had an unlimited supply of energy, we could ensure comfort even without a building. In most real cases, it is a mixture (or synergy) of the two kinds of control we would be relying on.

In this day and age, when it is realised that our traditional energy sources (coal, oil, gas) are finite and their rapidly increasing use has serious environmental consequences (CO_2 emissions, global warming, as well as local atmospheric pollution), it should be the designer's aim to ensure the required indoor conditions with little or no use of energy, other than from ambient or renewable sources.

Therefore the designer's task is:

1 to examine the given conditions (site conditions, climate, daylight, noise climate);
2 to establish the limits of desirable or acceptable conditions (temperatures, lighting and acceptable noise levels);
3 to attempt to control these variables (heat, light and sound) by passive means (by the building itself) as far as practicable;
4 to provide for energy-based services (heating, cooling, electric lighting, amplification or masking sound) only for the residual control task.

The building is not just a shelter, or a barrier against unwanted influences (rain, wind, cold), but the building envelope should be considered a *selective filter*: to exclude the unwanted influences, but admit the desirable and useful ones, such as daylight, solar radiation in winter or natural ventilation.

The book consists of four parts:

1 **Heat: the thermal environment**
2 **Light: the luminous environment**
3 **Sound: the sonic environment**
4 **Resources: energy, water, materials**

In each Part the relevant physical principles are reviewed, followed by a discussion of their relationship to humans (comfort and human requirements). Then the control functions of the building (passive controls) are examined as well as associated installations, energy-using 'active' controls. The emphasis is on how these can be considered in design. Part 1 (Heat) is the most substantial, as the thermal behaviour of a building has the greatest effect on energy use and sustainability and its design is fully the architect's responsibility. In other areas there may be specialist consulting engineers to provide assistance.

Each Part concludes with a series of data sheets relating to that Part, together with some 'methods sheets', describing some calculation and design procedures.

PART 1   HEAT: THE THERMAL ENVIRONMENT

CONTENTS

SYMBOLS AND ABBREVIATIONS (SYMBOL, DEFINITION, UNIT)

Symbol	Definition	Unit
asg	alternating solar gain factor	–
asp	aspect ratio	
b	breadth, thickness	m
clo	unit of clothing insulation	
dTe	sol-air excess temperature (difference)	K
er	evaporation rate	kg/h
f	response factor	–
k	linear heat loss coefficient	W/m.K
met	unit of metabolic heat (58.2 W/m^2)	
mr	mass flow rate	kg/s
p	pressure	Pa
pt	total atmospheric pressure	Pa
pv	vapour pressure	Pa

Symbol	Definition	Unit
pv_s	saturation vapour pressure	Pa
q	building conductance (spec. heat loss rate)	W/K
qa	total admittance	W/K
qc	envelope conductance	W/K
qv	ventilation conductance	W/K
h	surface conductance	W/m^{2}K
h_c	convective surface conductance	W/m^{2}K
h_r	radiative surface conductance	W/m^{2}K
sM	specific mass (per floor area)	kg/m^2
sQ	swing in heat flow rate (from mean)	W
sT	swing in temperature (from mean)	K

SYMBOLS AND ABBREVIATIONS (Continued)

t	time	hour	Q_e	evaporative heat loss rate	W	
v	velocity	m/s	Q_i	internal heat gain rate	W	
vr	volume flow rate (ventilation rate)	m^3/s, L/s	Q_s	solar heat gain rate	W	
vR	vapour resistance	$MPa.s.m^2$/g	Q_v	ventilation heat flow rate	W	
y	year		R	resistance	m^2K/W	
A	area	m^2	R_{a-a}	air-to-air resistance	m^2K/W	
AH	absolute humidity	g/kg	R_c	cavity resistance	m^2K/W	
ALT	solar altitude angle	°	Rd	radiation, radiated heat (from body)	W	
AZI	solar azimuth angle	°	RH	relative humidity	%	
C	conductance	W/m^2K	R_s	surface resistance	m^2K/W	
Cd	conduction, conducted heat (from body)	W	R_{si}	internal surface resistance	m^2K/W	
			R_{so}	outside surface resistance	m^2K/W	
CDD	cooling degree-days	Kd	SD	standard deviation		
CoP	coefficient of performance	–	SET	standard effective temperature	°	
CPZ	control potential zone		SH	saturation point humidity	g/kg	
Cv	convection, convected heat (from body)	W	SI	Système International (of units)		
			T	temperature	°C	
D	daily total irradiation Wh/m^2	MJ/m^2	T_b	balance point (base~) temperature	°C	
D_v	daily total vertical irradiation Wh/m^2	MJ/m^2	TIL	tilt angle	°	
DBT	dry bulb temperature	°C	T_i	indoor temperature	°C	
DD	degree-days	Kd	T_n	neutrality temperature	°C	
DEC	solar declination angle	°	T_o	outdoor temperature	°C	
Dh	degree-hours	Kh	T_s	surface temperature	°C	
DPT	dew-point temperature	°C	T_{s-a}	sol-air temperature	°C	
DRT	dry resultant temperature	°C	U	air-to-air (thermal) transmittance	W/m^2K	
E	radiant heat emission	W	V	volume	m^3	
EnvT	environmental temperature	°C	VSA	vertical shadow angle	°	
ET*	new effective temperature	°C	WBT	wet bulb temperature	°C	
Ev	evaporation heat transfer (from body)	W	Y	admittance	W/m^2K	
G	global irradiance	W/m^2				
GT	globe temperature	°C	α	absorptance, or thermal diffusivity	–	
H	enthalpy (heat content)	kJ/kg	δ	vapour permeability	µg/m.s.Pa	
HDD	heating degree-days	Kd	ε	emittance	–	
H_L	latent heat content	kJ/kg	η	efficiency	–	
H_s	sensible heat content	kJ/kg	θ	solar gain factor	–	
HSA	horizontal shadow angle	°	$θ_a$	alternating solar gain factor	–	
Htg	heating requirement	(kWh) Wh	κ	conductivity correction factor	–	
INC	angle of incidence	°	λ	conductivity	W/m.K	
Kd	Kelvin days	Kd	µ	decrement factor	–	
Kh	Kelvin hours	Kh	π	vapour permeance	$µg/m^2.s.Pa$	
L	length (linear thermal bridges)	m	ρ	density, or reflectance	kg/m^3 or –	
LAT	geographical latitude angle	°	τ	transmittance	–	
M	metabolic heat production	W	φ	time lag	h	
Mb	body mass	kg	σ	Stefan-Boltzmann constant	W/m^2K^4	
MRT	mean radiant temperature	°C	Σ	sum of . . .	–	
N	number of air changes per hour	–	Δp	pressure difference	Pa	
ORI	orientation angle	°	ΔS	rate of change in stored heat	W	
Q	heat flux or heat flow rate	W	ΔT	temperature difference, interval or increment	K	
Qc	conduction heat flow rate	W				

SUBSCRIPTS TO G AND D

first		b	beam~			v	vertical
		d	diffuse~			p	on plane p
		r	reflected~	for G only		n	normal to radiation
second		h	horizontal				

LIST OF FIGURES

LIST OF FIGURES (Continued)

LIST OF TABLES

LIST OF WORKED EXAMPLES

LIST OF EQUATIONS

1.1 PHYSICS OF HEAT

1.1.1 Heat and temperature

Heat is a form of energy, contained in substances as molecular motion or appearing as electromagnetic radiation in space. Energy is the ability or capacity for doing work and it is measured in the same units. The derivation of this unit from the basic MKS (m, kg, s) units in the SI (Système International) is quite simple and logical, as shown in Table 1.1.

Temperature (T) is the symptom of the presence of heat in a substance. The Celsius scale is based on water: its freezing point taken as 0°C and its boiling point (at normal atmospheric pressure) as 100°C. The Kelvin scale starts with the 'absolute zero', the total absence of heat. Thus 0°C = 273.15°K. The temperature interval is the same in both scales. By convention, a point on the scale is denoted °C (degree Celsius) but the notation for a temperature difference or interval is K (Kelvin), which is a certain length of the scale, without specifying where it is on the overall scale (Fig. 1.1). Thus 40°C–10°C = 30 K, and similarly 65°C–35°C is 30 K but 15°C, as a point on the scale, is 288.15°K.

The **specific heat** concept provides the connection between heat and temperature. This is the quantity of heat required to elevate the temperature of unit mass of a substance by one degree, thus it is measured in units of **J/kg.K**. Its magnitude is different for different materials and it varies between 100 and 800 J/kg.K for metals, 800–1200 J/kg.K for masonry materials (brick, concrete) to water, which has the highest value of all common substances: 4176 J/kg.K (see Data sheet D.1.1).

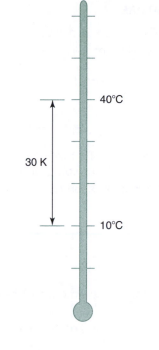

1.1

Temperature scale and interval

Table 1.1 Derivation of composite SI units for thermal quantities

length	m	(metre)
mass	kg	(kilogram)
time	s	(second)
velocity, speed	m/s	That is unit length movement in unit time, the everyday unit is km/h, which is 1000m / 3600 s = 0.278 m/s or conversely: 1 m/s = 3.6 km/h
acceleration	m/s^2	That is unit velocity increase in unit time: (m/s)/s
force	kg.m/s^2	That which gives unit acceleration to unit mass called newton (**N**)
work, energy	kg.m^2/s^2	Unit work is done when unit force is acting over unit length, i.e. N × m called joule (**J**)
power, energy flow rate	kg.m^2/s^3	unit energy flow in unit time or unit work done in unit time, i.e. J / s called watt (**W**)
pressure, stress	kg/m.s^2	unit force acting on unit area (kg.m/s^2)/m^2, i.e. N / m^2 called pascal (**Pa**)

Note: SI unit symbols, derived from personal names, are always capitalised.

EXAMPLE 1.1 SPECIFIC HEAT AND TEMPERATURE

Given 0.5 L (= 0.5 kg) of water at 20°C in an electric jug with an 800 W immersion heater element (efficiency: 1.0 or 100%). How long will it take to bring it to the boil?

   requirement: 0.5 kg × 4176 J/kg.K × (100 – 20) K = 167 040 J

   heat input 800 W, i.e. 800 J/s, thus the time required is

   167 040 J / 800 J/s ≈ 208 s » 3.5 minutes.

Latent heat of a substance is the amount of heat (energy) absorbed by unit mass of the substance at change of state (from solid to liquid or liquid to gaseous) without any change in temperature. This is measured in kJ/kg, e.g. for water:

the latent heat of fusion (ice to water) at 0°C = 335 kJ/kg (= J/g)
the latent heat of evaporation at 100°C   = 2261 kJ/kg
at about 18°C   = 2400 kJ/kg

At a change of state in the reverse direction, the same amount of heat is released.

Thermodynamics is the science of the flow of heat and of its relationship to mechanical work.

The *first law* of thermodynamics is the principle of conservation of energy. Energy cannot be created or destroyed (except in sub-atomic processes), but only converted from one form to another. Heat and work are interconvertible. In any system, the energy output must equal the energy input, unless there is a +/− storage component.

The *second law* of thermodynamics states that heat (or energy) transfer can take place spontaneously in one direction only: from a hotter to a cooler body, or generally from a higher to a lower grade state (same as water flow will take place only downhill). Only with an external energy input can a machine deliver heat in the opposite direction (water will move upwards only if it is pumped).Temperature can only be increased by energy (work) input, e.g. by a heat pump (see Fig. 1.98 on p. 85). Any machine to perform work must have an energy source and a sink, i.e. energy must flow through the machine: only part of this flow can be turned into work.

Heat flow from a high to a low temperature zone can take place in three forms: conduction, convection and radiation. The magnitude of any such flow can be measured in two ways:

1 as *heat flow rate* (Q), or heat flux, i.e. the total flow in unit time through a defined area of a body or space, or within a defined system, in units of J/s, which is a watt (W). (The most persistent archaic energy flow rate or power unit is the *horsepower*, but in fully metric countries even car engines are now rated in terms of kW.)

2 as *heat flux density* (or density of heat flow rate), i.e. the rate of heat flow through unit area of a body or space, in W/m². The multiple kW (kilowatt = 1000 W) is often used for both quantities. (The term 'density' as used here is analogous with e.g. population density, i.e. people per unit area, or with surface density, i.e. kg mass per unit area of a wall or other building element.)

A non-standard, but accepted and very convenient unit of energy is derived from this heat flux unit: the watt-hour (Wh). This is the amount of energy delivered or expended if a flow rate (flux) of 1 W is maintained for an hour.

As 1 hour = 3600 s
and 1 W = 1 J/s
thus 1 Wh = 3600s × 1 J/s = 3600 J = 3.6 kJ.

The multiple kWh (kilowatt-hour) is often used as a practical unit of energy (e.g. in electricity accounts). 1 kWh = 3 600 000 J = 3600 kJ = 3.6 MJ (megajoule).

1.1.2 Heat flow

As water flows from a higher to a lower position, so heat flows from a higher temperature zone (or body) to a lower temperature one. Such heat flow can take place in three forms:

1 *Conduction* within a body or bodies in contact, by the 'spread' of molecular movement.
2 *Convection* from a solid body to a fluid (liquid or gas) or vice versa (in a broader sense it is also used to mean the transport of heat from one surface to another by a moving fluid, which, strictly speaking, is 'mass transfer'). The magnitude of convection heat flow rate depends on
  a area of contact (A, m^2) between the body and the fluid;
  b the difference in temperature (ΔT, in K) between the surface of the body and the fluid;
  c a convection coefficient (h_c) measured in W/m^2K, which depends on the viscosity of the fluid and its flow velocity as well as on the physical configuration that will determine whether the flow is laminar or turbulent (see Section 1.1.2.2).
3 *Radiation* from a body with a warmer surface to another which is cooler. Thermal radiation is a wavelength band of electromagnetic radiation, normally taken as 700 nm* to 10 000 nm (10 μm)**

'short infrared' 700–2300 nm (2.3 μm) (see Section 1.3.1.2);
'long infrared' 2.3–10 μm (some suggest up to 70 μm).

The temperature of the emitting body determines the wavelength. The sun with its 6000°C surface emits short infrared (as well as visible and ultraviolet), bodies at terrestrial temperatures (<100°C) emit long infrared radiation. (Fig. 1.2 shows these bands in relation to the full electro-magnetic spectrum.) See also Fig. 2.4 in Section 2.1.1.1.

In all three forms, the magnitude of flux (or of flux density) depends on the temperature difference between the points (or surfaces) considered, while the flux (heat flow rate) in conduction also depends on the cross-sectional area of the body available.

---

* 1 nm (nanometre) = 10^{-9} m.
** 1 μm (micrometre) = 10^{-6} m.

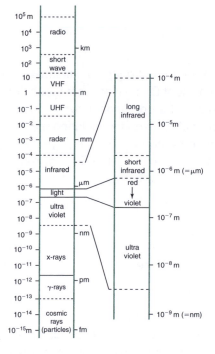

1.2
Electromagnetic radiation spectrum

WAVE-BAND SUMMARY:

< 280 nm	UV 'C'
280–315	UV 'B'
380–780	UV 'A'
380–780	light
–	overlap with thermal:
700–2300	short IR
2300–10000	long IR

1.1.2.1 Conduction

Conduction depends also on a property of the material known as *conductivity* (λ), measured as the heat flow density (W/m^2) in a 1 m thick body (i.e. the length of heat flow path is 1 m), with a 1 degree temperature difference, in units of W.m/m^{2}K = W/m.K.

As insulating materials are either fibrous or porous, they are very sensitive to moisture content. If the pores are filled with water, the conductivity will increase quite drastically. Take a porous, fibrous-cement insulating board:

	Density: kg/m³	*Conductivity: W/m.K*
Dry	136	0.051
Wet	272	0.144
soaked	400	0.203

Materials with a foam (closed pore) structure are not quite as sensitive.

Some conductivity values are given in Data sheet D.1.1. Note that these are 'declared values', based on laboratory testing. The operational conditions in transportation and on building sites are such that damage to insulating materials is often inevitable, reducing their insulating properties. Before using such λ values for U-value calculations, they should be corrected by one or more conductivity correction factors: κ (kappa), which are additive:

$$\lambda_{design} = \lambda_{declared} \times (1 + \kappa_1 + \kappa_2. ...)$$

If from Data sheet D.1.1, for EPS $\lambda_{declared} = 0.035$, and it will be used as external insulation over a brick wall, with cement rendering applied directly to it (with a wire mesh insert), from Table 1.2: $\kappa = 0.25$, then

$$\lambda_{design}. = 0.035 \times (1 + 0.25) = 0.0438 \text{ W/m.K.}$$

Conductivity is a material property, regardless of its shape or size. The corresponding property of a physical body (e.g. a wall) is the *conductance* (C) measured between the two surfaces of the wall. For a single layer, it is the conductivity, divided by thickness (λ/b). It is a rarely used quantity. *Transmittance*, or U-value, includes the surface effects and it is the most frequently used measure. This is the heat flow density (W/m^2) with 1 K temperature difference (DT) between air inside and air outside (see Fig. 1.3), in units of **W/m^{2}K.**

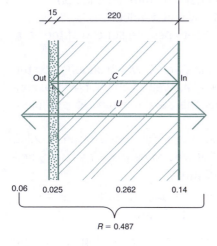

15   220

Out   C   In

U

0.06   0.025   0.262   0.14

R = 0.487

1.3

Example wall section: C and U

Table 1.2 Conductivity correction factors

Material	Condition of use	κ
Expanded polystyrene	Between cast concrete layers	0.42
	Between masonry wall layers	0.10
	In ventilated air gap (cavity)	0.30
	With cement render applied	0.25
Mineral wool	Between masonry wall layers	0.10
Polyurethane	In ventilated air gap (cavity)	0.15

For U-values, see Data sheets D.1.2 and D.1.3.

If ΔT is always taken as $T_o - T_i$, then a negative value (thus also a negative Q) will indicate heat loss, while a positive value would mean heat gain.

EXAMPLE 1.2   HEAT LOSS: THE U-VALUE

If the outside temperature is $T_o = 10°C$, and the inside is $T_i = 22°C$, thus $\Delta T = 10 - 22 = -12$ K (the negative indicating a heat loss).

Over a 10 m² brick wall (U = 1.5 W/m²K) the heat flow rate will be

$$\boxed{Q = A \times U \times \Delta T)}$$

(1.1)

$$Q = 10 \times 1.5 \times (-12) = -180 \text{ W}$$

It is often useful to do a 'dimensional check' for such expressions:

$$m^2 \times \frac{W}{m^2 K} \times K = W$$

The reciprocal of the U-value is the air-to-air *resistance* ($R_{a\text{-}a}$, in m²K/W), which is the sum of component resistances: resistances of the surfaces and of the body of the element (wall, roof, etc.), e.g. for a wall of two layers:

$$R_{a-a} = R_{si} + R_1 + R_2 + R_{so}$$

(1.2)

The R-value of any homogeneous layer is its thickness (b* for breadth) in m, divided by the conductivity of its material:

$$R = \frac{b}{\lambda}$$

(1.3)

The reciprocal of this resistance is *conductance*, C in W/m²K.

Layers, through which heat flows, can be represented as resistances in series, thus the resistances of layers are additive (see Fig. 1.56 on p. 44).

Various elements of an envelope are heat flow paths (with resistances) in parallel, and in this case the (area weighted) conductances (transmittances) are additive (see Fig. 1.55 in Section 1.4.3.1).

For example, Fig. 1.3 shows a 220 mm brick wall ($\lambda = 0.84$ W/m.K), with a 15 mm cement render ($\lambda = 0.6$ W/m.K) and surface resistances of $R_{si} = 0.14$ and $R_{so} = 0.06$ m²K.W (values taken from Data sheets D.1.1 and D.1.4).

$$R_{body} = \frac{0.220}{0.84} + \frac{0.015}{0.6} = 0.287 \text{ thus}$$

$$C = \frac{1}{R_{body}} = \frac{1}{0.287} = 3.484 \text{ W/m}^2\text{K}$$

$$R_{a-a} = 0.14 + \frac{0.220}{0.84} + \frac{0.015}{0.6} + 0.06 = 0.487$$

$$= 0.14 + 0.287 + 0.06 = 0.487, \text{ thus } U = \frac{1}{R_{a-a}} = \frac{1}{0.487} = 2.054 \text{ W/m}^2\text{K}$$

---

* 'b' is used for thickness (breadth) to distinguish it from 't' for time and 'T' for temperature in equation (1.3).

The surface resistance depends on the degree of exposure and – to some extent – on surface qualities.

The surface resistance combines the resistances to convection and radiation, thus it is affected by radiation properties of the surface, as discussed below in Section 1.1.2.3 on radiation.

1.1.2.2 Convection

Convection heat transfer is a function of the *convection coefficient*, h_c (in W/m^2K):

$$\boxed{Q_{cv} = A \times h_c \times \Delta T} \quad m^2 \times W/m^2K \times K = W \tag{1.4}$$

The magnitude of h_c depends on the position of the surface, the direction of the heat flow and the velocity of the fluid, e.g.

- for vertical surfaces (horizontal heat flow) $h_c = 3 \ W/m^2K$
- for horizontal surfaces:
  - heat flow up (air to ceiling, floor to room air) 4.3 W/m^2K
  - heat flow down (air to floor, ceiling to room air) 1.5 W/m^2K
  (as hot air rises, the upward heat transfer is stronger).

In the above, still air is assumed (i.e. air flow is due to the heat transfer only). If the surface is exposed to wind, or mechanically generated air movement (i.e. if it is forced convection), then the convection coefficient is much higher:

- $h_c = 5.8 + 4.1 \ v$ where v is air velocity in m/s.

1.1.2.3 Radiation

Radiation heat transfer is proportional to the difference of the 4th power of absolute temperatures of the emitting and receiving surfaces, and depends on their surface qualities:

- *Reflectance* ρ (rho) is a decimal fraction indicating how much of the incident radiation is reflected by a surface.
- *absorptance* α (alpha) is expressed as a fraction of that of the 'perfect absorber', the theoretical black body (for which $\alpha = 1$), and its value is high for dark surfaces, low for light or shiny metallic surfaces. For everyday surfaces, it varies between $\alpha = 0.9$ for a black asphalt and $\alpha = 0.2$ for a shiny aluminium or white painted surface. For any opaque surface, $\rho + \alpha = 1$.
- *emittance* ε (epsilon) is also a decimal fraction, a measure of the ability to emit radiation, relative to the 'black body', the perfect emitter. For an ordinary surface, $\alpha = \varepsilon$ for the same wavelength (or temperature) of radiation, but many surfaces have selective properties, e.g. high absorptance for solar (6000°C) radiation but low emittance at ordinary temperatures (< 100°C), e.g.:

$$\alpha_{6000} > \varepsilon_{60}$$

Such *selective surfaces* are useful for the absorber panels of solar collectors, but the reverse is desirable where heat dissipation (radiation to the sky) is to be promoted:

$$\alpha_{6000} < \varepsilon_{60}$$

The expression for radiant heat transfer between two opposed parallel surfaces is

$$Q = A \times \sigma \times \varepsilon \left[\left(\frac{T'}{100} \right)^4 - \left(\frac{T''}{100} \right)^4 \right]$$

where (sigma) $\sigma = 5.67 \ W/m^2K^4$ (it is the Stefan-Boltzmann constant) and T is in °K (°C + 273)
and (epsilon) ε is the effective emittance

$$\frac{1}{\varepsilon} = \frac{1}{\varepsilon'} + \frac{1}{\varepsilon''} - 1$$

for everyday calculations a radiation (h_r) coefficient can be derived

$$h_r = 5.7 \times \varepsilon \frac{(T'/100)^4 - (T''/100)^4}{t' - t''}$$

then $Qr = h_r \times A \times (t' - t'')$
typically $h_r = 5.7 \times \varepsilon$ at 20°C
$\qquad h_r = 4.6 \times \varepsilon$ at 0°C
$\varepsilon = 0.9$ for ordinary building surfaces
$\varepsilon = 0.2$ for dull aluminium
$\varepsilon = 0.05$ for polished aluminium

In the above T is in °K and t is in °C

White paints (especially a titanium oxide) have such properties.

A shiny metal surface is non-selective:

$$\alpha_{6000} = \varepsilon_{60}$$

Reflectance, ρ, may be the same for a white and a shiny metal surface, but emittance $\varepsilon_{white} > \varepsilon_{shiny}$, so e.g. in a hot climate a white roof is better than a shiny one.

The calculation of radiant heat exchange is complicated, but it is quite simple for the effect which is most important for buildings: solar radiation. If the flux density of incident radiation is known (referred to as global irradiance, G), then the radiant (solar) heat input rate will be:

$$Q_s = A \times G \times \alpha \qquad m^2 \times W/m^2 \times \text{non-dim.} = W \qquad (1.5)$$

1.1.3 Humid air: psychrometry

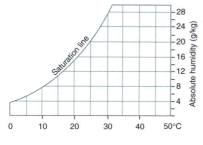

1.4

Structure of the psychrometric chart

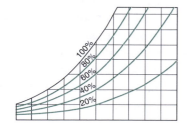

1.5

Relative humidity curves

(Not to be confused with 'psychometry', which means psychological measurement; this one has an '**r**' in the middle.)

Air is a mixture of oxygen and nitrogen, but the atmosphere around us is humid air, it contains varying amounts of water vapour. At any given temperature the air can only support a limited amount of water vapour, when it is said to be saturated. Fig. 1.4 shows the basic structure of the psychrometric chart: the dry bulb (air) temperature on the horizontal axis and moisture content (or *absolute humidity*, AH) on the vertical axis (in units of g/kg, grams of moisture per kg of dry air).

The top curve is the *saturation line*, indicating the maximum moisture content the air could support at any temperature, which is the *saturation humidity* (SH). Each vertical ordinate can be subdivided (Fig. 1.5 shows a subdivision into five equal parts) and the curves connecting these points show the relative humidity (RH) in percentage, i.e. as a percentage of the saturation humidity. In this case the 20, 40, 60 and 80% RH curves are shown.

For example (with reference to Fig. 1.9, the full psychrometric chart), at 25°C the saturation AH is 20 g/kg. Halving the ordinate we get 10 g/kg, which is half of the saturation humidity or 50% RH.

Another expression of humidity is the vapour pressure (pv), i.e. the partial pressure of water vapour in the given atmosphere. The saturation vapour pressure is pv_s. This can be estimated by the Antonine equation:

$$pv_s = 0.1333222 \times \exp\left[18.686 - 4030.183 / (T + 235)\right]$$

Thus, RH = (AH/SH) × 100 or (pv/pv_s) × 100 (in %). Vapour pressure is linearly related to AH and the two scales are parallel:

$$AH = \frac{622 \times pv}{pt - pv} \quad \text{conversely} \quad pv = \frac{AH \times pt}{622 + AH} \qquad (1.6)$$

where pt = total barometric pressure, taken as 101.325 kPa ('standard atmosphere').

e.g. if pv = 2 kPa, AH = (622 × 2) / (101.325−2) = 12.5 g/kg (see Fig. 1.9).

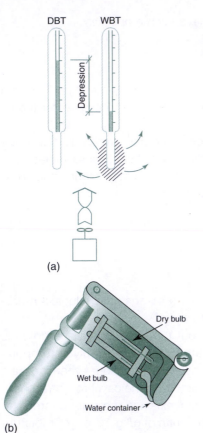

(a)

(b)

1.6

Psychrometer and whirling hygrometer

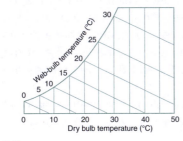

1.7

Wet bulb temperature lines

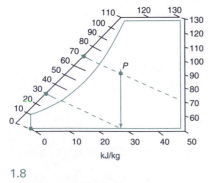

1.8

Enthalpy scales extrenally

Humidity is best measured by the wet-and-dry bulb (whirling) *psychrometer* or an aspirated psychrometer (Fig. 1.6). These contain two thermometers. One has its bulb wrapped in a gauze, which is kept moist from a small water container. When whirled around (or the fan is operated) to obtain maximum possible evaporation, this produces a cooling effect, showing the *wet bulb temperature* (WBT). The other thermometer measures the air or dry bulb temperature (DBT). The difference DBT − WBT is referred to as the *wet bulb depression* and it is indicative of the humidity. Evaporation is inversely proportional to humidity. In saturated air there is no evaporation, no cooling, thus WBT = DBT. With low humidity there is strong evaporation, strong cooling and a large wet bulb depression.

Fig. 1.7 shows the sloping WBT lines on the psychrometric chart. These coincide with the DBT at the saturation curve. When a measurement is made, the intersection of the DBT and WBT lines can be marked on the psychrometric chart; it will be referred to as the *status point*, which indicates both the RH (interpolated between the RH curves) and the AH values (read on the right-hand vertical scale).

For example, (from Fig. 1.9), if DBT = 29°C and WBT = 23°C have been measured and plotted, the two lines intersect at the 60% RH curve and on the vertical scale the AH is read as just over 15 g/kg.

For any point P of a wet-bulb line, the X-axis intercept will be:

$$T = T_P + AH_P \times (2501 - 1.805 \times 24)/1000 \; °C \tag{1.7}$$

e.g. if $T_P = 25$, $AH_P = 10$ g/kg

$$T = 25 + 10 \times (2501 - 1.805 \times 24)/1000$$

$$= 49.6°C \text{ (verifiable from Fig. 1.9).}$$

Enthalpy (H) is the heat content of the air relative to 0°C and 0 humidity. It is measured in kJ/kg, i.e. the heat content of 1 kg air. It has two components: *sensible heat* (H_S), taken up to increase the dry bulb temperature (approx. 1.005 kJ/kg.K) and *latent heat* (H_L), i.e. the heat that was necessary to evaporate liquid water to form the moisture content of the air. As the constant enthalpy lines almost coincide with the WBT lines (but not quite), to avoid confusion, it is indicated by duplicate scales on either side, outside of the body of the psychrometric chart, which are used with a straight edge (Fig. 1.8).

If enthalpy is the diagonal distance of the status point from the 0°C and 0 RH point, then the horizontal component is the H_S and the vertical component is the H_L.

Specific volume of air at any condition is also shown on the chart by a set of steeply sloping lines (Fig. 1.10). This is the volume of air occupied by 1 kg of air (at normal pressure), in m³/kg. It is the reciprocal of density, kg/m³.

Psychrometric processes or changes can be traced on the chart in Fig. 1.9.

Heating is represented by the status point moving horizontally to the right. As the DBT increases, with no change in moisture content, the relative humidity is reducing (Fig. 1.11).

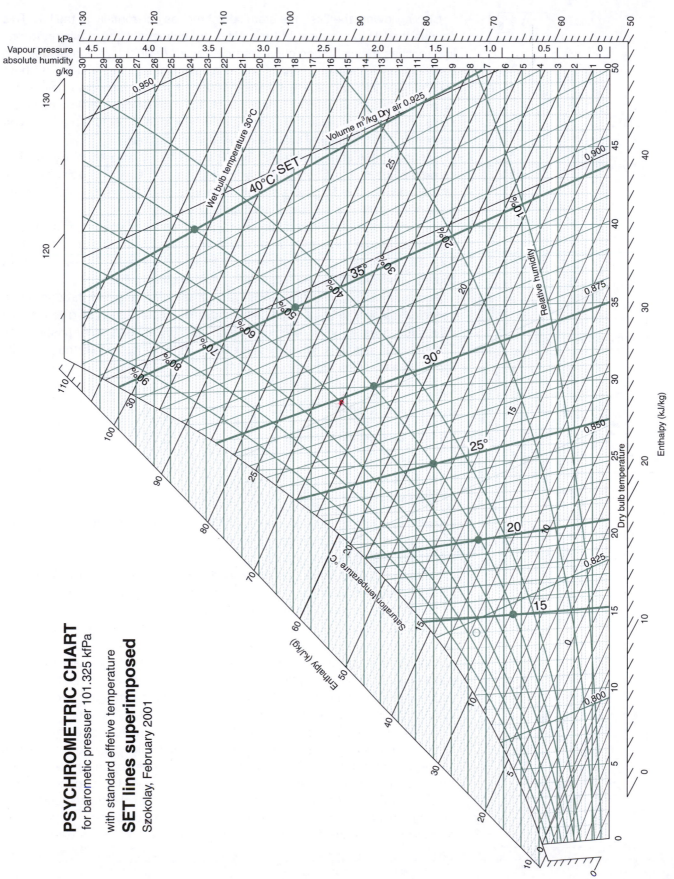

PSYCHROMETRIC CHART
for barometic pressuer 101.325 kfPa

with standard effetive temperature
SET lines superimposed
Szokolay, February 2001

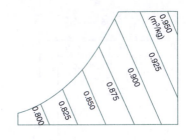

1.10
Specific volume lines

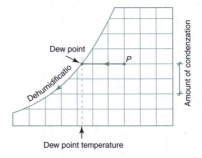

1.11
Cooling and heating

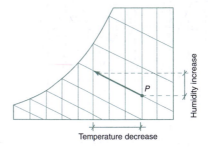

1.12
Cooling to reduce humidity

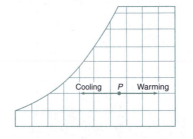

1.13
Evaporative cooling: humidification

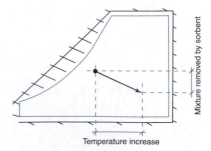

1.14
Adiabatic dehumidification

Cooling lowers the DBT, the status point moves horizontally to the left. This causes the RH to increase, but the AH is not changed. Where this horizontal line reaches the saturation curve, the *dew-point temperature* (corresponding to the given AH) can be read. For the above example this will be at about 20.5°C. At this point, the RH will be 100%. If the air is cooled below this point, condensation will start, dew will be formed. Below the dew point the status point moves along the saturation curve and the absolute humidity corresponding to the vertical drop will have condensed out.

Continuing the above example, the 29°C air of 15.2 g/kg AH (60% RH) has its dew-point at 20.5°C, and if it is cooled to, say, 15°C, at this point its (saturated) AH would be 10.5 g/kg, so the difference of 15.2 −10.5 = 4.7 g/kg will have condensed out in liquid form (Fig. 1.12).

Humidification, i.e. evaporation of moisture into an air volume, is said to be adiabatic, if no heat is added or removed. This causes a reduction of temperature (DBT) but an increase of humidity (both AH and RH). The status point moves up to the left, along a constant WBT line (Fig. 1.13).

Adiabatic *dehumidification* takes place when air is passed through some chemical sorbent (a solid, such as silica gel, or a liquid, such as glycol spray) which removes some of the moisture content (by absorption or adsorption). This process releases heat, thus the DBT will increase, while the humidity (both AH and RH) is reduced (Fig. 1.14).

1.1.4   Air flow

Air flow can be characterised by:

velocity	v	m/s
mass flow rate	mr	kg/s
volume flow rate	vr	m³/s or L/s

Volume flow rate through an opening of A area is **vr = v × A**, e.g. a velocity of v = 0.5 m/s, through a window of A = 1.5 m² will give a flow rate of vr = 0.5 × 1.5 = 0.75 m³/s or 750 L/s.

Natural air flow is caused by pressure difference: it will flow from a zone of higher pressure towards a lower pressure. Pressure differences may be due to two effects: stack effect or wind effect.

Stack effect occurs when the air inside a vertical stack is warmer than the outside air (provided that there are both inlet and outlet openings). The warmer air will rise and will be replaced at the bottom of the stack by cooler outside air. A good example of this is a chimney flue: when heated, it will cause a considerable 'draught'. Ventilating shafts are often used for internal bathrooms or toilets, which are quite successful in a cool climate.

The stack effect can also occur within a room of significant height, if it has both a high level outlet and a low level inlet. The air flow will be proportional to the height difference between the inlet and outlet openings and to the temperature difference between the air within the stack (or room air) and the outdoor air (Fig. 1.15). In low-rise buildings such stack effects are quite small, but, for example, in the staircase of a multistorey building, it can develop into a howling gale. In warm climates the outdoor air may be just as warm as the

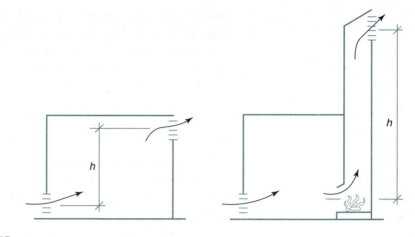

1.15
Stack effect

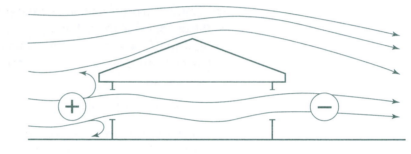

1.16
Wind effect: cross-ventilation

stack air, so there will be no air flow, or if the stack air is cooler, it can produce a down-draught.

A special case that could be considered as an 'enhanced stack effect' is the *solar chimney*, where at least one side of the stack is exposed to solar radiation and has a high absorptance. This will be heated, it heats the air inside, thus, the inside–outside temperature difference is increased, which in turn would increase the air flow.

Wind effects are normally much more powerful. On the windward side of a building a positive pressure field will develop, where the pressure is proportional to the square of the velocity. At the same time a negative (reduced) pressure field may develop on the leeward side and the difference between the two pressures can generate quite a strong cross-ventilation (Fig. 1.16).

Method sheet M.1.4 gives ways of estimating the air flow that would result from stack and wind effects.

1.2 THERMAL COMFORT

1.2.1 Thermal balance and comfort

The human body continuously produces heat by its metabolic processes. The heat output of an average body is often taken as 100W, but it can vary from

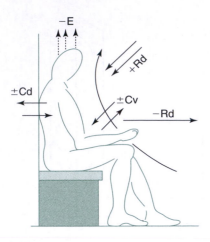

1.17
Heat exchanges of the human body

about 70 W (in sleep) to over 700 W in heavy work or vigorous activity (e.g. playing squash). This heat must be dissipated to the environment, or else the body temperature will increase. This deep-body temperature is normally about 37°C, while the skin temperature can vary between 31 and 34°C.

The body's thermal balance can be expressed as (see Fig. 1.17):

$$M \pm Rd \pm Cv \pm Cd - Ev = \Delta S \qquad (1.8)$$

where

M = metabolic heat production
Rd = net radiation exchange
Cv = convection (including respiration)
Cd = conduction
Ev = evaporation (including in respiration)
ΔS = change in stored heat.

A condition of equilibrium is that the sum (i.e. the ΔS) is zero and such an equilibrium is a precondition of thermal comfort. However, comfort is defined as 'the condition of mind that expresses satisfaction with the thermal environment, it requires subjective evaluation' (ASHRAE Standard 55). This clearly embraces factors beyond the physical/physiological.

1.2.2 Factors of comfort

The variables that affect heat dissipation from the body (and thus also thermal comfort) can be grouped into three sets:

Environmental	Personal	Contributing factors
Air temperature	Metabolic rate (activity)	Food and drink
Air movement	Clothing	Body shape
Humidity	State of health	Subcutaneous fat
Radiation	Acclimatization	Age and gender

Air temperature is the dominant environmental factor, as it determines convective heat dissipation. Air movement accelerates convection, but it also changes the skin and clothing surface heat transfer coefficient (reduces surface resistance), as well as increasing evaporation from the skin, thus producing a physiological cooling effect. This can be estimated by eq. (1.24), given in Section 1.4.2. Subjective reactions to air movement are:

< 0.1 m/s	stuffy
To 0.2	unnoticed
To 0.5	pleasant
To 1	awareness
To 1.5	draughty
> 1.5	annoying

but in overheated conditions, air velocities up to 2 m/s may be welcome.

Maslow (1984) proposed a 'hierarchy of human needs' and suggested that starting with the dominant item 1, any further needs can (and will) only be satisfied if all lower levels had been satisfied.

1 physical/ biological
2 safety/survival
3 affection/belonging
4 esteem (self- and by others)
5 self-actualisation.

Thermal comfort is one of the basic physical/biological needs. For survival, our deep-body temperature must stay around 37°C. It is therefore imperative to keep thermal conditions in buildings within acceptable limits, before any of the 'higher level' needs could even be considered.

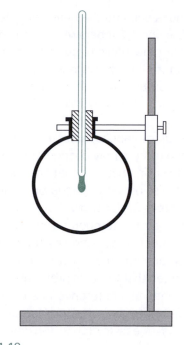

1.18
Globe thermometer

Medium humidities (RH 30–65%) do not have much effect, but high humidities restrict evaporation from the skin and in respiration, thus curbing the dissipation mechanism, while very low humidities lead to the drying out of the mucous membranes (in the mouth or throat) as well as the skin, thus causing discomfort.

Radiation exchange depends on the temperature of surrounding surfaces, measured by the MRT, or mean radiant temperature. This is the average temperature of the surrounding surface elements, each weighted by the solid angle it subtends at the measurement point.

The unit of solid angle is the steradian *(sr), that subtended by unit area (r^2) of the surface at the centre of a sphere of unit radius (r) (see also Fig. 2.7). As the surface area is $4\pi\ r^2$, the centre point will have a total of 4π sr (by analogy, the radian is an angular measure, a unit where the arc length is equal to the radius; as the circumference of a circle is 2π r, the complete circle (360°) is 2π radians).*

The MRT cannot be measured directly, only by a black globe thermometer, which responds to radiant inputs as well as to air temperature. This may be a 150 mm diameter copper ball, painted matt black, with a thermometer at its centre (Fig. 1.18) but recently matt black painted ping pong balls have been used to measure the GT (globe temperature), to the same effect. When the air velocity is zero, MRT = GT but there is a correction for air movement:

$$\text{MRT} = \text{GT} \times (1 + 2.35\sqrt{v}) - 2.35 \times \text{DBT}\ \sqrt{v}$$

where v = air velocity in m/s.

The effect of this MRT depends on clothing. In warm climates (with light clothing), it is about twice as significant as the DBT, which gave rise to

the environmental temperature: $\text{EnvT} = \dfrac{2}{3}\text{MRT} + \dfrac{1}{3}\text{DBT}$

but in cooler climates (people wear heavier clothing), it has about the same influence as the DBT, hence

the dry resultant temperature: $\text{DRT} = \dfrac{1}{2}\text{MRT} + \dfrac{1}{2}\text{DBT}.$

A comfort requirement is that the difference between DBT and MRT should be no greater than about 3 K.

Metabolic rate is a function of activity level. The unit devised for this is the *met*, which corresponds to 58.2 W/m² of body surface area.

Du Bois and Du Bois (1916) proposed the equation for body surface area (the Du Bois area) as: $A_D = 0.202 \times Mb^{0.425} \times h^{0.725}$, where Mb is body mass (kg) and h is height (m). For a man of Mb = 80 kg, h = 1.8 m, this area is 2 m².

For an average person this met unit would be about 115 W. With higher levels of met, a cooler environment will be preferred, to facilitate the heat dissipation.

Clothing is thermal insulation of the body. It is measured in units of *clo* which means a U-value of 6.45 W/m²K (or a resistance of 0.155 m²K/W) over the whole body surface. 1 clo corresponds to a three-piece business suit, with cotton underwear. Shorts and short-sleeved shirts would give about 0.5 clo, an overcoat may add 1 or 2 clo units to a business suit and the heaviest type of arctic clothing would be some 3.5 clo (see Section 1.2.4 below). If clothing can be freely chosen, it is an important adjustment mechanism, but if it is constrained (e.g. by social conventions or work safety) in a warm environment, it should be compensated for by a cooler air temperature. Acclimatisation and habit (being used to . . .) are a strong influence, both physiologically and psychologically.

Food and drink habits may have an influence on metabolic rates, thus have an indirect effect on thermal preferences. These effects may change in time, depending on food and drink intake. Body shape is significant in that heat production is proportional to body mass, but heat dissipation depends on body surface area. A tall and skinny person has a larger surface-to-volume ratio, can dissipate heat more readily, and can tolerate warmer temperatures than a person with a more rounded body shape. This effect is increased by the fact that subcutaneous fat is a very good insulator, and will thus lower the preferred temperatures. At one stage it was suggested that females prefer about 1 K warmer temperatures than males, but recently this difference has been attributed to differing clothing habits. Age does not make much difference in a preferred temperature, but older people have less tolerance for deviations from the optimum, probably because their adjustment mechanisms are impaired.

1.2.3 Adjustment mechanisms

The body is not purely passive, it is *homeothermic*, thus it has several thermal adjustment mechanisms. The first level is the vasomotor adjustments: *vasoconstriction* (in a cold environment) will reduce the blood flow to the skin, reduce skin temperature, reduce heat dissipation,* while *vasodilation* (in a warm situation) will increase blood flow to the skin, thus the heat transport will elevate the skin temperature and increase heat dissipation.

If, in spite of the appropriate vasomotor adjustment there remains an imbalance, in a warm environment, sweat production will start, providing an evaporative cooling mechanism. The sustainable sweat rate is about 1 L/h, which absorbs about 2.4 MJ/L of body heat (which constitutes a cooling rate of some 660 W). If this is insufficient, *hyperthermia* will set in, which is a circulatory failure, the body temperature may reach 40°C and heat stroke may occur. Conversely, in a cold environment, shivering will start, which is involuntary muscular work, increasing the heat production by up to a factor of 10. If this cannot restore equilibrium, *hypothermia* would set in, with possible fatal consequences. There are also longer-term adjustments, after a few days of exposure up to about six months. These may involve cardio-vascular and endocrine adjustments. In a hot climate this may consist of increased blood volume, which improves the effectiveness of vasodilation, enhanced performance of the sweat mechanism, as well as the readjustment of thermal preferences.

---

* This is a sacrificial mechanism: this may lead to freezing of extremities (ears, toes, fingers) in order to preserve deep body temperature.

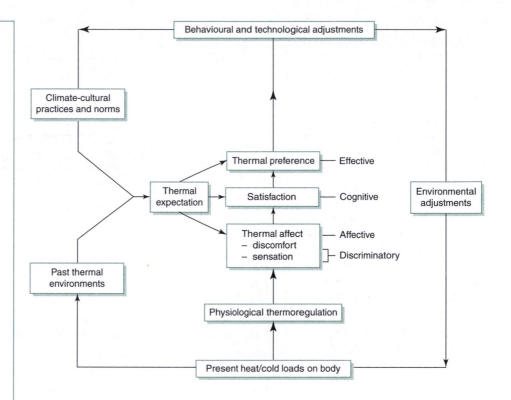

1.19

Auliciems' thermal perception model

ADAPTABILITY MODEL

Humphreys (1978) examined a large number of comfort studies, correlated thermal neutrality with the prevailing climate and for free-running buildings suggested the equation

$$Tn = 11.9 + 0.534\, To_{av}$$

(where To_{av} is the month's mean outdoor temperature).

Thus he laid the foundation of the adaptability model.

Auliciems (1981) reviewed the above data, supplemented it by others and proposed the equation

$$Tn = 17.6 + 0.31\, To_{av}$$

Since then, many other workers have found similar correlations, e.g. Griffiths (1990):

$$Tn = 12.1 + 0.534\, To_{av}$$

Nicol and Roaf (1996):

$$Tn = 17 + 0.38\, To_{av}$$

A very large study by De Dear *et al.* (1997) produced correlations and suggested eq. 1.9, which is practically the same as the Auliciems expression. This is the one here adopted.

With continued underheated conditions the vasoconstriction may become permanent, with reduced blood volume, while the body metabolic rate may increase. These adjustments are, however, not only physiological, there is a strong psychological aspect as well: getting used to the dominant conditions, accepting the prevailing conditions as 'normal'.

The adjustment of seasonal preferences can be quite significant, even over a period of a month. Extensive studies showed that the 'neutrality temperature' (the median of many people's votes) changes with the mean temperature of the month, as

$$Tn = 17.8 + 0.31 \times T_{o.av} \tag{1.9}$$

where $T_{o.av}$ is the mean temperature of the month.

Auliciems (1981) offered a psycho-physiological model of thermal perception, which is the basis of the adaptability model (Fig. 1.19).

1.2.4 Comfort indices, the comfort zone

The range of acceptable comfort conditions is generally referred to as the comfort zone. The temperature limits of such a comfort zone can be taken relative to the above Tn (the neutrality temperature) for 90% acceptability as

from (Tn −2.5)°C to (Tn + 2.5)°C.

but +/−3.6K will still be acceptable for 80% of people.

Yagloglou (1923) devised the ET (effective temperature) scale to recognise the effect of humidity on thermal sensation. ET coincides with DBT at the saturation curve of the psychrometric chart and 'equal comfort lines' are sloping down to the right.

This and the nomogram derived have been widely used, not only in the USA (e.g. by most ASHRAE publications) but also in the UK (e.g. Vernon and Warner 1932; Bedford 1936; Givoni 1969; Koenigsberger *et al.* 1973).

Gagge *et al.* (1974), in the light of more recent research, created the 'new effective temperature' scale, denoted ET* (ET star). This coincides with DBT at the 50% RH curve. Up to 14°C humidity has no effect on thermal comfort (ET* = DBT) but beyond that the ET* lines have an increasing slope. The slopes were analytically derived, differing for various combinations of activity and clothing.

Recognising this difficulty, Gagge *et al.* (1986) devised the SET (standard effective temperature) scale, which is also adopted here.

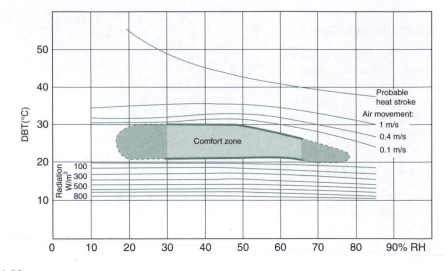

1.20
Olgyay's bioclimatic chart

As thermal comfort is influenced by another three environmental variables, attempts have been made since the early 1900s to create a single figure comfort index, which would express the combined effect of all four (or at least several) of these variables. The first one was proposed by Houghten and Yagloglou in 1923, the 'effective temperature'. At least 30 different such indices have been produced over the years by various research workers, all based on different studies, all with different derivations and names.

Olgyay (1953) introduced the 'bioclimatic chart' (Fig. 1.20) which has the RH on the horizontal and the DBT on the vertical axis, and the aerofoil shape in the middle is the 'comfort zone'. Curves above show how air movement can extend the upper limits and lines below it show the extension by radiation.

The latest comfort index now generally accepted, is the ET* (ET star) or new effective temperature and its standardised version, the **SET**. The ET* constructed for 0.57 clo and 1.25 met has been found to be valid for pairs of conditions such as (an increase in met could be compensated for by a decrease in clo):

met	clo
1	0.67
1.25	0.57
2	0.39
2	0.26
4	0.19

so this is now referred to as SET (Standard Effective Temperature).*

The SET isotherms are shown in Fig. 1.9 drawn on the psychrometric chart. The SET coincides with DBT at the 50% RH curve. The slope of the SET lines

---

* See *Architectural Science Review*, 44(2): 187.

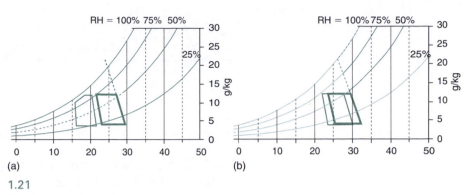

1.21

Comfort zones for Budapest and Darwin

For example, for Budapest, the warmest month, July. $T_{o.av}$ = 23°C

$Tn = 17.8 + 0.31 \times 23 = 24.9°C$

thus the comfort limits are:

$T_L = 22.4$ and $T_U = 27.4°C$ mark these on the 50% RH curve.

For the side boundaries either follow the slope of SET lines

or

note the AH for these two points: 8.5 and 11.5 g/kg then the base line intercepts will be

for $T_L = 22.4 + 0.023 \times$
$(22.4 - 14) \times 8.5$
$\approx 24°C$

for $T_U = 27.4 + 0.023 \times$
$(27.4 - 14) \times 11.5$
$\approx 31°C$

Draw the side boundaries (extend these above the 50% curve).

The top and bottom boundaries are at the 12 and 4 g/kg level

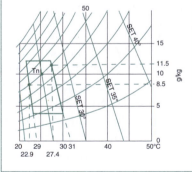

indicates that at higher humidities the temperature tolerance is reduced, while at lower humidities higher temperatures are acceptable. Up to 14°C, the SET lines coincide with the DBT. Above that, the slope of these isotherm lines is progressively increasing, with the slope coefficient taken as X/Y or DBT/AH = 0.023 × (T −14) which gives the deviation from the corresponding vertical DBT line for each g/kg AH, positive below the 50% and negative above it. For example, for DBT = 30°, RH = 50%, thus AH = 13.4 g/kg, the X-axis displacement of 30° SET will be 13.4 × 0.023 × (30 −14) = 4.93 K, i.e. at DBT = 34.93°C.

The SET thus defined combines the effect of temperature and humidity, the two most important determinants. The comfort zone can be plotted on Fig. 1.21 that will vary with the climate and be different for each month. The procedure may be as follows:

Find the thermal neutrality (as eq. 1.9: $Tn = 17.8 + 0.31 \times T_{o.av}$) for both the warmest and the coldest month and take the comfort limits as $Tn \pm 2.5$ °C. Mark these on the 50% RH curve. These will define the 'side' boundaries of the comfort zone as the corresponding SET lines. The humidity limits (top and bottom) will be 12 and 4 g/kg respectively (1.9 and 0.6 kPa vapour pressure). Fig. 1.21 shows the comfort zones for Darwin and Budapest, for January (summer) and July (winter). (See also Method sheet M.1.7.)

Note that Darwin has very little seasonal variation (a warm humid climate), while in Budapest (a cool temperate climate), there is a big difference between winter and summer.

1.3 CLIMATE

Weather is the set of atmospheric conditions prevailing at a given place and time. **Climate** can be defined as the integration in time of weather conditions, characteristic of a certain geographical location.

1.3.1 The sun

The climate of the Earth is driven by the energy input from the sun. For designers there are two essential aspects to understand: the apparent movement of the sun (the solar geometry), and the energy flow from the sun and how to handle it (exclude it or make use of it).

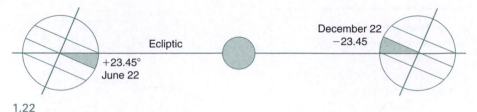

1.22

Two-dimensional section of the Earth's orbit and DEC

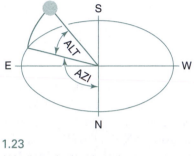

1.23

Altitude and azimuth angles

The Earth moves around the sun on a slightly elliptical orbit. At its maximum (aphelion) the Earth–sun distance is 152 million km, and at its minimum (perihelion) is 147 million km. The Earth's axis is not normal to the plane of its orbit, but tilted by 23.5°. Consequently the angle between the Earth's equatorial plane and the Earth–sun line (or the ecliptic, the plane of the Earth's orbit) varies during the year (Fig. 1.22).

This angle is known as the declination (DEC) and varies as

- +23.45° on June 22 (the northern solstice)
- 0 on March 21 and Sept. 22 (the equinox dates)
- −23.45° on December 22 (the southern solstice).

While the above heliocentric view is necessary to understand the real system, in building problems the *lococentric* view provides all the necessary answers. In this view the observer's location is at the centre of the sky hemisphere, on which the sun's position can be determined by two angles (Fig. 1.23):

- the altitude (ALT): measured upwards from the horizon, 90° being the zenith;
- the azimuth (AZI): measured in the horizontal plane from north (0°), through east (90°), south (180°) and west (270°) to north (360°).

These angles can be calculated for any time of the year by the trigonometrical equations given in Method sheet M.1.1. Conventionally α is used for ALT and γ is used for AZI, but here three-letter abbreviations are adopted for all solar angles to avoid confusion with other uses of the Greek letters.

The sun has the highest orbit and will appear to be on the zenith at noon on June 22 along the Tropic of Cancer (LAT = +23.45°, see Fig. 1.22) and along the Tropic of Capricorn (LAT = −23.45°) on December 22. Fig. 1.24 shows the lococentric view of sun paths for a northern and a southern hemisphere location (drawn for LAT = 28° and −28°).

The sun rises at due east on the equinox dates. In the northern hemisphere it travels through south in a clockwise direction but in the southern hemisphere (for an observer facing the equator), it travels through the north in an anticlockwise direction, to set at due west.

1.3.1.1 Sun-path diagrams

Sun-path diagrams or solar charts are the simplest practical tools used to depict the sun's apparent movement. The sky hemisphere is represented by a circle (the horizon). The *azimuth* angles (i.e. the direction of the sun) are given along the perimeter and the *altitude* angles (from the horizon up)

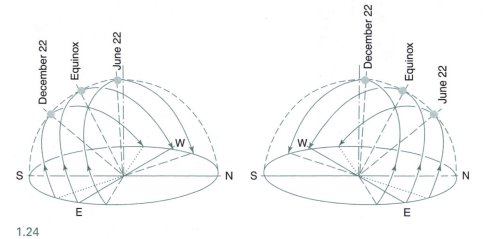

1.24
Lococentric view of sun paths

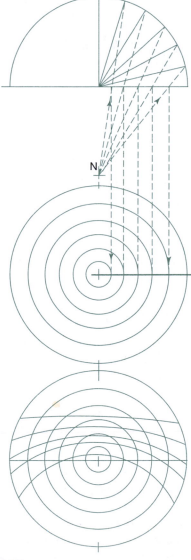

1.25
Stereographic projection method

are shown by a series of concentric circles, with 90° (the zenith) being the centre.

Several methods are used for the construction of these charts. The orthographic, or parallel projection method is the simplest, but it gives very compressed altitude circles near the horizon. The equidistant method is in general use in the US, but this is not a true geometrical projection. The most widely used are the stereographic charts. These are constructed by a radial projection method (Fig. 1.25) in which the centre of projection (N) is vertically below the observer's point, at a distance equal to the radius of the horizon circle (the nadir point).

The sun-path lines are plotted on this chart for a given latitude for the solstice days, for the equinoxes and for any intermediate dates as described in Method sheet M.1.2. For an equatorial location (LAT = 0°), the diagram will be symmetrical about the equinox sun-path, which is a straight line; for higher latitudes the sun-path lines will shift away from the equator.

For a polar position the sun-paths will be concentric circles (or rather an up and down spiral) for half the year, the equinox path being the horizon circle, and for the other half of the year the sun will be below the horizon. The shifting of sun-paths with geographical latitudes is illustrated in Fig. 1.26.

The date-lines (sun-path lines) are intersected by hour lines. The vertical line at the centre is noon. Note that on equinox dates the sun rises at due east at 06:00 and sets at due west at 18:00. As an example, a complete sun-path diagram for latitude 36° is given in Fig. 1.27.

The time used on solar charts is solar time, which coincides with local clock time only at the reference longitude of each time zone. Every 15° longitude band gives one hour difference (360/24 = 15), therefore every degree longitude means a time difference of 60/15 = 4 minutes.

For example, for Brisbane, longitude 153°E, the reference longitude is 150° (10 hours ahead of Greenwich); the 3° difference means that the local clock time is 3 × 4 = 12 minutes behind solar time (i.e. at solar noon, the clock shows only 11:48).

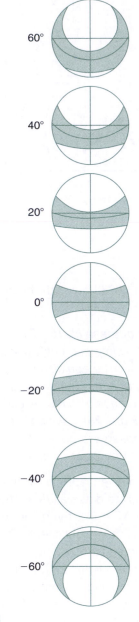

1.26
Sun-paths vs latitudes

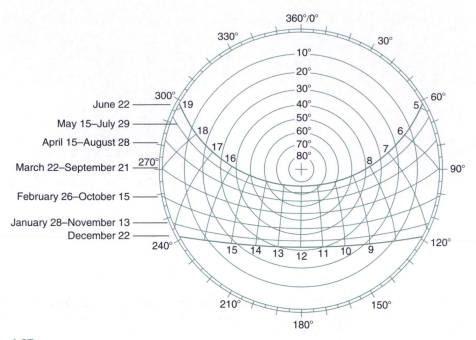

1.27
Example sun-path diagram

1.3.1.2 Solar radiation

The quantity of solar radiation can be measured in two ways (Fig. 1.28):

1 irradiance, in W/m^2 (in older texts referred to as 'intensity');
2 irradiation, in J/m^2 or Wh/m^2, an energy quantity integrated over a specified period of time (hour, day, month or year).

See also Section 1.4.1.

The sun's surface is at a temperature of some 6000°C, thus the peak of its radiant emission spectrum is around the 550 nm wavelength, extending from 20 to 3000 nm.

According to human means of perception we can distinguish:

1 ultraviolet radiation, 20–380 nm, (most of the UV below 200 nm is absorbed by the atmosphere, thus some sources give 200 nm as the lower limit), which produces photochemical effects, bleaching, sunburn, etc.;
2 light, or visible radiation, from 380 (violet) to 700 nm (red);
3 short infrared radiation, 700–3000 nm, or thermal radiation, with some photochemical effects.

For wavelengths, see also Fig. 1.2.

If a graph of continuously changing solar radiation is drawn against time (Fig. 1.28), the ordinate represents irradiance and the area under the curve is irradiation (the 10 a.m. irradiance (W/m^2 average from 9.30 to 10.30) is numerically the same as irradiation (Wh/m^2) for the hour 9.30–10.30).

At the outer limits of the Earth's atmosphere the annual mean value of irradiance is 1353 W/m^2, measured at normal incidence, i.e. on a plane perpendicular to the direction of radiation. This is referred to as the 'solar constant',

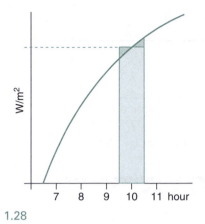

1.28
Irradiance and irradiation

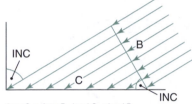

INC

B

C

INC

Area C > Area B   irrad C < irrad B
C = B/cos INC $G_C = G_B \times \cos$ INC

1.29
Angle of incidence

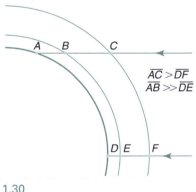

A B   C

$\overline{AC} > \overline{DF}$
$\overline{AB} \gg \overline{DE}$

D E   F

1.30
Radiation path-lengths

though it varies ±2% due to variations in the sun's emission itself and ±3.5% due to the changing Earth–sun distance.

As the Earth's radius is 6376 km (6.376×10^6m), its circular projected area is $(6.376 \times 10^6)^2 \times 3.14 \approx 127 \times 10^{12}$ m², it continuously receives a radiant energy input of $1.353 \times 127 \times 10^{12} \approx 170 \times 10^{12}$ kW. Some 50% reaches the Earth's surface and enters the terrestrial system. Ultimately all of it is re-radiated, this being a condition of equilibrium (see Fig. 1.36 on p. 28).

There are large variations in irradiation among different locations on the Earth, for three reasons:

1 the angle of incidence: according to the cosine law (Fig. 1.29), the irradiance received by a surface is the normal irradiance times the cosine of the angle of incidence (INC);
2 atmospheric depletion, a factor varying between 0.2 and 0.7, mainly because at lower altitude angles the radiation has to travel along a much longer path through the atmosphere (especially through the lower, denser and most polluted layer), but also because of variations in cloud cover and atmospheric pollution (Fig. 1.30);
3 the duration of sunshine, i.e. the length of daylight period (sunrise to sunset) and to a lesser extent also on local topography.

The maximum irradiance at the Earth's surface is around 1000 W/m² and the annual total horizontal irradiation varies from about 400 kWh/m²y near the poles to a value in excess of 2500 kWh/m²y in the Sahara Desert or north-western inland Australia.

1.3.2 Global climate, the greenhouse effect

At the global level, climates are formed by the differential solar heat input and the almost uniform heat emission over the Earth's surface. Equatorial regions receive a much greater energy input than areas nearer to the poles. Up to about 30° N and S latitudes the radiation balance is positive (i.e. the solar 'income' is greater than the radiant loss), but at higher latitudes the heat loss far exceeds the solar input. Differential heating causes pressure differences and these differences are the main driving force of atmospheric phenomena: winds, cloud formations and movements (but also ocean currents), which provide a heat transfer mechanism from the equator towards the poles.

As Fig. 1.31 shows, some 31% of solar radiation arriving at the Earth is reflected, the remaining 69% enters the terrestrial system. Some is absorbed in the atmosphere and a little more than 50% reaches the ground surface.

At points of strong heating the air rises and at a (relatively) cold location it sinks. The movement of air masses and of moisture-bearing clouds is driven by temperature differentials, but strongly influenced by the *Coriolis force*, explained below (Fig. 1.32).

In the absence of such heat transfer the mean temperature at the North Pole would be −40, rather than the present −17°C and at the equator it would be about 33 and not 27°C as at present.

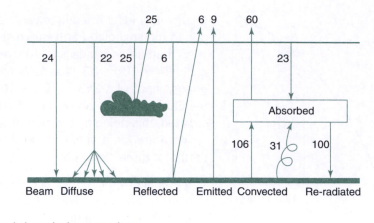

1.31

Radiation balance in the atmosphere
INPUT: 24 + 22 + 25 + 6 + 23 = 100%   Reflected: 25 + 6 = 31%
OUT: 25 + 6 + 9 + 60 = 100%   Emitted: 9 + 60 = 69% = 100%

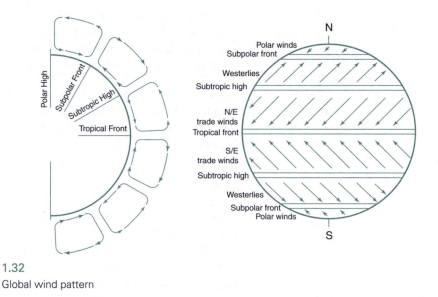

1.32
Global wind pattern

A 'stationary' air mass e.g. at the subtropics moves with the Earth's rotation and as it has a certain circumferential velocity, hence it has a moment of inertia. As it moves towards the poles, the circumference of the Earth (the latitude circle) decreases, therefore, the air will overtake the surface. Conversely an air mass at the subtropics when moving towards the equator (a larger circumference) will lag behind the Earth's rotation. This mechanism causes the N/E and SE trade winds.

The tropical front, or **ITCZ** (inter-tropical convergence zone), moves seasonally north and south (with a delay of about one month behind the solar input, thus the extreme north in July and south in January), as shown in Fig. 1.33. Note that the movement is much larger over continents than over the oceans.

The atmosphere is a very unstable three-dimensional system, thus small differences in local heating (which may be due to topography and ground cover) can have significant effects on air movements and influence the swirling patterns of low and high pressure (cyclonic and anti-cyclonic) zones.

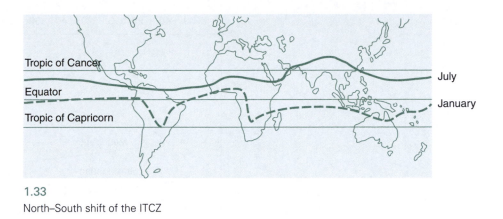

1.33
North–South shift of the ITCZ

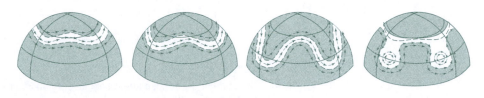

1.34
Development of mid-latitude cyclonic cells

Note that the parallel pressure zones implied by Fig. 1.32 gradually develop into cells of cyclonic circulation, as shown in Fig. 1.34.

Earth, which has an average radius of 6376 km, is surrounded by a very thin atmosphere. Its depth is usually taken as 80 km, which is the top of the mesosphere, where the pressure drops to practically zero, although some trace gases can still be found up to about 160 km. If the Earth were to be represented by a sphere of the size of a soccer football, the thickness of its atmosphere would be only about 1.5 mm.

The first 9 km thick layer contains about half of the total mass of the atmosphere and an 18 km layer (the *troposphere*) houses practically all life. All our climatic phenomena take place within this thin layer. To continue the football analogy, this would correspond to a layer of 0.3 mm thickness. Indeed, it is a very delicate, highly vulnerable and fragile mantle.

Fig. 1.35 shows the sectional structure of the atmosphere. The pressure is practically zero at the *mesopause* (80 km) and it increases downwards, to about 1010 hPa (1.01 kPa) at the ground level. The temperature reduces upwards through the troposphere to some −60°C (at 20 km), but increases above that through the stratosphere to about 80°C at the *stratopause*, then reducing again to −40°C, the mesopause.

The **greenhouse effect** is caused by the following mechanism. The solar radiation input (I in Fig. 1.36) into the terrestrial system is at the rate of some 170×10^{12} kW (as shown above in Section 1.3.1.2). Equilibrium is maintained with an equal rate of energy emission (E) to space (E = I, input). E is determined by the Earth's surface temperature (t) and the optical transparency (the retardation effect) of the atmosphere. The optical transparency of the atmosphere is quite high for short-wave solar radiation, but much less so for long-wave infrared, emitted by the Earth's surface.

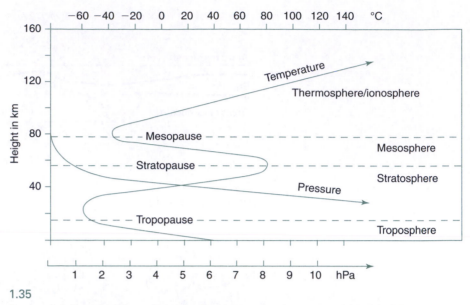

1.35

Structure of the atmosphere. Changes of temperature and pressure with height (hPa = hectoPascal = 100 Pa. ! hPa = 1 millibar)

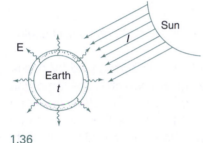

1.36

Earth's heat balance: greenhouse effect

1.37

A precision pyranometer

If this is further reduced by an increased CO_2 content (or other greenhouse gases), the t will increase until E is restored to gain a new equilibrium. This is referred to as the *greenhouse effect*, and it is the cause of *global warming*.

1.3.3   Elements of climates: data

The main climatic elements regularly measured by meteorological organisations and published in summary form are:

1   Temperature (DBT), measured in the shade, usually in a ventilated box, the Stevenson screen, 1.2–1.8 m above ground level.
2   Humidity, usually measured by an aspirated *psychrometer* (see Fig. 1.6a) which can be expressed as RH or AH, or the WBT or dew-point temperature can be stated.
3   Air movement, i.e. wind, normally measured at 10 m above ground in open country, but higher in built-up areas, to avoid obstructions; both velocity and direction are recorded.
4   Precipitation, i.e. the total amount of rain, hail, snow or dew, measured in rain gauges and expressed in mm per unit time (day, month, year).
5   Cloud cover, based on visual observation, expressed as a fraction of the sky hemisphere ('octas' = eighths, or more recently tenths) covered by clouds.
6   Sunshine duration, i.e. the period of clear sunshine (when a sharp shadow is cast), measured by a sunshine recorder, in which a lens burns a trace on a paper strip; shown as hours per day or month.
7   Solar radiation, measured by a *pyranometer* (solarimeter), on an unobstructed horizontal surface (Fig. 1.37) and recorded either as the continuously varying irradiance (W/m²), or through an electronic integrator as

irradiation over the hour or day. If the hourly value of irradiation is given in Wh/m², it will be numerically the same as the average irradiance (W/m²) for that hour (see Fig. 1.28 on p. 25).

Four environmental variables directly affect thermal comfort: temperature, humidity, radiation and air movement. These are the four constituents of climate most important for the purposes of building design.

The problem in the presentation of climatic data is to strike a balance between the two extremes of:

- too much detail: e.g. hourly temperatures for a year, $24 \times 365 = 8760$ items; it would be very difficult to glean any meaning from such a mass of numbers and, if many years are to be considered, it would be an impossible task.
- oversimplification: e.g. the statement of the annual mean temperature of, say, 15°C, which may indicate a range between 10 and 20°C or between -10 and $+40$°C. The greater the simplification, the more detail is concealed.

For all but the most detailed thermal performance analysis, the following data are adequate, as a minimum requirement (see tabulation, as in Fig. 1.39 on p. 30):

- Temperature monthly means of daily maxima (°C)
  - standard deviation of its distribution (K)
- monthly means of daily minima (°C)
  - standard deviation of its distribution (K)
- Humidity
  - early morning RH (%) approx. maximum
  - early afternoon RH (%) approx. minimum
- Rainfall monthly totals (mm)
- Irradiation monthly mean daily total (Wh/m²).

Such data may also be presented in graphic form, e.g. as Figs 1.38 and 1.45.

Fig. 1.39 is in fact a sample of the climatic database of the program package ARCHIPAK, that is briefly described in Method sheet M.1.9. The inclusion of standard deviations of temperatures allows the calculation of various percentile values of the variable.

Much more detailed data may be required for the purposes of some thermal response simulation programs, such as hourly data for a year, which itself may be a composite construct from many years of actual data. Such data are available for some locations in digital format, referred to as 'weather-tapes or files'. A great deal of effort has been spent on producing a year of hourly climatic data, variously referred to as TRY (test reference year), or TMY (typical meteorological year) or WYEC (weather year for energy calculations). These are required and used by various computer programs to simulate the thermal performance of buildings and consequent energy use.

The US program DoE-2 (http://doe2.com) includes a large number of 'weather files', hourly data for a sample year of a whole range of variables. TMY2 is derived from the SAMSON data-base of NREL (National Renewable

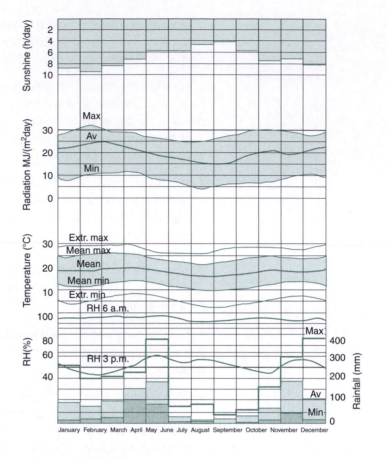

1.38
A climate graph example (Nairobi)

Climatic data for NAIROBI												Latitude: −1.2°	
	Jan	Feb	Mar	Apr	May	Jun	Jul	Aug	Sep	Oct	Nov	Dec	
T.max	25	26	26	24	23	22	21	22	24	25	23	23	°C
SD. max	1.7	1.7	1.5	1.1	1.7	1.6	1.5	1.5	1.5	1.1	1.1	1.2	K
T.min	11	11	13	14	13	11	9	10	10	12	13	13	°C
SD min	2	1.7	1.2	1.2	2.2	2.5	2.5	2	1.6	1.2	1.7	2	K
RH a.m.	95	94	96	95	97	95	92	93	95	95	93	95	%
RH p.m.	48	42	45	55	61	55	57	53	48	45	56	55	%
Rain	88	70	96	155	189	29	17	20	34	64	189	115	mm
Irrad	6490	6919	6513	5652	4826	4664	3838	4047	5245	5629	5489	6024	Wh/m²

(standard deviations are estimated only)

1.39
Simplest set of climatic data

Energy Laboratories). The primary source is the US NCDC (National Climatic Data Center). Typical Weather Years (TWY) for Canada have been developed by the University of Waterloo. Many TRY sets do not include solar radiation. In Australia, the Bureau of Meteorology provides data (http://www.bom.gov.au). The most comprehensive database is METEONORM (www.kornicki.com/meteonorm/EN/) containing data for over 7400 locations world-wide.

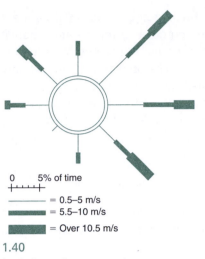

0   5% of time
+++++
——— = 0.5–5 m/s
▬▬▬ = 5.5–10 m/s
██ = Over 10.5 m/s

1.40
A wind rose for one month

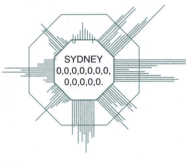

SYDNEY
0,0,0,0,0,0,0,
0,0,0,0,0.

1.41
Annual wind rose

There are many levels of simplification, such as using 3-hourly data or representing each month by a typical sequence of three days of hourly data. For the purposes of all calculations in this book, the above described monthly mean data are adequate.

1.3.3.1 Wind data

Wind data are best presented graphically. Several different types of wind roses can be used for this purpose. One method presents a separate wind rose (Fig. 1.40) for each month (or sometimes one wind rose representing three months, i.e. four wind roses representing the four seasons of the year). The length of lines radiating from a small circle are proportionate to the frequency of wind from that direction. Different line thicknesses may indicate wind velocity categories.

For architectural purposes the most useful form of wind rose is an octagon, with 12 lines on each side, corresponding to the 12 months, from January to December in a clockwise direction, where the length of a line is proportional to the frequency (% of observations) of wind from that direction in that month. If the winds were evenly distributed, all lines would extend to the outer octagon, which indicates a line length of 12.5%. Small dashes on the inside of the base octagon indicate that there is no wind in that month from that direction (Fig. 1.41).

The 12 numbers inside the graph give the percentage of total calm periods for the 12 months. It is usual to give a wind rose for an early morning and one for a mid-afternoon hour. Often two such graphs are shown, one for 9 a.m. and one for 3 p.m.

These may be supplemented by a tabulated wind frequency analysis, such as that shown in Fig. 1.42 for one month (Australia Bureau of Meteorology, 1988).

9 a.m. January calm 25 km/h	N	NE	E	SE	S	1859 observations SW	W	NW	All
1–10	1	1	1	9	22	3	1	1	39
11–20	1	–	–	5	21	2	–	1	30
21–30	–			1	4	–	–	–	6
>30				–	–	–			1
all	2	1	1	15	47	5	1	2	100

3 p.m. January calm 5 km/h	N	NE	E	SE	S	1854 observations SW	W	NW	All
1–10	6	5	3	2	2	2	–	1	20
11–20	12	14	9	8	4	–	–	1	50
21–30	2	3	5	10	3	–	–	–	23
>30	–		–	2	–	–	–		3
all	20	22	17	22	10	1	1	2	100

–	less than 1%		no wind from that direction

1.42
Wind frequency analysis

Degree-days (DD or Kd, Kelvin-days) or heating degree-days (HDD) are a climatic concept that can be defined as 'the cumulative temperature deficit below a set base temperature (Tb)'. In other words: the temperature deficit times its duration, summed up for the year. It can be obtained if from January 1 we go through the year day by day and whenever the mean temperature of the day (T_{av}) is less than this Tb, we write down the difference and add these up (negative differences are ignored). Thus, for the year, if Tb = 18°C:

DD = Kd = Σ (18 − T_{av}) (from day 1 to 365)

or generally

$$\boxed{DD = Kd = \Sigma\ (Tb - T_{av})}\tag{1.10}$$

Such sums can be produced separately for each month. Data sheet D.1.9 gives some typical degree-day data.

Degree-hours can be estimated as Dh = Kh = Kd × 24, but more accurately a summation similar to the above can be carried out on an hourly basis. If T_h = hourly temperature:

$$Kh = \Sigma\ (18 - T_h)\ \text{(from hour 1 to 8760)}\tag{1.11}$$

or, indeed, separately for each month.

This can also be visualised from a continuous temperature graph (Fig. 1.43) as the area under the curve measured below the Tb level, where the ordinate is in K (degrees temperature difference) and the abscissa in h (hours), therefore the (shaded) area is Kh, Kelvin-hours or degree-hours. Kd and Kh are the preferred terms, to avoid confusion with American DD data given in terms of °F.

Method sheet M.1.5 shows the calculation for converting degree-days into degree-hours from monthly mean data, to any base temperature, which can be used if the standard deviation of the temperature distribution is known.

The concept is useful for estimating the annual (or monthly) heating requirement. Kelvin-hours is the climatic parameter used and the building parameter is the *building conductance* (specific heat loss rate) (q). The heating requirement (Htg) is the product of the two:

$$Htg = Kh \times q\ (Kh \times W/K = Wh)\tag{1.12}$$

Sometimes the 'cooling degree-days' (or degree-hours) concept is used for the estimation of cooling requirements. This is conceptually similar to the above, but the base temperature is usually taken as 26°C and the temperatures in excess of this base are considered

CDD = Σ (T_{av} − 26) (from day 1 to 365)

1.3.4 Classification of climates

Many different (and some very complex) systems of climate classification are used, for different purposes. Some are based on vegetation, others on evapotranspiration. Some serve the purposes of agriculture, some are found in human health studies. The most generally used system is the Köppen-Geiger classification, which distinguishes some 25 climate types. This is shown in Fig. 1.44, followed by a tabulation of the main types.

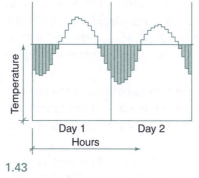

1.43
Definition of degree-hours (kh)

COOLING DD

This is nowhere near as reliable as the heating requirement calculation, but can be taken as indicative. Cooling requirements depend also on solar heat gain (which is different for each building surface and also depends on fenestration), internal heat gain and on atmospheric humidity (the determinant of latent heat load). There are methods of making some allowance for these (making assumptions of 'average conditions') but these have no general validity.

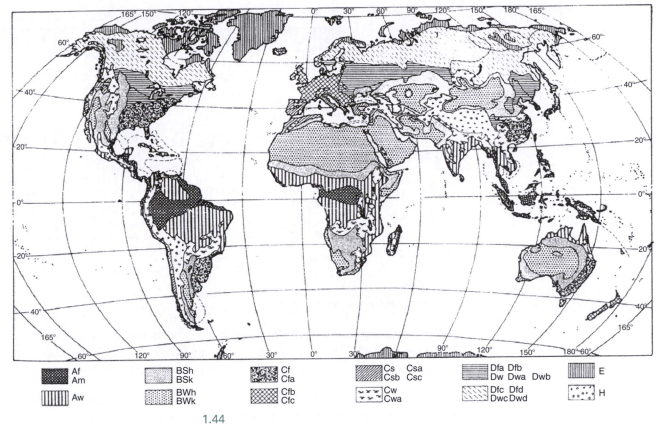

1.44
The Köppen-Geiger climate zones

Legend:
- Af, Am
- Aw
- BSh, BSk
- BWh, BWk
- Cf, Cfa
- Cfb, Cfc
- Cs, Csa, Csb, Csc
- Cw, Cwa
- Dfa, Dfb, Dw, Dwa, Dwb
- Dfc, Dfd, Dwc, Dwd
- E
- H

The Köppen–Geiger climate classification (main types)

Type	Main group	Sub-group	Second sub-group
Af	hot	rainy all seasons	
Am		monsoonal rain	
As		dry summer	
Aw		dry winter	
Bsh	dry	semi-arid steppe	very hot
Bsk			cold or cool
Bwh		arid	very hot
Bwk			cold and cool
Cfa	mild winter	moist all seasons	hot summer
Cfb			warm summer
Cfc			cool short summer
Cwa		dry winter	hot summer
Cwb			warm summer
Csa		dry winter	hot summer
Csb			warm summer
Dfa	severe winter	moist all seasons	hot summer
Dfb			warm summer
Dfc			short cool summer
Dfd			very cold winter
Dwa		dry winter	hot summer
Dwb			cool summer
Dwc			short cool summer
Dwd			very cold winter
ET	polar climate	short summer allows tundra vegetation	
EF		perpetual ice and snow	

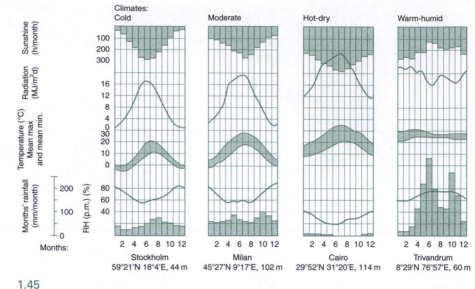

1.45

Climate graphs: four climate types

For the purposes of building design, a simple system is adequate (after Atkinson, 1953), that distinguishes only four basic types. This is based on the nature of the human thermal problem in the particular location:

1 *Cold* climates, where the main problem is the lack of heat (underheating), or an excessive heat dissipation for all or most of the year.
2 *Temperate* (moderate) climates, where there is a seasonal variation between underheating and overheating, but neither is very severe.
3 *Hot-dry* climates, where the main problem is overheating, but the air is dry, so the evaporative cooling mechanism of the body is not restricted. There is usually a large diurnal (day–night) temperature variation.
4 *Warm-humid* climates, where the overheating is not as great as in hot-dry areas, but it is aggravated by high humidities, restricting the evaporation potential. The diurnal temperature variation is small.

Sometimes we consider also the following sub-types:

• island or trade-wind climate
• maritime desert climate
• tropical highland climate

or indeed 'composite climates', with seasonally changing characteristics.

Use of the composite climate graphs allows a visual appreciation at a glimpse of the differences of the four basic climates (Fig. 1.45).

There are distinct seasonal variations in the first three. Both the temperature and the solar radiation curves are stepping up, except the last one, which shows very small seasonal variations. The width of temperature bands indicates short-term (diurnal) variability: very narrow at both extremes: in cold and in warm-humid climates. Hot-dry climates (Cairo) have the most sunshine hours and solar radiation, the widest temperature-band and the lowest relative humidity and rainfall. Contrast the rainfall histogram and humidity curves of Cairo and Trivandrum (southern India).

1.4 THERMAL BEHAVIOUR OF BUILDINGS

A building can be considered as a thermal system, with a series of heat inputs and outputs (analogous to eq. 1.8 for the human body):

Qi – internal heat gain
Qc – conduction heat gain or loss
Qs – solar heat gain
Qv – ventilation heat gain or loss
Qe – evaporative heat loss.

The system can be depicted by the following equation:

$$Qi \pm Qc + Qs \pm Qv + Qe = \Delta S \qquad (1.13)$$

where ΔS is a change in heat stored in the building.

Thermal balance exists when the sum of all heat flow terms, thus ΔS is zero: if the sum is greater than zero, the temperature inside the building is increasing, or if it is less than zero, the building is cooling down.

The system can be analysed assuming *steady state* conditions, i.e. both the indoor and the outdoor conditions are steady, non-changing (taking a representative point in time), or we can consider the building's dynamic response. The former may be valid when the diurnal changes are small compared with the indoor-outdoor temperature difference, or as the basis of finding the required heating or cooling capacity, under assumed 'design' conditions, or, indeed, as a first approach to fabric design.

The most significant energy input into a building is solar radiation. The next section examines the solar heat input and its control, this will be followed by the other components of eq. 1.13 above.

1.4.1   Solar control

The first task in solar control is to determine when solar radiation would be a welcome input (solar heating for the underheated period) or when it should be excluded (the overheated period). This overheated period can then be outlined on the sun-path diagram: take the sun path dates as the Y axis and the hours as the X axis, the only difference being that here both axes are curved (see Method sheet M.1.8). The performance of a shading device is depicted by a *shading mask*, which can be constructed with the aid of the shadow angle protractor (Fig. 1.46). This is then superimposed on the diagram, corresponding to the window's orientation. A device is to be found, the shading mask of which covers the overheated period.

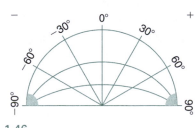

1.46
Shadow angle protractor

1.4.1.1   Shading design

Shading design for the exclusion of solar input is a geometrical task. External shading devices are the most effective tools to control sun penetration. Three basic categories of shading devices can be distinguished:

1 *Vertical devices*, e.g. vertical louvres or projecting fins. These are characterised by *horizontal shadow angles* (HSA) and their shading mask will be of a sectoral shape (Fig. 1.47). By convention, the HSA is measured

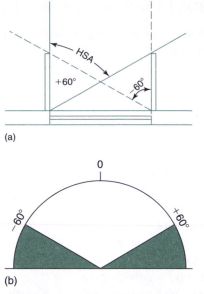

(a)

(b)

1.47

Vertical devices, HSA and mask

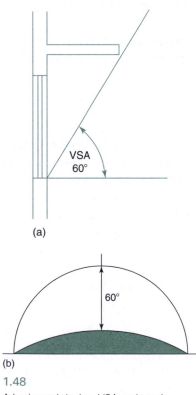

(a)

(b)

1.48

A horizontal device, VSA and mask

from the direction of orientation (i.e. from the surface normal), positive in clockwise and negative in the anticlockwise direction. The HSA cannot be greater than 90° or less than −90°, as that would indicate that the sun is behind the building. These devices may be symmetrical, with identical performance from left and right, or asymmetrical. They are most effective when the sun is towards one side of the direction the window is facing. We may distinguish the 'device HSA' (as above) and the 'solar HSA', which is the required performance at a given time.

2 *Horizontal devices*, e.g. projecting eaves, a horizontal canopy or awning, or horizontal louvres (Fig. 1.48). These are characterised by a *vertical shadow angle* (VSA). One large or several small elements may give the same performance, the same vertical shadow angle. Their shading mask, constructed by using the shadow angle protractor (see Method sheet M.1.2), will be of a segmental shape. They are most effective when the sun is near-opposite to the window considered.

The 'solar VSA' is the same as the ALT (altitude) only when the sun is directly opposite the window (when AZI = ORI, or solar HSA = 0). When the sun is to one side of the surface normal, its altitude must be projected onto a vertical plane perpendicular to the window (Fig. 1.49). For the calculation of these angles, see Method sheet M.1.1.

3 *Egg-crate devices*, e.g. concrete grille-blocks or metal grilles. These produce complex shading masks, combinations of the above two and cannot be characterised by a single angle. An example of this is shown in Fig. 1.50.

A window facing the equator (south in the northern hemisphere and due north in the southern hemisphere) is the easiest to handle, it can give an automatic seasonal adjustment: full shading in summer but allowing solar heat gain in winter (Fig. 1.51). For complete summer six months sun-exclusion (for an equinox cut-off) the vertical shadow angle will have to be VSA = 90°-LAT; e.g. for LAT = 36° it will be VSA = 90−36 = 54°.

This shading mask exactly matches the equinox sun-path line. For other dates the match is not so exact, but still quite similar to the sun-path line. For orientations other than due north the situation is not so simple. A combination of vertical and horizontal devices may be the most appropriate answer.

The suggested procedure is the following (Fig. 1.52):

1 Draw a line across the centre of the sun-path diagram, representing the plan of the wall face considered (i.e. the surface normal being the orientation). During any period when the sun is behind this line, its radiation would not reach that wall, thus it is of no interest. Fig. 1.52 shows a north-east orientation (LAT =−36°, ORI = 45°).

2 Mark on the sun-path diagram the period when shading is desirable. In Fig. 1.52, this shading period is taken as the summer six months, i.e. its boundary is the equinox sun-path line (heavy outline).

3 Select a shading mask, or a combination of shading masks which would cover this shading period, with the closest possible match.

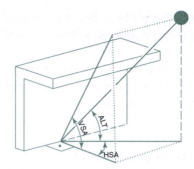

1.49

Relationship of ALT and VSA

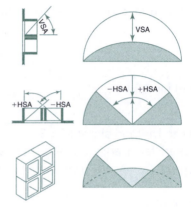

1.50

An egg-crate device and its shading mask built up from its horizontal and vertical components

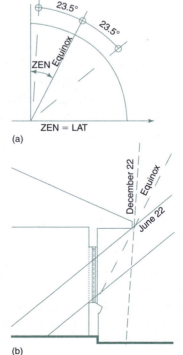

(a)

(b)

1.51

Equinox cut-off (sections)

Several combinations of vertical and horizontal shadow angles may give satisfactory results:

- a combination of VSA = 30° and HSA = +20° would give the required shading but would also exclude the winter sun from about 10:00, which is undesirable;
- a combination of VSA = 47° and HSA = 0° would also provide complete shading for 6 months (shaded area in Fig. 1.52), but still exclude the mid-winter sun after 12:00 noon (or 11:55);
- a combination of VSA = 60° and HSA = +20° may be an acceptable compromise: on Feb. 28 the sun would enter from 09:20 to 11:00 (a little longer in early March).

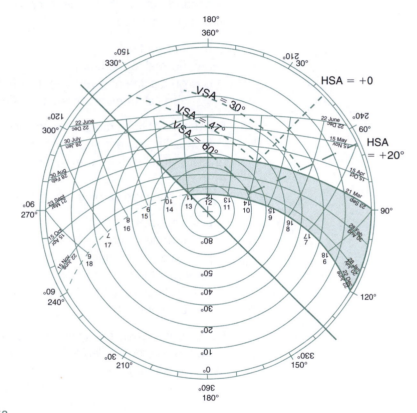

1.52

Design procedure for composite shading

1.4.1.2 Radiation calculations

At any location and with respect to a surface of any orientation (ORI) and any tilt angle (TIL), the angle of incidence (INC) is continuously changing. For any desired point in time it can be calculated by the expressions given in Method sheet M.1.1.

The global irradiance (G) incident on a particular surface consists of two main components:

- Gb = beam or direct component, reaching the surface along a straight line from the sun (this is a vectorial quantity and depends on the angle of incidence).
- Gd = diffuse component, i.e. the radiation scattered by the atmosphere, thus arriving at the surface from the whole of the sky hemisphere (depends on how much of the sky hemisphere is 'seen' by the surface).

Possibly also:

- Gr = reflected component; if the surface is other than horizontal, it may be reached by radiation reflected from the ground or nearby surface.

G = Gb + Gd (+ Gr).

A second subscript is necessary to specify the surface on which the irradiance is considered:

h = horizontal
n = normal to the beam
p = on a plane of given orientation (ORI) and tilt (TIL)
v = vertical, of given orientation (ORI).

For details of such radiation calculations, refer to Method sheet M.1.3.

In the literature the symbol H is often used for irradiation (e.g. hourly or daily total). Here the symbol D is adopted, to avoid confusion with enthalpy.

D can have the same subscripts as G (except n), i.e.:

b = beam component
d = diffuse component
p = on a given plane
r = reflected component
v = vertical plane of given ORI
no subscript = total.

Gb is continuously changing but it can be integrated over the day to get Db.

Very often the available data give only the horizontal total irradiation for an average day of each month. Before this can be transposed to other planes it must be split into beam and diffuse components, then the hourly values of both components must be estimated. This is a lengthy calculation, more suited to computer programs, but Method sheet M.1.3 gives the appropriate algorithms.

1.4.1.3 Solar heat gain

Solar heat gain is considered differently for transparent and opaque surfaces. The global irradiance incident on the surface (Gv or Gh, in W/m^2) must be known in both cases.

Transparent elements (windows): the solar gain is the product of this G, the area of the window and the *solar gain factor* (θ or sgf). This is a decimal fraction indicating what part of the incident radiation reaches the interior. (In the USA this is referred to as SHGC, solar heat gain coefficient.) Values of sgf for different glazing systems are given in Data sheet D.1.3.

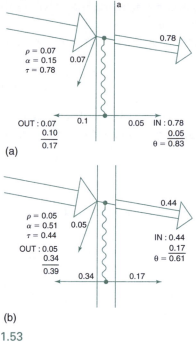

1.53

Transmission through glass

Some part of the incident radiation is transmitted (t), some is reflected (r) and the remainder is absorbed (a) within the body of the glass.

$$\tau + \rho + \alpha = 1$$

The absorbed part will heat up the glass, which will emit some of this heat to the outside, some of it to the inside, by re-radiation and convection (Fig. 1.53). The θ is the sum of this inward re-emitted heat and the direct transmission. Therefore the solar gain through a window is:

$$Qs = A \times G \times \theta \tag{1.14}$$

In the USA the ASHRAE *Handbook of Fundamentals* defines a 'solar factor' with a similar meaning, as the sum of direct transmittance and some part of the absorptance:

$$F = \tau + \alpha \times U/h_o$$

It also gives a series of tables of solar heat gain factors (SHGF) for various latitudes, orientations and times of day, for the 21st of each month. These are not really 'factors', but calculated values of solar irradiance, in W/m². These will have to be multiplied by the shading coefficient (SC) of the particular fenestration. This is defined as

$$SC = \frac{\text{solar heat gain of the fenestration considered}}{\text{solar heat gain through reference glass}}$$

The reference glass is defined as 'double strength glass' (DSA) of about 3 mm thickness, having the properties of:

$$\tau = 0.86$$
$$\rho = 0.08$$
$$\alpha = 0.06.$$

If $U = 5$ W/m²K and $h_o = 16.66$ W/m²K, we get a value for the reference glass of:

$$F_{DSA} = 0.86 + 0.06 \times 5 / 16.66 = 0.86 + 0.018 = 0.878$$

SC can also be defined in terms of solar factors as

$$SC = \frac{\text{F of fenestration}}{F_{DSA}}$$

and the solar heat gain will be

$$Qs = A \times SHGF \times SC$$

This roundabout method has been superseded by using the solar heat gain coefficient (SHGC), that is a non-dimensional term (same as our sgf or θ):

$$SHGC = \frac{\text{solar heat transmitted}}{\text{solar irradiance of the window surface}}$$

and the solar heat gain will be

$$Qs = A \times G \times SHGC$$

and G must be found from other sources or by some other method.

Opaque elements: the solar heat input is treated by using the sol-air temperature concept. This can be explained as follows:

The radiant heat input into a surface depends on its absorptance (α, see Data sheet D.1.4).

$$Qin = G \times A \times \alpha \tag{1.15}$$

This heat input will elevate the surface temperature (T_s), which will cause a heat dissipation to the environment. The heat loss depends on the surface conductance (h)

$$Qloss = A \times h \times (T_s - T_o)$$

As the surface temperature increases, equilibrium will be reached when

$Qin = Qloss$
i.e. $G \times A \times \alpha = A \times h \times (T_s - T_o)$.

and then the temperature will stabilise (Fig. 1.54).

From this the T_s can be expressed as:

$$
\begin{aligned}
T_s &= T_o + G \times \alpha / h \text{ or} \\
&= T_o + G \times \alpha \times R_{so} \text{ (as } 1/h = R_{so})
\end{aligned}
\tag{1.16}
$$

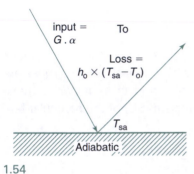

1.54
Derivation of sol-air temperature

This derivation neglects any heat flow from the surface into the body of the element, thus T_s is not a true surface temperature; it is the notional *sol-air temperature* (T_{sa}), which is the driving force of the heat flow.

For surfaces exposed to the sky (roofs), a radiant emission term should be included in the sol-air temperature expression:

$$T_{sa} = T_o + (G \times \alpha - E) / h \text{ or } \quad T_o + (G \times \alpha - E) \times R_{so} \tag{1.17}$$

and the radiant emission is usually taken as between $E = 90$ W/m^2 for a cloudless sky and 20 W/m^2 for a cloudy sky. For walls, no such emission term is necessary, as these face surfaces of a similar temperature.

The heat flow through a sun-lit opaque element will then be

$$Qc = A \times U \times (T_{sa} - T_i)$$

The air temperature T_o is taken as the same all around but the T_{sa} is different for each side of the building. It is therefore convenient to split this sol-air temperature into air temperature and sol-air excess temperature (dTe, in K) which is the temperature equivalent of the solar heat input, over and above the air temperature effect. The effect of air temperature is evaluated by the conduction expression (Qc), as eq. 1.26, using $qc = \Sigma (A \times U)$ and $\Delta T = T_o - T_i$ for the whole building and the extra heat flow caused by solar radiation will be calculated separately for each side:

$$Qs = qc \times dTe \tag{1.18}$$

where

$$dTe = (G \times \alpha - E) \times R_{so} \text{ for roofs}$$

$dTe = G \times \alpha \times R_{so}$ for walls

and qc is as defined by eq. 1.25.

taken for elements on that side of the building.

There may be a situation where Qc through an element is negative, but Qs is positive.

1.4.1.4 Special glasses

Special glasses are an important tool for solar control. Data sheet D.1.3 shows that glass quality can significantly affect solar gain while it has little or no effect on the U-value. Surface tinting (single, 6 mm glass) can reduce the solar gain factor (q) from 0.76 to 0.6 but body tinting will reduce it to 0.52. This last one has several varieties, referred to as 'heat-absorbing glass'. This would reduce solar gain by $(0.76 - 0.52)/76 = 0.32$, or 32%. However, the glass itself will become hot and will contribute to heat gain by convection.

The 'solar control' glasses may reduce sgf to 0.18, by selective reflection of the infra-red. The problem with all these is that they are fixed, whereas the circumstances may require adjustment: normally to exclude solar heat gain but make use of it in winter, similar to the use of adjustable shading devices, as opposed to fixed ones.

A new development is the introduction of 'smart glasses'. *Photochromic* glasses darken when exposed to strong radiation (as e.g. some sunglasses). *Thermochromic* glass darkens when its temperature increases, or e.g. a vanadium dioxide (VO_2) coating (tungsten-doped) turns the glass reflective when it reaches 29°C. The most promising type is the *electrochromic* glass, e.g. the 'Switchglass' turns the transparent glass into translucent when a small voltage is applied. It is marketed for 'privacy' purposes (e.g. for glazed office partitions). Some switchable glasses use an LED film laminated between two sheets of glass, which becomes reflective when a voltage is switched on. Others are based on some form of liquid crystal.

1.4.2 Ventilation

The term 'ventilation' is used for three totally different processes and it serves three different purposes:

1 the supply of fresh air, to remove smells, CO_2 and other contaminants
2 the removal of some internal heat when $T_o < T_i$
3 to promote heat dissipation from the skin, i.e. physiological cooling.

The first two require quite small air exchange rates (volume flow rates, vr, in m^3/s or L/s), while for the last one, it is the air velocity at the body surface which is critical (in m/s).

Both deliberate ventilation and incidental air infiltration cause a heat flow, e.g. when in a heated building, warm air is replaced by cold outside air. If the ventilation rate (volume flow rate, vr) is known, then the *ventilation conductance* (or specific ventilation heat flow rate) of the building can be found as

$$qv = 1200 \times vr \qquad (1.19)$$

where 1200 J/m³K is the average volumetric heat capacity of moist air.

Often only the number of air changes per hour (N) is known (i.e. the number of times the total building volume of air is replaced in an hour), but from this the ventilation rate can be found:

$$vr = N \times V / 3600 \text{ (m}^3/\text{s)}$$

where V is the volume of the room or building (m³).

Substituting:

$$qv = 0.33 \times N \times V \qquad (1.20)$$

where 0.33 is 1200 J / 3600 s.

Incidental air infiltration in a poorly built house can be as much as N = 3 air changes per hour, but with careful detailing and construction it can be reduced to N = 0.5. The fresh air, i.e. deliberate ventilation requirement (for the above purpose 1) is usually N = 1 for habitable rooms, N = 10 for a kitchen (when in use) but up to N = 20 for some industrial situations or restaurant kitchens (see Data sheet D.1.8).

The ventilation heat flow rate (which may serve the above purpose 2) will be

$$Qv = qv \times \Delta T \qquad (1.21)$$

where $\Delta T = T_o - T_i$

In practice, qc and qv are often added to get the *building conductance* (or building heat loss coefficient in some sources, a term that assumes a heat loss condition, whereas building conductance is valid for heat gain as well).

Note that this is not the same as 'conductance' (C) defined in Section 1.1.2.1.

$$q = qc + qv \qquad (1.22)$$

and then multiplied by ΔT to get the total heat flow rate

$$Q = Qc + Qv = q \times \Delta T \qquad (1.23)$$

where Qc is as eq. 2.26.

For purpose 3, physiological cooling, the apparent cooling effect of air movement (dT) can be estimated as

$$dT = 6 \times v_e - 1.6 \times v_e^2 \qquad (1.24)$$

where the effective air velocity is $v_e = v - 0.2$, v is air velocity (m/s) at the body surface and the expression is valid up to 2 m/s.

For the estimation of ventilation, refer to Method sheet M.1.4, but for a more accurate calculation or depiction of air-flow pattern, a CFD (Computational Fluid Dynamics) program or wind tunnel measurements must be used.

Heat flow into or out of a building may be predicted by using a steady state or a dynamic model. The **steady state model** is based on the assumption of steady conditions of temperatures both inside and outside (as well as unchanging occupancy). The use of this may be valid if the outdoor diurnal changes are small compared to the indoor–outdoor temperature difference. Then the daily mean temperatures can be used. It will give reasonably reliable results in the case of a building with large thermal capacity.

It is normally used for the calculation of the required heating capacity (e.g. in the winter of a moderate climate) or the annual heating requirement. It may be considered as a 'snap-shot' of the building's thermal behaviour under assumed (or 'recommended') conditions. It is useful as a first approach to fabric design. It is less reliable for finding the cooling requirement under summer conditions, due to the large influence of solar heat gain. It may be used just to find the peak load.

Dynamic models would use hourly climatic data for at least one day, hourly data for internal heat gains and these would take into account the thermal capacitance of the building fabric. Such models are used as the algorithm of computer programs and would predict the dynamic thermal response of a given building. This would give realistic results if the inputs accurately depict the real conditions.

The first step in any thermal response calculation is to identify the various heat-flow channels between inside and outside, both for a steady state model and for the dynamic analysis of periodic heat flow.

1.4.3   Steady state heat flow

Internal gains include any heat generated inside the building: the heat output of occupants, appliances and lighting. Data sheet D.1.7 gives the output of human bodies (at various activity levels) and of appliances. Both for appliances and for electric lighting the total consumption rate (power, in W) must be taken into account as heat output, for the duration of their use (power $\times$ time = energy, W $\times$ h = Wh).

For the purposes of steady state analysis it is usual to take the daily average internal heat gain rate, i.e. add all gains for the day (in Wh) and divide it by 24 hours to get the average rate in W.

1.4.3.1   Conduction heat flow

Conduction heat flow is found as eq. 1.1, except that the sum of A $\times$ U products is found for the whole building envelope. This will be referred to as the *envelope conductance* (Fig. 1.55).

$$\boxed{qc = \Sigma \ (A \times U)} \quad (\text{m}^2 \times \text{W/m}^2\text{K} = \text{W/K}) \tag{1.25}$$

This is the heat flow rate by conduction through the total envelope of the building with a $\Delta T = 1$ K temperature difference between inside and outside.

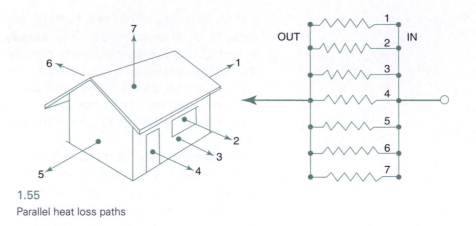

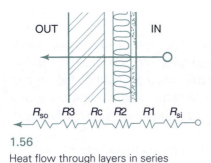

1.55

Parallel heat loss paths

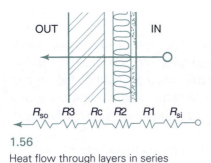

1.56

Heat flow through layers in series

The resistance to heat flow of a layer of material is R = b/λ, i.e. thickness, divided by conductivity (see Section 1.1.2.1 and eq. 1.3). For a multi-layer building element the **resistances** of all layers must be added. The surfaces provide additional resistances (air-to-surface and surface-to-air) which must be added to this sum. Data sheet D.1.4 gives the appropriate surface resistance values (R_{si} and R_{so}) for inside and outside surfaces. The reciprocal of this surface resistance is the surface conductance (h), which is itself the sum of convective (h_c) and radiative (h_r) components. In each case the surface resistance is

$$R_s = 1/h = 1/(h_c + h_r) \text{ (in } m^2K/W)$$

Any cavity or air gap may also offer a resistance (Rc), thus the air-to-air resistance of an element will be (Fig. 1.56):

$$R_{a-a} = R_{si} + R1 + R2 + Rc + R3 + R_{so}$$

where

R1, R2 = resistance of material layers
Rc = the resistance of any cavity

Data sheet D.1.4 gives also cavity resistance values.

The U-value is the reciprocal of this R_{a-a}.

U-values of many elements are given in Data sheets D.1.2 and D.1.3, but they can also be calculated from their component resistances.

The actual total conduction heat flow rate of the building will be

$$\boxed{Qc = qc \times \Delta T} \quad (W/K \times K = W) \tag{1.26}$$

or

$$Qc = \Sigma (A \times U) \times \Delta T$$

where $\Delta T = T_o - T_i$, the difference between outside and inside air temperature, ΔT, therefore Qc are negative for heat loss, positive for heat gain.

Any heat loss (or gain) calculation must start by identifying the possible heat flow paths (as Fig.1.55) and it is useful to tabulate this as in Example 1.3.

EXAMPLE 1.3   ELEMENT CONDUCTANCES

Refer to Fig. 1.55 (assuming the window faces north).

Element	Dimensions	Area	Transmittance	Conductance
	m	A (m²)	U (W/m²K)	qc = A × U (W/K)
1 west wall	5 × 3.4 *	17	1.53	26.01
2 window	2 × 1.2	2.4	2.9	6.96
3 north wall**	7 × 2.8 − (2.4+1.6)	15.6	1.53	23.87
4 door	0.76 × 2.1	1.6	2.2	3.52
5 east wall	5 × 3.4	17	1.53	26.01
6 south wall	7 × 2.8	19.6	1.53	29.99
7 roof	7 × 5	35	0.51	17.85
8 floor	7 × 5	35	0.85	29.75

Envelope conductance 163.96 ≈ 164 W/K.

Notes:
* height 2.8 at eaves, 4 m at ridge, av, 3.4 m
** net area, door and window subtracted
Assuming the following constructions (from data sheet D.1.2 and 1.4):

walls   270 mm cavity brick
window   20% timber frame, double clear glass
door   45 mm solid core
roof   tiled, sarking,50 EPS with 25 timber sloping ceiling

Volume = 35 × 3.4 =119 m³, then assuming three air changes, from eq. 1.20

  qv = 0.33 × 3 × 119 = 117.81 ≈ 118 W/K

Thus total conductance q = 164 + 118 = **282 W/K.**

 If this building is located in Canberra, where winter 'design' outdoor temperature is 0.5 °C and the indoor temperature is 22°C, the annual number of degree-hours is 64125 Kh (see eq. 1.12).

 The heating requirement will be Htg = 64125 Kh × 282 W/K = 18083 Wh ≈ **18 kWh**.

 As the 'design' ΔT is 0.5 – 22 = −21.5 K, the required heating capacity will be (eq. 1.21–eq. 1.23). (The negative implies heat loss.)

  Q = 282 W.K × −21.5 K = 6063 W = **6.1 kW**.

1.4.3.2   Insulation

Insulation means the control of heat flow, for which three different mechanisms can be distinguished: reflective, resistive and capacitive.

 Reflective insulation: where the heat transfer is primarily radiant, such as across a cavity or through an attic space, the emittance of the warmer surface and the absorptance of the receiving surface determine the heat flow.

 A shiny aluminium foil has both a low emittance and a low absorptance, it is therefore a good reflective insulator. It will be effective only if it is facing a cavity, so it does not itself have an R-value, but it modifies the R-value of the cavity. For example, a cavity at least 25 mm wide, in a wall, would have the following resistances:

with ordinary building materials	0.18 m²K/W
if one surface is lined with foil	0.35
if both surfaces are lined with foil	0.6 (see Data sheet D.1.4 for further data).

A reflective surface in contact with another material would have no effect, as heat flow would take place by conduction.

An often asked question (in hot climates) is: which would be more effective to reduce downward heat flow in an attic space: to have a foil (a) on top of the ceiling, with its face upwards (relying on its low absorptance) or (b) under the roof skin, with face down (relying on its low emittance)? The two would be equally effective, when new. However, in less than a year the foil over the ceiling would be covered in dust, so its reflectance (low absorptance) is destroyed, therefore solution (b) would be better in the long run.

In a hot climate, where the downward heat flow is to be reduced, this solution (b) could be very effective, but almost useless in a cold climate, in reducing upward heat flow. Here the top of the ceiling (of a heated room) is warm, and will heat the air adjacent to it, which will then rise and transmit its heat to the underside of the roof. So the upward heat transfer is dominantly convective, unaffected by the foil.

Fig. 1.57 shows that the downward heat transfer is primarily radiant (strongly affected by the foil): there will be practically no convective transfer, the heated air will remain adjacent to the roof skin, as it is lighter than the rest of the attic air.

On this basis some authors suggest that in a hot climate such a foil insulation under the roof skin is preferable to resistive insulation. It will reduce downward heat flow, but will allow the escape of heat at night, thus permitting the building to cool down; acting practically as a 'thermal diode'. A diode is an electronic device that allows current flow in one direction only. A resistive insulation would affect the up and down heat flow almost equally.

Resistive insulation: of all common materials, air has the lowest thermal conductivity: 0.025 W/m.K (other values are given in Data sheet D.1.1) – as long as it is still. However, in a cavity, convection currents will effectively transfer heat from the warmer to the cooler face. The purpose of resistive insulation is just to keep the air still, dividing it into small cells, with the minimum amount of actual material. Such materials are often referred to as

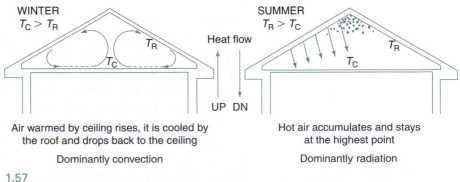

1.57

Heat flow through an attic space

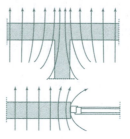

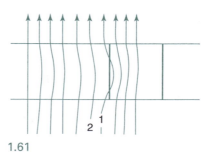

1.58
Thermal bridge due to geometry

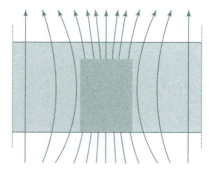

1.59
Thermal bridge in mixed construction

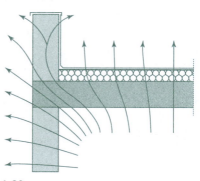

1.60
The two effects combined

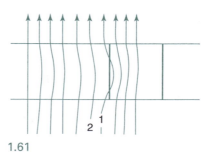

1.61
Concrete column in a brick wall

Table 1.3 Summary of steady state heat flow expressions

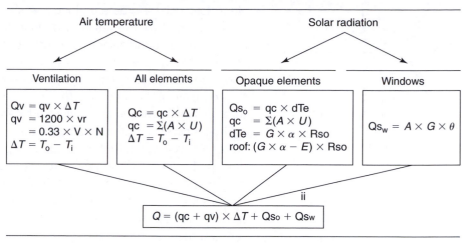

	Air temperature		Solar radiation	
Ventilation	All elements	Opaque elements	Windows
$Q_v = q_v \times \Delta T$ $q_v = 1200 \times v_r$ $\quad= 0.33 \times V \times N$ $\Delta T = T_o - T_i$	$Q_c = q_c \times \Delta T$ $q_c = \Sigma(A \times U)$ $\Delta T = T_o - T_i$	$Q_{s_o} = q_c \times dT_e$ $q_c \;= \Sigma(A \times U)$ $dT_e = G \times \alpha \times R_{so}$ roof: $(G \times \alpha - E) \times R_{so}$	$Q_{s_w} = A \times G \times \theta$

ii

$$Q = (q_c + q_v) \times \Delta T + Q_{s_o} + Q_{s_w}$$

'bulk insulation'. The best ones have a fine foam structure, consisting of small closed air cells separated by very thin membranes or bubbles, or consist of fibrous materials with entrapped air between the fibres.

The most common insulating materials are expanded or extruded plastic foams, such as polystyrene or polyurethane or fibrous materials in the form of batts or blankets, such as mineral wool, glass fibres or even natural wool.

Loose cellulose fibres or loose exfoliated vermiculite can be used as cavity fills or as poured over a ceiling. Second-class insulators include strawboard, wood wool slabs (wood shavings loosely bonded by cement), wood fibre softboards and various types of lightweight concrete (either using lightweight aggregate or autoclaved aerated concrete).

Heat flow into (and out of) buildings is driven by two external (climatic) forces: air temperature and solar radiation. The expressions used for calculating these heat flows are summarised in Table 1.3.

1.4.3.3 Thermal bridges

Thermal bridges usually cause multidimensional (steady state) heat flow. In the above discussion the assumption was made that heat flows through an envelope element with the flow path being perpendicular to the plane of that element, i.e. the phenomenon is analysed as a *one-dimensional heat flow*. Strictly speaking, this is true only for infinitely large elements with parallel plane surfaces and a uniform cross-section. The results obtained with calculation techniques presented above are therefore approximate only.

In real building elements the criteria of one-dimensional heat flow are often not fulfilled. Where the boundaries are other than plane parallel surfaces, or the material is not homogeneous, two- or three-dimensional heat flows develop. Areas where increased, multidimensional heat flow occurs are called *thermal bridges*. These may be the consequences of the geometric form (Fig. 1.58), including corner effects, the combination of materials of different conductivities (Fig. 1.59), or both (Fig. 1.60).

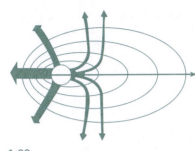

1.62
Heat flow 'downhill'

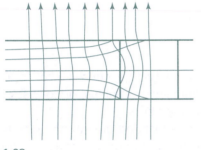

1.63
Temperature isotherms near a thermal bridge

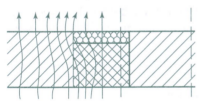

1.64
Flow paths: insulation over a column

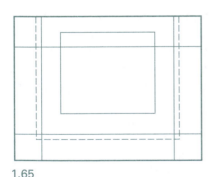

1.65
A wall module: thermal bridge bands

Temperature distribution and thermal bridges

Heat flow will be greatest along the shortest path, the path of least resistance. In Fig. 1.61 the resistance along flow path 1 is less than it would be along a line perpendicular to the surface, due to the higher conductivity of the column. Along flow path 2 the resistance is also reduced, due to the bigger 'cross-section', not 'occupied' by other flows. In a heat loss situation, the heat flow density will be greater at thermal bridges, therefore the surface temperature outside increased and inside reduced.

Heat flows in the direction of the steepest temperature gradient, as water flows in the direction of the steepest slope (Fig. 1.62). Thus the heat flow paths are at right angles to the isotherms (an isotherm is the locus of points of equal temperature). In Fig. 1.63 the density of heat flow paths indicates an increased heat flow, while the isotherms show an increased outside surface temperature at the column and a reduced inner surface temperature.

If, as in Fig. 1.64, an insulating element is inserted (here: on the outside face of the concrete column), which blocks the heat flow, the temperature in the highly conductive column will be higher than in the adjoining wall, therefore a sideways heat flow will occur, increasing the flow density near the column. The outside surface temperature over the insulating insert will be lower and next to this insert higher than of the plain wall.

As a rule of thumb, the effect of thermal bridges reduces to negligible levels beyond a strip of a width of twice the wall thickness. If the wall thickness is 300 mm, the width of this strip is approx. 600 mm, in both directions from the edge.

Viewing a usual room size facade element and marking these strips along the joints with abutting elements and around the window, it can be seen that there is no area on this element that would be free of thermal bridge effects and of multidimensional temperature distribution (Fig. 1.65). For a further discussion of thermal bridges, see Section 1.5.1 (Example 1.7) and Data sheet D.1.6.

Capacitive insulation will be considered in Section 1.4.4.

1.4.3.4 Steady state balance

With reference to the thermal balance equation (eq. 1.13), it can be seen that most items have been included in Example 1.3 but not internal heat gain Q_i and solar gain Q_s. The former was discussed in Section 1.4.3 above and the latter in Section 1.4.1.3 but not in a form that could be used in this equation. Both these would reduce the heating requirement. For both, the daily average value should be estimated and included as constant for the day and for the building. The heat loss is variable as a function of the building conductance (q). It is convenient to compare the total losses with the total gains in a graphic form, which can become an important design tool to examine the benefit of different improvements.

Thus Example 1.3 can be continued:

EXAMPLE 1.4   HEAT LOSSES AND GAINS

Qi:	2 persons × 120W =	240 W
	computers etc. 320	600 W × 10 h = 6000 Wh
	urn	600 W × 1 h = 600
	lights: 400 lux × 0.04* × 35 m² = 560 W × 4 h = 2240

| | | | 8840 |
| Qs | exposed area 52 m² × 550 W/m² × 0.4 × 5 h = | 57200 | Wh |

66040 / 24 = 2752 W
say   2.75 kW

Note: * From Table 2.5 for a fluorescent lamp in an open trough.

Draw a graph with kW on the vertical axis and temperature on the horizontal. Plot the (constant) Qs + Qi horizontal line at **2.75** kW.

Mark the lowest acceptable Ti (take e.g. 18°C) as the set point on the horizontal axis. At the origin point (in this case, −5°C) ΔT = 18 + 5 = 23 K.

From Example.1.3, q = 282, thus heat loss Q = 282 W/K × 23 = 6486 W ≈ **6.5** kW. Mark this on the vertical axis and connect to the set point, this sloping line shows the heat loss at any outdoor temperature.

The intersection of the two lines gives the 'balance point' temperature, where the heat loss is the same as the heat gains (Q = Qs + Qi), in this case, **8.4** °C. This means that at this temperature, there is no heating requirement (Fig. 1.66).

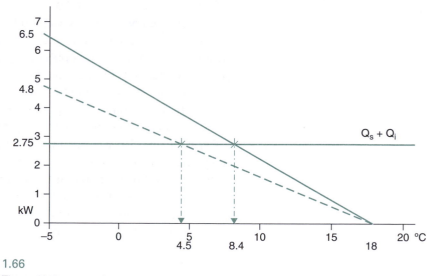

1.66

Thermal balance graph

The effect of various improvements can then be examined. Reducing the ventilation to N = 2.25 would give a qv = 0.33 × 2.25 × 119 = **88.36** W/K.

For the south, east and west walls, insert a 25 mm EPS in the cavity (from Data sheet D.1.2) U = 0.72 W/m.K, thus the tabulation of Example 1.3 would be:

1	west wall	17 m²	0.72	12.24 W/K	
2	window			6.96	from Ex.1.3
3	north wall			23.87	from Ex.1.3

> **EXAMPLE 1.4 CONTINUED**
>
> | | | | | |
> |---|---|---|---|---|
> | 4 door | | | 3.52 | from Ex.1.3 |
> | 5 east wall | 17 | 0.72 | 12.24 | |
> | 6 south wall | 19.6 | 0.72 | 14.11 | |
> | 7 roof | | | 17.85 | from Ex.1.3 |
> | 8 floor | | | 29.75 W/K | from Ex.1.3 |
>
> $$qc = 120.54$$
> $$qv = 88.36$$
> $$\text{total } q = \mathbf{208.9} \text{ W/K}$$
>
> The vertical axis intercept will become 208.9 × 23 = 4804 W, say, **4.8** kW. This can then be connected to the set point, and the balance-point temperature will become 4.5°C.

1.4.4 Dynamic response of buildings

Capacitive insulation, i.e. envelope-layers of a high thermal capacity material (massive construction), affects not only the magnitude of heat flow, but also its timing. Both reflective and resistive insulation respond to temperature changes instantaneously. As soon as there is a heat input at one face, a heat output on the other side will appear, albeit at a controlled rate. Not so with capacitive insulation. This relies on the thermal capacity of materials and their delaying action on the heat flow.

In a non-steady, randomly varying thermal environment the tracing of heat flows requires sophisticated and lengthy calculation methods, which are feasible only if included in computer programs. There is a sub-set of non-steady heat flow regimes, the *periodic heat flow*, the analysis of which is relatively easy. Fortunately, most meteorological variables (temperature, solar radiation) show a regular variation, a repetitive 24-hour cycle, The following discussion relates to such a periodic heat flow analysis.

Periodic heat flow is illustrated in Fig. 1.67 over a 24-hour period. The solid line is the heat flow through an actual masonry wall and the dashed line is the heat flow through a 'zero-mass' wall of the same U-value. This curve would be the result if we calculated the heat flow by a steady state method for each hour and connected the points.

Both curves show a 24-hour cycle, but they differ in two ways:

1 The actual heat flow curve is delayed behind the zero-mass curve by some time. This delay of the peak of the solid curve behind the peak of the dashed-line curve is referred to as the **time-lag**, (or phase-shift, denoted ϕ) measured in hours.

2 The amplitude or swing of the peak from the daily average heat flow is smaller for the solid line (sQ), than for the dashed line, showing the wall of zero mass (sQ_0). The ratio of the two amplitudes is referred to as the **decrement factor**, or amplitude decrement, denoted μ:

$$\mu = \frac{sQ}{sQ_0}$$

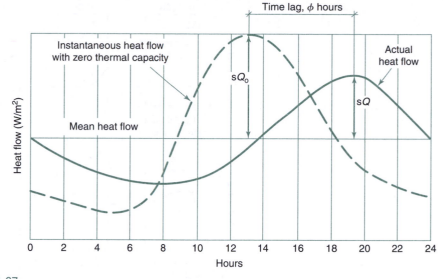

1.67

Heat flow (inwards) through a mass wall (m and f)

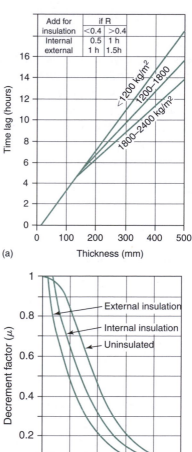

(a)

(b)

1.68

Time lag and decrement factors

A similar diagram could be drawn with the temperature on the vertical scale. The dashed line would then show the temperatures of the outer surface and the solid line indicating temperatures at the inside surface. From this, the same two properties could be derived.

The calculation of these two properties is fairly involved, particularly for multi-layer elements, but Data sheets D.1.2 and D.1.3 give these values for numerous everyday constructions, alongside their U-values. Fig. 1.68 shows graphs for the time lag and decrement factor properties of solid, homogeneous massive walls (brick, masonry, concrete or earth) and the effect of insulation applied to the inside or the outside of the massive wall. These are based on the work of Danter (1960) at the BRE (Building Research Establishment, UK), also given in Petherbridge (1974), often quoted in many publications, but seem to have been superseded by Milbank and Harrington-Lynn (1974) and for a more accurate and reliable calculation of these factors, see Method sheet M.1.11. This method was used to find the ϕ and μ values in Data sheets D.1.2 and D.1.3.

If we take a 220 mm brick wall with a U-value of 2.26 W/m²K and take a polystyrene slab of about 10 mm thickness, which would have about the same U-value, under steady state conditions the heat flow through these two would be identical and the calculations based on steady state assumptions would give the same results. In real life, their behaviour will be quite different. The difference is that the brick wall has a surface density of about 375 kg/m² and the polystyrene slab only some 5 kg/m². The respective thermal capacities would be 300 kJ/m² and 7 kJ/m². In the brick wall each small layer of the material will absorb some heat to increase its temperature before it can transmit any heat to the next layer. The stored heat would then be emitted with a considerable time delay.

A time sequence of temperature profiles through this wall is shown in Fig. 1.69. It can be observed that from evening hours (from about 16:00 h) onwards the middle of the wall is the warmest and the stored heat will also

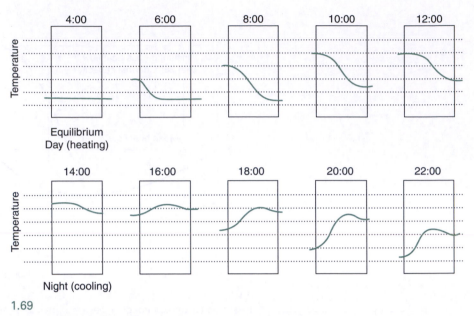

Equilibrium
Day (heating)

Night (cooling)

1.69
Time sequence of temperature profiles

start flowing backwards. So (assuming inward heat flow) only a part of the heat that had entered the outside surface will reach the inside surface. In the polystyrene slab the temperature profile would be a sloping straight line moving up and down as the temperature changes on the input side.

The procedure to calculate periodic heat flow consists of two parts, e.g. for a solid element:

1 Find the daily mean heat flow, $\overline{Q}c$.
2 Find the deviation from (or swing about) this mean flow for time (hour) 't' of the day:

sQc_t

First find the mean sol-air temperature of the outside surface, $\overline{T}_{sa}$, then find the mean temperature difference ΔT, then

$$\overline{Q}c = qc \times \Delta\overline{T} \qquad (1.27)$$

Then calculate the swing in heat flow at time t due to the deviation of conditions ϕ hours earlier (at time $t - \phi$) from the day's average:

$$sQc_t = qc \times \mu \times (T_{sa \cdot (t-\phi)} - \overline{T}_{sa}) \qquad (1.28)$$

e.g. if the calculation is done for 14:00 and $\phi = 5$ h, then take the sol-air temperature at $14 - 5 = 9$ o'clock ($T_{sa.9:00}$).

The heat flow at time t will then be the sum of the mean and the swing:

$$Qc_t = \overline{Q}c + sQc_t$$

substituting:

$$Qc_t = A \times U \times [(\overline{T}_{sa} - T_i) + \mu \times (T_{sa.(t-\Phi)} - \overline{T}_{sa})] \qquad (1.29)$$

Table 1.4 Expressions for the swing in heat flow

	Building parameter	Environmental parameter
1 Ventilation	$sQv = qv$	$\times\ (T_{o.t} - T_{o.av})$
2 Conduction, glass	$sQc_g = A \times U$	$\times\ (T_{o.t} - T_{o.av})$
3 Conduction, opaque	$sQc_o = A \times U \times \mu$	$\times\ (T_{o(t-\phi)} - T_{o.av})$
4 Solar, glass	$sQs_g = A \times \theta_a$	$\times\ (G_t - G_{av})$
5 Solar, opaque	$sQs_o = A \times U \times \mu \times \alpha \times R_{so}$	$\times\ (G_{t-\phi} - G_{av})$
6 Internal gain	$sQi = Qi_t - Qi_{av}$	

Notes: Where μ = decrement factor, ϕ = time lag, θ_a = alternating solar gain factor
$qv = 0.33 \times N \times V$ or $1200 \times vr$ (N = number of air changes, vr = volume rate).

The deviation from the mean heat flow rate (sQc_t) at time t can be calculated on the basis of eq. 1.28 (included in eq. 1.29) for a single element.

Table 1.4 summarises the six components of such flow swing. Items 3, 4 and 5 will have to be repeated for each envelope element of a different orientation.

The benefits of capacitive insulation (or mass effect) will be greatest in hot-dry climates, which show large diurnal temperature variations. Some sources suggest that a mean range (the range between monthly mean maximum and minimum, averaged for the 12 months) of 10 K would warrant heavy construction, others put this limit at 8 K. Capacitive insulation has a dampening, stabilising effect; it can improve comfort or, if the building is air-conditioned, it can produce energy savings.

The dynamic properties (time-lag, decrement factor and admittance) of multilayer elements depend not only on the material and thickness of layers, but also on the sequence of these layers with respect to the direction of heat flow. This is best illustrated by an example (Fig. 1.70).

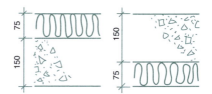

1.70
Sequence of layers (roof)

EXAMPLE 1.5   A ROOF SLAB: POSITION OF INSULATION

Take a roof slab of 150 mm reinforced concrete, with 75 mm of EPS insulation (the waterproof membrane is thermally negligible) and consider a summer (heat gain) situation.

The air-to-air resistance will be

$$
\begin{aligned}
R_{a-a} &= R_{so} + R_{EPS} + R_{CONCR} + R_{si} \\
&= 0.04 + \frac{0.075}{0.035} + \frac{0.150}{1.4} + 0.14 = 2.43
\end{aligned}
$$

$U = 1/R_{a-a} = 1 / 2.43 = 0.41$ W/m²K.

This is the same, regardless of the sequence of layers, but for dynamic properties:

	Φ	μ	Y_{inside}
EPS externally	6.28 h	0.3	5.41 W/m²K
EPS internally	5.03 h	0.56	0.44
difference	1.25 h	0.26	4.97

The last column (Y) is the *admittance* of the element, which is the measure of its ability to pick up (and release) heat from the indoors, as the temperature changes (swings). Y has a strong influence when indoor temperatures are to be calculated which result from the heat flows.

The total admittance of a building (or of a room) is

$$qa = \Sigma(A \times Y) \text{ in W/K} \tag{1.30}$$

The EPS externally produces a time lag some 1.25 hour longer, reduces the decrement factor from 0.56 to a little over half (to 0.3) and gives an inside surface admittance some 4.97 W/m^2K more than the reverse order of layers. So, the mass inside of a resistive insulation will reduce the heat gain, delay it more and result in a more stable indoor temperature.

For a summary of dynamic thermal properties, see Method sheet M.1.10.

1.4.4.1 Dynamic heat flow

This was first analysed by Fourier (1768–1830), a French mathematician. He developed the expression for heat flow through a thin slab:

$$\frac{\partial T}{\partial t} = \alpha \times \left[\frac{\partial^2 T}{\partial x^2} + \frac{\partial^2 T}{\partial y^2} \right]$$

where

T = temperature at any point (x,y) at time t
α = thermal diffusivity (see Method sheet M.1.10) of the material

and the heat flow rate will be

$$Q = -\lambda \times A \times \frac{\partial T}{\partial x}$$

which became known as Fourier's law.

The thermal system of a building can be depicted by a network of differential equations of this type. Solutions of these simultaneous differential equations can be of two main types:

1 *Finite difference methods*, where the heat flows induced by environmental or occupational changes are traced from point-to-point, with energy balances calculated for each point at frequent intervals. In some systems this may involve the solution of up to 10 000 simultaneous differential equations.
2 *Response factor methods*, where the thermal response of a building element to a unit pulse is first calculated, i.e. the response factor of that element and then the actual environmental and occupational changes are applied to these response factors. A later development of this produces a *building response factor*.

Manual execution of these calculations is impracticable but these form the basis of the algorithms for numerous computer-based simulation programs.

1.4.4.2 Thermal response simulation

Thermal response simulation of buildings has become an everyday design tool with the rapid development of computers, since the 1970s. PCs are now more powerful than the early mainframe computers and can run the most sophisticated simulation programs. Relatively simple programs have also been produced, which use basically steady-state type calculations adding some 'fudge factor' to approximate dynamic behaviour, e.g. QUICK or BREDEM (BRE domestic energy model).

A number of programs are based on the time-lag and decrement factor concepts introduced above (a harmonic analysis), and using the 'admittance procedure' of the UK BRE (e.g. ADMIT and ARCHIPAK) to find the temperatures resulting from such heat flows. These analyse the dynamic thermal response, but in a strict sense, do not 'simulate' the various heat flows. The most refined of these is ECOTECT, with graphic inputs of the building and graphic outputs which allow optimisation of sub-systems.

There are numerous programs which trace the heat flow hour-by-hour through all components of the building, using an annual hourly climatic data base (such as those mentioned in Section 1.3.3). These can predict hourly indoor temperatures or the heating/cooling load if set indoor conditions are to be maintained. Some go further and simulate the mechanical (HVAC) systems, thus predicting the energy consumption for the hour, the day, the month or the year.

CHEETAH (of the CSIRO) became the basis of the Australian NatHERS (National House Energy Rating Scheme) and AccuRate (accurate rating). ENERGY10 or EnergyPlus of NREL (pronounced 'enrel', National Renewable Energy Laboratory, Colorado) is a design tool especially for passive solar, but generally for low energy buildings. The most sophisticated of these is probably ESPr, of the University of Strathclyde and it is now the European reference simulation program (it was originally written for mainframe computers, but can now be run on PCs under the LINUX operating system).

The most widely used one is the US DoE-2 (it has reached its 46th version and it is 'freeware', and can be downloaded from http://doe2.com/DOE2). This is now available to run on PCs, under Windows. Hong *et al.* (2000) reviewed more than a dozen such programs.

Computer graphics systems have developed to such an extent that most, if not all, architectural offices now use them for drawing production. On the other hand, thermal (and other) simulation programs are rarely used by architects, it is suggested that this is engineers' territory. For such simulations the most laborious task is the description of ('inputting') the building. So to kill two birds with one stone, it is desirable: to attempt to use the graphics (drafting) system also as the basis of simulations. Recently several such integrated packages have appeared. The package called TAS of EDSL (Environmental Design Solutions Ltd of Milton Keynes, UK) has a fully-fledged 3-D CAD module, as a front end for simulations, down to a CFD (computerised fluid dynamics) module for air flow studies.

COMBINE (of the EU Joule program) integrates a number of CAD and simulation programs, including ESPr, SUPERLITE and VENT. In a similar manner, in America EnergyPlus combines DOE2, BLAST (Building Loads and System Thermodynamics) and COMIS, a multi-zone air flow program.

Probably the most comprehensive package is the IES-VE, Integrated Environmental Solutions (NOT the Illuminating Engineering Society) Virtual Environment program system. Its key units are the CUI (Common User

Interface) and the IDM (Integrated Data Model). The main modules that use these are:

- Model IIT, model builder, to create and edit the building geometry.
- SunCast, visualisation and analysis of shading.
- ApacheSim, thermal simulation, coupled with ApacheHVAC for mechanical systems.
- ApacheCALC for load analysis and MacroFlo for simulation of natural ventilation.
- MicroFlow, for three-dimensional CFD (computational fluid dynamics).
- FlucsPro and RadianceIES for electric and daylighting. The latter can produce photo-realistic interior modelling of daylighting, including luminance distribution.
- LifeCycle for energy and cost life cycle analysis.

More detailed discussion of this topic is beyond the scope of this book.

1.4.5   Application

The whole is more than the sum of its parts – a statement as true for the thermal behaviour of buildings as in perception psychology.

In perception psychology there are two main schools of thought: the behaviourists who analyse simple stimulus-reaction relationships and try to build up an overall picture from such building blocks, while followers of the Gestalt School profess that the 'configuration', i.e., the totality of experience, the interaction of all sensory channels is important. In a similar way one can discuss the thermal effect of individual building components, but the thermal behaviour of any building will be the result of the interaction of all its elements, the thermal system embodied in the climate–building–services–user relationship. In this sense we can speak of the 'thermal Gestalt' of a building.

A simple example of this interdependence is the question of roof insulation in a warm climate. There is no doubt that increased roof insulation would reduce daytime (solar) heat gain, but it will also prevent night-time dissipation of heat. Only a careful analysis will give the right answer, the best for both situations.

The distinction must be made between a fixed and a variable (adjustable) element. In the latter case we can have ample roof insulation, if there is little thermal mass and any stored heat can be dissipated in the evening by ventilation.

One can quote the example of equator-facing windows, which are desirable in winter, but if the building is lightweight, without adequate thermal storage mass, the resulting heat gain may produce overheating during the day; the user will get rid of this by opening the windows, so there will be no heat left to soften the coldness of the night.

In some texts the use of skylights is advocated as an effective energy conservation measure. It is undoubtedly useful for daylighting, but it produces more solar heat gain in the summer (with high angle sun) than in winter, and in winter in most cases it will be a net loser of energy. Such loss can be avoided by using insulated shutters, controlled from the inside. In the summer it may cause overheating. It depends how it is done. It may have its own adjustable shading device, possibly even with an automated (sensor-driven) control.

Over the last ten years or so, there has been a battle raging over the usefulness of courtyards in hot dry climates. Both the protagonists and adversaries produced measured results, which seem to support their contention. The resolution is that *it depends* on how the courtyard is treated. It can be both good and bad. Even the 'bad' can be improved by shading, a shade tree, vegetation and water (a pond or a spray).

It is often said that *to any difficult question there is a simple answer*, however, it is usually wrong. The right answer is usually quite complicated, and often it is of the 'if . . . then . . .' type. When the designer asks a consultant (e.g. an architectural science expert) what the width of eaves of a house should be, the answer can only be: '*It depends* . . .' and a long sequence of counter-questions, such as, where is the house? In what climate? When is the overheated period? What is the orientation? Is it single- or double-storey? Is a window considered or a door with glass down to floor level?

The architect must make thousands of (larger or smaller) decisions during the design of even the simplest building. There is no time to analyse every single question in detail. However, the analytical attitude is important. The designer working in a given climate, given the culture and the given building industry, will probably examine such questions once and remember the answer. Many such answers derived from serious analysis will enrich his/her experience. Education is (or should be) accelerated experience. Studying architectural science (*inter alia*) should provide such experience, the details of which may be forgotten but the 'experience' will influence subsequent design thinking.

Accumulated experience (including experience of failures or the experience of others) may make quick decisions possible but would also suggest what factors, what conditions would have a bearing on a given question. And this is what constitutes professional know-how.

1.5 THERMAL DESIGN: PASSIVE CONTROLS

The first step in any bioclimatic design approach is to examine the given climate and establish the nature of the climatic problem and relate the climate to human requirements. A good way of doing this is to use the psychrometric chart as the base.

Once the comfort zone for winter and summer has been plotted (as in Section 1.2.4, Fig. 1.21), the climate can be plotted on the same diagram.

Mark on the chart two points for each of the 12 months: one given by the mean maximum temperature with the afternoon RH and the other by the mean minimum temperature with the morning RH. Connect the two points by a line (Fig. 1.71c). The 12 lines thus produced would indicate the median zone of climatic conditions.

The relationship of these lines to the comfort zone indicates the nature of the climatic problem. Lines to the right of the comfort zone indicate overheating, to the left underheating. Lines above the 12 g/kg limit indicate that humidity may be a problem. Long lines indicate large diurnal variations, short ones are characteristic of humid climates with small diurnal variations.

Fig. 1.71 (printouts of the ARCHIPAK program) shows psychrometric plots for each of the four basic climate types. (Fig. 1.71c shows how a climate line is generated.)

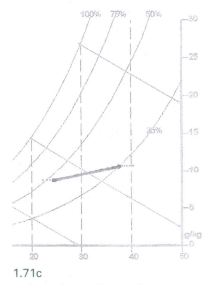

1.71c

A climate line for Tennant Creek, January

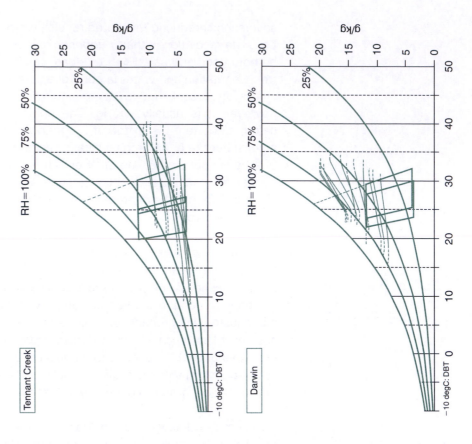
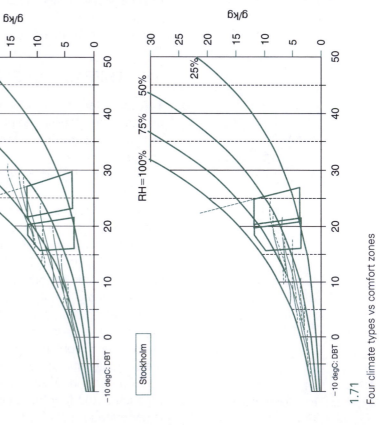

1.71

Four climate types vs comfort zones

The next step would then be the choice of passive control strategy. Four basic strategies can be distinguished, with some subdivisions in each:

1 passive solar heating (with efficiency or *utilisability* of 0.5 and 0.7);
2 mass effect (summer and winter + for summer with night ventilation);
3 air movement (physiological cooling) effect, for 1 and 1.5 m/s;
4 evaporative cooling (direct and indirect).

The range of outdoor conditions, for which each of these strategies has the potential to ensure indoor comfort (referred to as the CPZ or control potential zone) can be outlined on the psychrometric chart. The method is described in Method sheet M.1.7 but introduced here for each of these strategies.

1.5.1 Passive control of heat flows

In climates where there is a large temperature difference between the inside and the outside (the climate lines extend far from the comfort zone), where some form of heating or cooling will be necessary, thermal insulation of the envelope is the most important means of control. In most countries there are regulatory requirements for the insulation of envelope elements, walls, roofs and windows. These may stipulate a maximum U-value (which must not be exceeded) or a minimum R-value (R_{a-a}) which must be achieved by the construction (see e.g. Table 1.5 in Section 1.5.3.2).

EXAMPLE 1.6   R-VALUE AND ADDED INSULATION

Assume that we propose to have a 260 mm cavity brick wall (105 + 50 + 105), with 10 mm plastering on the inside. Conductivities are:

facing brick (outer skin) $\lambda = 0.84$ W/m.K
inner skin of brick $\lambda = 0.62$
plastering $\lambda = 0.5$

inside	R_{si}	$= 0.12$ m²K/W
10 mm plastering 0.010/0.5		$= 0.02$
105 mm inner brick 0.105/0.62		$= 0.17$
cavity	R_c	$= 0.18$
105 mm outer brick 0.105/0.84		$= 0.12$
outside surface	R_{so}	$= \underline{0.06}$
	R_{a-a}	$= 0.67$

$U = 1/0.67 = 1.49$ W/m²K

The regulations require, say:
$U <= 0.8$ W/m²K $R_{a-a} > 1/0.8$ $= \underline{1.25}$
additional R required: $1.25 - 0.67 = 0.58$.

Consider using EPS boards inside the cavity, held against the inner skin of brick, which has a conductivity of $\lambda = 0.033$ W/m.K.
The required thickness (b for 'breadth') will be:
as $R = b/\lambda$
we need 0.58 m²K/W $= b/0.033$ $b = 0.58 \times 0.033 = 0.019$ mm
that is, we must install a 20 mm EPS board.

This method can be generalised, to say that, take the resistance of the construction selected for reasons other than thermal and find the additional resistance required. From that the necessary thickness of added insulation can be found.

EXAMPLE 1.7   THE EFFECT OF THERMAL BRIDGES: $U_{AVERAGE}$

Assume that a wall element of 5 m length and 3 m height is at the corner of a building and it incorporates a window of 2.5 × 1.5 m dimensions. There is an internal partition joining at the other end. The wall is of the construction examined above (U = 0.8 W/m²K) and the window is double-glazed, with a U-value of 3.6 W/m²K (Fig. 1.72).

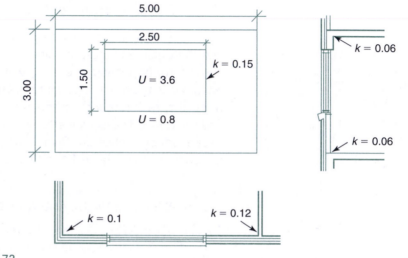

1.72

Thermal bridges, linear k coefficients

The wall is 5 × 3 = 15 m² minus the window: 2.5 × 1.5 = 3.75 m² net wall area = 11.25 m².

The A × U products are:

wall	11.25 × 0.8	=	9 W/K
window	3.75 × 3.6	=	13.5
			22.5 W/K

The following linear losses must be added (values from Data sheet D.1.5):

for the window perimeter	8 m × 0.15	=	1.2
for the outer corner	3 m × 0.1	=	0.3
for the wall/partition junction	3 m × 0.12	=	0.36
for the wall/floor slab joints	2 × 5 m × 0.06	=	0.6 W/K
			2.46 W/K

$$U_{av} = \frac{22.5 + 2.46}{15} = 1.66 \text{ W/m}^2\text{K}$$

in a generalised form:

$$U_{av} = \frac{\Sigma(A \times U) + \Sigma(L \times k)}{\Sigma A}$$

where L is the length of each linear component.

Thermal bridge effects (discussed in Section 1.4.3.3) can be allowed for by using linear heat loss coefficients, k (see Data sheet D.1.6) in addition to the U-value-based calculation. Dimensionally these coefficients are W/m.K and are to be multiplied by the length, to give W/K. This is illustrated by Example 1.7.

A quick look at any table of U-values would show that the weakest point of any building envelope is the window. While even an uninsulated brick wall (as in Example 1.4) would have a U-value around 1.5 W/m²K, an ordinary single-glazed window would be about four times as much, 5.5–6.5 W/m²K.

The U-value of a window depends on the following:

1 the glazing: single, double, low-e, etc.
2 the frame: wood, metal, discontinuous metal
3 frame thickness:10–30% of the elevational area of the window
4 exposure: sheltered, normal, exposed.

A window with a sealed double glazing unit would have a U-value of 2.7 to 4.5 W/m²K, depending on the frame. A wooden frame has a lower U-value than a metal one, but the latter can be improved by a built-in discontinuity (which would break the thermal bridge effect of the frame).

A low emittance coating inside a sealed double glazing unit would reduce the radiant heat transfer and a low pressure inert gas (krypton or argon) fill (partial vacuum) would reduce the conductive transfer. Such glazing, with a discontinuous 10% metal frame (where the frame takes up 10% of the overall window area) would have a U-value as low as 2.0 W/m²K. For a discussion of special glasses, see Section 1.4.1.4.

A good window must perform five functions:

1 provide a view;
2 admit daylight;
3 reduce heat loss;
4 admit solar heat (in a cold situation);
5 allow a controllable ventilation.

In a cold situation a large window may be a liability. It would cause a large heat loss, but it could also produce a significant solar heat gain. A comparison can be made between heat loss and gain in a very simple way, based on a unit area of window, as in Example 1.8.

EXAMPLE 1.8   WINDOWS: HEAT LOSS VS SOLAR GAIN

Taking Canberra as an example, calculate the gains and losses over a day of the coldest month (July). Comparison can be made for a unit area:

$T_{o.av}$ = 5.8°C. Take T_i as 23°C, thus the ΔT is 17.2 K.

Take a single-glazed window:

U = 5.3 W/m²K and solar gain factor: θ = 0.76
orientation: North
daily vertical irradiation $D_{V.360}$ = 2801 Wh/m².

Assume a solar 'efficiency' (utilisability) of 0.7.

GAIN: 2801 × 0.76 × 0.7 = 1490 Wh/m²
LOSS: 5.3 × 17.2 × 24 = 2188
Loss > Gain, thus the window is not beneficial.

However, if double glazing is used:

U = 3 W/m²K, θ = 0.64
GAIN: 2801 × 0.64 × 0.7 = 1255 Wh/m²
LOSS: 3 × 17.2 × 24 = 1238
Loss < Gain, thus it is beneficial (marginally).

If we look at the same window, facing East:

Dv_{90} = 1460 Wh/m²
GAIN: 1460 × 0.64 × 0.7 = 654 Wh/m²
LOSS: same as above = 1238
Loss >> Gain, the window would be a liability.

The situation changes if we use an insulating shutter overnight.
Assume one that would reduce the U-value with single glazing to 1.5 and with double glazing to 1.3 W/m²K and that it would be closed for 14 hours. The (daytime) gain is the same as above. The loss will be:

single glazing: (1.5 × 14 + 5.3 × 10) = 1272 Wh/m² 1490 > 1272 ∴ OK
double glazing: (1.3 × 14 + 3 × 10) = 829 1255 > 829 ∴ OK

1.5.1.1   Passive solar heating

Passive solar heating, in its simplest form, requires no more than a good window, facing the equator. An appropriate horizontal shading device could provide shading in the summer but allow the entry of solar radiation in the winter (see Fig. 1.51). Adjustable shading could also be considered (a 'direct gain' system).

The performance of such a system would also depend on the available thermal storage mass. In a lightweight building the solar heat input would over-heat the interior, which may lead to discomfort, but also to a large heat loss.

Heavy walls and floor (especially where it is reached by the solar beam) would absorb much heat, reduce the overheating and the stored heat would be released at night. The mass need not be very much. For the 24-hour cycle, the depth of heat penetration (i.e., the effective storage, where the heat input and release surface are the same, so there would be a cyclic reversal of heat flow) may not be more than 100–120 mm.

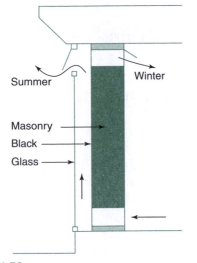

1.73

Principles of the Trombe–Michel wall

A massive wall exposed to solar radiation would also act as a heat collector and storage device, but much heat would be lost through the outside surface, both while it is heated by the sun and after sunset. Such loss could be reduced by a glazing or a transparent insulation cover on the outside. This would be recognised as a passive solar 'mass wall' heating system. However, as the wall surface behind the glass is heated, it will heat the air in the gap and cause a large heat loss, backwards, through the glazing.

This can be reduced by the 'Trombe–Michel' system (named after Jacques Michel (architect) and Felix Trombe (physicist)) (Fig. 1.73), which incorporates vent openings near the floor and near the ceiling. As the heated air rises, it would enter the room through the top vent, drawing in cooler air from the room near the floor level, forming a thermosiphon circulation.

Another passive solar heating system is the 'attached greenhouse'. This can be considered as an enlargement of the air gap of the above system (of about 100 mm) to perhaps 2 m or more. The thermal function is the same as for the Trombe–Michel wall, but while it heats the room behind it, it also provides a useable space for plants and even for sitting, as a 'winter garden' or conservatory. At night, such a greenhouse can lose much heat, so it is essential to provide for closing off the room it serves, or else it becomes a net loser of heat.

The CPZ (see Section 1.5) for passive solar heating (by whatever system) can be estimated on the following basis. The critical parameter is solar radiation on the equator-facing vertical surface, for the average day of the coldest month (D_V). Find the lowest temperature at which the solar gain can match the heat losses.

The limiting condition will be:

$$D_V \times A \times \eta = q \times (T_i - T_o) \times 24$$

where

D_V = vertical irradiation (Wh/m²day)
A = area of solar aperture
η = efficiency (utilisability), taken as 0.5 or 0.7
q = qc + qv, building conductance (W/K)
T_i = indoor temperature limit, taken as Tn-2.5
T_o = the limiting temperature to be found.

Assume a simple house of 100 m² floor area and 20% (= 20 m²) solar window and a building conductance of 115 W/K.

Substituting:

$$D_V \times 20 \times 0.5 = 115 \times (T_i - T_o) \times 24$$

rearranging for T_o

$$T_i - T_o = D_V \times 20 \times 0.5 / (115 \times 24) = D_V \times 0.0036$$
$$T_o = T_i - 0.0036 \times D_V$$

or with the higher efficiency:

$$T_i - T_o = D_V \times 20 \times 0.7 / (115 \times 24) = D_V \times 0.005$$

$$T_o = T_i - 0.005 \times Dv$$

The use of this estimating coefficient (0.0036 and 0.005) is illustrated by Example 1.9.

EXAMPLE 1.9   CPZ: PASSIVE SOLAR HEATING (LOS ANGELES)

If in Los Angeles in January

$D_{V..180} = 3774$ Wh/m² and $T_{o.av} = 13°C$, Tn $= 21.6°C$

Thus, the lower limit of $T_i = 19.1°C$, then with $\eta = 0.5$, the lowest T_o that the solar gain can compensate for is

$T_o = 19.1 - 0.0036 \times 3774 = 5.5°C$

or with $\eta = 0.7$

$T_o = T_i - 0.005 \times D_V$
$T_o = 19.1 - 0.005 \times 3774 = 0.2°C$

which means that down to 5.5°C (or even 0.2°C) outdoor temperature the passive solar heating system has the *potential* to keep the indoors comfortable.

The results are shown in Fig. 1.74. depicting the Control Potential Zone (CPZ) for passive solar heating

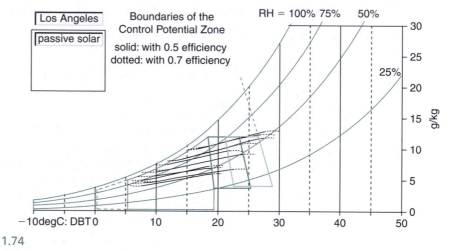

1.74
CPZ: passive solar heating

1.5.1.2   *The mass effect*

The mass effect provided by a heavy construction is beneficial in many situations, even without any such special devices: it is especially useful in a cold climate, for a continuously occupied building (e.g. a house or a hospital), where it would allow the use of intermittent heating and still keep a stable temperature. In an intermittently used and heated building (an office or a school), lightweight (insulated) construction may be better. Massive construction would have a longer heating-up period in the morning and the stored heat would be dissipated overnight, and thus be wasted.

The same argument is valid for an air-conditioned building in a hot-humid climate, where even the nights are too warm.

The 'mass effect' is one of the most important passive control strategies. If there is a storage mass, it can be manipulated according to the climatic needs. In a typical hot-dry climate, with a large diurnal variation, where the temperature varies over the daily cycle between too high and too cold, (where the day's mean is within the comfort zone), massive construction may provide the full solution, it may ensure comfortable indoor conditions without any mechanical cooling (or night heating).

What is the definition of a 'massive, heavyweight' and a 'lightweight' building? The criterion may be the *specific mass* of the building:

$$sM = \frac{\text{total mass of the building}}{\text{floor area of the building}} \frac{kg}{m^2}$$

or the CIBSE 'response factor' (f), which is defined as

$$f = \frac{qa + qv}{qc + qv} \tag{1.31}$$

where

qa = total admittance (see Section 1.4.4, eq. 1.30)
qv and qc have been defined in Sections 1.4.2 and 1.4.3.1.

the boundaries for two or three (arbitrary) divisions are

	sM	f		sM	f
light	<150 kg/m²	<3	light	<=250 kg/m²	<= 4
medium	150–400	3–5			
heavy	> 400	>5	heavy	>250	> 4

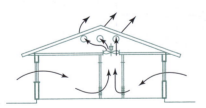

1.75
An attic fan or 'whole house' fan

Night ventilation can be used to modify the mass effect, where the day's average is higher than the comfort limit, to assist the heat dissipation process. This may rely on natural ventilation through windows and other openings, but can also be assisted by a 'whole-house fan' (or attic-fan), operated when $T_o < T_i$ (Fig. 1.75).

This is a large diameter, slow-moving fan, built into the ceiling around the centre of the house. The arrangement should be such that it draws air through all rooms (fresh air inlets in the rooms served) and pushes the air out through the attic, expelling the hot air of that space. This will not provide any sensible air movement, but would help in dissipating any heat stored in the building fabric.

The potential of such a mass effect (the extent of the CPZ or control potential zone) can be estimated by the following reasoning: in a very massive building the indoor temperature would be practically constant at about the level of the outdoor mean.

The outdoor mean can be taken as $(T_{o.max} + T_{o.min}) \times 0.5$.

The amplitude (mean-to-maximum) would be $(T_{o.max} - T_{o.min}) \times 0.5$ but as the building will not quite cool down to the minimum, it is taken as $(T_{o.max} - T_{o.min}) \times 0.3$.

If the mean is to be within the comfort zone, the outdoor maximum must be less than the comfort limit plus the amplitude. So the limit of the control potential zone (the CPZ) will be the upper comfort limit + the amplitude. This is illustrated by Example 1.10.

In a climate, where air temperatures are below comfort, solar radiation can be relied on to supplement the mass effect, to improve the indoor conditions, possibly ensuring comfort, but certainly reducing any heating requirement.

EXAMPLE 1.10   CPZ: MASS EFFECT (PHOENIX)

If in Phoenix, Arizona, in the hottest month (August)

$T_{o.max} = 38°C$, $T_{o.min} = 25°C$, $T_{o.a} = 31.5°C$
$Tn = 27.3°C$

thus, the upper comfort limit = 29.8°C

amplitude $= (38 - 25) \times 0.3 = 3.9$ K
limit of the CPZ $= 29.8 + 3.9 = 33.7°C$.

If the mass effect is assisted by night ventilation, the fabric will be cooled down more effectively, so the amplitude will be taken as $(T_{o.max} - T_{o.min}) \times 0.6$, thus

amplitude $= (38 - 25) \times 0.6 = 6.5$ K
limit of the CPZ $= 29.8 + 6.5 = 36.3°C$

All these temperatures are taken at the 50% RH curve and the corresponding SET lines are the boundaries of the CPZ. Fig. 1.76 illustrates the above example.

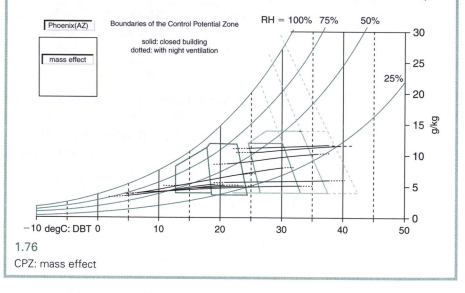

1.76
CPZ: mass effect

1.5.1.3   Air movement

Air movement, i.e. a sensible air velocity (as discussed in Section 1.4.2) can provide physiological cooling. It is an important tool of passive thermal control. Its apparent cooling effect can be estimated using eq. 1.24 (or as per Data sheet D.1.8). An air velocity at the body surface of the occupants is necessary either by cross-ventilation, relying on the wind effect, or by electric fans, most often by low-power ceiling fans. A stack effect, relying on the rise of warm air cannot be relied on for this purpose. First, it would only occur when $T_i > T_o$. and if T_o is high, then T_i would be far too high. Second, even if it works, it may give a mass flow but it would not be of a noticeable velocity. (Method sheet M.1.4 gives an estimation method for both.) Cross-ventilation demands that there should be both an inlet and an outlet opening. The difference between positive pressure on the windward side and negative pressure on the leeward side provides the driving force. The inlet opening should face within 45° of the wind direction dominant during the most overheated periods.

The potential of air movement cooling effect is found using eq. 1.24, thus it will be:

for 1 m/s air velocity: $v_e = 1 - 0.2 = 0.8$ $dT = 6 \times 0.8 - 1.6 \times 0.8^2 = 3.8$ K
for 1.5 m/s $v_e = 1.5 - 0.2 = 1.3$ $dT = 6 \times 1.3 - 1.6 \times 1.3^2 = 5.1$ K

To define the CPZ for air movement effect, these dT values are added to the upper comfort limit along the 50% RH curve. Above that, the boundary will be the corresponding SET line, but below 50% there is a cooling effect even without air movement, as the air is dry, so the additional effect of the air movement is taken as only half of the above: thus, the boundary line will be nearer to the vertical. These boundaries define the range of outdoor conditions under which air movement has the potential to render indoor conditions comfortable.

EXAMPLE 1.11   CPZ: AIR MOVEMENT EFFECT (MOMBASA)

In Mombasa (latitude = −4°), the warmest month is March, with

$T_{o.av}$ = 29°C, thus Tn = 17.6 + 0.31 × 29 = 26.6°C

and

upper comfort limit = 29.1°C

Limits of the air movement CPZs will thus be

for 1 m/s: 29.1 + 3.8 = 32.9°C
for 1.5 m/s: 29. 1 + 5.1 = 34.2°C as illustrated by Fig. 1.77.

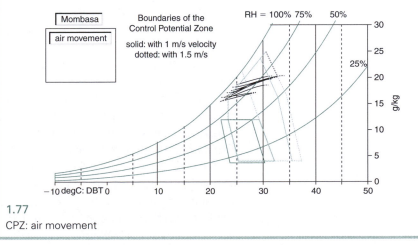

1.77
CPZ: air movement

To produce the maximum total air flow through a space, both inlet and outlet openings should be as large as possible. The inlet opening will define the direction of the air stream entering. To get the maximum localised air velocity, the inlet opening should be much smaller than the outlet. Positioning the inlet opening, its accessories (e.g. louvres or other shading devices) as well as the aerodynamic effects outside (before the air enters) will determine the direction of the indoor air stream.

1.5.1.4 Evaporative cooling

Evaporative cooling can be provided as part of a passive system, e.g. by a roof pool or a courtyard pond, or by a spray over the roof or some other building surface. If evaporation occurs within an enclosed space, it may lower the dry bulb temperature, but it increases the humidity, therefore the latent heat content, in effect, it converts sensible heat to latent heat. The total heat content of the system does not change, i.e. it is said to be adiabatic.

Indirectly, evaporation loss occurs if there is some evaporation within the space or room, which is adiabatic, but the moist air is then removed by ventilation. This process is referred to as 'mass transfer' and must be considered in air conditioning load calculations.

If the evaporation rate (er, in kg/h) is known, the corresponding heat loss will be

$$Qe = (2400 / 3600) \times er = 666 \times er \text{ (W)} \qquad (1.32)$$

where 2400 kJ/kg is the latent heat of evaporation of water.

A *direct evaporative cooler* (Fig. 1.78) would draw air in through fibrous pads, which are kept moist by a perforated pipe, and feed it into the space to be cooled. In the process the latent heat of evaporation is taken from the air, so it is cooled, but the humidity (thus also the latent heat content) of the supply air is increased. The status point on the psychrometric chart will move up and to the left along a constant WBT line (see Fig. 1.13).

For this reason, the CPZ for evaporative cooling can be defined by the WBT line tangential to the upper and lower corners of the comfort zone. It is impractical to achieve more than about 11 K cooling effect (from the Tn temperature), thus the CPZ is delimited by a vertical line at the Tn + 11°C temperature (Fig. 1.79).

The effectiveness of this system is limited by the evaporation potential of the humid air but can be improved by using an indirect evaporative cooler. This uses two fans and a plate heat exchanger (see Fig. 1.120). It can still be considered as a 'passive' system, as the cooling is done by evaporation. The return air stream is evaporatively cooled and passed through the heat exchanger, to cool the fresh air intake to be supplied to the space, without the addition of any moisture. The exhaust air is then discharged. A slight increase in humidity tolerance (to 14 g/kg) can be accepted if the air is cooled, hence the upper boundary of the CPZ is a horizontal line at this level, while the temperature limit would be at Tn + 14 (Fig. 1.79).

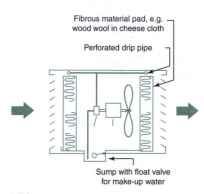

Fibrous material pad, e.g.
wood wool in cheese cloth

Perforated drip pipe

Sump with float valve
for make-up water

1.78
Principles of a direct evaporative cooler

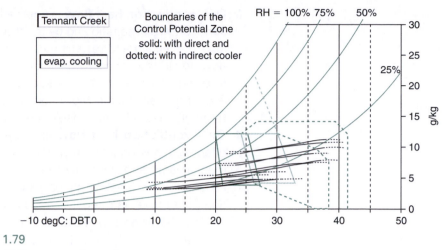

1.79
CPZ for evaporative cooling

1.5.2 Control functions of design variables

In this section, as a summary of previous discussions, answers to two questions will be attempted:

1 Which factors influence the magnitude of each of the components of eq. 1.13?
2 Which attributes of major design variables affect the building's thermal behaviour?

1.5.2.1 Component heat flows

Which building variables determine or affect the component heat flows?

1 **Qi – internal heat gain** can be influenced only in a minor way, by planning: by separating any heat-emitting functions from occupied spaces, or attempting to dissipate the generated heat at or near the source. The condensing coil of a refrigerator may be placed outside, or at least ventilated separately, or the control gear of fluorescent lighting could be outside the habitable space. A local exhaust could be used next to a heat-generating appliance, such as a kitchen stove.
2 **Qs – solar heat gain** on opaque surfaces is influenced not only by surface properties (reflectance), but also by the shape and orientation of the building. If it is to be reduced, the solar geometry should determine the shape: larger surfaces should face the least solar exposure. Solar heat gain through windows provides the most powerful passive control. It is affected by window size, orientation, glazing material and shading devices.

  Adjustable shading can provide flexibility in variable climatic situations. The sun's apparent seasonal movement can provide an automatic summer/winter adjustment. Vegetation and surrounding objects can have a strong influence on sun penetration. Deciduous plants are often used to give summer shade but allow the entry of winter sun. While fenestration determines the admission of solar radiation, the thermal mass of the building affects its retention and release.

3 **Qc – conduction heat flow** is affected by the shape of the building, by the surface-to-volume ratio and by the thermal insulating qualities of the envelope. Reflective and resistive insulation affect the magnitude of the heat flow, while the capacitive insulation also affects the timing of heat input. In a multi-layer element the sequence of resistive and capacitive layers is an important factor. More stable internal conditions are achieved if the thermal mass is located inside the resistive insulation.

4 **Qv – ventilation heat flow** is influenced by the fenestration and other openings, their orientation with respect to the wind direction, their closing mechanisms and generally the air-tightness or wind permeability of the envelope. The building shape can have a strong influence on the creation of positive and negative pressure zones, which in turn influence air entry. External objects, such as fences, wing walls or even vegetation can also have an effect. In cold conditions the unwanted but unavoidable air exchange is referred to as *infiltration*. This can be kept to a minimum by well-closing windows and doors and by sealing any cracks or gaps at construction joints.

5 **Qe – evaporative cooling** is a useful technique, especially under hot-dry conditions. It can be provided by mechanical equipment, but also by purely passive systems, such as a pond or a spray. It cannot be considered in isolation: the cooled air must be retained, if it is not indoors, then e.g. by a courtyard or some other outdoor space enclosed by a solid fence. The designer must ensure that the cooling effect occurs where it is needed and that it is not counteracted by wind or solar heating.

1.5.2.2 Design variables

The design variables that have the greatest influence on thermal performance are: shape, fabric, fenestration and ventilation. These will now be briefly considered as a summary of previous discussions.

1 **Shape**

a *surface-to-volume ratio*: as the heat loss or gain depends on the envelope area, particularly in severe climates it is advisable to present the least surface area for a given volume. From this point of view, the hemisphere is the most efficient shape, but a compact plan is always better than a broken-up and spread-out arrangement.

b *orientation:* if the plan is other than a circle, orientation in relation to solar gain will have a strong effect. The term 'aspect ratio' (Fig. 1.80) is often used to denote the ratio of the longer dimension of an oblong plan to the shorter. In most instances the North and South walls should be longer than the East and West and the ratio would be around 1.3 to 2.0, depending on temperature and radiation conditions. It can be optimised in terms of solar incidence and wanted or unwanted solar heat gain or heat dissipation.

2 **Fabric**

a *shading* of wall and roof surfaces can control the solar heat input. In extreme situations a 'parasol roof' can be used over the roof itself to provide shading, or a west-facing wall may be shaded to eliminate the

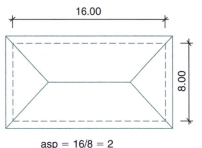

16.00

8.00

asp = 16/8 = 2
roof plan

1.80
Definition of aspect ratio

In many countries insulation is specifie d in terms of its R-value, rather than its reciprocal, the U-value. In cold climates R3 or R4 are not uncommon (U-value of 0.33 or 0.25) and 'superinsulated houses' have been built with up to R8 (U-values down to 0.125).

    See Table 1.5.

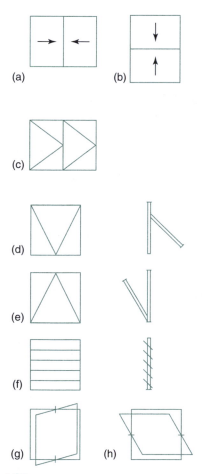

(a)
(b)
(c)
(d)
(e)
(f)
(g)   (h)

1.81

Window types by closing mechanism

(a) horizontal sliding
(b) vertical sliding (double hung)
(c) casements
(d) top hung (friction stays)
(e) bottom hung (drop-in hopper)
(f) glass louvres
(g) vertical pivot
(h) horizontal pivot

late afternoon solar input. If the plan shape is complex, then the shading of one surface by another wing should be considered.

b *surface qualities*: absorptance/reflectance will strongly influence the solar heat input; if it is to be reduced, reflective surfaces are preferred. A white surface and a shiny metal surface may have the same reflectance, but the white would have an emittance similar to a black body at terrestrial temperatures while the emittance of the shiny metal is practically negligible. Thus if heat dissipation is the aim, a white surface would be preferred.

c *resistive insulation* controls the heat flow in both directions, it is particularly important in very cold climates (heated buildings) or in very hot climates (air-conditioned buildings). Usually the roof is the most exposed element, thus its insulation is most important.

d *reflective insulation*; the best effect is achieved if the (double-sided) foil is suspended in the middle of a cavity, so that both the high reflectance and low emittance are utilised. This is rarely achievable. There is no difference in magnitude between the low emittance and high reflectance effects. Deterioration in time, e.g. dust deposit, should be considered, hence a foil under the roof skin, face down is better than one on top of the ceiling, face up. It affects downward heat flow more than the upward flow. See discussion of attic insulation in Section 1.4.3.2 (and Fig. 1.57).

e *capacitive insulation* provides a very powerful control of the timing of heat input especially in climates with a large diurnal temperature swing, as it can store the surplus heat at one time, for release at another time, when it is needed. It is important in all buildings, except those of very short occupancy.

3 Fenestration

a *size, position and orientation of windows* affect sun penetration, thus solar heat input, but also affect ventilation, especially where cross-ventilation (physiological cooling) is desirable.

b *glass*: single, double, multiple and *glass quality*: special glasses (e.g. heat-absorbing, heat-reflecting or low-e glasses) may be used to ameliorate an otherwise bad situation, by reducing the solar heat input. Their qualities are constant, they would reduce solar heating even when it would be desirable and would reduce daylighting. They should be considered as a last resort.

c *closing mechanism:* fixed glass, louvres, opening sashes, type of sashes used (Fig. 1.81).

d *internal blinds and curtains* can slightly reduce the solar heat input, by reducing the beam (direct) radiation, but they become heated and will re-emit that heat, thus causing convective gains.

e *external shading devices* are the most positive way of controlling solar heat input. The effect of such devices on wind (thus ventilation) and on daylighting and views must be kept in mind.

f *insect screens* (part of fenestration) may be a necessity in hot-humid climates, but their effect on air flow and on daylighting must be recognised. Air flow may be reduced by 30% even by the best, smooth nylon screen and daylighting may also be reduced by 25%. To keep the same effect, the window size may have to be increased.

4 Ventilation

a airtight construction to reduce air infiltration is important both in a cold climate and in a hot climate in air-conditioned buildings;

b beyond the provision of fresh air, ventilation can be relied on to dissipate unwanted heat, when $T_o < T_i$.

c physiological cooling can be provided even when $T_o > T_i$ (slightly, i.e. $T_o < T_i + 4$) and for this not the volume flow but the air velocity is important. This can only be achieved by full cross-ventilation (or mechanical means, e.g. by fans) and it may be the main determinant of not only fenestration and orientation but also of internal layout (e.g. single row of rooms) or partitions not extending to the ceiling.

1.5.3 Climatic design archetypes

1.5.3.1 Cold climates

In cold climates where the dominant problem is underheating, where even the best building will need some active heating, the main concern is to minimise any heat loss. The surface-to-volume ratio is important and, though we cannot always build Eskimo igloos (Fig. 1.82) (which have the best surface-to-volume ratio), the idea should be kept in mind. In any case, a compact building form is desirable.

Insulation of the envelope is of prime concern. U-values of less than 0.5 W/m²K are usual in most locations in this climate. Windows should be small, at least double-glazed, but preferably triple-glazed, or double-glazed with low-e treatment and partially evacuated with inert gas fill.

Where heating is necessary, capacitive insulation (massive construction) can be beneficial in continuously occupied buildings as it may allow intermittent heating (keeping the building reasonably warm during non-heating periods). For intermittent occupancy a lightweight, well-insulated building is preferable, as it has a shorter heating-up period. Night temperatures in such a building can be very low, and if equipment protection or freezing (e.g. of water in pipes) is a risk, then a massive construction could save overnight heating.

Winter sunshine for an equator-facing vertical window, at low altitude sun angles may be significant. All other windows should be kept as small as possible. A check should be made whether a well-oriented window could be beneficial, but it is very likely that solar heating would only work if there is some form of night insulation. Any such passive solar heating would work only if there is an adequate thermal storage mass available. An externally insulated massive wall may be a good choice.

Attention should be paid to the air-tightness of the envelope, to ensure that air infiltration is not greater than about 0.5 air changes per hour. If it is very well done, and it is reduced to less than this value, ventilation should be provided to bring it up to 0.5 ach. Inadequate ventilation may lead to the accumulation of undesirable gases (formaldehydes or even radon) emitted by building materials. Entrances should be fitted with an air-lock and should be protected externally from cold winds.

1.82

Eskimo igloos

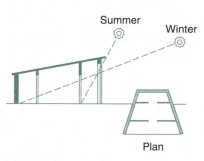

1.83
The house proposed by Socrates for temperate climates

1.5.3.2 Temperate climates

In temperate climates, the winter requirements would be similar to those mentioned above for cold climates, but may be somewhat less strict, depending on the severity of the winter. U-values of the order of 0.7 are usual. The building solutions would be different, to allow for the summer requirements. Any large (equator-facing) windows used for winter solar heating may cause summer overheating.

Overhanging eaves or other shading devices may ensure summer shading but allow winter entry of solar radiation (see Figs 1.51 and 1.83). A full cut-off at the equinox would be provided with a VSA of 90° minus latitude, but this should be adjusted according to temperatures. For a cool-temperate climate a higher VSA would allow increased solar radiation entry, which may be welcome for the winter half-year, but not for the summer. If overheating occurs in the summer, ventilation could be relied on to dissipate the unwanted heat, as air temperatures are unlikely to be too high. No special provisions are necessary for ventilation beyond facilities for fresh air supply.

In most temperate climates the night-time temperatures are too low even in the summer. For this reason a heavy construction (capacitive insulation) may be preferable. The time-lag of a solar heated massive wall can be set to equal the time difference between the maximum of solar input and the time when heating would be welcome.

In most temperate climate countries there are now regulatory requirements for insulation. In the UK there were no such requirements up to 1965. Then an upper limit of acceptable U-value was introduced, as 1.7 W/m²K for walls and 1.42 for roofs. Since then, this requirement has been tightened several times and at present it is 0.35 W/m²K (= R2.8) for walls and 0.25 (= R4) for roofs. In Australia, the first attempts at regulatory controls were in the 1990s. It may be of some interest to compare the ranges of U-values prescribed in some groups of OECD countries. Table 1.5 compares the U-values not to be exceeded, (as well as the 'overall U-value', which is defined by the EU as $U_{r/c} + U_w + U_{fl} + 0.2\ U_{wi}$).

Table 1.5 Comparison of maximum U-values permitted

	EU	North America	AUS/NZ
Roof/ceiling	0.13–0.55	0.12–0.22	0.20–0.35
Walls	0.19–0.82	0.20–0.42	0.45–1.25
Floors	0.16–1.20	0.19–0.42	0.63–1.42
Windows	1.40–2.80	1.60–3.70	3.20–3.80
U overall*	0.80–2.60	0.90–1.95	2.45–2.60

Note: Sweden 0.7, Denmark 0.77, Norway 0.84, Finland 0.94, Ontario 0.93.
The broad ranges of values (especially for the EU) are due to the very large climatic differences (e.g. between Sweden and Spain). Some countries require insulation up to twice as good for lightweight elements than for heavyweight construction, others vary the roof U-value requirement as a function of roof surface absorptance.

In the USA there are local variations, different regulations set by states, or even local authorities, but most states follow the ASHRAE Standard 90.1. The requirements may be stated as a function of climate characteristics (e.g. degree-days). The BCA (Building Code of Australia, 2003 amendment) divides the country into eight climatic zones and sets different requirements for each. In all cases the option is to comply with such elemental prescriptions (DTS, deemed to satisfy) clauses or to produce energy calculations (by an authorised person or accredited software) to show that the proposed building will be as good as one complying with the elemental prescriptions. This is also discussed in Section 4.4.4.

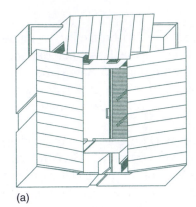

(a)

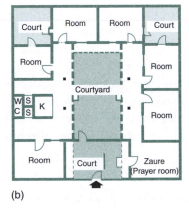

(b)

1.84
A modern courtyard house for a hot-dry climate: isometric view and planv

1.5.3.3 Hot-dry climates

In hot-dry climates, the daytime temperatures can be very high but the diurnal range is large, often more than 20 K. Night temperatures may be too cold. Consequently the single most important characteristic should be a large thermal mass: massive walls but also a roof with high thermal capacity.

Building surfaces should be white, which would act as a selective surface. This is most important for roofs exposed to the night sky. The radiant cooling effect can help to dissipate the heat stored during the day. White paint has a high emittance, unlike a shiny metallic surface (see also Section 1.1.2.3).

The outdoor environment is often hostile, hot and dusty, so the best solution may be an inward-looking, courtyard type building. The air mass enclosed by the building, by solid walls or fences is likely to be cooler than the environment, and heavier, thus it would settle as if in a basin. This air can be evaporatively cooled by a pond or a water spray. The reservoir of cool air thus created can then be used for fresh air supply to habitable spaces. With adequate vegetation such a courtyard can become quite a pleasant outdoor living space (Fig. 1.84).

Much depends, however, on how the courtyard is treated. An unshaded courtyard, without water, can be a liability, warmer than the external environment, not only in 'winter' but also during the hottest periods. Such unwanted heating up to 5 K above the ambient has been recorded. The traditional courtyards with shading, trees and some water element can be substantially cooler than the ambient at the height of summer.

Ventilation, beyond the small fresh air supply from the courtyard, is undesirable as the outdoor air is hot and dusty.

1.5.3.4 Warm humid climates

Warm humid climates are the most difficult ones to design for. The temperature maxima may not be as high as in the hot-dry climates, but the diurnal variation is very small (often less than 5 K), thus the 'mass effect' cannot be relied on. As the humidity is high, evaporation from the skin is restricted and evaporative cooling will be neither effective nor desirable, as it would increase the humidity. Indirect evaporative cooling may be used, as it does not add moisture to the supply air and produces some sensible cooling.

Typical of these climates is the elevated house (to 'catch the breeze' above local obstructions) of lightweight construction. The best the designer can do is to ensure that the interior does not become (much) warmer than the outside (it cannot be any cooler), which can be achieved by adequate ventilation removing any excess heat input. Warm-humid climates are located around the equator, where the sun's path is near the zenith, so the roof receives very strong irradiation. Keeping down the indoor air temperature is not enough. The ceiling temperature may be elevated due to solar heat input on the roof, thus the MRT would be increased. When people wear light clothing, the MRT has double the effect of the DBT.

Undue increase of ceiling temperature can be prevented by the following measures:

(a)

(b)

1.85
A house for warm-humid climates

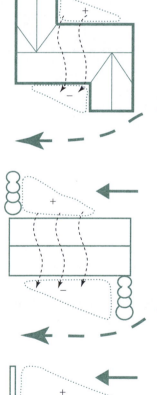

1.86
Projecting building wings

1 using a reflective roof surface;
2 having a separate ceiling, forming an attic space;
3 ensuring adequate ventilation of the attic space;
4 using a reflective surface for the underside of the roof skin;
5 using some resistive insulation on the ceiling.

East and west walls should have no windows, to avoid heat input from a low-angle sun, and should be reflective and insulated. The sol-air temperature of these walls could be much higher than the air temperature.

Beyond the prevention (or reduction) of heat gains the only passive cooling strategy possible is the physiological cooling effect of air movement. In order to ensure maximum cross-ventilation, the major openings should face within 45° of the prevailing wind direction. It should, however, be remembered that there are possibilities to influence the wind, but not the solar incidence.

Therefore, solar orientation should be dominant. North and south walls could have large openings. The rooms could be arranged in one row, to allow both inlet and outlet openings for each room (thus cross-ventilation). Fig. 1.85 shows such a typical tropical house.

With a north-facing wall, if the wind comes from the east or near-east a wing wall placed at the western end of a window would help create a positive pressure zone (Fig. 1.86).

At the same time, a wing wall placed at the eastern edge of a south-facing window could help creating a negative pressure zone. The difference between the positive and negative pressure would drive cross-ventilation, probably better than with a normal wind incidence. It can work even if the wind direction is due east or west. A projecting wing of the building or even vegetation (e.g. a hedge) may achieve the same result.

The above discussion applies to a reasonably free-standing house. With urban developments and increasing densities in warm-humid tropical areas, the ventilation effect disappears. The solution then is to use a low-power, low velocity, slow-moving ceiling fan, which can generate the required velocity for physiological cooling. This is a useful standby in any case, for times when there is no breeze available.

In such a dense situation (when all other houses are also elevated) the benefit of the elevated house may also disappear. A concrete slab-on-ground

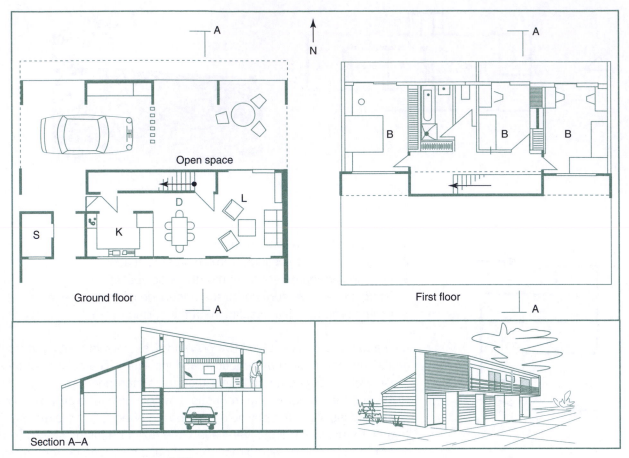

1.87
A hybrid house for warm-humid climates

floor may provide a desirable heat sink. For daytime rooms (living, dining, kitchen), a heavy construction may ensure indoor temperatures close to the day's minimum.

Bedrooms should cool down quickly after sunset, therefore a lightweight construction and cross-ventilation would be desirable. On this basis a house form and hybrid construction have been suggested to get the best of both worlds (Fig. 1.87).

1.5.4   Condensation and moisture control

Condensation occurs whenever moist air is cooled to, or comes into contact with, a surface below its dew-point temperature (DPT). The process can be followed on the psychrometric chart and is best illustrated by an example. This can often be observed on the bathroom mirror or the inside of windows in winter. Surface condensation can be allowed for, e.g. a 'condensation trough' may be included on the bottom rail of a window, which is drained to the outside. More difficult to handle and potentially damaging is the interstitial condensation, which may occur within the materials of envelope elements, especially in winter.

EXAMPLE 1.12 CONDENSATION

Mark the status point on the chart corresponding to, say, 26°C and 60% RH (Fig. 1.88). The absolute humidity is 12.6 g/kg and the vapour pressure is just over 2 kPa. If this horizontal line is extended to the saturation curve, the DPT is obtained as 17.5°C. This means that if this air comes into contact with a surface of 17.5°C or less, condensation will occur.

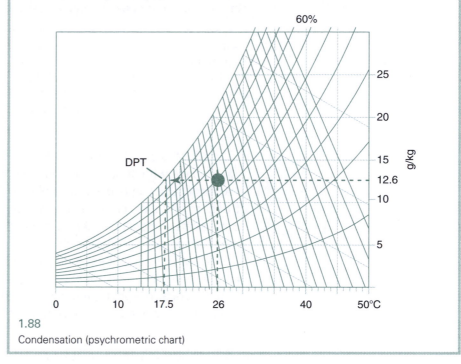

1.88

Condensation (psychrometric chart)

Vapour will permeate the envelope fabric, driven by the indoor-outdoor vapour pressure difference. The cross-section of an envelope element, such as a wall, has a temperature gradient between the warm inside and the cold outside. When the vapour reaches a layer of temperature at or below the DPT, condensation will occur within the pores of the material. This liquid water may fill the pores, thus reducing the insulating qualities of the material, the fabric will become colder, which will further increase the condensation. In many cases in cold winters a roof leak has been suspected, which subsequently proved to be 'only' condensation.

Condensation may lead to mould growth over such damp surfaces and may damage the construction (e.g. the plastering may fall off). In cold situations the risk is greatest at the outer edge of roof/wall junction, where the fabric is cold (due to the thermal bridge effect), especially in low-income housing, where bedrooms may not be heated at all, any vents may be sealed 'to preserve the heat', but the kitchen door is left open to allow the warm (moisture-laden) air to go up to the bedrooms.

The causes of condensation are:

1 Moisture input, increased humidity of the room air. An average person would exhale some 50 g of water vapour in an hour. A shower may

contribute 200 g and cooking or indoor drying of clothes are large producers of vapour (see Data sheet D.1.5 for moisture production rates).

2 Lack of ventilation, which means that the vapour generated stays in the room.

3 Inadequate heating and poor insulation can produce very cold inside surface temperatures.

Vapour flow quantities are analogous to heat flow quantities:

Heat	J	Vapour quantity	g	(usually $\mu g = 10^{-6}$ g)
Temperature	T	Vapour pressure	pv	Pa
Conductivity	λ	Permeability	δ	μg/m.s.Pa
Transmittance	U	Permeance	π	μg/m^2.s.Pa
Resistance	R	Vapour resistance	vR	MPa.s.m^2/g*

See Method sheet M.1.6 for the calculation process.

In a space with large vapour production (e.g. a place of assembly), which in winter could lead to uncontrollable condensation, a simple passive method of dehumidification is the use of a 'condenser window'. If all windows are double-glazed, install one (or several) narrow, single glazed windows, fitted with a condensation trough on the inside, which is drained to waste. As this window will be the coldest surface in the space, this is where condensation will start and if it works properly, it will precipitate much of the vapour content of the indoor atmosphere, thus reducing humidity and condensation risk elsewhere. It is clearly a simple form of passive dehumidification.

1.5.5 Microclimatic controls

Most published climatic data has been collected from meteorological stations, usually located on an open site, often at airports. The climate of a given site may differ from that indicated by the available data, quite significantly. On-site measurements are impractical, as nothing less than a year would suffice, and such time is rarely available for a project. The best one can do is to obtain data from the nearest meteorological station and use a qualitative judgement as to how and in what way the site climate would differ.

Local factors that will influence the site climate may be the following:

• *topography*, slope, orientation, exposure, elevation, hills or valleys at or near the site;
• *ground surface*, natural or man-made, its reflectance (often referred to as *albedo*), permeability, soil temperature, paved areas or vegetation;
• *3D objects*, such as trees, tree-belts, fences, walls and buildings as these may influence the wind, cast shadows and may subdivide the area into smaller distinguishable climate zones.

Solar radiation is affected by the clarity of the atmosphere: it will be reduced by pollution, smog and dust. Slope and the orientation of such a slope have an effect on irradiation. Slopes of equatorial orientation receive more and slopes of polar orientation receive less radiation. Hills, trees and buildings around

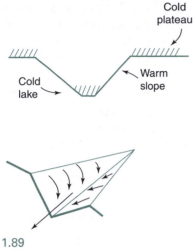

1.89
Katabatic wind

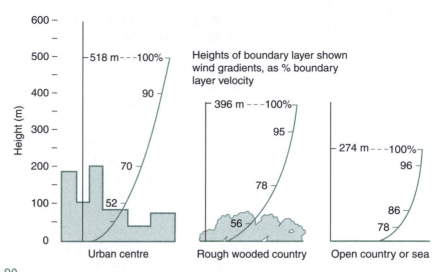

Heights of boundary layer shown wind gradients, as % boundary layer velocity

1.90
Wind velocity profiles

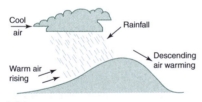

1.91
Rainfall on hill

the site also affect the apparent sunrise/sunset times, therefore the length of day, thus the daily irradiation. Temperature during the day is likely to be higher near the ground than at higher levels. This is taken as the 'normal' layering. At night, particularly with clear skies, as the surface radiates to the sky, the near-ground temperature drops and an 'inversion' will occur. Such cooling can be more pronounced on hills and mountains; this cool air will behave as water: flow downhill, collect in a valley and constitute a *katabatic wind* (Fig. 1.89).

Wind is retarded by the ground surface and turbulent flow is caused near the ground, forming a boundary layer. The depth of this boundary layer depends on the surface and on objects sitting on the surface; it can vary from about 270 m over open country to over 500 m over a city area (Fig. 1.90). All our buildings and most of our activities take place in this boundary layer. Topography may deflect the wind, but may also affect precipitation. As Fig. 1.91 indicates, a hill deflects the flow of warm, humid air upwards, it cools and precipitation will be generated. On the leeward side of the hill, the descending air flow would rarely produce any precipitation.

Coastal winds occur near the sea or other large bodies of water (unless they are suppressed by macroclimatic winds). During the day land surfaces heat up, causing the heated air to rise, drawing in cooler air from the water, as an on-shore wind. At night the water remains warmer than the land, causing the warm air to rise, drawing in a land-breeze, an off-shore wind (Fig. 1.92).

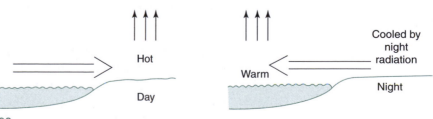

1.92
Coastal winds

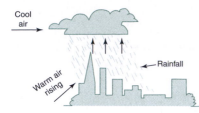

1.93
Urban heat island effect

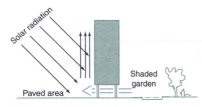

1.94
Local wind at one building

The phenomenon of urban heat islands is now well documented. The air mass over cities is likely to be warmer than in the surrounding countryside, differences (heat island intensities) up to 10 K have been measured. This effect is most pronounced when there is little or no wind. It may be caused by more absorbent surfaces, radiation losses are reduced by pollution, but also by energy seepage from buildings, cooling towers and vehicles, referred to as *anthropogenic* heat. A rising, upward air current is likely to produce more rain than in the nearby countryside, a process which may be assisted by the presence of urban pollution: particulate emissions that will 'seed' the humid air and start the precipitation (Fig. 1.93).

Quite strong local air flow can be caused by a single building. The equator-facing side of a large slab-type building can be strongly heated up by solar radiation, which causes an upward air flow. If the building is on *pilotis* (the ground floor is open), cooler air will be drawn in from the shaded side, reaching considerable velocities under the building (Fig. 1.94).

Recent studies show that differences can occur within a building site. Most of our calculations assume that the temperature around a house is uniform and this has now been shown to be incorrect. An air pocket between two buildings can have temperatures quite different to the air near an exposed side. Heat loss through the floor of an elevated house is assumed to flow to a T_o same as all around the building, but in fact the underfloor air temperature may be quite different.

The microclimate around a building can show substantial variations, but such variation can also be produced deliberately, and referred to as 'microclimatic controls'. These can serve two purposes:

1 to control conditions (sun, wind) in outdoor spaces;
2 to assist building performance by ameliorating outdoor conditions adjacent to the building.

Microclimatic controls may affect winter and summer conditions, but they are most effective in the 'shoulder' seasons (spring, autumn) when they can significantly extend the period of purely passive operation of the building.

At the urban design scale it is useful in all streets to attempt to keep one side footpath shaded in the summer and one side sunny in the winter to allow people a choice of which side to walk on. Similarly, in parks or public gardens, seats should be provided in both shaded and sunny areas.

Such 'controls' may be of two kinds:

• vegetation, trees, shrubs, vines and ground covers
• built objects, fences, walls, screens, pergolas, shade structures and pavements.

In a cold climate, protection from cold winds may be provided by a tree-belt. The selection of plants is critical. Experts should be consulted. Deciduous trees will not offer much protection when it would be most wanted. Some trees have a tall trunk, which would allow free passage of the wind near ground level. If protection is the purpose, these should be supplemented by shrubs. A fence or a screen, even well-positioned outbuildings can serve the same purpose.

In a hot climate the shadow cast by trees can be a great relief. The surface temperature of a roof can be over 70°C, but in the shade it may not go above 35°C. The temperature of ground surfaces can show a similar difference, but it depends on the nature of these surfaces. Pavements will be much warmer than grass or other green ('soft') ground cover. At night, pavements become much cooler than soft covers. Pavements show a large diurnal swing, black asphalt is even worse than concrete.

Another advantage of soft ground covers is that they are permeable, thus they reduce stormwater run-off and allow the ground water to be replenished. The use of deciduous trees is recommended by many authors, to provide shade in summer but allow solar radiation to reach the building in winter. This may be so in some climates, but in many instances trees do not follow the calendar (especially in climates with a mild 'winter'), and may cast too much shadow in winter and not enough in the summer.

One additional point that many architects tend to forget, is that trees grow, thus their effect will change over the years. If any trees are to be planted, landscape advice should be sought on what they would look like in 10, 20 or even more years' time. However, some cynics say that trees (and vegetation in general) are the architect's best friends: they cover up many mistakes and much ugliness.

1.5.6 Free-running buildings

This is a term used for buildings which can operate without any 'active' (energy-based) thermal controls. These would be designed for the given climate, with the best use of microclimatic controls and passive thermal controls (perhaps incorporating the appropriate passive systems), to ensure indoor thermal conditions for the users. The task here is to control not only the magnitude, but also the timing of heat flows. Some adjustments on both the daily and annual time-scale may be incorporated.

The most clear-cut situation occurs in very cold climates, where the main thermal problem is the lack of heat, the task being to avoid heat loss and make use of any indoor or solar heat gain. Example 1.4 (and Fig. 1.66) show how to examine the 'balance-point' temperature (when gains balance the losses), e.g. for the daily average condition. Shading design, either fixed or adjustable devices, provides an important tool for any climate. It must be related to orientation and room use. It must be considered together with thermal mass, as discussed in Section 1.5.1.2.

Mass can be used two ways: for heat input from outside or inside. With the former the heat input at the outside surface of walls of roof (from hot air or solar radiation) will have an effect at the inside surface with a delay of time-lag (ϕ) hours (refer to Fig. 1.67). The designer must relate the time of input to the room, the time a heat input is required (e.g. depending on room use).

Heat input to inside surfaces may be due to solar radiation entering through a window. Here the heating effect is almost simultaneous, but if the radiation is received by a solid surface, a massive floor or wall, or a solid dwarf wall, then these would store much of the heat and release it gradually, a reduced (improved) decrement factor, but the main benefit is the strongly increased admittance.

Example 1.5 (and Fig. 1.70) show the importance of the sequence of layers. A massive inner layer (insulated outside) gives a slightly greater time lag, a smaller (better) decrement factor and a substantially greater admittance than the reverse. Insulation on the top reduces the external, especially solar heat input. The large admittance allows it to pick up heat from the inside. On a hot day this may keep the interior sufficiently cool without 'active' cooling. It will certainly ensure a thermally more stable indoor environment.

Is this desirable? Certainly so, for a room of continuous occupancy, but not for, say, a breakfast room facing east, where an almost instantaneous heating is very welcome on a cold winter morning.

The role of thermal mass cannot be over-emphasised. Having a good thermal mass, allows the manipulation of other variables, such as shading (solar input) or ventilation. In some cases heat dissipation would need to be assisted, e.g. in a hot climate for a bedroom.

Fig. 1.119 on p. 97 indicates the 'balancing act' performed by thermal mass in an air-conditioned building. It will shift the load, certainly reducing the required plant capacity and possibly even reducing the load. In many cases it may result in a free-running building. A free-running building (a 'zero energy house') may be the ideal, but even if such design efforts are not 100% successful, energy use of the building will have been minimised.

1.6 ACTIVE CONTROLS: HVAC

Generally, where passive controls cannot fully ensure thermal comfort, some energy-based system can be used to supplement their performance. This may be heating, ventilation or air conditioning (HVAC) and the task of mechanical engineers. Here only a brief overview is attempted, partly to aid an understanding of what these systems do, partly to introduce some of the language of engineers, thus encouraging cooperation.

The required performance of such systems is usually referred to as the 'load' (heating load, air conditioning load). From the mechanical engineering viewpoint the task of the building design (i.e. of the passive controls) is to reduce such a load as far as practicable.

1.6.1 Heating

The design of heating systems, after the choice of an appropriate system, aims to establish two quantities:

1 the size (capacity) of the system;
2 the annual (seasonal) or monthly heating requirement.

The first of these is based on a heat loss calculation under assumed design conditions, and the heating capacity will have to match that heat loss. If the building conductance (q, as in Section 1.4.2, eq. 1.23) is known, then the heat loss rate will be

$$Q = q \times \Delta T$$

where $\Delta T = T_o - T_i$ (W/K × K = W)

...s a value near the 'worst conditions', to make sure that the
... with such conditions.
...ere conditions the system can be operated at partial capac-
...nfort requirements for the given building type and T_o values
...us reference publications as *outdoor design temperatures*.
...taken as the 10th or 20th percentile temperature value,
...thermal inertia of the building.
...quick response building even short-term very low tempera-
...noticeable effect, thus the system sizing should be based
...the 10th percentile value. A massive building can smooth
...troughs, thus it is enough to use the 20th percentile value

...ve an *overload capacity*, which could be activated under
...s, so the sizing can use a higher temperature. Table 1.6
...values for the UK.

$$(W/K \times Kh = Wh) \text{ (same as eq. 1.12)}$$

...d for continuous heating and should be adjusted by the
...e 1.7, for duration of occupancy, building thermal mass

...ign outdoor temperatures (for the UK)

...ui inertia	If overload capacity	Then design To
High e.g. multistorey buildings with solid floors and partitions	20%	−1°C
	Nil	−4°C
Low, most single-storey buildings	20%	−3°C
	Nil	−5°C

Note: The annual (or seasonal) heating requirement can be estimated as in Section 1.3.3.2.

Table 1.7 Correction factors for heating requirement

For length of working week:	7 days		1
	5 days massive buildings		0.85
	lightweight buildings		0.75
For building and plant response:	continuous heating		1

intermittent heating (night shut-down)		if plant response	
		quick	slow
If building mass	light	0.55	0.70
	medium	0.70	0.85
	heavy	0.85	0.95

For intermittent heating only, length of heating day		if building mass	
		light	heavy
	4 hours	0.68	0.96
	8 hours	1	1
	12 hours	1.25	1.02
	16 hours	1.4	1.03

1.6.1.1 Local heating

In some instances heat can be generated in the space where it is needed. This is referred to as 'local heating'. The available energy sources and the mode of energy delivery for such local heating may be:

electricity	by cables
gas	piped, from grid or externally located bottle
liquid fuel (oil, kerosene)	piped from an external tank or in batch (cans, bottles)
solid fuel	(coal, coke, firewood) in batch (cans, bins, baskets)

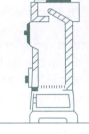

1.95
A typical cast iron stove

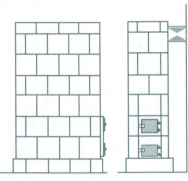

1.96
A ceramic stove built in situ

In all these (except electrical appliances) heat is produced by the combustion of some fuel. This uses oxygen, thus an air supply must be ensured and the combustion products must be removed. This requires that they should be connected to a flue.

Oil heaters are available in small portable form. These use the room air and discharge their combustion products into the room. One point, often forgotten, is that the combustion of 1 L of oil produces about 1 kg of water vapour, which increases vapour pressure in the room and thus the risk of condensation. Adequate ventilation is therefore essential.

Solid fuel appliances (or stoves) may be industrial products made of metal (e.g. cast iron, Fig. 1.95) or may be built in situ of ceramic blocks (these have a large thermal inertia, Fig. 1.96). Both are connected to a flue. Such flues can remove a significant quantity of air and will operate well only if the room air can be replenished through appropriate vents. Open fireplaces are often used as decorative elements (many people love to look at the fire) but cannot be considered as serious heating devices because of their very low efficiency.

Gas heaters may have a 'balanced flue' (Fig. 1.97) where the fresh air supply and the discharge of combustion products form a circuit separated from the room air. In large spaces (a church or industrial buildings) flueless gas-fired radiators may be used, usually mounted overhead, in a tilted position. The burners heat a refractory plate (of shaped, perforated ceramic elements) to 800–900°C, which thus becomes incandescent and emits heat primarily by radiation.

Electric heaters have the greatest variety in terms of heat output (radiant/convective) and form, though all of them are based on resistance heater elements. Table 1.8 lists the basic types of electric heaters, but a wide variety of products exists within each type.

Electricity is often referred to as the most convenient 'fuel', because of its ease of transport, as it can be readily controlled ('at the flick of a switch'), as it has no combustion products at the point of heat delivery and as its efficiency at conversion to heat is practically 100%. It is rather seductive, but this view is deceptive. Its adverse characteristics are only shifted to the generating stations, with their emissions polluting the atmosphere and contributing to the greenhouse effect as well as the low efficiency of conversion from heating fuel to electricity of around

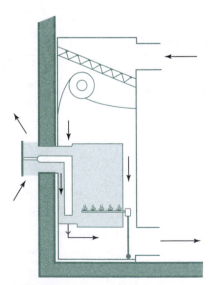

1.97
A gas convector heater with a balanced flue

Table 1.8 Types of electric heaters

Type	Heat emission (%)		Convective
	Radiant		
Infrared lamps	100		
Incandescent radiators	80		20
Medium temperature (tube or panel) radiators	60		40
Low temperature panels (oil-filled) convectors	40		60
Fan-convectors			100
Storage (block) heaters	10		90
Floor warming	20		80
Ceiling warming	70		30

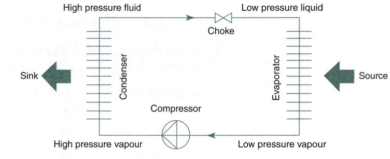

1.98
Principles of a heat pump

33% (on average). So 1 kWh of electricity used means the use of fuel of some 3 kWh energy content and the release of some 3 kg of CO_2 into the atmosphere.

A special form of electric heating is based on the *heat pump*, where the input of electricity at the rate of 1 kW can produce heating of up to 4 kW. This appears to contravene the first law of thermodynamics, but the heat is not actually produced by the heat pump. The input of 1 kW to drive the compressor facilitates the delivery of heat from a low grade (low temperature) source, upgrading and delivering it at a useful temperature at the rate of 4 kW. Fig. 1.98 shows the principles of such a heat pump.

A working fluid or refrigerant (such as an organic fluoride or a hydrocarbon) is circulated in a closed loop by the compressor. A pressure release valve (choke) keeps the condenser side under high pressure and the evaporator side under low pressure and low temperature. When the fluid is compressed, it becomes hot and liquefies, while it will emit heat to the *sink*, in this case, the room air. Passing through the choke it evaporates and its temperature drops, so that it can pick up heat from a *source*. This heat source may be the atmosphere (with the evaporator shaped as an air-to-liquid heat exchanger), or may be warm 'grey' water discharged into a sump or a natural body of water (a river or the sea), where the evaporator is shaped as a liquid-to-liquid heat exchanger.

Organic fluorides (freons, CFCs) were largely responsible for ozone depletion in the upper atmosphere (the ozone holes) and consequent increase in UV radiation at ground level. These have now almost completely been phased out, as a result of the Montreal Protocol of 1987, and have been replaced by hydrocarbons.

If the purpose of using this machine is to gain heat, then the coefficient of performance is defined as

$$CoP = \frac{Q}{W} = \frac{\text{heat delivered to sink}}{\text{compressor work input}} \qquad (1.33\ a)$$

This CoP is higher for a small temperature increment (or step-up) but it reduces if the necessary step-up is large. In the ideal (Carnot) cycle the CoP is inversely proportionate to the temperature increment:

$$CoP \propto \frac{T'}{T' - T''}$$

where

T' = sink temperature
T'' = source temperature (in °K)

but a real cycle will give 0.82 to 0.93 (average 0.85) of the Carnot performance. This will be further reduced by the actual component efficiencies, such as

electric motor   0.95
compressor   0.8
heat exchangers   0.9

If the same machine is used for cooling, i.e. to remove heat, then the definition of CoP is slightly different:

$$CoP = \frac{Q}{W} = \frac{\text{heat removed from source}}{\text{compressor work input}} \qquad (1.33\ b)$$

The difference is that in a heat pump application the compressor input is added to the heat gained, it is included in the value of Q, but in a cooling application it is not.

EXAMPLE 1.13   COP CALCULATION

If there is a source of 10°C (= 283°K) and the heat is to be delivered at 55°C (= 328°K)

$$CoP = 0.85 \times 0.95 \times 0.8 \times 0.9 \times \frac{328}{328 - 283} = 4.24$$

but if the source is 0°C (= 273°K) and 60°C (333°K) is wanted, then

$$CoP = 0.85 \times 0.95 \times 0.8 \times 0.9 \times \frac{333}{333 - 273} = 3.23$$

1.6.1.2   Central heating

Heat may be produced centrally in a building (or group of buildings), distributed to the occupied spaces by a heat transport fluid and emitted to provide the required heating.

Schematically:

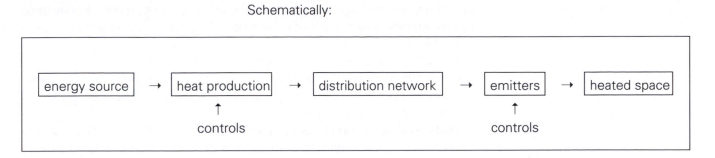

The energy source may be fossil fuels: coal, oil or gas, or electricity, produced from fossil fuels, nuclear or hydro power, or renewable energy sources, such as solar, wind, tidal, wave, ocean-thermal or geothermal energy or biogas. At one stage coal was the most often used source, but today oil or gas is most frequently relied on. The transport fluid may be water or air. Heat is produced in boilers for a water system and in a furnace for an air system.

Architectural implications are the accommodation of any fuel storage, the heat production plant and its flue, the routing and accommodation of the distribution network: pipes for a water system and ducts for an air system, as well as the choice and placement of emitters.

Fig. 1.99 shows an outdoor storage arrangement for a bank of gas cylinders. Gas leaks indoors mixed with air can produce a highly explosive mixture, which can be ignited by the smallest spark. Fig. 1.100 shows the section of an oil storage tank chamber. Here fire precautions are dominant: note the foam inlet valve and the high threshold, which must be high enough for the chamber to contain the full tank volume of oil in case of leakage. Storage for heavier oils may have to be heated to at least the following temperatures:

class E – 7°
class F – 20°C
class G – 32°C

The emitter for a warm air system may be a grille or a diffuser (on rare occasions a directional jet). This system has the disadvantage that the room surface temperatures are below the air temperature, whereas human preference is for an MRT slightly (1–2 K) warmer than the air temperature.

Fig. 1.101 shows the ducting arrangement for a domestic warm air system. The volume flow rate (m³/s) in a duct is

$$vr = A \times v$$

where

A = duct cross-sectional area (m²)
v = air velocity (m/s)

Air velocities in ducts may be 2.5 to 7.5 m/s for low velocity systems, but up to 25 m/s for high velocity (high pressure) systems. The latter would require smaller ducts, but would result in a much larger flow resistance,

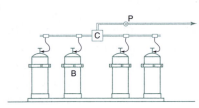

1.99
Gas bottles

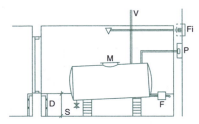

1.100
Oil storage tank room V = vent, P = filling pipe, S = sludge valve, D = depth to contain full volume, Fi = foam inlet, M = manhole, F = fire shut-off

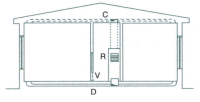

1.101
Domestic warm air system

would need a greater fan power and would tend to be noisier. In habitable rooms an outlet velocity of not more than 2.5 m/s is preferred and in no case should it exceed 4 m/s.

In modern systems, especially where summer air conditioning is necessary, the warm air central heating system is combined with air conditioning. Most often a boiler is used to produce hot water, which will feed a heating coil included in the air handling unit.

Water-based systems (called 'hydronic' in the USA) can rely on gravity (thermosiphon) circulation, or can be pumped. The former requires larger pipe sizes and is rarely (if ever) used today. For pumped systems small-bore copper pipes are normally used. For a single-storey house a two-pipe ring-main system is usual (Fig. 1.102).

For a house of two or more storeys two-pipe systems are the most suitable, which can be up-feed (Fig. 1.103) or down-feed (Fig. 1.104), but a one pipe system is also possible (Fig. 1.105). In domestic systems small-bore (13–20 mm) pipes are usual, but recently the micro-bore (6 mm) system has gained popularity, where each emitter is served by a separate flow and return pipe, connected to a manifold. The design of larger systems is the task of mechanical consultants.

Emitters are most often pressed steel 'radiator' panels (at least half the emission is by convection) (Fig. 1.106) but various convector units can also be used (Fig. 1.107). Practically all forms of local heaters can also be adapted for use in central hot water heating systems, including floor warming, with embedded pipe coils (instead of electric heating cables). Floor warming is essentially a very slow response system and it is often designed to provide background heating (to, say, 16°C) with local, quick response heaters or emitters for topping-up heating, as required.

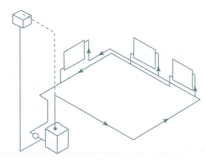

1.102
Central heating ring main system

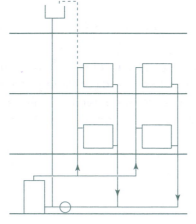

1.103
Two-pipe up-feed system

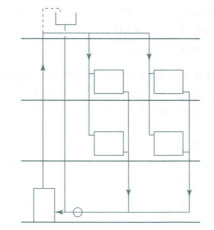

1.104
Two-pipe, down-feed system

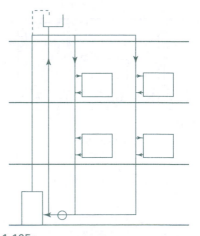

1.105
A one-pipe down-feed system

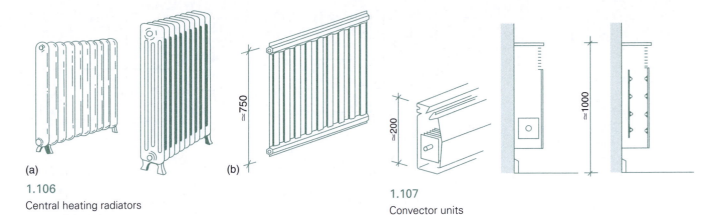

1.106
Central heating radiators

1.107
Convector units

1.6.2 Hot water supply

The very large range of hot water supply systems available can be categorised according to four facets:

1 by heat source:
 — coupled to the space heating system
 — independent
 — separate boiler
 — electric
 — gas
 — solar
2 by operational mode:
 — storage type
 — semi-storage
 — instantaneous
3 by pressure:
 — mains pressure
 — reduced pressure
 — low pressure
 — free outlet (inlet valve only)
4 by heat input mode:
 — direct
 — indirect.

Fig. 1.108 shows the ten most popular systems in diagrammatic terms, the following alphabetical designations of explanatory paragraphs refer to the diagrams.

a *Coupled, storage type, low pressure, direct*: a branch of the central heating water circuit is led through a heat exchanger submerged in the hot water cylinder. The consumed hot water is replaced from a header tank (cistern). Water pressure at the outlets is only that of the header tank height.

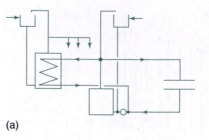

(a)

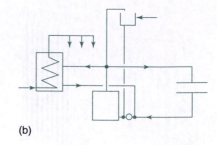

(b)

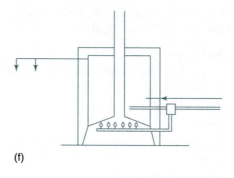

(d)

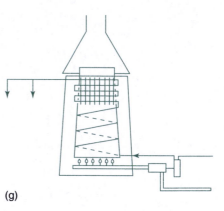

(e)

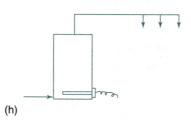

(f)

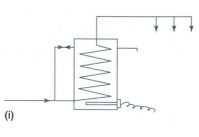

(g)

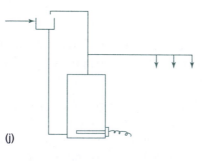

(h)

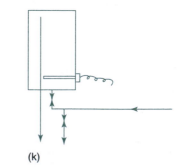

(i)

(j)

(k)

1.108

Hot water systems (a–k)

b *Coupled, storage type, mains pressure, indirect:* as above, but without the header tank, fed directly off the mains; the water is heated while passing through the heat exchanger.

c *Separate boiler, storage type, low pressure, direct:* (not shown) same as (a) above, without the emitter circuit (not shown).

d *Gas, storage type, low pressure, direct:* a modest size gas heater circulates water through a heat exchanger submerged in the hot water cylinder.

e *Gas, storage type, mains pressure, indirect:* same as (d), but the gas 'circulator' is connected to the tank (not the coil). The coil is fed directly off the mains; the water is heated while passing through the heat exchanger.

f *Gas, semi-storage, reduced or low pressure, direct:* a modest size gas heater with a storage volume of 60–80 L. The burner starts as soon as there is a draw-off. When the contents are used, it can give a slow instantaneous warm flow (not hot). Full recovery will take some 20 minutes.

g *Gas, instantaneous, free outlet, direct:* a powerful burner heats the water while flowing through. Water flow is controlled at the inlet. A 10–15 kW unit can serve a single draw-off point. Multi-point units up to 35 kW are under mains pressure. A 30 kW unit can heat water from 10 to 65°C at a rate of 0.1 L/s. Gas ignition is controlled by a water pressure-operated gas valve. Older models have a gas pilot flame, new units have electric spark ignition.

h *Electric, storage type, mains pressure, direct:* both cylinder and pipework are exposed to mains pressure. If the mains connection is fitted with a pressure-reducing valve, it becomes a *reduced pressure unit* and a lighter gauge cylinder can be used.

i *Electric, storage, mains pressure, indirect:* the tank volume heated by an immersion heater is not consumed. Mains pressure water is heated while flowing through the coil.

j *Electric, storage, low pressure, direct:* similar to (h) but it is fed from a header tank.

k *Electric, semi-storage, free outlet, direct:* a tap controls the cold water inlet, the outlet is free. Usually a small volume unit (15–50 L), with 15–20 minutes recovery time.

Some washing machines and dishwashers can only operate with mains pressure water. The indirect types (b, e, i) have the advantage that mains pressure is provided without the expense of a heavy cylinder. In most of the UK these systems have no relevance as the whole of the water installation must be fed from a storage cistern (mains connection allowed only for one tap in the kitchen).

Electric storage type units can be used with off-peak electricity, which is much cheaper. The distance between the water heater and draw-off points should be kept to a minimum, to avoid the 'dead-leg' water wasted (as it cools down) each time the hot tap is opened.

In larger installations a secondary hot water circulation system (flow and return) can be installed, such as that shown in Fig. 1.109 with well-insulated

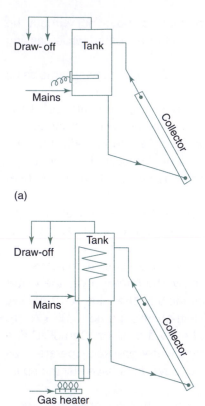

(a)

(b)

(c)

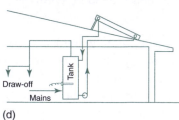

(d)

1.110

Solar hot water systems (a–d)

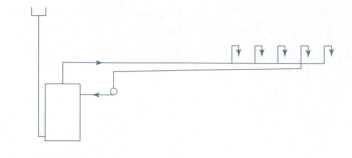

1.109

Secondary H/W circulation

pipes. This would ensure instant hot water at every draw-off point. The return pipe can be quite small.

The use of solar water heaters is becoming increasingly widespread. The most successful systems use *flat plate collectors*. These consist of an absorber plate (usually copper) with attached tubes (or waterways formed by the sheet) with a selective black finish ($\alpha_{solar} >> \varepsilon_{100}$) in a tray-form casing with a glass top.

Fig. 1.110 shows some arrangements for connecting such a collector to a hot water tank and providing an auxiliary (booster) heater.

a thermosiphon system (gravity-driven circulation) with an electric booster;
b the same with a gas-fired 'circulator' booster';
c a *close-coupled* thermosiphon system (with an integral tank) – this seems to be the most successful system, but rather expensive;
d a pumped installation, where the tank is at ground floor level.

Many combinations and permutations result in a wide variety of systems, from mains-pressure units to low pressure (inexpensive) systems, fed from an elevated cistern, and solar pre-heaters connected to a conventional hot water system of some kind. It is suggested that of the above system (b) is the ecologically most sound one.

A good system in a favourable climate can provide up to 90% of a household's hot water demand, at 60–65°C (100% if the user is willing to compromise to have less hot, say, 50°C water), but 50% is quite possible even in less sunny climates.

1.6.3 Ventilation and air conditioning

Both these systems must be capable of providing a sufficient fresh air supply to occupied spaces. If natural ventilation is relied on, the requirements can be stated in qualitative terms only, but for closed buildings served by a mechanical system fresh air requirements are set by regulations. Ventilation requirements are usually given as a function of occupancy density (in either volumetric or floor area terms) in L/(s.pers), or if no such information is available, then in terms of air changes per hour (number of times the whole volume of air must be exchanged every hour). See Data sheet D.1.9 for typical ventilation requirements. These values are for general guidance only, and may vary according to locally valid regulations.

1.6.3.1 Mechanical ventilation systems

These may be of three types:

1 extract
2 supply
3 balanced.

Extract systems are useful near a source of contamination, such as toilets, kitchen cooker hoods, laboratory fume cupboards. These create a negative pressure; relief should be provided by vent openings.

Supply systems bring in filtered outside air and create a positive pressure. Air must be released through vents. This is useful where the entry of dust should be prevented. A special form of this is the fire ventilation, which forces air at high pressure (some 500 Pa) into staircases and corridors, to keep the escape route free of smoke.

Balanced systems have both supply and exhaust provided by mechanical means. These can provide a great degree of control, but are expensive. The supply flow is usually kept higher than the exhaust, to keep a slight positive pressure and thus prevent unwanted dust entry.

The ventilation heat loss (Q_v, in a cool climate) can be reduced by a ventilation heat recovery system. This would employ a heat exchanger (rotary, as Fig. 1.111, or a plate type) or a heat transfer loop (Fig. 1.112), to pre-heat the air intake by the exhaust air, without mixing the two air streams. The latter may be assisted by a heat pump to upgrade the temperature of exhaust air before it heats the intake. This could be a reversible system, to assist cooling. The technique presupposes a balanced ventilation system, i.e. the use of two fans.

Fans are used to drive the air. Two main types can be distinguished:

1 propeller or axial flow fans; very effective when working against small back-pressure (flow resistance). The latter term is used when fitted inside a cylindrical casing.
2 centrifugal (or radial flow) fans: the intake is axial, the output is tangential. The impellers may have straight radial blades, forward or backward

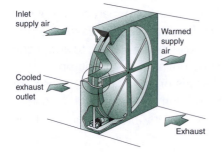

1.111

Rotary heat exchanger

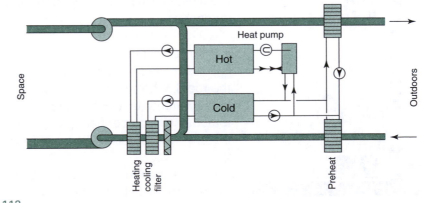

1.112

A ventilation heat recovery system

curved or aerofoil-shaped blades. These can be optimised for the particular installation, with emphasis on flow quantity, or to work against large back-pressure, or on quietness. Large fans ('blowers') are almost always of this type and for extensive ductworks the second type must be used.

Filters can be one of three types:

1 dry filters, 25–50 mm thick, usually disposable, panel or roller type, using a fabric or porous paper or other fibrous material. Some types can be cleaned by water. Dry filters tend to be more efficient than the wet ones, but usually become 'loaded' (clogged up) quicker.
2 wet filters, 12 to 100 mm thick pads, e.g. metal turnings between wire meshes, oil-coated ('viscous impingement filters'). These are washable, re-usable and are effective down to 10 μm particle sizes
3 'air washers', fine sprays against the air intake stream, particularly useful where the air is very dry and needs humidification, but also used as a pre-cooler. These must be followed by a set of 'eliminator plates', to arrest any water droplets carried by the air stream and drain these to a sump
4 electrostatic filters, up to 12 kV static charges on metal plates. These are effective down to 0.01 μm particle size, and normally used with a coarser pre-filter. These are the best filters for particularly clean areas, such as laboratories or operating theatres.

Ducts are used to convey and distribute the air. Usually they were made of sheet metal of rectangular cross-section, but in recent times plastic materials are often used in circular or oval sections. For larger sizes 'builder's work' ducts may be used, formed in brick or concrete, or framed and sheeted. These may have a greater surface friction (suitable for lower flow velocities) and it is difficult to prevent air leakages.

1.6.3.2 Air conditioning systems

These control the temperature and humidity as well as the purity of the air. The simplest system is the room conditioner: a packaged unit which can be installed in a window or an external wall. Its capacity may be up to 10 kW. It has a direct expansion evaporator-cooling coil and a condenser cooled by the outdoor air.

Such a unit is shown in Fig. 1.113 in diagrammatic terms and Fig. 1.114 is a similar unit in console form. Both are adaptations of the circuit shown in Fig. 1.98. The split units have the cooling coil (evaporator, E) and fan inside the room, while the more noisy compressor and condenser (C) are included in the outdoor unit (Fig. 1.115). Some models have a reverse-cycle facility, to act as (air-source) heat pumps for heating in winter. These are the most effective way of using electricity for heating, even if the CoP is no more than 2.

In larger systems the air is treated in an air handling unit, which includes the fan and is distributed by a ductwork. The heating coil of the air handling unit is served by a boiler, which delivers hot water. The cooling coil can be of a direct expansion type, i.e. the evaporator of the cooling machine itself, or the

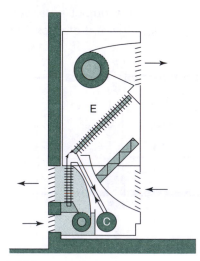

1.113
A window air conditioner unit

1.114
A console-type a/c unit

cooling machine can become a chiller (the evaporator shaped as a refrigerant-to-water heat exchanger), supplying chilled water to the cooling coil.

Fig. 1.116 shows a central air handling unit and Fig. 1.118 presents the four basic system types in diagrammatic form.

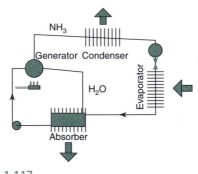

1.115

An air conditioner 'split unit'

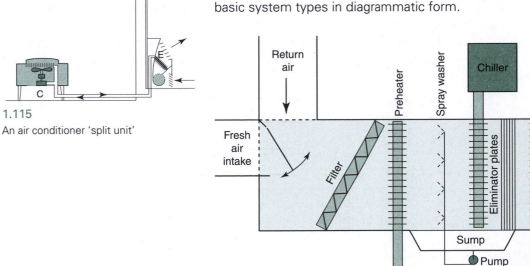

1.116

A typical central air handling unit

The chiller machine of an air conditioner may be a compressor type, such as that shown in Fig. 1.98 or an absorption chiller. Fig. 1.117 is a schematic diagram of such a chiller, using ammonia as the refrigerant and water as the absorbent. A heat input (e.g. a gas flame) expels the ammonia from the solution. The hot ammonia gas is cooled to the atmosphere through the condenser. This high pressure gas is released to the evaporator, where it expands and cools, ready to pick up heat from its environment. It is then re-absorbed in the water.

1.117

An ammonia/water absorption chiller

Both chillers can be used to produce chilled water, which is then circulated to the air conditioner unit cooling coil, or in a direct expansion coil, where the evaporator becomes the cooling coil.

In an *all-air system* (Figure 118a), the plant is centralised and the treated air is distributed by a network of ducts. This is a rather inflexible system, using quite large ducts for both supply and return. The air volume flow rate to each room is constant and the required condition is set at the central plant. It may include a terminal re-heat facility, to provide some flexibility, but at a cost in energy.

A significant improvement is the variable air volume (VAV) system, where the supply air condition is constant and the cooling requirement of each room can be matched by reducing or increasing the air flow at the diffuser. This is the most energy-efficient system.

At the other extreme is the local air-handling system (Fig. 118d), where each room or group of rooms would have its own fan-coil unit, supplied by chilled and hot water from a central plant. Each room may have its own controls. The decentralised air handling is similar to the above, but a whole zone or a floor may have its air handling unit.

In an induction system the central plant may produce over-cooled and very dry air and supply this to induction units in each room, where the supply air jet

F   Filter
W   Washer
C   Chiller
B   Boiler

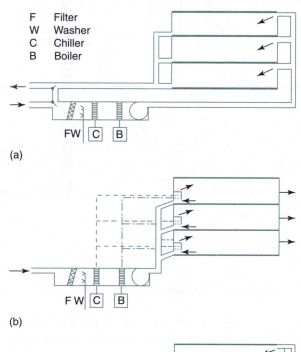

(a)

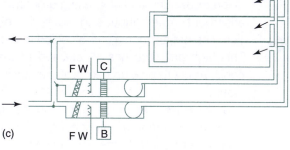

(b)

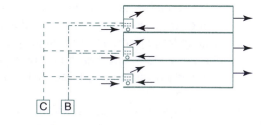

(c)

(d)

1.118

Four basic a/c systems (a–d)

induces a flow and mixing with room air, thus creating a recirculation. Heating and cooling coils may or may not be included in these units, which may be supplied from a central chiller and boiler (Fig. 118b).

In a dual duct system there may be two central air handling units, supplying cooled or heated air respectively, which are ducted to each room and can be mixed at the outlet to the desired condition. A very flexible but in energy terms very wasteful system (Fig. 118c).

These are only the basic types: a very large number of variations and permutations are available, both in terms of system arrangement and in size. In large systems the air-handling units would be room-size and may provide conditioned air supply to a number of separate zones. A building of any size could (and should) be divided into zones, according to exposure to external load, to occupancy variations and the timing of such loads.

Significant energy savings can be achieved by the control of air conditioning systems. All systems must provide a fresh air supply, at least as much as required for ventilation purposes. However, internal loads can be removed, if the outdoor air is cooler than the indoors, with an increased outdoor air supply, without running the chiller plant. This is often referred to as an *economy cycle*.

In many instances it is advisable to provide a *night flush* of (cool) outdoor air to remove the heat stored in the building fabric, thus reducing the following day's cooling requirement. Storage of heat in the fabric of the building can also be relied on to reduce the peak cooling requirement, as indicated by Fig. 1.119. Another possibility is to provide individual work-station controls: providing a minimum of general conditioning (e.g. in a large office) with individually controllable supplementary air supply to each work station.

Such controls may become parts of a BEMS (building energy management system) which would coordinate all the building's energy using equipment in a responsive manner, to minimise energy use. Ultimately such systems can produce what has been referred to as *intelligent buildings*.

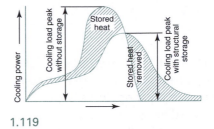

1.119
Structural storage effect on a/c load

1.6.4 Open cycle cooling systems

In conventional cooling machines (such as Fig. 1.98) the refrigerant (or coolant) fluid circulates in a closed loop. Its evaporation provides cooling and it is then 'reactivated' (condensed) by the action of a compressor. As opposed to this, in the open cycle systems water is the coolant, its evaporation provides cooling and it is then discharged. The whole system is open to the atmosphere.

The simplest open cycle system is the *direct evaporative cooler* (Fig. 1.78), which has been discussed in Section 1.5.1.4. It was considered a 'passive system', though it may use a small pump and a fan, but the cooling is provided by natural evaporation. Its disadvantage is that it increases the humidity of the supply air (see Fig. 1.13).

This is avoided by the indirect evaporative cooler, where the exhaust air is cooled and in turn it cools the intake air through a heat exchanger, without adding moisture to the supply air. The crucial element is the plate heat exchanger, shown in Fig. 1.120.

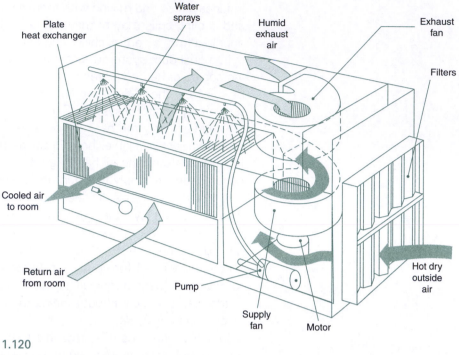

1.120
Indirect evaporative cooler

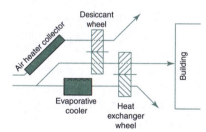

1.121
Open cycle a/c: solid sorbents

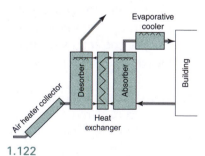

1.122
Open cycle a/c: liquid desiccant

A more sophisticated system is shown in Fig. 1.121. This uses a 'desiccant' or moisture transfer wheel, which is packed with silica gel (or some other absorbent or adsorbent) between two wire meshes. In its upper position it is dried out (reconditioned) by solar heated air. Slowly turning, this dry sorbent will come into the path of the supply air and will pick up much of its moisture content. Sorption is an exothermic process (see Fig. 1.114), thus both the wheel and the air become warm. This air will be passed through and cooled by a rotary heat exchanger (heat transfer wheel). This, in its lower half, is cooled by the evaporatively cooled air stream, which is then discharged. Besides the supply air passage, the system has two auxiliary passages open to the atmosphere: one to remove moisture, the other to provide cooling.

Another open cycle system is shown in Fig. 1.122. This is using a liquid sorbent (such as a glycol) in aqueous solution. This is sprayed downwards in the 'desorber', against an upward-moving solar-heated air stream, which 'dries out' the solution, evaporating much of the water. The warm enriched solution passes through a heat exchanger and is sprayed downwards in a second column (the absorber) against an upward air stream (return air from the house, possibly mixed with fresh air) where much of its moisture content is absorbed by the rich solution (which becomes diluted and returns to the desorber). The air is then supplied to the house through an evaporative cooler.

These two and several other open cycle systems have been produced and a few have reached the commercial development stage. Their electricity consumption for a given cooling capacity is only 15–20% of that of a conventional air conditioner. Unfortunately they tend to be bulky and the performance of sorbent materials tends to be reduced in time, over thousands of cycles.

1.6.5 Integration/discussion

HVAC services must be integrated with the architectural design in two ways:

1 in performance;
2 in hardware.

Examples of performance integration have been given throughout this chapter. The last of these was in conjunction with Fig. 1.119, which showed that building mass can reduce the necessary installed capacity of the AC system.

Table 1.6 and the associated discussion showed the interdependence of occupancy pattern, building mass and plant response. Tables 1.7 and 1.8 imply that even electric heaters should be matched to occupancy pattern and building fabric.

Floor warming is appropriate for continuously and uniformly occupied buildings. Convectors can be used where the air should be heated up quickly, but with heavy construction this would leave the room surfaces colder. Panel radiators are good where a quick response is not required, but steady warmth is welcome. Infrared lamps and incandescent radiators are the choice where there is no chance of heating up the fabric, or the room air, but the instantaneous heating effect on the body surface of people can ameliorate the situation (e.g. in a church).

In buildings larger than houses, active systems are normally designed by mechanical engineers. Cooperation with these is important both in terms of performance and in the integration of hardware. This includes the provision of adequate space, which can cause professional arguments and mutual complaints. Where should service spaces be located, without being 'squeezed into' leftover nooks and crannies? There is an architectural logic which may not coincide with an engineering logic. Understanding each other's thinking may avoid problems.

'Accommodation of services' is not enough, it is no substitute for 'integration'. Early discussions may avoid later problems. In very large buildings services provisions may become a dominant factor for architectural design. It may be beneficial to include a complete intermediate floor for services, but even in smaller buildings space is to be provided for fuel storage, plant rooms, cooling towers (or dry condensers) and, last but not least, the required ductwork. This is most often under the floor slab and covered by a suspended ceiling, but can also be located on top of a floor slab, with an elevated raised floor. In both cases such a service space would add to the building height.

Such ducts could be quite bulky. The volume flow rate is the product of air velocity and cross-sectional area, thus the two are inversely related. Velocities may be between 10 and 20 m/s. Higher velocities require smaller ducts (easier to accommodate) but produce greater friction and need a larger fan power; they may also be noisy. Often two sets of ducts are required: for supply air and return/exhaust air. The two should never cross each other, as that would set the depth of ceiling space necessary.

Ducts should also be coordinated with the structural system, e.g. to avoid crossing deep beams. Structural elements themselves may be used as ducts, e.g. hollow beams. Sometimes, such as when a long row of offices is served by a central corridor, the corridor could serve as the return air duct (large cross-section, low velocity) and the return air is picked up by a riser duct near the lift lobby.

These are just examples, by no means treating the subject systematically, but indicating the kind of thinking required.

At the early stages of design one can get a rough idea of the necessary duct size. This is best illustrated by an example: see Example 1.14.

There are also economic implications. It is not unusual for the ceiling spaces required for ductwork to be so large that over 10 floors they would add up to the height of an extra floor. This would imply extra cost for structure and envelope, which will not produce any returns. Reducing the ceiling space would allow an extra floor for the same overall building height. In a medium-to-large air conditioning system the condenser may be cooled to the outside air (dry condenser) or it may be water-cooled. The cooling water will then dissipate its heat through a *cooling tower*. These provide an ideal breeding ground for legionella bacteria. Regular maintenance with disinfectant is necessary. Using dry condensers may avoid this, but these are less efficient in energy terms than the cooling towers. The choice is one of the critical strategic decisions.

At an early stage of the design strategic decisions should be reached in consultation with the services engineer, such as where to put the plant room(s), the outline of the distribution system, any need for major riser ducts, etc. A good start would save many problems later and avoid having a patched-up job.

EXAMPLE 1.14   DUCT SIZES ESTIMATE

In an office building there will be 6000 m² space per floor. Data sheet D.1.9 shows that one person should be counted for every 10 m², thus there will be 600 persons on this floor. The ventilation (fresh air) requirement is 10 L/s per person, i.e. 6000 L/s or 6 m³/s. To remove or deliver heat, at least twice that flow would be required, say, 12 m³/s.

Assuming a medium velocity of 15 m/s, the duct cross-section required would be 12/15 = 0.8 m², which could be a 1 m × 0.8 m size. To minimise the ceiling space depth, an oblong shape would be used, but the ratio of the two sides should not exceed 2. Something like 1.25 m wide and 0.64 high would be the limit. From the aerodynamic viewpoint a circular duct would be preferable (air flows in a spiral motion), as this gives the least resistance, and needs the least fan power. The area of a circle is r²p, which gives an r of some 0.5 m, i.e. a diameter of 1 m (!). However, in a circular duct (with lesser resistance), a higher velocity may be acceptable.

DATA SHEETS AND METHOD SHEETS

DATA SHEETS

METHOD SHEETS

DATA SHEET D.1.1

Thermal properties of materials

		conductivity W/m.K	density kg/m³	spec.heat J/kg.K
WALL MATERIALS	adobe blocks	1.250	2050	1000
	brickwork, outer leaf	0.840	1700	800
	brickwork, inner leaf	0.620	1700	800
	brick, sand-lime	1.080	1840	840
	brick, silica	0.890	2240	840
	same but dense	1.900	2300	840
	concrete, cast, dense	1.400	2100	840
	lightweight	0.380	1200	1000
	aerated	0.140	400	1000
	concrete, cellular, light	0.084	320	960
	dense	0.650	1600	1050
	concrete, clinker aggreg.	0.330	1520	75
	exp.clay aggr.	0.290	800	
	up to	0.480	1280	
	vermiculite aggr.	0.190	580	
	up to	0.430	2340	
	concrete block, heavy	1.630	2300	1000
	concrete block, medium	0.510	1400	1000
	concrete block, light	0.190	600	1000
	fibreboard (softboard)	0.060	300	1000
	fibrous cement sheet	0.360	700	1050
	fibrous cement decking	0.580	1500	1050
	glass	1.100	2500	840
	plasterboard	0.160	950	840
	plywood	0.138	620	1300
	hardboard (Masonite)	0.220	1025	1675
	sand (dry)	0.300	1500	800
	stone: marble	2.000	2500	900
	sandstone	1.300	2000	800
	granite	2.300	2600	820
	slate	1.530	2950	750
	tile hanging	0.840	1900	800
	timber softwood (fir)	0.115	544	1220
	softwood	0.130	610	1420
	hardwood	0.150	680	1200
	wood chipboard, light	0.078	592	1300
	average	0.108	660	1300
	heavy	0.170	1000	1300
SURFACING	external rendering	0.500	1300	1000
	plastering, dense	0.500	1300	1000
	lightweight	0.160	600	1000
ROOF & FLOOR MATERIALS	concrete slab, dense	1.130	2000	1000
	aerated	0.160	500	840
	metal deck	50.000	7800	480
	linoleum	0.220	1300	840
	sand/cement screed	0.410	1200	840
	asphalt	1.200	1550	1600
	bituminous felt	0.500	1700	1000
	stone chippings	0.960	1800	1000
	tiles	0.840	1900	800
	thatch (straw)	0.070	240	1420
	timber boarding	0.140	640	1200

Data Sheet D.1.1 (continued)

		conductivity W/m.K	density kg/m³	spec.heat J/kg.K
	wood blocks (parquetry)	0.140	650	1200
	terrazzo	1.600	2440	1000
INSULATING MATERIALS	cork	0.038	144	1800
	cork, dense	0.049	224	1800
	cotton fibre	0.042	150	1340
	EPS (exp'ded. polystyrene)	0.035	25	1400
	up to	0.038	50	1675
	glass fibre quilt	0.040	12	840
	batt	0.035	25	880
	up to	0.040	80	880
	mineral fibre slab	0.035	35	1000
	same, denser	0.044	150	920
	phenolic foam	0.040	30	1400
	polyurethane board	0.025	30	1400
	urea formaldehyde foam	0.040	10	1400
	strawboard	0.037	250	1050
	eel grass	0.046	21	
	same compr, paper faced	0.081	320	1450
	textile blanket	0.035	12	
	up to	0.045	48	
	wood wool slab	0.100	500	1000
	rubber sheet	0.160	930	2010
	rubber, cellular	0.040	80	1670
	up to	0.084	480	1670
LOOSE FILLS	sawdust	0.059	192	
	jute fibre	0.036	107	
	cellulose fibre (fireproofed)	0.039	42	
	same, denser	0.047	83	
	coconut fibre husk	0.053	48	
	perlite fill, loose	0.046	65	
	vermiculite, exfoliated	0.069	128	
	up to	0.110	270	
METALS	aluminium	236	2700	877
	copper	384	8900	380
	zinc	112	7200	390
	iron	78	7900	437
	tin	64	7300	230
	nickel	59	8890	440
	steel, mild	47	7800	480
	stainless steel	24	7900	510
	lead	37	11300	126
MISCELLANEOUS	air (25°C, 50% RH, still)	0.025	1.15	1063
	water (still)	0.58	1000	4187
	ice (−1°C)	2.200	918	
	soil loose	0.370	1200	1100
	medium	0.710	1300	1170
	dense	1.210	1500	1260

Note that the above are 'declared' conductivity values based on laboratory tests. Before they could be used for calculating U-values, they should be corrected by κ factors as shown in Section 1.1.2.1 and Table 1.2.

DATA SHEET D.1.2

Thermal properties of walls

Note: EPS = expanded polystyrene fc = fibrous cement sheet		U-value W/m²K	admittance W/m²K	φ time lag hours	μ decrement factor
BRICK & BLOCK					
brick, single skin	105 mm	3.28	4.2	2.6	0.87
	220 mm	2.26	4.7	6.1	0.54
	335 mm	1.73	4.7	9.4	0.29
single skin	105 mm plastered	3.02	4.1	2.9	0.83
	220 mm plastered	2.14	4.5	6.5	0.49
	335 mm plastered	1.79	4.5	9.9	0.26
single skin	105 mm + 13 mm LW plaster	2.59	3.3	3.0	0.82
	220 mm + 13 mm LW plaster	1.91	3.6	6.6	0.46
	335 mm + 13 mm LW plaster	1.50	3.6	10.0	0.24
single skin	105 mm + 10 mm plasterb'd	2.70	3.5	3.0	0.83
	220 mm + 10 mm plasterb'd	1.98	3.8	6.5	0.47
	335 mm + 10 mm plasterb'd	1.60	3.8	10.0	0.25
cavity	270 mm	1.53	4.2	6.9	0.52
	270 mm plastered	1.47	4.4	7.4	0.47
	– same, + 25 mm EPS in cav.	0.72	4.6	8.9	0.34
	– same, + 40 mm EPS in cav.	0.55	4.7	9.1	0.32
	– same, + 50 mm EPS in cav.	0.47	4.7	9.2	0.31
	270 mm + 13 mm LW plaster	1.36	3.4	7.5	0.44
	+ 10 mm plasterb'd	1.12	2.3	8.1	0.36
	+ UF foam cav.fill	0.57	4.6	8.7	0.35
brick 105, cavity, 100 Lw concr. block, Lw plaster		0.92	2.2	7.0	0.55
– same + 25 mm EPS		0.55	2.3	8.0	0.43
– same but 50 mm EPS		0.40	2.4	9.0	0.41
concrete block, solid 200, plasterboard		1.83	2.5	6.8	0.35
– same, but foil-backed plasterboard		1.40	1.82	7.0	0.32
– same, but 25 cavity, 25 EPS, plasterb'd		0.70	1.0	7.3	0.29
– same, but lightweight concrete		0.69	1.8	7.4	0.46
– same, but foil-backed plasterboard		0.61	1.5	7.7	0.42
– same, but 25 cavity, 25 EPS, plasterb'd		0.46	1.0	8.3	0.34
concrete block, LW 200, 25 cav.+10 plasterb'd		0.69	1.8	7.0	0.47
– same but foil-back plasterboard		0.64	1.6	8.0	0.44
– same but 20 mm EPS		0.55	1.2	8.0	0.39
– same but 25 mm EPS		0.51	1.1	8.0	0.37
– same but 25 polyurethane		0.45	1.0	8.0	0.34
concrete block, hollow, 100 mm + plasterboard		2.76	3.4	1.8	0.93
200 mm + ins. plasterboard		2.42	4.1	3.0	0.83
concrete, dense, cast, 150 mm		3.48	5.3	4.0	0.70
– same + 50 mm woodwool slab, plastered		1.23	1.7	6.0	0.50
– same, but lightweight plaster		1.15	1.7	6.3	0.49
concrete, dense, cast, 200 mm		3.10	5.5	5.4	0.56
– same + 50 mm woodwool slab, plastered		1.18	2.2	7.7	0.36
– same, but lightweight plaster		1.11	1.7	6.2	0.35
concrete, precast panel, 75 mm		4.28	4.9	1.9	0.91
– same + 25 cavity + 25 EPS + plasterboard		0.84	1.0	3.0	0.82
concrete, precast, 75 +25 EPS +150 LW concrete		0.58	3.8	9.5	0.41
– same, but 50 mm EPS		0.49	3.8	9.2	0.26

Data Sheet D.1.2 (continued)

Note: EPS = expanded polystyrene fc = fibrous cement sheet	U-value W/m²K	admittance W/m²K	φ time lag hours	μ decrement factor
BRICK / BLOCK VENEERS				
brick 105 + cavity (frame) + plasterboard	1.46	2.4	3.6	0.99
– same, but foil-backed plasterboard	1.35	1.7	3.7	0.75
– same with 25 mm EPS or glass fibre	0.72	1.1	4.0	0.77
– same with 50 mm EPS or glass fibre	0.47	0.8	4.2	0.72
– same, 25 EPS + foil-backed plasterboard	0.64	1.0	4.1	0.81
block 100 + cavity (frame) + plasterboard	1.57	2.1	4.1	0.72
– same, but foil-backed plasterboard	1.24	1.7	4.3	0.69
– same with 25 mm EPS or glass fibre	0.74	1.1	4.7	0.65
– same with 50 mm EPS or glass fibre	0.48	0.9	4.9	0.62
– same, 25 EPS + foil-backed plasterboard	0.66	1.0	4.7	0.64
FRAMED				
framed, single fc or galvanised steel	5.23	5.2	0	1
– same + cavity + plasterboard	2.20	2.2	0.3	1
– same with 25 mm EPS or glass fibre	0.86	1.1	0.5	0.99
– same with 50 mm EPS or glass fibre	0.53	0.9	0.7	0.99
framed, 20 mm timber boarding	3.19	3.2	0.4	1
– same + cavity + plasterboard	1.68	1.8	0.8	0.99
– same with 25 mm EPS or glass fibre	0.68	1.0	0.9	0.99
– same with 50 mm EPS or glass fibre	0.46	0.8	1.0	0.98
framed, tile-hanging + paper+cavity + 50 EPS + plast'bd	0.54	0.78	1.0	0.99
– same, but 100 EPS or glass fibre	0.32	0.71	1.0	0.99
reverse brick veneer: 5 mm fc + cavity + 105 brick	1.39	4.13	3.70	0.97
– same + 25 mm EPS in cavity	0.70	4.53	4.50	0.68
– same but 50 mm EPS	0.47	4.62	4.80	0.61
– same but only aluminium foil in cavity	1.14	4.22	3.90	0.99
– same but both foil and 25 mm EPS	0.63	4.54	4.50	0.70
reverse block veneer: 5 fc + cavity + 100 hollow block	1.41	3.14	2.20	1.00
– same but 100 mm solid concrete block	1.63	6.05	4.40	0.79
– same but 50 EPS in cavity + 100 hollow blck	0.47	3.59	3.20	0.85
– same but 50 EPS in cavity + 100 solid block	0.49	6.45	5.20	0.46
– same but 50 EPS in cavity + 200 solid block	0.48	6.16	7.70	0.21
SANDWICH PANELS				
6 mm fibrous cement + 25 EPS + 6 mm fc.	1.20	1.1	0.5	1
6 mm fibrous cement + 50 polyurethane + 6 fc	0.45	0.9	0.7	1

DOORS			U-value	admittance	φ time lag	μ decrement
Timber	35 mm	10 mm inset panels	3.24	3.24	0.6	1
	45 mm	hollow core, flush	2.44	2.44	0.4	1
	45 mm	solid core, flush	2.20	2.10	1.0	0.97
metal (roller shutter, tilt-a-door)			5.54	5.00	0	1

DATA SHEET D.1.3

Thermal properties of windows, roofs and floors

				U-value W/m²K	admittance W/m²K	sgf θ	asg1 light	asg2 heavy
WINDOWS								
wood frame,	10%	single	6 mm clear glass	5.3	5.3	0.76	0.64	0.47
			surface tinted glass	5.3	5.3	0.60	0.53	0.41
			body tinted glass	5.3	5.3	0.52	0.47	0.38
			reflective glass	5.3	5.3	0.18	0.17	0.15
		double	clear glazing	3.0	3.0	0.64	0.56	0.42
			surf. tinted + clear	3.0	3.0	0.48	0.43	0.34
			body tinted + clear	3.0	3.0	0.40	0.37	0.30
			reflective + clear	3.0	3.0	0.28	0.25	0.21
			sealed, reflect.+clear	3.0	3.0	0.15	0.14	0.11
	20%	single	6 mm clear glass	5.0	5.0	0.76	0.64	0.42
			surface tinted glass	5.0	5.0	0.60	0.53	0.41
			body tinted glass	5.0	5.0	0.52	0.47	0.38
			reflective glass	5.0	5.0	0.18	0.17	0.15
		double	clear glazing	2.9	2.9	0.64	0.56	0.42
			surf. tinted + clear	2.9	2.9	0.48	0.43	0.34
			body tinted + clear	2.9	2.9	0.40	0.37	0.30
			reflective + clear	2.9	2.9	0.28	0.25	0.21
			sealed, reflect.+clear	2.9	2.9	0.15	0.14	0.11
	30%	single	6 mm clear glass	4.7	4.7	0.76	0.64	0.47
			surface tinted glass	4.7	4.7	0.60	0.53	0.41
			body tinted glass	4.7	4.7	0.52	0.47	0.38
			reflective glass	4.7	4.7	0.18	0.17	0.15
		double	clear glazing	2.8	2.8	0.64	0.56	0.42
			surf. tinted + clear	2.8	2.8	0.48	0.43	0.34
			body tinted + clear	2.8	2.8	0.40	0.37	0.30
			reflective + clear	2.8	2.8	0.28	0.25	0.21
			sealed, reflect.+clear	2.8	2.8	0.15	0.14	0.11
metal frame	10%	single	6 mm clear glass	6.0	6.0	0.76	0.64	0.47
			surface tinted glass	6.0	6.0	0.60	0.53	0.41
			body tinted glass	6.0	6.0	0.52	0.47	0.38
			reflective glass	6.0	6.0	0.18	0.17	0.15
		double	clear glazing	3.6	3.6	0.64	0.56	0.42
			surf. tinted + clear	3.6	3.6	0.48	0.43	0.34
			body tinted + clear	3.6	3.6	0.40	0.37	0.30
			reflective + clear	3.6	3.6	0.28	0.25	0.21
			sealed, reflect.+clear	3.6	3.6	0.15	0.14	0.11
	20%	single	6 mm clear glass	6.4	6.4	0.76	0.64	0.47
		double	clear glazing	4.3	4.3	0.64	0.56	0.42
metal frame	10%		discontinuous frame, single	5.7	5.7	0.76	0.64	0.47
			same, body tinted	5.7	5.7	0.52	0.47	0.38
			discontinuous frame, double	3.3	3.3	0.64	0.56	0.42
	20%		discontinuous frame, single	5.8	5.8	0.76	0.64	0.47
			discontinuous frame, double	3.7	3.7	0.64	0.56	0.42
vinyl frame			bronze + clear glass	2.8	2.8	0.58	0.50	0.39
			double (clear + clear) glazing	2.8	2.8	0.48	0.43	0.34
			argon filled clear+clear glazing	1.9	1.9	0.55	0.49	0.39
			argon filled low-e clear + clear	1.7	1.7	0.32	0.28	0.23

Data Sheet D.1.3 (continued)

		U-value W/m²K	admittance W/m²K	sgf θ	asg1 light	asg2 heavy
insulated vinyl frame	krypton fill, triple clear glass	1.9	1.9	0.5	0.47	0.38
	krypton fill, triple(2 low-e)glass	0.9	0.9	0.37	0.34	0.27
roof	single glazing 6 mm glass	6.6	6.6	0.76	0.64	0.47
	body tinted glass	6.6	6.6	0.52	0.47	0.38
	double clear glazing	4.6	4.6	0.64	0.56	0.42
	body tinted + clear	4.6	4.6	0.40	0.37	0.30
horizontal	laylight + skylight, ventilated	3.8	3.8	0.60	0.56	0.42

Note: fc = fibrous cement	U-value W/m²K	admittance W/m²K	time lag hours	decrement factor
FLAT ROOFS				
150 concr. slab, plastered,75 screed +asphalt	1.80	4.50	8	0.33
– same, but lightweight concrete	0.84	2.30	5	0.77
25 timber deck, bit. felt, plasterboard ceiling	1.81	1.90	0.9	0.99
– same + 50 mm EPS	0.51	0.80	1.3	0.98
10 fc. deck, 13 fibreboard, asphalt, fc.ceiling	1.50	1.90	2	0.96
– same + 50 mm EPS	0,49	0.88	1.93	0.95
50 ww,13 screed, 20 asph, plasterboard ceiling	1.00	1.40	3	0.93
13 fibreb'd, 20 asph,10 foil-back plasterboard	1.20	1.30	1	0.99
– same + 50 mm EPS	0.44	1.1	1.2	0.98
metal deck, 25 EPS,bitumenous felt	1.10	1.20	1	0.99
– same+ 13 fibreboard +plasterboard ceiling	0.73	0.91	1	0.99
– same, but 50 mm EPS	0.48	0.75	1	0.98
– same, but 75 mm EPS	0.38	0.86	1.4	0.98
PITCHED ROOFS				
corrugated fibrous cement sheet	4.9	4.9	0	1
– same + attic + plasterboard ceiling	2.58	2.6	0.3	1
– same + 50 mm EPS or glass fibre	0.55	1	0.7	0.99
– same but 75 mm EPS or glass fibre	0.4	0.73	0.77	0.99
tiles, sarking + attic + plasterboard ceiling	2.59	2.6	0.5	1
– same + 50 mm EPS or glass fibre	0.54	1.0	1.5	0.97
– same but 75 mm EPS or glass fibre	0.39	0.86	1.07	0.99
tiles, sarking, 25 timber ceiling (sloping)	1.91	2.1	1.0	0.99
– same + 50 mm EPS or glass fibre	0.51	1.5	1.4	0.97
– same but 75 mm EPS or glass fibre	0.4	1.5	1.77	0.96
metal sheet (corrugated or profiled)	7.14	7.1	0	1
metal sheet + attic + plasterboard ceiling	2.54	2.6	0.3	1
– same but 75 mm EPS or glass fibre	0.39	0.86	1.07	0.99
– same + 50 mm EPS or glass fibre	0.55	1.0	0.7	0.99
FLOORS				
suspended timber, bare or linoleum				
3 × 3 m	1.05	2.0	0.7	0.99
same + 50 EP{S	0.44	1.35	1.6	1
7.5 × 7.5 m	0.68	2.0	0.8	0.98

Data Sheet D.1.3 (continued)

	U-value W/m²K	admittance W/m²K	time lag hours	decrement factor
15 × 7.5 m	0.61	2.0	0.8	0.98
15 × 15 m	0.45	2.0	0.9	0.97
same + 50 EPS	0.30	1.35	1.59	1
30 × 15 m	0.39	2.0	0.9	0.97
60 × 15 m	0.37	2.0	1.0	0.97
concr. slab on ground, 2 adjacent edges exposed				
3 × 3 m 18 28	1.07	6.0	-	0.01
6 × 6 m	0.57	6.0	-	0
7.5 × 7.5 m	0.45	6.0	-	0
10 × 10 m	0.30	6.0	-	0
15 × 7.5 m	0.36	6.0	-	0
15 × 15 m	0.26	6.0	-	0
30 × 15 m	0.21	6.0	-	0
60 × 15 m	0.18	6.0	-	0
100 × 40 m	0.09	6.0	-	0
concr. slab on ground, 2 parallel edges exposed				
3 × 3 m	1.17	6.0	-	0.01
6 × 6 m	0.58	6.0	-	0
7.5 × 7.5 m	0.48	6.0	-	0
15 × 7.5 m	0.32	6.0	-	0
10 × 10 m	0.30	6.0	-	0
15 × 15 m	0.29	6.0	-	0
30 × 15 m	0.25	6.0	-	0
60 × 15 m	0.21	6.0	-	0
100 × 40 m	0.13	6.0	-	0
4 edges exposed (see corrections below)				
3 × 3 m	1.47	6.0	-	0.02
6 × 6 m	0.96	6.0	-	0.01
7.5 × 7.5 m	0.76	6.0	-	0.01
15 × 7.5 m	0.62	6.0	-	0
10 × 10 m	0.62	6.0	-	0
15 × 15 m	0.45	6.0	-	0
30 × 15 m	0.36	6.0	-	0
60 × 15 m	0.32	6.0	-	0
100 × 40 m	0.16	6.0	-	0

corrections for edge insulation (min. R = 4) of concr. slab-on-ground floors (4 edges exp.) multipliers for the U-value

	depth or width 0.5	1 m
3 × 3 m	0.82	0.72
6 × 6 m	0.85	0.75
10 × 10 m	0.86	0.78
15 × 15 m	0.87	0.80
60 × 15 m	0.88	0.82
100 × 40 m	0.89	0.83

DATA SHEET D.1.4

Thermal properties of surfaces and cavities

		for 6000°C solar radiation		at 50°C
		absorptance & emittance α or ε	reflectance ρ	absorptance & emittance α and ε
RADIATION PROPERTIES				
brick	white, glazed	0.25	0.75	0.95
	light colours	0.40	0.60	0.90
	dark colours	0.80	0.20	0.90
roofs	asphalt or bitumen	0.90	0.10	0.96
	red tiles	0.65	0.35	0.85
	white tiles	0.40	0.60	0.50
	aluminium, oxidised	0.30	0.80	0.11
	bright aluminium, chrome, nickel	0.10	0.90	0.05
	bright (new) aluminium foil	0.03		
weathered building surfaces, light		0.50	0.50	0.60
	medium	0.80	0.20	0.95
paint	white	0.30	0.70	0.92
	matt black	0.96	0.04	0.96
generally:	reflectance = (V × V−1) / 100 where V = Munsell value of the paint			

SURFACE RESISTANCES (m^2K/W)		*normal surfaces*	*low emittance surfaces*
inside	walls	0.12	0.30
	ceiling, floor: heat flow up	0.10	0.22
	heat flow down	0.14	0.55
	45° ceiling		
	heat flow up	0.11	0.24
	heat flow down	0.13	0.39
outside	walls, sheltered	0.08	0.11
	normal exposure	0.06	0.07
	severe exposure	0.03	0.03
roofs	sheltered	0.07	0.09
	normal exposure	0.04	0.05
	severe exposure	0.02	0.02

CAVITY RESISTANCES ($m^2 K/W$)		*normal surfaces*	*low emittance surfaces*
unventilated:			
5 mm cavity	any position	0.10	0.18
>25 mm cavity	heat flow horizontal	0.18	0.35
	heat flow up	0.17	0.35
	heat flow down	0.22	1.06
	45°, heat flow up	0.19	0.40
	45°, heat flow down	0.20	0.98
multiple foil	heat flow horizontal or up	–	0.62
	heat flow down	–	1.76
ventilated:			
between fibrous cement sheet ceiling & dark metal roof		0.16	0.30
between fibrous cement sheet ceiling & fibrous cement roof		0.14	0.25
between fibrous cement sheet ceiling & tiled roof		0.18	0.26
between tiles and sarking		0.12	–
air space behind tile hanging (incl. the tile)		0.12	–
in ordinary cavity walls		0.18	

DATA SHEET D.1.5

Moisture movement data

A INDOOR MOISTURE PRODUCTION

one person	at rest	40 g/h
	sedentary activity	50 g/h
	active	200 g/h
cooking (gas)	breakfast	400 g ⎫
	lunch	500 g ⎬ ≈ 3000 g/day
	dinner	1200 g ⎭
dishwashing	breakfast	100 g
	lunch	100 g
	dinner	300 g
floor mopping		1100 g
clothes washing		2000 g
clothes drying (indoors)		12 000 g
shower		200 g
bath		100 g
oil (kerosene, paraffin)	heater (flueless)	1 kg per kg oil burnt
Animal houses:		
dairy cows	per kg body mass	1–1.5 µg/s

B PERMEABILITY (δ) OF SOME
MATERIALS

	mg/s.m.kPa or µg/s.m.Pa
brickwork	0.006–0.042
cement render	0.010
concrete	0.005–0.035
cork board	0.003–0.004
expanded ebonite (Onozote)	< 0.0001
expanded polystyrene	0.002–0.007
fibreboard (softboard)	0.020–0.070
hardboard (Masonite)	0.001–0.002
mineral wool	0.168
plastering	0.017–0.025
plasterboard	0.017–0.023
plywood	0.002–0.007
polyurethane foam	open cell	0.035
	closed cell	0.001
strawboard		0.014–0.022
timber	air dry	0.014–0.022
	wet	0.001–0.008
urea formaldehyde foam		0.031–0.053
wood wool slab		0.024–0.070

SURFACE COEFFICIENTS *(permeance)*		*µg/s.m²Pa*
with still air	if h = 4.5 W/m²K	25.5
with moving air	if h = 11.4 W/m²K	62.3
	if h = 17 W/m²K	96.3

Data Sheet D.1.5 (continued)

C permeance (π) of some elements and surfaces

		$mg/s.m^2kPa$ or $\mu g/s.m^2Pa$
acrylic sheet	1.5 mm	0.007
aluminium foil		< 0.006
bituminous paper		0.090
brickwork	105 mm	0.04–0.060
concrete blocks	200 mm hollow	0.140
cellulose acetate	0.25 mm	0.260
	3 mm	0.018
cement render, or screed,		
	25 mm, 4:1	0.670
	25 mm, 1:1	0.400
corkboard	25 mm	0.40–0.540
fibreglass sheet	1.2 mm	0.003
fibrous cement sheet	3 mm	0.20–0.500
same with oil paint		0.02–0.030
glazed brick	105 mm	0.007
hardboard (Masonite)	3 mm	0.630
same, tempered		0.290
kraft paper	single	4.540
	3-ply	2.000
	5-ply	1.600
oil paint, 2 coats	on plaster	0.09–0.170
3 coats	on wood	0.02–0.060
plaster on lath	25 mm	0.630
	20 mm	0.830
	12 mm	0.930
plasterboard	10 mm	1.70–2.800
plywood		
external quality	6 mm	0.026–0.041
internal quality	6 mm	0.106–0.370
polyethylene film	0.06 mm	0.009
	0.1 mm	0.005
	0.2 mm	0.002
PVC sheet	0.05 mm	0.040
same, plasticised	0.1 mm	0.050–0.080
softwood (pine)	25 mm	0.080
	12 mm	0.10–0.170
strawboard	50 mm	0.13–0.260
wood wool slab	25 mm	3.08–4.140
surface	internal	25
	external	100

Note: any layer of less than 0.067 mg/s.m²kPa (μg/s.m²Pa) permeance is taken as a vapour barrier.

Vapour resistance is the reciprocal of permeance: $vR = 1/\pi$ or $vR = b/\delta$.

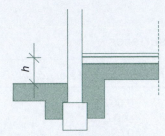

h = ground level to
floor level distance

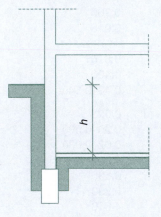

DATA SHEET D.1.6

Thermal bridges, ground floors and basement walls

LINEAR HEAT LOSS COEFFICIENTS	k
window perimeter	0.15 W/m.K
same, but if window is in the plane of insulation and joint sealed	0
outer corner of homogeneous wall	0.10
outer corner of wall with external insulation	0.15
external wall with internal insulation	0
joint of homogeneous external wall and internal wall (both edges counted)	0.12
joint of ext. wall with ext. insulation and internal wall (both edges counted)	0.06
joint of homog. ext. wall & floor slab with insul. strip (both edges counted)	0.15
joint of ext. wall with ext. insulation and floor slab (both edges counted)	0.06
parapet wall, cornice	0.20
projecting balcony slab	0.3

ON-GROUND FLOOR LOSSES
linear heat transmission coefficients. **W/m.K**

height [h] relative to ground level (m)	if floor thermal resistance is [m²K/W]							
	no insul.	0.2–0.35	0.4–0.55	0.6–0.75	0.8–1.0	1.05–1.5	1.55–2	2.05–3
> |6.0|	0	0	0	0	0	0	0	0
−6.00 to −4.05	0.20	0.20	0.15	0.15	0.15	0.15	0.15	0.15
−4.00 to −2.55	0.40	0.40	0.35	0.35	0.35	0.35	0.30	0.30
−2.50 to −1.85	0.60	0.55	0.55	0.50	0.50	0.45	0.45	0.40
−1.80 to −0.25	0.80	0.70	0.70	0.65	0.60	0.60	0.55	0.45
−1.20 to −0.75	1.00	0.90	0.85	0.80	0.75	0.70	0.65	0.55
−0.70 to −0.45	1.20	1.05	1.00	0.95	0.90	0.80	0.75	0.65
−0.40 to −0.25	1.40	1.20	1.10	1.05	1.00	0.90	0.80	0.70
−0.20 to +0.20	1.75	1.45	1.35	1.25	1.15	1.05	0.95	0.85
+0.25 to +0.40	2.10	1.70	1.55	1.45	1.30	1.20	1.05	0.95
+0.45 to +1.00	2.35	1.90	1.70	1.55	1.45	1.30	1.15	1.00
+1.05 to +1.50	2.55	2.05	1.85	1.70	1.55	1.40	1.25	1.10

LOSSES THROUGH EARTH SHELTERED WALLS
linear heat transmission coefficients. **W/m.K**

height [h] below ground level (m)	if U-value of wall itself is [W/m²K]							
	0.4–0.49	0.5–0.59	0.6–0.79	0.8–0.99	1–1.19	1.2–1.49	1.5–1.79	1.8–2.2
>6.0	1.40	1.65	1.85	2.05	2.25	2.45	2.65	2.80
6.00 to 5.05	1.30	1.50	1.70	1.90	2.05	2.25	2.45	2.65
5.00 to 4.05	1.15	1.35	1.50	1.65	1.90	2.05	2.24	2.45
4.00 to 3.05	1.00	1.15	1.30	1.45	1.65	1.85	2.00	2.20
3.00 to 2.55	0.85	1.00	1.15	1.30	1.45	1.65	1.80	2.00
2.50 to 2.05	0.70	0.85	1.00	1.15	1.30	1.45	1.65	1.80
2.00 to 1.55	0.60	0.70	0.85	1.00	1.10	1.25	1.40	1.55
1.50 to 1.05	0.45	0.55	0.65	0.75	0.90	1.00	1.15	1.30
1.00 to 0.75	0.35	0.40	0.50	0.60	0.65	0.80	0.90	1.05
0.70 to 0.45	0.20	0.30	0.35	0.40	0.50	0.55	0.65	0.75
0.40 to 0.25	0.10	0.15	0.20	0.25	0.30	0.35	0.40	0.45

DATA SHEET D.1.7

Heat emission of people and appliances

HEAT OUTPUT OF HUMAN BODIES in W *(watts)*	Total	at 20°C sensible latent		at 26°C sensible latent	
seated at rest	115	90	25	65	50
sedentary work	140	100	40	70	70
seated, eating	150	85	65	70	80
slow walking	160	110	50	75	85
light bench-type work	235	130	105	80	55
medium work	265	140	125	90	175
heavy work	440	190	250	105	335
very heavy work (gymnasium)	585	205	380	175	420

ELECTRIC LIGHTING LOAD		**W / (m² lux)**
Incandescent	open enamelled reflector	0.125–0.160
	general diffusing	0.160–0.225
Florescent	white, open trough	0.037
	enclosed, diffusing	0.050
	de luxe warm white, enclosed, diffusing	0.075–0.100
	louvred, recessed	0.085–0.110
Mercury MBF industrial reflector		0.050–0.075

ELECTRICAL APPLIANCES		sensible W	latent W
hair dryer (blower)		700	100
hair dryer (helmet type)		600	100
coffee urn	14–23 L	800–1000	900–1200
computer (PC)	main unit	200–300	–
	VDU (CRT), VGA	150–300	–
	printer	30–300	–
food	per m² top surface	1000	1000
frying	(300 × 350 mm)	1100	1700
grill, meat	(250 × 300 cooking area)	1200	600
grill, sandwich	(300 × 300 cooking area)	800	200
jug or kettle		≈1800	500
microwave oven		≈1300	–
	1 door, manual	150–260	–
	2 door,–auto defrost	350–400	–
	2 door,–frost-free	500–600	–
sterilizer, bulk	(600 × 600 × 900)	10000	6500
sterilizer, water	45 L	1200	4800
sterilizer, instrument	(150 × 100 × 450)	800	700
toaster, pop-up	(2 slices)	700	200
toaster, continuous	(4 slices)	1800	800
vacuum cleaner		600–1200	–
waffle iron		400	200
water heater (domestic)		2400–3600	–

GAS APPLIANCES			
coffee urn	14–23 L	900–1200	900–1200
food warmer	per m² top surface	2700	1600
frying pot, mm	280 × 410	2100	1400
grill, top burner, surface	0.13 m²	4400	1100
toaster, continuous	(2 slices)	2200	1000
stove, short order, closed top	per m² top surface	11000	11000
laboratory burners (bunsen)	10 mm dia.(natural gas)	500	100

DATA SHEET D.1.8

Typical ventilation requirements

air inhaled	at sedentary activity	0.5 m³/h
	at heavy work, up to	5 m³/h
limitation	CO_2 content, absolute limit	0.5%
	markedly 'used air' effect	0.15%

apparent cooling effect of air flow past the skin

$$dT = -1.2844 v^2 + 5.9331 v - 1.0136$$

or

$$dT = 6 \times (v - 0.2) - 1.6 \times (v - 0.2)^2$$

or approximately

$$dT = 3.2 v \qquad \text{where v is in m/s and dT in K}$$

if room volume per person (m³)	*then fresh air supply rate*	*per person*
	minimum	recommended
3	12	17
6	7	11
9	5	8
12	4	6

kitchen, other than domestic	20 air changes per hour
kitchen, domestic	10
laundry, boiler room, operating theatre	15
canteen, restaurant, dance hall	10–15
cinema, theatre, lavatory	6–10
bathroom, bank hall, parking station	6
office, laboratory	4–6
library	3–4
staircase, corridor (non-domestic)	2
all other domestic rooms	1

For ventilation rates as a function of density or on a floor area basis see the following page.

For estimation of ventilation rates produced by wind and stack effects see M.1.4.

requirement	*If density: (area/pers.)*	*room occupancy type (examples only)*
4 L/s.pers	given number	sauna, steam room
10 L/s.pers	given number	dormitory, ticket booth
	0.6 m²	transport concourse, platform, funeral chapel
	1 m²	rest room, shops fitting room, kiosk, funeral reception room
	1.5 m²	medical waiting room, museum exhibition area, broadcast studio
	2 m²	school classroom >16y, music room, locker room, waiting area
	2.5 m²	prison, guard rooms
	5 m²	shops sales floor, arcade, office art room, physiotherapy room drawing office, library, coin-op. laundry, pharmacy

Data Sheet D.1.8 (continued)

requirement	If density: (area/pers.)	room occupancy type (examples only)
	10 m²	photo dark room, florist, dry cleaner, hotel bedroom, general office bank vault, residential buildings
	20 m²	warehouse
	25 m²	computer room
	50 m²	hangar
	100 m²	greenhouse
12 L/s.pers	2 m²	school classrooms < 16y.
15 L/s.pers	0.6 m²	theatre, opera, concert hall, foyer, lecture hall
	1 m²	cafeteria, fast food, large assembly room, disco, conference room
	1.5 m²	hotel dining room, ball room, casino
	2 m²	small conference room
	4 m²	theatre, concert hall, lecture hall, hairdresser shop, beauty salon
	5 m²	hotel suite living room, theatre 'green room', prison cell block
20 L/s.pers	1 m²	bar, cocktail lounge
	1.5 m²	cabaret
	2 m²	air traffic control room,
	5 m²	medical buildings: delivery and operating room
25 L/s.pers	1.5 m²	smoking room
50 L/s.pers	5 m²	autopsy room

On a floor area basis:

	1 L/s.m²	corridor, foyer, lobby, stairs, pedestrian tunnel, utility room
	3.5 L/s.m²	pool area, deck
	4 L/s.m²	electricity meter or switch room, fire control room
	5 L/s.m²	veterinary kennel, animal room, operating room, pet shop

DATA SHEET D.1.9

Degree-days of some locations

Kelvin-days, base 18°C

AUSTRALIA			NORTH AMERICA	
Adelaide		1000	Chicago	3311
Alice Springs		618	Dallas	1260
Brisbane		245	Denver	3456
Canberra		2186	Los Angeles	771
Hobart		2063	Miami	112
Kalgoorlie		914	New York	2375
Melbourne city		1378	Phoenix	609
	airport	1629	St Louis	2504
Newcastle		681	Montreal	4137
Perth		778	Ottawa	4338
Port Headland		24	Toronto	3450
Sydney		642	Vancouver	2934

EUROPE		SOUTH AMERICA	
Amsterdam	2795	Brasilia	170
Berlin	3076	Buenos Aires	930
Bern	3666	Campo Grande (Br)	156
Budapest	3005	Cordoba (Argentina)	1145
Copenhagen	3238	Florianopolis	260
Geneva	2463	Lima	226
Hamburg	3160	Porto Allegre	622
Lausanne	3375	Rio de Janeiro	8
Lucerne	3654	Rio Gallegos (Arg)	3823
Paris	2544	Santiago de Chile	1841
St Gallen	4644	São Paolo	343
Vienna	2974	Chile Valparaiso	1841

UNITED KINGDOM			ASIA / AFRICA	
England	Yorkshire	2987	Altai (Mongolia)	7806
-	Midlands	2922	Beijing	2967
-	West	2332	Islamabad	781
-	South	2509	Kushiro	4121
-	London	2610	Novosibirsk	6254
Scotland	West	3244	Osaka	1504
-	South/East	3112	Seoul	2995
Wales	Cardiff	2634	Shanghai	1645
-	Swansea	2711	Tokyo	2795
-	Holyhead	2811	Cape Town	909
N. Ireland	Belfast	3080	Johannesburg	1131
	Londonderry	2631	Nairobi	327

Conversion factors for bases other than 18°C (multipliers)

For 17 °C: 0.91	for 15 °C: 0.72	for 12 °C: 0.44
16 °C: 0.82	14 °C: 0.63	10 °C: 0.25

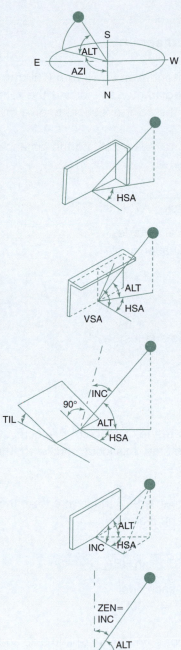

ZEN = zenith angle (from vertical)

METHOD SHEET M.1.1

Solar geometry

DEFINITIONS:

AZI = solar azimuth (0 to 360°)
ALT = solar altitude (from horizontal; zenith = 90°)
ZEN = zenith angle (from the vertical); ZEN = 90–ALT
ORI = orientation (azimuth of the surface normal, 0 to 360°)
HAS = horizontal shadow angle (azimuth difference)
VSA = vertical shadow angle (on perpendicular normal plane)
INC = angle of incidence (from the surface normal)
LAT = geographical latitude (south negative)
DEC = declination (between the earth-sun line and the equator plane)
HRA = hour angle from solar noon, 15° per hour
SRA = sunrise azimuth, i.e. azimuth at sunrise time
SRT = sunrise time

EXPRESSIONS:

DEC = 23.45 × sin[0.9836 × (284 + NDY)]   (result in degrees)
    where NDY = number of day of year
        0.9836 = 360° / 365 days
    or more accurately:
DEC = 0.33281 − 22.984 × cosN + 3.7872 × sinN−
    −0.3499 × cos(2 × N) + 0.03205 × sin(2 × N)−
    −0.1398 × cos(3 × N) + 0.07187 × sin(3 × N)
where N = 2 × π × NDY/366 in radians (if trig. functions set for radians)
    N = 0.9836 × NDY   in degrees (if trig. functions set for degrees)
                    (in any case DEC results in degrees)

HRA = 15 × (hour−12)
ALT = arcsin(sinDEC × sinLAT + cosDEC × cosLAT × cosHRA)

$$AZI = arcos\frac{\cos LAT \times \sin DEC - \cos DEC \times \sin LAT \times \cos HRA}{\cos ALT}$$

gives result 0–180°, i.e. for a.m. only, for p.m., take AZI = 360–AZI (as found)

HSA = AZI–ORI
    if 90° < abs|HSA| < 270° then sun is behind the facade, it is in shade
    if HSA > 270° then HSA = HSA−360°
    if HSA <−270° then HSA = HSA+360°

$$VSA = arctan\frac{\tan ALT}{\cos HSA}$$

INC = arcos (sinALT × cosTIL + cosALT × sinTIL × cosHSA)
    where TIL = tilt angle of receiving plane from the horizontal

For vertical planes, as TIL = 90, cosTIL = 0, sinTIL = 1:
INC = arcos(cosALT × cos HSA)

For a horizontal plane:
INC = ZEN = 90−ALT
SRA = arcos (cosLAT × sinDEC + tanLAT × tanDEC × sinLAT × cosDEC)

$$SRT = 12-\frac{arcos(-\tan LAT \times \tan DEC)}{15}$$

METHOD SHEET M.1.2

Construction of stereographic sun-path diagrams

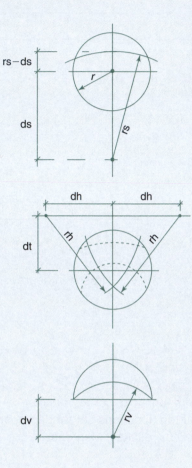

1 Draw a circle of selected radius (r), most often taken as 75 mm (150 mm diameter). Draw a horizontal and a vertical diameter to indicate the four compass points. Extend the vertical one in the polar direction, to give the locus for the centres of all sun-path arcs.

2 For each sun-path arc (each date) calculate its radius (rs) and the distance of its centre from the centre of the circle (ds)

$$rs = r \times \frac{\cos DEC}{\sin LAT + \sin DEC} \qquad ds = r \times \frac{\cos LAT}{\sin LAT + \sin DEC}$$

where   LAT = geographical latitude
              DEC = solar declination angle

March 21 and Sep 23:   DEC = 0
June 22   DEC = 23.45°
December 22   DEC = −23.45°

for intermediate lines the following dates are suggested:
May 12 + Aug.1   DEC = 18°
Apr 14 + Aug 28   DEC = 9°
Nov 11 + Jan 30   DEC = −18°
Oct 14 + Feb 27   DEC = −9°

3 For the construction of the hour lines calculate the distance of the locus of centres from the centre of the circle (dt) and draw this locus parallel to the east-west axis:

dt = r × tanLAT

For each hour calculate the horizontal displacement of the centre from the vertical centreline (dh) and the radius of the hour-arc: (rh):

$$dh = \frac{r}{\cos LAT \times \tan HRA} \qquad rh = \frac{r}{\cos LAT \times \sin HRA}$$

where   HRA hour angle from noon, 15° for each hour
        e.g. for 8:00 h: HRA = 15 × (8−12) = −60°
        for 16:00 h: HRA = 15 × (16−12) = 60°

Draw the arcs for afternoon hours from a centre on the right-hand side and for the morning hours from the left-hand side. A useful check is that the 6:00 and 18:00 h lines should meet the equinox sun-path at exactly the east and west points respectively.

4 Mark the azimuth angles on the perimeter at any desired increments from 0 to 360° (north) and construct a set of concentric circles to indicate the altitude angle scale. For any altitude (ALT) the radius will be

$$ra = r \times \frac{\cos ALT}{1 + \sin ALT}$$

Method Sheet M.1.2 (continued)

5 For a **shadow angle protractor** draw a semi-circle to the same radius as the chart, extend the vertical axis downwards to give the locus for the centres of all VSA (vertical shadow angle) arcs. For each chosen increment of VSA find the displacement of the centre (dv) and the radius of the arc: (rv):

$$dv = r \times \tan VSA \qquad rv = \frac{r}{\cos VSA}$$

6 Mark the HSA (horizontal shadow angle) scale along the perimeter: the centreline is zero, then to 90° to the right (clockwise) and to −90° to the left (anticlockwise).

A useful check is that along the centreline of the protractor the VSA arcs should coincide with the corresponding altitude circles of the sun-path diagram.

METHOD SHEET M.1.3

Solar radiation calculations

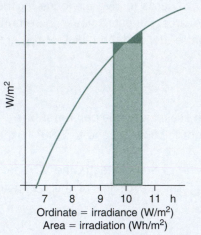

Ordinate = irradiance (W/m²)
Area = irradiation (Wh/m²)

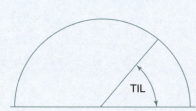

Notation

G = irradiance or power density (W/m²)

D = irradiation (Wh/m²) over a specified period, e.g. day or month

first subscript

b = beam (direct)

d = diffuse

r = reflected if none, then it means Global

second subscript (surface of incidence)

n = normal to the direction of the beam

p = on a plane (to be defined)

v = vertical (e.g. G_{v270} = irradiance of a west-facing vertical plane)

h = horizontal (may be omitted)

TIL = tilt angle of a plane from the horizontal

ρ = (rho) reflectance

If daily total horizontal irradiation (Dh) is given for an average day of the month

1 estimate beam and diffuse components of the total

a) find extraterrestrial irradiance (W/m²) normal to the direction of radiation

$$G_{on} = 1353 \times [1 + 0.033 \times \cos(2 \times \pi \times NDY/365.24)$$

where NDY = number of day of the year, taken for mid-month

b) the daily total irradiation (Wh/m²) on a horizontal plane will be

$$D_h = (24/\pi) \times G_{on} \times \cos LAT \times \cos DEC \times (\sin SSH - SSH \times \cos SSH)$$

where   LAT = latitude,

DEC = solar declination (see M.1.3)

SSH = sunset hour angle = $\arccos(-\tan LAT \times \tan DEC)$

c) the atmospheric clearness index is $k' = Dh / D_{oh}$

d) the diffuse fraction will be

if $j = SSH - 0.5 \times \pi$

$$df = 0.775 + 0.347 \times j - (0.505 + 0.261 \times j) \times \cos[2 \times (k'-0.9)]$$

e) then the diffuse component will be $D_{dh} = Dh \times df$

f) and the beam component $D_{bh} = Dh - D_{dh}$

2 estimate hourly values of global radiation and of diffuse component

a) pre-calculate five factors

$$f1 = \sin(SSH - 1.047)$$
$$f2 = 0.409 + 0.5016 \times f1$$
$$f3 = 0.6609 - 0.4767 \times f1$$
$$f4 = (\pi/24)/[\sin SSH - (SSH \times \cos SSH)]$$

b) for each hour from sunrise to sunset the fraction of the day's total for that time r $(_t)$ will be

$$f5 = \cos HRA - \cos SSH$$

Method Sheet M.1.3 (continued)

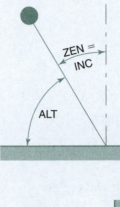

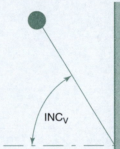

fraction of total: $rt_t = f4 \times f5 \times (f2 + f3 \times cosHRA)$

fraction of diffuse: $rf_t = f4 \times f5$

c) total irradiation for the hour $Dh_t = Dh \times rt_t$

diffuse irradiation for the hour $Dd_t = Ddh \times rf_t$

the beam component will be the difference between the two

$$Db_t = Dh_t - Dd_t$$

generally	$G = Gb + Gd (+ Gr)$
diffuse	$Gdv = Gdh \times 0.5$
	$Gdp = Gdh \times (1 + cosTIL) / 2$
	when TIL = 0, then cosTIL = 1, (1+1)/2 = 1
	when TIL = 90° then cosTIL = 0, (1+0)/2 = 0.5
reflected	$Grv = Gh \times \rho \times 0.5$
	$Grp = Gh \times \rho \times (1 - cosTIL)/2$
	when TIL = 0, then cosTIL = 1, (1−1)/2 = 0
	when TIL = 90° then cosTIL = 0. (1−0)/2 = 0.5
horizontal/normal	$Gh = Gn \times cosZEN$
	$Gn = Gh / cosZEN$
	$= Gh \times sinALT$ (as ALT = 90° − ZEN)

beam:

vertical/normal	$Gbv = Gn \times cosINCv$
	$= Gh \times cosINCv / sinALT$
	$Gbp = Gh \times cosINCp / sinALT$

total:

$Gp = Gh \times cosINCp / sinALT + Gdh \times (1+cosTIL)/2 + Gh \times \rho \times (1-cosTIL)/2$

$Gv = Gh \times cosINCv / sinALT + Gdh \times 0.5 \times Gh \times \rho \times 0.5$

METHOD SHEET M.1.4

Stack and wind effects

STACK EFFECT

Air flow in a stack is driven by the density difference between inside and outside air.

The density of air at 0°C is $\qquad$ $d_o = 1.293$ kg/m³

and at any other temperature T: $\boxed{d_T = 1.293 \times 273/T.}$ (1)

where T is absolute temperature in °K

The gravitational acceleration is $g = 9.81$ m/s²

The 'stack pressure' $(p_i - p_o)$ is $\Delta p = h \times g \times (d_o - d_i)$

substituting from eq.1 $\qquad \Delta p =$

$h \times 9.81 \times (1.293 \times 273/T_o - 1.293 \times 273/T_i)$

$\boxed{\Delta p = h \times 3462 \times (1/T_o - 1/T_i).}$ (2)

(as $9.81 \times 1.293 \times 273 = 3462$)

where $\quad$ T is in K

$\qquad$ height (h) is in m (between centres of inlet and outlet)

then Δp is in Pa (Pascal)

The volume flow rate will then be $.vr = 0.827 \times A \times \sqrt{\Delta p}.$ (3)

where A is in m² and vr is in m³/s

if apertures are in series (e.g. inlet and outlet)

then the effective area will be $A' = \dfrac{A_1 + A_2}{\sqrt{A_1^2 + A_2^2}}$

e.g: $\quad$ if $T_o = 28°C = 301°K$, which gives a density of $1.293 \times 273/301 = 1.173$ kg/m³

$\qquad$ Ti = 32°C = 305°K, which gives a density of $1.293 \times 273/305 = 1.157$ kg/m³

and if $\quad h = 4$ m

then $\qquad \Delta p = 4 \times 3462 \times (1/301 - 1/305) = 0.6$ Pa or $\Delta p = 4 \times 9.81 \times (1.173 - 1.157) = 0.6$ Pa

and if $\quad$ inlet = outlet = shaft cross sectional area: A = 0.5 m²

then $\qquad vr = 0.827 \times 0.5 \times \sqrt{0.6} = 0.32$ m³/s or 320 L/s

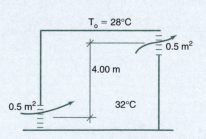

$T_o = 28°C$

0.5 m²

4.00 m

0.5 m²

32°C

WIND EFFECT

The pressure of wind is $\qquad p_w = 0.5 \times d \times v^2$

where $\quad$ d = density, as above (often taken as 1.224 kg/m³ corresponding to 15.5°C)

v = velocity in m/s

thus generally taken as $\qquad \boxed{p_w = 0.612 \times v^2}$ (4)

Method Sheet M.1.4 (continued)

For a building surface this must be multiplied by a pressure coefficient c_p typical values of which are

on windward side $c_{pW} = 0.5$ to 0.8
on leeward side $c_{pL} = -0.3$ to -0.5

Cross ventilation is driven by the wind pressure difference

$$\Delta p_w = p_w \times (c_{pW} + c_{pL}) \qquad (5)$$

and the resulting volume flow rate will be

$$vr = 0.827 \times A \times c_e \times \sqrt{\Delta p_w}. \qquad (6)$$

where   A = effective area of openings (as above)
         c_e = 'effectiveness coefficient'

values of which are
from   0.1   if windows in one wall only (no cross ventilation)
to   1   with full cross-ventilation, equal inlet and outlet, no partitions

e.g.   if $v = 3$ m/s $c_{pW} = 0.8$ $c_{pL} = -0.4$
then $\Delta_{pW} = 0.612 \times 3^2 \times [0.8-(-0.4)]$
                                  $= 0.612 \times 9 \times 1.2$
                                  $= 6.61$ Pa

and if $A = 3$ m^2 $c_e = 1$ (full cross-ventilation)
then $vr = 0.827 \times 3 \times 1 \times \sqrt{6.61} = 6.38$ m^3/s

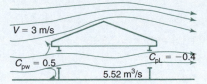

$V = 3$ m/s
$C_{pw} = 0.5$ $C_{pL} = -0.4$
              5.52 m^3/s

METHOD SHEET M.1.5

Calculation of degree-hours

HEATING DEGREE-HOURS FOR A MONTH

data required: $\overline{T}$ = outdoor mean temperature
Tsd = standard deviation of temperatures
Tb = base temperature (e.g. the lower comfort limit)

let   dT be Tb $-$ $\overline{T}$
X be dT / Tsd

The probability density function is

$$\varphi = \frac{1}{\sqrt{2 \times \pi} \times \exp[-(X^2/2)]} \tag{1}$$

if t is taken as

$$t = \frac{1}{1 + 0.33267 \times X} \tag{2}$$

then the 'tail area' will be

$$AT = \varphi \times (0.43618 \times X - 0.12016 \times X^2 + 0.93729 \times X^3) \tag{3}$$
(a numerical approximation of the integral)

The fraction below the base temperature will be
if dT > 0 then Φ = 1 $-$ AT
otherwise Φ = AT

Finally   Kh = 24 $\times$ N $\times$ ($\Phi \times$ dT + Tsd $\times \varphi$)   (4)
where N = number of days in the month

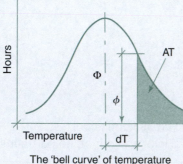

The 'bell curve' of temperature distribution (normal or Gaussian distribution is assumed)

---

e.g. for Canberra, July   T = 5.3°C

Tsd = 2.7 K

Tb = 15.4°C

dT = 15.4 $-$ 5.3 = 10.1

$X = \dfrac{10.1}{2.7} = 3.74$

as $\dfrac{1}{\sqrt{2*\pi}} = 0.3989$

$\varphi = 0.3989 \times \exp[-(3.74^2/2)] = 0.000365$

$t = \dfrac{1}{1 + 0.33267 \times 3.74} = 0.45$

$AT = 0.000365 \times (0.43618 \times 0.45 - 0.12016 \times 0.45^2 + 0.93729 \times 0.45^3)$
$= 9.25 \times 10^{-5}$

as dT = 10.1 > 0   P = 1 $-$ AT = 0.9999

Kh = 24 $\times$ 31 $\times$ (0.9999 $\times$ 10.1 + 2.7 $\times$ 0.000365) = **7514**

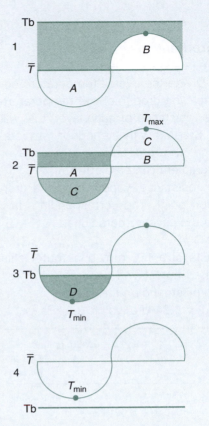

Note: two semicircles represent the sine curves of temperature variation

Method Sheet M.1.5 (continued)

The assumption behind eq.4 above is that $Kh = 24 \times Kd$ (or $24 \, h \, N \, (Tb - T)$) is not always true. A correction term may have to be added to the Kh value thus obtained. The criteria will be the relative position of Tb, T, T_{max} and T_{min} and intersections with the diurnal temperature curve. (N = number of days in month)

1 if $Tb > T_{max}$ then $Kh = 24 \times Kd$, area A compensates for area B, the assumption is OK

2 $T_{max} > Tb > T$ then A compensates for B, but C must be added
assume semicircle, $r = T_{max} - Tb$, thus $C = r^2\pi/2$
Thus $Kh = 24 \times Kd + N \times C$

3 if $T > Tb > T_{min}$ then $Kd = 0$ but area D indicates heating requirement if semicircle the $r = Tb - T_{min}$
thus $Kh = N \times D = N \times r^2\pi / 2$

4 if $Tb < Tmin$ then $Kh = 0$, $Kh = 0$, no heating requirement

in the above example (Canberra, July) $Tmax = 11.1°C$, $Tb = 15.4$, $Tb > Tmax$, so case 1 (the first case) is applicable

METHOD SHEET M.1.6

Temperature and vapour pressure gradient

Add the thermal resistances of all layers. Divide the overall temperature difference by this total resistance. This is the 'unit drop', i.e. the temperature drop per unit resistance. Multiplied by the resistance of each layer, this will give the temperature drop for each layer. Starting with the indoor temperature, subtract the temperature drops to get the temperature at each layer junction point. From this the temperature gradient can be plotted.

Repeat the same procedure for vapour resistance, vapour pressure drop and vapour pressure at each layer junction point. The corresponding dew point temperature (DPT) is to be read from the psychrometric chart.

The method is illustrated by an example.

Take a simple cavity wall, which consists of a 110 mm brick outer skin and an inner skin of 100 mm AAC (aerated autoclaved concrete, such as Thermalite or Hebel blocks), with a 12 mm plastering on the inside.

Assume $T_i = 22°C$ and $T_o = 0°C$, $\qquad vp_i = 1.34$ kPa, $vp_o = 0.4$ kPa

	temperature gradient				vapour pressure gradient			
	R	ΔT	T at junction		vR	Δvp	vp	DPT at junct'n
outside air			0 °C				0.4 kPa	−5.0 °C
external surface	0.06	1.42 K			0.01	0.001 kPa		
			1.42				0.401	−4.8
brick $\frac{b}{\lambda} = \frac{0.110}{0.84} =$	0.13	3.07			$\frac{b}{\delta} = \frac{0.110}{0.02} = 5.50$	0.538		
			4.49				0.939	6.4
cavity	0.18	4.26			0.02	0.002		
			8.75				0.941	6.5
AAC $\frac{0.100}{0.24} =$	0.42	9.94			$\frac{0.100}{0.03} = 3.33$	0.326		
			18.69				1.267	10.6
plaster $\frac{0.012}{0.5} =$	0.02	0.47			$\frac{0.012}{0.017} = 0.71$	0.069		
			19.16				1.336	11.5
internal surface	0.12	2.84			0.04	0.004		
inside air			22				1.340	11.7
	0.93	22 K			9.61	0.94 kPa		

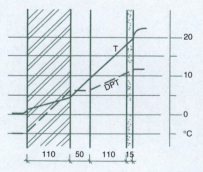

as ΔT = 22 K, the 'unit drop is' $\frac{22}{0.93} = 23.65$

the T drop in each layer is R × 23.65

as Δvp = 1.34 − 0.4 = 0.94 kPa thus the 'unit drop' is $\frac{0.94}{9.61} = 0.098$ thus the drop in vapour pressure in each layer is vR × 0.098

The R, λ, vR and δ values are taken from Data sheets D 1.2 and D 1.6.

Where the temperature T drops below the DPT, there is a risk of condensation.

From the plot of the T and DPT profiles on a cross-section of the wall, it will be seen that there is a condensation risk at the inside face of the brick skin.

The gradients can also be determined graphically. This is best introduced by continuing the above example.

Method Sheet M.1.6 (continued)

The overall vapour resistance is 9.61. Draw the thickness of the wall and its layers to a suitable vapour resistance scale. Here we assume a scale of 5 mm = 1 vR unit, so the total "thickness" is 48 mm. Draw this section (**A**) alongside a part of the psychrometric chart, so that the vapour pressure scale of that chart (in kPa) can be used for the vertical scale in this section. Mark the level of internal vapour pressure on the inside surface of this section and the outdoor vapour pressure on the outside surface. Connect these two points by a straight line: the intersection with each boundary line will mark the vapour pressure at that plane.

To convert these vapour pressures to dew-point temperature values, project all intersection points across to the saturation curve of the psychrometric chart. Project these intersections vertically down to the base line, where the dew point temperatures can be read.

It may be convenient to use this (horizontal) temperature scale also in a vertical position, with the physical section of the wall. In the diagram below quadrant arcs have been used to translate the scale into vertical, to an actual section of the wall (**B**), here drawn to a scale of 1:10. The dew-point temperatures can be transferred to this section, and will define the dew-point temperature gradient.

A third section should be drawn alongside the above, where the thickness is scaled to the thermal resistance of each layer. A scale of 10 mm to 0.1 resistance unit (m²K/W) is convenient. (**C**) The vertical (temperature) scale should be shared with the actual section. If the indoor and outdoor temperature points are marked on the surfaces and connected by a straight line, the intersection of this with each layer boundary will determine the temperature at that point. The line connecting these points will be the temperature gradient across the wall. Wherever the dew-point gradient drops below the temperature gradient, there will be a condensation risk (in this case at the inside surface of the outer brick skin).

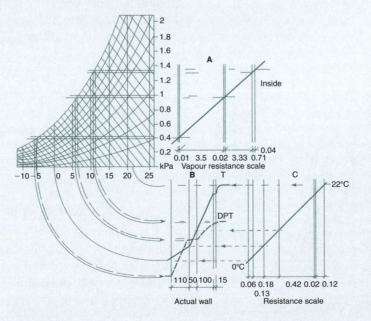

METHOD SHEET M.1.7

Construction of comfort zone and CPZs

1 establish the mean temperature of the warmest and coldest months (Tav).
2 find the neutrality temperature for both $Tn = 17.6 + 0.31 \times Tav \,°C$
   and the limits of comfort lower: $T_L = Tn - 2.5 \,°C$
   upper: $T_U = Tn + 2.5 \,°C$

   mark these on the 50% RH curve.

3 construct the corresponding sloping SET lines by determining the X-axis
   intercept from $T = T_L + 0.023 \times (T_L - 14) \times AH_{50}$
   where AH_{50} is the abs. humidity (g/kg) at the RH 50% level at the T_L temperature, this can be read from the psychrometric chart (Fig.1.9) or calculated as half of the saturation humidity. The saturation vapour pressure is
   $$p_{vs} = 0.133322 \times exp[18.6686 - 4030.183 /(T_L + 235)]$$
   saturation humidity will be sh $= 622 \times p_{vs} / (101.325 - p_{vs})$
   and $AH_{50} = 0.5 \times sh$
   repeat for T_U and repeat both for the warmest month.

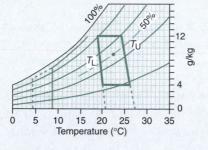

Passive solar heating CPZ

in relation to the July comfort zone (see also example 1.7 in section 1.5.1.1)
the extension is if $\eta = 0.5$ then $0.0036 \times D_{v.360}$
$\eta = 0.7$ $0.005 \times D_{v.360}$
draw vertical lines at these limiting temperatures
the upper limit will be the 95% RH curve

Mass effect CPZ

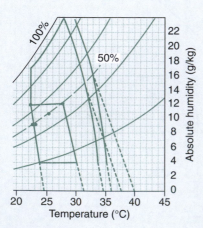

for summer, in relation to the January comf. zone
if 'amplitude' $= (T_{max} - T_{min})$ then for mass: dT = amplitude $\times 0.3$
with night vent dT = amplitude $\times 0.6$

limiting temperature $= T_U + dT$
draw corresponding SET lines as in (3) above
the upper boundary of the CPZ is the 14 g/kg

repeat for 'winter' in relation to the July comfort zone CPZ to the left
mark the limiting temperature on the 50% RH curve
find the X-axis intercept as in (3) above; draw the (near vertical) side
   boundary
the top boundary cannot be higher than the 95% RH curve

Air movement effect CPZ

for summer, in relation to the January comf. zone for 1 & 1.5 m/s
effective velocities 0.8 & 1.3 m/s
apparent cooling effects dT (from eq. 1.21) limiting temperatures: $T_U + dT$
mark these on the 50% RH curve
find the notional X-axis intercept as in (3) above
draw the boundary from this intercept upwards from the 50% curve only
for the lower half take half of this increment
the top limit is the 95% RH curve

Method Sheet M.1.7 (continued)

Evaporative cooling CPZ
take lower left corner of January comfort zone (the S-point)
draw the corresponding WBT line to the X-axis
$$\text{X-intercept} = S + AH \times (2501 - 1.805 \times T)/1000$$
draw parallel line from top right corner of comfort zone
the temperature limit is the vertical at $Tn + 11°C$
for indirect this is at $Tn+14°C$ and the upper boundary is the 14 g/kg horizontal line e.g. for **Brisbane**

Passive solar
July: mean temperature $T = 15.1°C$ north vertical irradiation $D_{v.360} = 3094$ Wh/m²

$Tn = 17.8 + 0.31 \times 15.1 = 22.5°C$
$T_L = 20°C$
$T_U = 25°C$
limiting outdoor temperatures for passive solar heating:
$20 - 0.005 \times 3094 = 4.5°C$
$20 - 0.0036 \times 3094 = 8.9°C$

Mass effect

July (as above)		$T_{ampl} = 20.4 - 9.8 = 10.6$ K	
$T_L = 20$	$p_{vsL} = 2.3$ kPa	$sh_L = 14.6$ g/kg	$AH_{50}:_L = 7.3$ g/kg
$T_U = 25$ °C	$p_{vsU} = 3.15$ kPa	$sh_U = 20$ g/kg	$AH_{50}:_U = 10$ g/kg
	intercepts:	$T1 = 20 + 0.023 \times (20 - 14) \times 7.3 = 21°C$	
		$T2 = 25 + 0.023 \times (25 - 14) \times 10 = 27.5°C$	

lower limit: $20 - (10.6 \times 0.3) = 16.8°C$

January mean temperature $\qquad T = 25°C \qquad T_{ampl} = 29.1 - 21 = 8.1$ K
$Tn = 17.8 + 0.31 \times 25 = 25.5°C$

$T_L = 23°C$	$p_{vsL} = 2.79$	$sh_L = 17.6$	$AH_{50}:_L = 8.8$
$T_U = 28°C$	$p_{vsU} = 3.75$ kPa	$sh_U = 23.9$ g/kg	$AH_{50}:_U = 11.9$ g/kg
	intercepts:	$T3 = 23 + 0.023 \times (23 - 14) \times 8.8 = 24.4°C$	
		$T4 = 28 + 0.023 \times (28 - 14) \times 11.9 = 31.8°C$	

upper limit: $28 + (14.5 \times 0.3) = 32.3°C$
with night vent: $28 + (14.5 \times 0.6) = 36.7°C$

Air movement effect
January (as above)
$T_L = 23°C$
$T_U = 28°C$
upper limits: for 1 m/s $T1 = 28 + 6 \times 0.8 - 1.6 \times 0.8^2 = 31.8°C$
$AH1 = 15.2$ g/kg
for 1.5 m/s $T2 = 28 + 6 \times 1.3 - 1.6 \times 1.3^2 = 33.1°C$
$AH2 = 16$ g/kg
for notional intercept $\quad dT1 = 0.023 \times (31.8 - 14) \times 15.2 = 6.2$ K
$$dT2 = 0.023 \times (33.1 - 14) \times 16 = 7 \text{ K}$$

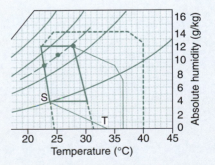

Method Sheet M.1.7 (continued)

notional intercept	$T1 = 31.8 + 6.2 = 38.0°C$
	$T2 = 33.1 + 7 = 40.1°C$
actual intercept	$T1 = 31.8 + 6.2 / 2 = 34.7°C$
	$T2 = 33.1 + 7 / 2 = 36.3°C$

Evaporative cooling
January (as above)
$Tn = 25.5°C$
indirect cooler: $25.5 + 14 = 39.5°C$
$T_L = 23°C$ AH diff $= AH_L - 4 =$ $9 - 4 = 5$ g/kg
S-point: $23 + 0.023 \times (23 - 14) \times 5 = 24°C$
lower X-axis intercept (as AH dif $= 4$):
$T = 24 + 4 \times (2501 - 1.805 \times 24) / 1000 = 33.8°C$

METHOD SHEET M.1.8

Determine shading (overheated) period

Comfort limits (Phoenix):

	January	July
$T_U =$	23.5	30.2
Tn =	21.0	27.7
$T_L =$	18.5	25.2

Solar heat input can be tolerated up to To = Tn (as long as outdoor temperature is less than the neutrality) and it is definitely desirable when To is below the lower comfort limit (as per eq. 1.9 in section 1.2.3).

Take Phoenix (AZ) as an example. The printout shows hourly temperatures for an average day of each month, as well as the neutrality with the ±2.5 K upper and lower comfort limits (as per eq. 1.9 in section 1.2.3). Tn varies between 21°C (Jan) and 27.7°C (July). The lower limit in January is. Below 21°C solar heat input is welcome, but definitely below. 18.5C Above 27.7°C shading is a must, These three isopleths are plotted on a month × hour chart. (the overheated period is printed **bold**).

mth\hr	1	2	3	4	5	6	7	8	9	10	11	12	13	14	15	16	17	18	19	20	21	22	23	24	av
1	7.1	6.1	5.2	4.5	4.1	4.0	4.5	6.1	8.3	11.0	13.7	15.9	17.5	18.0	17.9	17.5	16.8	15.9	14.9	13.7	12.4	11.0	9.6	8.3	11.0
2	9.3	8.2	7.3	6.6	6.1	6.0	6.6	8.2	10.6	13.5	16.4	18.8	20.4	21.0	20.9	20.4	19.7	18.8	17.7	16.4	15.0	13.5	12.0	10.6	13.5
3	11.6	10.3	9.3	8.6	8.2	8.0	8.6	10.3	12.9	16.0	19.1	21.7	23.4	24.0	23.9	23.4	22.7	21.7	20.4	19.1	17.6	16.0	14.4	12.9	16.0
4	14.6	13.5	12.7	12.2	12.0	12.5	13.9	16.0	18.6	21.4	24.0	26.1	**27.5**	28.0	27.8	27.3	26.5	25.4	24.0	22.5	20.8	19.2	17.5	16.0	20.0
5	18.8	17.6	16.7	16.2	16.0	16.5	18.0	20.2	23.0	26.0	**28.8**	**31.0**	**32.5**	**33.0**	**32.8**	**32.3**	**31.4**	**30.2**	**28.8**	27.1	25.4	23.6	21.9	20.2	24.5
6	22.9	21.8	21.2	21.0	21.4	22.6	24.5	26.9	**29.5**	**32.1**	**34.5**	**36.4**	**37.6**	**38.0**	**37.8**	**37.2**	**36.1**	**34.8**	**33.2**	**31.4**	**29.5**	**27.6**	25.8	24.2	29.5
7	27.5	26.4	25.6	25.2	25.0	25.5	26.8	**28.8**	**31.2**	**33.8**	**36.2**	**38.2**	**39.5**	**40.0**	**39.8**	**39.4**	**38.6**	**37.5**	**36.2**	**34.8**	**33.3**	**31.7**	39.2	28.8	32.5
8	26.3	25.3	24.6	24.2	24.0	24.4	25.6	27.5	**29.8**	**32.2**	**34.5**	**36.4**	**37.6**	**38.0**	**37.8**	**37.4**	**36.7**	**35.7**	**34.5**	**33.2**	**31.7**	**30.3**	28.8	27.5	31.0
9	23.5	22.4	21.6	21.2	21.0	21.5	22.8	24.8	27.2	**29.8**	**32.2**	**34.2**	**35.5**	**36.0**	**35.8**	**35.4**	**34.6**	**33.5**	**32.2**	**30.8**	**29.3**	**27.7**	26.2	24.8	28.5
10	16.8	15.5	14.4	13.6	13.2	13.0	13.6	15.5	18.2	21.5	24.8	27.5	**29.4**	**30.0**	**29.8**	**29.4**	**28.6**	27.5	26.2	24.8	23.2	21.5	19.8	18.2	21.5
11	10.8	9.5	8.4	7.6	7.2	7.0	7.6	9.5	12.2	15.5	18.8	21.5	23.4	24.0	23.8	23.4	22.6	21.5	20.2	18.8	17.2	15.5	13.8	12.2	15.5
12	8.2	7.0	6.0	5.1	4.5	4.1	4.0	4.7	6.8	9.8	13.2	16.2	18.3	19.0	18.9	18.5	17.9	17.0	16.0	14.8	13.6	12.2	10.8	9.4	11.5

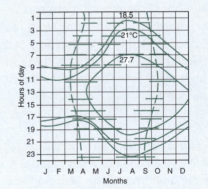

On the sun-path diagram the long east-west arcs correspond to the month lines of the above and the short north-south curves are the hour lines. So the above isopleths can be transferred onto this 'twisted' chart base, except that each sun-path curve is valid for two dates, thus two solar charts must be used, one from December to June and the other from July to December.

Outside the top (18.5°C) isopleth solar input is desirable. Inside the 27.7°C curve solar input must be prevented, but the boundary of the shading period may be as low as the 21°C isopleth, depending on the particular conditions. It can be noted that the Dec.–June half year requires less shading than the June – Dec. half (temperatures are lagging behind solar input by 4–6 weeks) thus the solution will have to be a compromise between the spring and autumn limits. The final decision can only be made when building (window) orientation and the kind of shading system are considered. Shading design has been discussed in Section 1.4.1.1 and an example was shown in Fig.1.52, with the protractor laid over the solar chart.

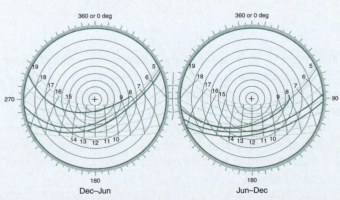

Dec–Jun   Jun–Dec

METHOD SHEET M.1.9

Outline of the program 'ARCHIPAK'

A series of small programs had been written by the author over the 1980s, for solar geometry, solar radiation, climate data handling, degree-day, building heat loss calculations, etc. These were put together in the early 1990s to form an architectural package (hence the name ARCHIPAK) and supplemented by a data-base system. The package has been re-shaped from 1995 on, using VisualBasic, to run under Windows. There are many more powerful and user-friendly programs available today, but it is suggested that this is useful as a teaching tool, as the user can follow each step: it is just a COMPUTERISED MANUAL METHOD.

Data-base

This includes almost 200 **climatic data** files, of the form shown in Fig.1.39 (Section 1.3.3 above). A **materials** file contains data of the kind given here in data sheet D.1.1, with a 2-digit code for each. The **elements** file contains sheets D.1.2 and 3 above) with a 3-digit code for each. New items can be created by specifying the thickness and materials code for each and properties (U-value, time-lag, decrement factor and admittance) are calculated and listed under the code assigned. There are facilities for creating, editing and retrieving any entry.

Climate analysis

The 'Mahoney-table' analysis can be carried out (c.f. Koenigsberger et al.1973) producing some simple design recommendations. The climatic data can be tabulated or graphically presented. Frequency distributions of temperatures (bell-curves) can be produced. An analysis based on the **CPZ method** can be carried out (e.g. Figs.1.70, 73, 75, 76, 79 and method sheet M.1.7) to get strategic guidance. It can calculate degree-hours and estimate the fraction of time overheated, underheated or excessively humid.

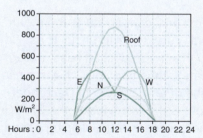

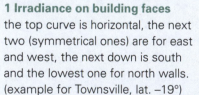

1 Irradiance on building faces
the top curve is horizontal, the next two (symmetrical ones) are for east and west, the next down is south and the lowest one for north walls. (example for Townsville, lat. −19°)

Solar design

This section can produce a stereographic **sun-path diagram** for the exact location specified, and has an interactive facility for shading design (see e.g. calculate daily or hourly values of irradiance for any time of the year and any orientation).

Thermal design

This section allows the input of a house (or a similarly simple building), a steady-state and a dynamic thermal analysis. A house is described in a tabular form: one line for each element, inputting sizes, element codes and orientation (horizontal is stated as −1 and all roofs are taken as the horizontal projected area: assuming that if one part the roof gets more solar input, another part will get less, i.e. the total solar input is the same as on the horizontal projected area). The line is then extended by data picked up from the elements file and some attributes calculated (e.g. A × U, or A × Y).

Method Sheet M.1.9 (continued)

The steady-state analysis (for heating design) 'QBALANCE' calculates the envelope and ventilation conductances and shows the heat loss rate as a function of outdoor temperature. Where this heat loss function has the same value as any heat gain (Qs +i, i.e. solar + internal heat gain), the 'balance-point' temperature is obtained. A sequence of alternatives can be tested and the best one selected (see below).

HARMON, that incorporates a dynamic analysis, is based on the BRE method (as in Section 1.4.4 above) and performing the 'admittance procedure'. Here the result is given as a 24-hour graph of indoor and outdoor temperature profiles, with the comfort band superimposed, or in tabulated form: 24 columns of the 'driving forces' (outdoor temperatres and solar input on each building face) and the result: the indoor temperature. This can be supplemented by the indoor temperatures resulting from 14th%-ile of minima and 86th %-ile of maxima. Tabulations can be obtained of the hourly heat flows and of heat flow swings. Alternatively hourly values of air conditioning load can be tabulated or shown in graphic form (3 below), both for controlled mode, in kWh and free-running mode in K.h. An annual summary table can also be produced (4 below).

Output of QBALANCE

dotted sloping line: version 1
solid line: improved version 2:
the heat loss function q × dT
X-axis intercept at the 16°C
set-point temperature (optional)
    horizontal line Qs + i, solar
and internal gain, 24 h average
    intersection of this and
the heat loss line gives the
balance-point temperature
(hence the name of the
module: QBALANCE). At any
To (X-axis) the heat loss line
gives the heating requirement
from the Qs + i line upwards

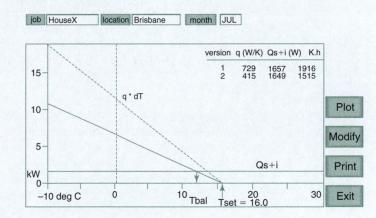

Air conditioning load estimate

Lower thin line: To, solid line Ti
    Dotted curve is what Ti
would be (7:30–16:00) if free
running.
    Histogram: a/c load: lower
part sensible, upper part talent
    Two parallel horizontal lines:
Comfort band

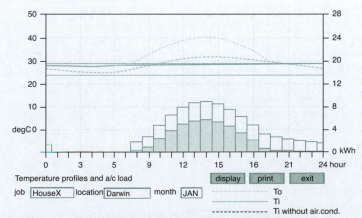

histogram: top of bars = total hourly load, lower (shaded) bars = sensible load

Method Sheet M.1.9 (continued)

4 Example: annual summary

SUMMARY for House Y *in Brisbane*

month	To_{av}	Ti_{min}	Ti_{max}	*Controlled*		*free running*	
				heating kWh	cooling kWh	underheated K.h	overheated K.h
JAN	25.0	22.9	27.9	–	3931	–	400
FEB	24.8	22.8	27.8	–	2883	01	304
MAR	23.6	22.4	27.4	–	1592	108	111
APR	21.8	21.9	26.9	423	–	445	–
MAY	18.4	20.8	25.8	843	–	1545	–
JUN	16.2	20.1	25.1	1130	–	2468	–
JUL	15.0	19.8	24.8	1378	–	3149	–
AUG	16.5	20.2	25.2	1158	–	2331	–
SEP	18.6	20.9	25.9	826	–	1389	–
OCT	21.1	21.6	26.6	529	–	661	–
NOV	23.0	22.2	27.2	–	1794	217	101
DEC	24.1	22.6	27.6	–	2988	66	263

METHOD SHEET M.1.10

Dynamic thermal properties

Diffusivity is a composite index of material properties:

$$\alpha = \frac{\lambda}{\rho \times c} \tag{1}$$

dimensionally $\dfrac{W/m.K}{kg/m^3 \times Wh/kg.K} = m^2/h$

or if c is in J/kg.K then it is in m^2/s

Decrement factor (non-dimensional) and the **time-lag** (hour) are discussed in Section 1.4.4 and method sheet M.1.11.

Specific admittance (or heat penetration coefficient or 'effusivity')

$$\beta = \sqrt{\lambda \times \rho \times c} = \sqrt{\frac{W}{m.K} \times \frac{kg}{m^3} \times \frac{Wh}{kg.K}} = \frac{W}{m^2K}h^{\frac{1}{2}} \tag{2}$$

Admittance, for a solid homogeneous element
where ω is angular velocity, for 1 cycle per day: 2 /24 = 0.2618 rad/h

$$Y = \sqrt{\lambda \times \rho \times c \times \omega}$$

as $\sqrt{\omega} = \sqrt{0.2618} = 0.5117\,h^{-1/2}$ $\tag{3}$

as β has $h^{1/2}$ in its dimension $h^{1/2} \times h^{-1/2} = 0$, the h cancels out

$$Y = 0.5117 \times \beta\ \ W/m^2K$$

Some authors use the concept of **time constant**, the product of resistance and thermal capacity:

$$\gamma = \frac{b}{\lambda} \times b \times \rho \times c = \frac{b^2 \times \rho \times c}{\lambda}$$

and if the α term is substituted it becomes

$$\gamma = \frac{b^2}{\alpha}, \text{ and taken for unit area, its dimension will be} \tag{4}$$

s (second) if α is in m^2/s, or in h (hour) if α is in m^2/h
for the latter

if ρ is density, kg/m^3
S is surface density kg/m^2
H is surface thermal capacity Wh/m^2K
   Time constant has two derivations:

– capacity/ transmittance ratio $\dfrac{H}{U} = \dfrac{Wh/m^2K}{W/m^2K} = h$

– resistance-capacity product $R \times H = m^2K/W \times Wh/m^2K = h$

The **thermal inertia index** is a non-dimensional index number, the ratio of admittance (Y) to the U-value (both are in units of W/m^2K)

METHOD SHEET M.1.11

Calculate time-lag and decrement factor

Symbols (other than earlier or generally used)
M resultant matrix coeff. i imaginary number   m matrix coefficient
t temperature   T time period   p (a sub-sum)

The temperature and energy flow cycles can be linked by using matrix algebra

$$\begin{bmatrix} t_1 \\ q_1 \end{bmatrix} = \begin{bmatrix} m_1 m_2 \\ m_3 m_1 \end{bmatrix} \times \begin{bmatrix} t_2 \\ q_2 \end{bmatrix}$$

For a homogeneous material the matrix coefficients are given as:

$$m_1 = \cosh(p + ip) \tag{1}$$

$$m_2 = \frac{b \sinh(p + ip)}{\lambda(p + ip)} \tag{2}$$

$$m_3 = \frac{\lambda(p + ip) \sinh(p + ip)}{b} \tag{3}$$

For a multilayer wall the matrices of each layer and the two surface matrices must be multiplied:

$$\begin{bmatrix} t_i \\ q_i \end{bmatrix} = \begin{bmatrix} 1 & R_{si} \\ 0 & 1 \end{bmatrix} \times \begin{bmatrix} m_1 m_2 \\ m_3 m_1 \end{bmatrix} \times \begin{bmatrix} n_1 n_2 \\ n_3 n_1 \end{bmatrix} \times \ldots \ldots \ldots \begin{bmatrix} 1 & R_{so} \\ 0 & 1 \end{bmatrix} \tag{4}$$

The hyperbolic trigonometric functions of (1), (2) and (3) above can be solved as

$$\sinh(x) = \tfrac{1}{2}[e^x - e^{-x}] \qquad \cosh(x) = \tfrac{1}{2}[e^x + e^{-x}]$$

for an imaginary number

$$\sinh(i.x) = i \sin(x) \qquad \cosh(i.x) = \cos(x)$$

and the exponential function is in trigonometric terms

$$\exp(i.x) = e^{i.x} = \cos(x) + i.\sin(x)$$

but if x is a complex number (here (p + ip), these can be resolved as:

$$\cosh(p + ip) = \tfrac{1}{2}[(e^p + e^{-p})\cos p + i(e^p - e^{-p})\sin p] \tag{5}$$

$$\sinh(p + ip) = \tfrac{1}{2}[(e^p - e^{-p})\cos p - i(e^p + e^{-p})\sin p] \tag{6}$$

$$\text{where } p = b\sqrt{\frac{\pi}{86400}}\sqrt{\frac{\rho c}{\lambda}} \qquad (\text{as } 24 \times 3600 = 86\,400) \tag{7}$$

The matrix coefficients will thus be: [from (5) and (6)]

$$m_1 = \frac{1}{2} \times [(e^p + e^{-p})\cos p + i(e^p - e^{-p})\sin p] \tag{8}$$

Method Sheet M.1.11 (continued)

$$m_2 = \frac{b[(e^p - e^{-p})\cos p + (e^p + e^{-p})\sin p - i(e^p - e^{-p})\cos p + i(e^p + e^{-p})\sin p]}{4\lambda p}$$

$$(9)$$

$$m_3 = \frac{\lambda p[(e^p - e^{-p})\cos p - (e^p + e^{-p})\sin p + i(e^p - e^{-p})\cos p + i(e^p + e^{-p})\sin p]}{2b}$$

$$(10)$$

then

$$\mu = \frac{1}{U \times \mu_{imaginary}} \quad \text{and} \quad \varphi = \frac{12}{\pi} \times atn\,\frac{\mu}{\mu_{real\,part}}$$

and for multiplying matrices

$$\begin{bmatrix} a & b \\ c & d \end{bmatrix} \times \begin{bmatrix} A & B \\ C & D \end{bmatrix} = \begin{bmatrix} aA + bC & aB + bD \\ cA + dC & cC + dD \end{bmatrix}$$

Take an example of a single skin brick wall:

$\rho = 1700$ kg/m^3

$\lambda = 0.84$ W/m.K   taking surface resistances as:

$c = 800$ J/kg.K $R_{si} = 0.12$ m^{2}K/W

$b = 0.22$ m (220 mm) $R_{so} = 0.06$

from (7):

$$p = \left(0.22\sqrt{\frac{\pi}{86400}}\sqrt{\frac{1700 \times 800}{0.84}}\right) = (0.22 \times 0.006 \times 1272.418) = 1.688$$

from (8): $m_1 = \frac{1}{2}[(e^{1.688} + e^{-1.688})\cos 1.688 + i(e^{1.688} - e^{-1.688})\sin 1.688]$ (radians)

$$= \frac{1}{2}[(5.4 + 1.849)(-0.1169) + i(5.4 - 0.1849)0.9931]$$

$$= \frac{1}{2}(-0.6531 + i\,5.179)$$

$m_1 = -0.3265 + i\,2.5896$

from (9)

$m_2 = b[(e^{1.688} - e^{-1.688})\cos 1.688 + (e^{1.688} + e^{-1.588})\sin 1.688 - i(e^{1.688} - e^{-1.688})\cos 1.688 + i(e^{1.688} + e^{-1.688})\sin 1.688)]/4 \times 0.84 \times 0.8$

$$m_2 = \frac{b[(5.4 - 0.1849)(-0.1169) + (5.4 + 0.1849)0.9931 - i(5.4 - 0.1849)(-0.1169) + i(5.4 + 0.1849)0.9931]}{4 \times 0.84 \times 1.688}$$

$= 0.22[5.2151 \times (-0.1169) + 5.5849 \times 0.9931 - i.5.2151 \times (-0.1169) + i.5.5849 \times 0.9931]/2.69$

$= 0.22[-0.6096 + 5.5464 - i\,0.6096 + i\,5.5464]/5.67$

$= 0.22[0.8707 + i\,1.0857]$

Method Sheet M.1.11 (continued)

$m_2 = 0.1916 + i\,0.2389$

from (10)

$m_3 = \lambda\,1.868[\,(e^{1.688} - e^{-1.688})\cos 1.688 - (e^{1.688} + e^{-1.688})\sin 1.688 + i(e^{1.688} - e^{-1.688})\cos 1.688 + i(e^{1.688} + e^{-1.688})\sin 1.688]\,/2\,b$

$m_3 = \lambda\,1.688\,[(5.4 - 0.1849)(-0.1169) - (5.4 + 0.1849)\,0.9931 + i(5.4 - 0.1849)(-0.1169) + i(5.4 + 0.1849)0.9931]2 \times 0.22$

$\quad = 0.84 \times 1.688\,[5.2151 \times (-0.1169) - 5.5849 \times 0.9931 + i\,5.2151 \times (-0.1169) + i\,5.5849 \times 0.9931]\,/\,0.44$

$\quad = 1.4179\,[-0.6096 - 5.5464 + i\,0.6096 + i\,5.5464]\,/\,0.44$

$\quad = 1.4179\,(-13.99 + i\,11.2199)$

$m_3 = -19.8377 + i\,15.9087$

Resistance: $\qquad\qquad\qquad\qquad R = 0.12 + \dfrac{0.22}{0.84} + 0.06 = 0.4419 \text{ m}^2\text{K/W}$

Transmittance: $U = 1/R = 1/0.4419 = 2.2629 \text{ W/m}^2\text{K}$

The resulting matrix is to be multiplied by the internal surface matrix, in which all four imaginary components will be zero.

$$\begin{bmatrix} 1 & R_{si} \\ 0 & 1 \end{bmatrix} \times \begin{bmatrix} 0.3265 + i\,2.59 & 0.1916 + i\,0.239 \\ -19.84 + i\,15.9 & 0.3265 + i\,2.59 \end{bmatrix} = \begin{bmatrix} -2.72 + i\,4.5 & 0.15 + i\,0.551 \\ -19.84 + i\,15.9 & 0.3265 + i\,2.59 \end{bmatrix}$$

Finally this is to be multiplied by the external surface matrix (it is sufficient to obtain the products of the second column only (M_2 and M_4). Note that the matrix coefficients are denoted 'm', but the product matrices are 'M'

thus we have $\begin{bmatrix} M_1 & M_2 \\ M_3 & M_4 \end{bmatrix}$

$$\begin{bmatrix} -2.72 + i\,4.5 & 0.15 + i\,0.551 \\ -19.84 + i\,15.9 & -0.3265 + i\,2.59 \end{bmatrix} \times \begin{bmatrix} 1 & 0.06 \\ 0 & 1 \end{bmatrix} = \begin{bmatrix} * & -0.013 + i\,0.821 \\ * & -1.52 + i\,3.54 \end{bmatrix}$$

as $\mu = \dfrac{1}{U.M_2}$ $\qquad\qquad\qquad\qquad \mu = \dfrac{1}{2.263(-0.013 + i\,0.821)}$

To eliminate 'i' from the denominator, to 'rationalise' it), multiply both numerator and denominator by $(-0.013 + i\,0.821)$:

$\mu = \text{abs}\dfrac{-0.013 + i\,0.821}{2.263\,(0.013^2 + 0.821^2)} = \text{abs}\dfrac{-0.013 + i\,0.821}{1.5257} = \text{abs}\,[0.0085 + i\,0.5381]$

$\mu = 0.538$

$\varphi = 12/\pi \times \text{atn}(\mu\,/\mu_{(real)}) = 3.82 \times \text{atn}\,(0.538\,/\,0.0085) = 3.82 \times 1.556 = 5.94$

$\varphi \approx 6$ hour

PART 2 LIGHT: THE LUMINOUS ENVIRONMENT

CONTENTS

SYMBOLS AND ABBREVIATIONS

a	acuity (visual)
asb	apostilb (luminance measure)
c	velocity of light (3×10^8 m/s)
cd	candela (source intensity)
d	distance
f	frequency (or a 'factor')
g	glare constant
lm	lumen (light flux)
lx	lux (illuminance)
p	position index
A	area

ALT	solar altitude angle
B	bars (framing) factor
BRE	Building Research Establishment (UK)
C	contrast
C	colour temperature
CCT	correlated colour temperature
CIE	Commission International d'Éclairage
CR	colour rendering index
DF	daylight factor
DFF	downward flux fraction
DLOR	downward light output ratio
DUF	daylight utilisation factor

SYMBOLS AND ABBREVIATIONS (Continued)

E	illuminance (éclairage), lux		UF	utilisation factor
ERC	externally reflected component (of DF)		UFF	upward flux fraction
F	luminous efficacy		UGR	unified glare rating
FFR	flux fraction ratio		ULOR	upward light output ratio
G	glass factor		V	value (Munsell)
GI	glare index			
H_m	mounting height		α	absorptance
I	intensity (of light source) cd		β	angle of incidence
INC	angle of incidence		γ	altitude angle on sky
IRC	internally reflected component (of DF)		η	efficiency
L	luminance (cd/m²)		θ	viewing or vertical displacement angle
LED	light emitting diode		λ	wavelength
LOR	light output ratio		ρ	reflectance
LT	lighting and thermal (pre-design) analysis		σ	visual angle
M	maintenance factor (glass cleaning)		τ	transmittance
MF	maintenance factor (lumen method)		ω	solid angle
PSALI	permanent supplementary lighting the interior		Δ	difference
RI	room index		Φ	light flux (lm)
SC	sky component (of DF)			

LIST OF FIGURES

LIST OF FIGURES (Continued)

LIST OF TABLES

LIST OF WORKED EXAMPLES

LIST OF EQUATIONS

2.1 PHYSICS OF LIGHT

A narrow wavelength-band of electromagnetic radiation (from about 380 nm to 780 nm, as shown in Fig.1.2) is perceived by our eyes as light.

2.1.1 Attributes of light

As for any other electromagnetic radiation, the velocity of light (c) is approximately 3×10^8 m/s (or 300 000 km/s). Its two main attributes are its quantity and its quality. Its quantitative aspects are discussed in Section 2.1.3 (photometry). Its quality is characterised by wavelength (λ) and its reciprocal, the frequency (f). The product of these two, by definition, gives the velocity:

$$c = f \times \lambda \qquad (2.1)$$

so, if one is known, the other can be found by dividing the known one into the velocity.

2.1.1.1 The colour of light

The colour of light is determined by its spectrum or spectral composition. Light of a particular wavelength, or a narrow band of wavelengths, is referred to as *monochromatic*. The colour of broad-band light depends on the relative magnitude of its components, on its spectral composition. A continuous spectrum white light can be split by a prism into its components, which are perceived as colours, shown in Table 2.1.

The three-colour theory of light distinguishes red, green and blue as the primary colours, and any colour can be defined in terms of its redness, greenness and blueness. If these are decimal fractions, the three must add up to 1. This has been depicted by a 'colour triangle' (Fig. 2.1), which has the three primary colours at the three vertices and any mixture will be within the triangle. At the centre is the 'white point' (W), equidistant from the three vertices, indicating an equal contribution from the three primaries. For colour mixes, the magnitude of contribution by each primary is proportional to the distance from the opposite side (b, g and r). This was later developed into a 3-D coordinate system (Fig. 2.2), set up to represent the three components. In its 2-D representation the red (X) and green (Y) axes are drawn and the

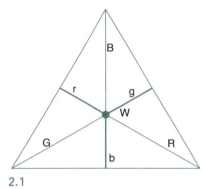

2.1

The colour triangle If B = G = R then b + g + r = white Always b + g + r = 1

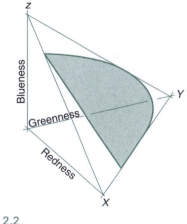

2.2

Framework of the CIE chromaticity chart

Table 2.1 Colour of light

Colour	Wavelength band (in nm)
Red	780–660
Orange	660–610
Yellow	610–570
Green/yellow	570–550
Green	550–510
Blue/green	510–480
Blue	480–440
Violet	440–380

blue is implied, as Z = 1 − (X + Y). This diagram is referred to as the CIE*
chromaticity chart (Fig. 2.3).

This is a very clever device: the outer parabola-like curve is the locus of
spectral (pure) colours, from red to violet, in an anti-clockwise direction (with
wavelengths in nm indicated); the straight line connecting the two ends of this
curve indicates non-spectral colours (mixtures) magentas, from pink to purple.

The centre of the diagram is the 'white point', where the light would contain
equal amounts (1/3) of all three components. A straight-edge laid across the
W point will indicate (at opposite sides of the spectral locus) a pair of spectral
colours which would add up to white (e.g. a 600 nm yellow-orange mixed
with a 490 nm blue-green would be perceived as white light). These pairs are
referred to as complementary colours.

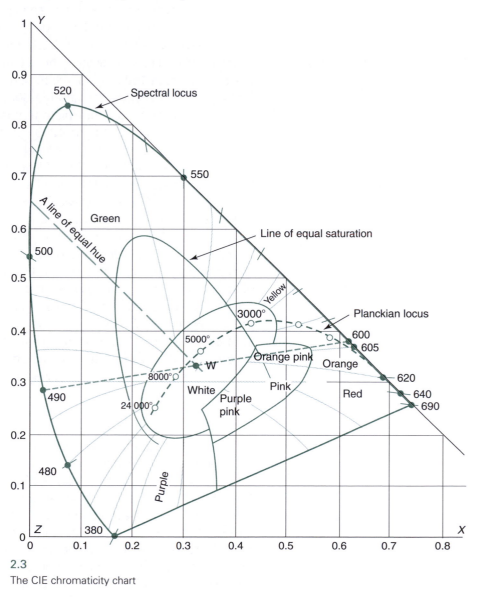

2.3

The CIE chromaticity chart

---

* Commission International d'Éclairage = International Lighting Commission.

The spectral locus indicates colours of full saturation and the radius from the W-point gives a scale of saturation. 'Equal saturation' contours can be interpolated between the W-point and the spectral locus. One such (parabolic) line of equal saturation is shown in Fig. 2.3. The oval-shaped area around the W-point indicates colours perceived as 'white' but with a slight tinge of the adjacent colours.

A heated body emits radiation, the wavelength composition of which depends on the body's temperature. Up to about 1500°K the wavelengths are longer than the visible band, i.e. infrared radiation, perceived as radiant heat. Beyond this it becomes visible and its colour is a function of the body's temperature, thus the colour can be defined by this *colour temperature* (CT). Fig. 2.4 shows the spectral emission of a black body at various temperatures, as a function of wavelength. The visible range (light) is indicated by the two vertical lines. The temperature of the emitter within this band is taken as the CT.

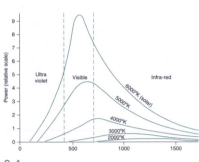

2.4

Spectral emission of black body at various temperatures

The heavy dashed line of Fig. 2.3 is the Planckian locus (named after the physicist Max Planck), indicating the colour temperatures of black body emissions, from about 1500°K (orange) through the 3000K (yellow-white) of a low wattage incandescent lamp, and the 6000°K solar emission (up to 24000°K of a blue sky). (Note that the colour temperature is the inverse of the everyday colour designation, e.g. the 1200°K red would be referred to as a 'warm' colour, and the 24000°K blue as a 'cool' colour.)

Colours other than those of the Planckian locus can be referred to by their CCT, or *correlated colour temperature*, i.e. where the radial direction of the colour from the W-point intersects the Planckian locus, e.g. the dashed line of Fig. 2.3 marked as the 'line of equal hue' (green) intersects the Planckian locus at about 6000°K, which will be its CCT designation.

The colour of light depends on the source (the spectral composition of the emission), but can also be produced by filters. A filter may reflect or absorb most of the given wavelengths and transmit only a specified narrow wavelength band. For example, a red filter would admit only a narrow band around 690 nm, absorbing or reflecting all other components. As filtering is a subtractive process, if the incoming light had no red component, no light will be transmitted. A yellow filter may be one that admits red and green (but not blue or violet), which will be perceived as yellow.

2.1.2 Surface colours

While coloured light from various sources would be additive (e.g. the above mentioned blue-green and yellow-orange, or any other pair of complementary colours, would add up to white), surface colours are subtractive, or rather their absorptances are additive. A surface painted red appears to be this colour, as it absorbs everything else, reflects only the red component of the incident light. If a red surface is illuminated by white light, which is the addition of the above yellow-orange and blue-green, it will appear to be a dirty grey, as the light has no red component, no red will be reflected. The lighting would need to be of a continuous spectrum white to reveal all colours, including the red thus to produce good *colour rendering*.

The most comprehensive classification of surface colours is the *Munsell system*. This distinguishes three attributes (Fig. 2.5):

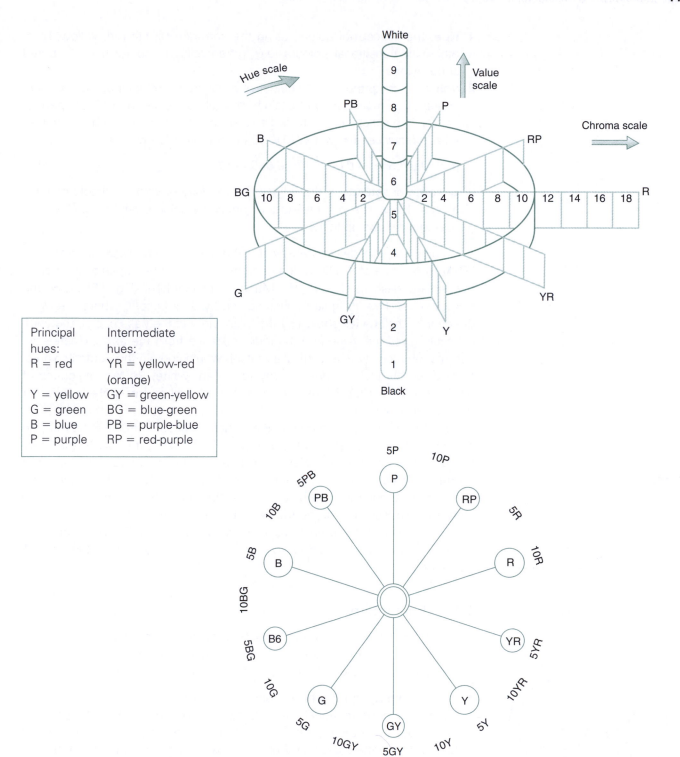

Hue scale

White

Value scale

Chroma scale

PB   P

B   RP

BG   10 8 6 4 2   2 4 6 8 10 12 14 16 18   R

G   YR

GY   Y

Black

Principal hues:	Intermediate hues:
R = red	YR = yellow-red (orange)
Y = yellow	GY = green-yellow
G = green	BG = blue-green
B = blue	PB = purple-blue
P = purple	RP = red-purple

5P

10P

5PB

PB   P   RP

10B

5B   B   R   5R

10R

10BG

5BG   B6   YR

5YR

10G   G   Y   10YR

5G   GY   5Y

10GY   5GY   10Y

2.5

The Munsell colour wheel and its 'plan' view

1 **Hue**: the concept of colour, using the common terms: red, yellow, blue, etc. with transitional colours (e.g. green/yellow) and further numbered subdivisions.

2 **Value** (V) or lightness: the subjective measure of reflectance, light or dark appearance, measured on a scale from 0 (absolute black) to 10 (the perfect white). In practice, values from 1 to 9 are encountered. It can be converted into *reflectance*: $\rho = V \times (V-1)/100$ or more accurately

$$\rho = (0.5796\ V^2 + 0.0435\ V^3 - 0.089\ V) / 100 \tag{2.2}$$

3 **Chroma** or saturation: the fullness or intensity of colour. All colours have at least 10 classes (e.g. blue-green), but some colours can be very 'strong', having a chroma up to 18.

Any colour can be designated by the three facets, *hue-value/chroma*, e.g. **5R-4/10** = a hue of red 5 – value of 4/chroma of 10 (the separators must be hyphen and slash, as shown). The Munsell 'colour wheel' (Fig. 2.5) shows the framework of two (irregular) cones (joined by their bases), where the radial direction is the hue (as shown by the 'plan' view of the base circle), the vertical scale gives the value and the radial distance from the axis indicates the chroma, or intensity. The vertical axis itself would contain the neutral colours, from black, through shades of grey to brilliant white. Better catalogues of paints would give the Munsell designation as well as the more 'poetic' (or gimmicky) colour names.

If such precision is not required, then British Standard 4800 can be referred to, which also has a set of colour samples. In the USA, the ISCC-NBS (Inter-Society Color Council – the National Bureau of Standards) publishes a set of 'Centroid Colour Charts'. These are numbered 1 to 267 and have common-sense names (such as pale blue, or emerald green). Some sources use the Ostwald colour system or the Maerz and Paul Dictionary of Colour.

Some paint manufacturers have their own systems, e.g. Dulux or Goodlass. The latter refers to the BS 2600 '101 Colour Range', but also gives the Munsell designation.

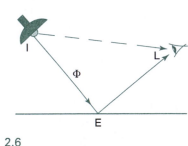

2.6
A simple luminous system

2.1.3 Photometry

The simplest luminous system consists of a light source (a lamp), a surface illuminated and an eye perceiving the light, both from the source and reflected by the surface (Fig. 2.6). The four measurable photometric quantities are:

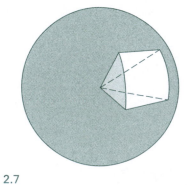

2.7
Definition of the steradian (sr)

• **I**, the **luminous intensity** of a source, measured in units of *candela* (cd), which is the international standard candle, defined as the intensity of a black body of 1/60 cm², when heated to the melting point temperature of platinum. It is the basic unit, from which all others are derived. **Φ** (phi), the **luminous flux** (or flow of light), measured in the unit *lumen* (lm), which is defined as the flux emitted within 1 steradian (sr) by a point source of I = 1 cd, emitting light uniformly in all directions (Fig. 2.7). Therefore, 1 cd emits a total of 4π lumens.

• **E**, or **illuminance** (the symbol E comes from the French *Éclairage*), the measure of the illumination of a surface (note that *illumination* is the

As the unit of 2-D angle is the *radian*, where the length of arc is the same as the radius (a full circle is 2π radians), so the *steradian* (stereo-radian), sr is the unit of (3-D) solid angle, that is subtended by an r^2 area of the surface of a sphere of r radius. As the surface area of a sphere is $4\pi r^2$, the centre of a sphere contains 4p steradians.

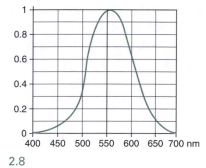

2.8

The CIE luminous efficacy curve: spectral sensitivity of the human eye F vs l

process, *illuminance* is the product). The unit is the *lux*, (lx) which is the illuminance caused by 1 lm incident of 1 m² area (i.e. the incident flux density of 1 lm/m²).

- **L**, or **luminance**, is the measure of brightness of a surface, when looked at from a given direction. Its unit is *cd/m²* (sometimes referred to as a *nit*, rarely used in English), which is the unit intensity of a source of unit area (source intensity divided by its apparent area viewed from the nominated direction).

(1cd pint source enclosed in a 1 m radius spherical diffuser has a projected area of π m², therefore its luminance will be $1/\pi$ cd/m².)

- For illuminated surfaces, the non-SI metric unit is often used, the *apostilb* (asb). This is the luminance of a fully reflective ($\rho = 1$) diffusing surface which has an illuminance of 1 lux. Thus asb $= \rho \times$ E. Both units measure the same quantity, but asb is a small unit: 1 cd/m² = asb.

Luminous flux (lm) is of the same physical dimension as watt (W), and illuminance (lx) is the same as irradiance (W/m²) but the latter are energy units, the former are luminous quantities (i.e. applicable to radiation in the visible wavelengths).

Energy quantities are not directly convertible into photometric quantities without specifying the wavelength, as the human eye's sensitivity varies with the wavelength of light. It is most sensitive to a yellow light of 555 nm, but its sensitivity (or efficacy, F) reduces in both directions, as shown by the CIE luminous efficacy curve (Fig. 2.8) This indicates the weighting of any narrow band of radiant energy (in W) into light flux (lm). Table 2.2 gives some typical values of flux output of light sources, illuminances and the luminance of some sources and surfaces, just to give a 'feel' of the magnitude of these quantities.

Table 2.2 Some typical photometric values

Total flux output of some sources	lm	Typical illuminance	Lux
Bicycle lamp	10	Bright sunny day, outdoors	80 000
40 W incandescent lamp	325	Overcast day, outdoors	5000
30 W fluorescent lamp	2800	Moderately lit desk	300
140 W sodium lamp	13000	Average general lighting	100
400 W mercury lamp	20000	Full moonlit night	0.1

Typical luminance values	cd/m²
Sun (1650 Mcd/m²)	1 650 000 000
Filament in clear incandescent lamp	7 000 000
Fluorescent lamp (tube surface)	8000
Full moon	2500
Paper with 400 lx illuminance:	

White ($\rho = 0.8$)	$\approx$ 100 or 400 $\times$ 0.8	= 320 asb
Grey ($\rho = 0.4$)	$\approx$ 50 or 400 $\times$ 0.4	= 160 asb
Black ($\rho = 0.04$)	$\approx$ 5 or 400 $\times$ 0.04	= 16 asb

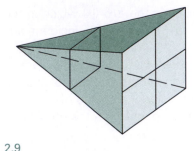
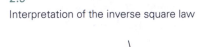

2.9
Interpretation of the inverse square law

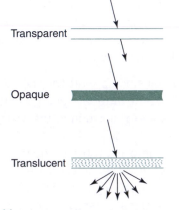

Transparent

Opaque

Translucent

2.11
Transmission of light

(a) Specular

(b) Spread

(c) Semi-diffuse

(d) Diffuse

2.12
Reflective surfaces

2.1.4 Transmission of light

In a vacuum or in a transparent homogeneous medium (air), light travels in a straight line. The *inverse square law* states that illuminance reduces in proportion to the square of the distance from the source. Fig. 2.9 shows that the flux which at a given distance goes through a unit area, at double that distance will go through four times that area, so the flux density (= illuminance) reduces to one quarter.

A source of 1 candela intensity (I) emits 1 lumen within a steradian and produces an illuminance of 1 lux at 1 m distance, thus numerically E = I, thus at a distance d

$$E = \frac{I}{d^2} \qquad (2.3)$$

The *cosine law* relates illuminance of a surface (E) to the illuminance normal to the direction of the light beam (E_n, E_{normal}), which depends on the angle of incidence. If the angle of incidence is β, (Fig. 2.10) and the surface area normal to the beam is A_n, then $A > A_n$ thus $E < E_n$

$$A = \frac{A_n}{\cos \beta} \text{ and } E = E_n \times \cos \beta$$

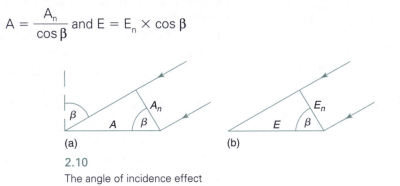

(a)   (b)

2.10
The angle of incidence effect

Material bodies exposed to light behave in various ways. A sheet of glass is said to be *transparent*, a sheet of plywood is *opaque*. A sheet of 'opal' perspex is *translucent* (Fig. 2.11). Light incident on the surface can be distributed in three ways: reflected, absorbed or transmitted. The corresponding properties are reflectance (ρ), absorptance (α) and transmittance (τ) and in all cases $\rho + \alpha + \tau = 1$ (as discussed in Sections 1.1.2.3 and 1.4.1.3 in relation to solar radiation). All three terms are functions of radiation wavelength, and when applied to the visible wavelengths (light), they may be referred to as 'optical', e.g. optical transmittance or optical absorptance.

Materials which in a small thickness may be transparent may become opaque in a large thickness. The term *absorptivity* is a property of the material, indicating the absorption per unit thickness, while *absorptance* is the property of a body of given thickness.

Surfaces may be classified in terms of their reflective properties (Fig. 2.12) as *specular* (a mirror), or *diffuse* (ordinary building surfaces), or transitional: (*spread or semi-diffuse*) giving a *diffuse* (all diffuse, but with some directional bias).

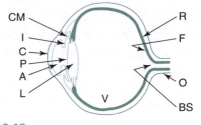

2.13
Section of the human eye

2.2 VISION

2.2.1 The eye and brain

Light is perceived by the eye. Its diagrammatic section (Fig. 2.13) can be compared to a camera:

- The aperture, controlled by a light-meter: the pupil (P), the size of which is varied by the iris (and controlled by the retina), which is the eye's main *adaptation* mechanism.
- Focusing, controlled by a coupled range-finder: changing the shape of the lens by the ciliary muscles (CM), thus varying its focal length, which is the *accommodation* mechanism.
- The adaptability of the retina can only be likened to using films of different 'speeds' or ISO (ASA) rating.

The retina (which is in fact an extension of the visual cortex and optical nerve) incorporates two kinds of nerve endings: cones and rods. A normal eye has some 6.5 million *cones* (in and around the *fovea*), which are sensitive to both quantity and quality (colour) of light, but operate only in good lighting (*photopic vision*). The retina also has some 125 million *rods*, which are more sensitive than the cones, but perceive only quantity of light, and do not distinguish colour (*scotopic vision*).

The pupil's response is practically instantaneous. A second adaptation mechanism of the eye is the variation of the retina's sensitivity by varying the photochemical compounds present (e.g. of the *visual purple*). While the pupil's response to changed lighting conditions is almost instantaneous, adaptation of the retina to dark conditions may take up to 30 minutes, as more visual purple is produced. Adaptation to brighter light is no more than about 3 minutes, as the visual purple is being removed.

Both adaptation mechanisms respond to the average luminance of the field of vision. Starting from darkness:

at 0.001 cd/m^2	the pupil is wide open and the rods start to operate;
at about 3 cd/m^2	the cones start to operate;
at 1000 cd/m^2	the pupil closes to its minimum.

Without light there is no vision, but visual perception depends as much on the brain as on the eye. It is largely dependent on recognition. Life is continuous learning (quickest at the cradle and gradually slowing), new visual images are compared to and built into relationships with images already stored and with percepts from other senses. Visual perception relies on memory to such an extent that expectation can influence perception itself.

As an old Arab saying has it: 'The eye is blind to what the mind can't see.'

2.2.2 Visual performance

The *contrast sensitivity* of the eye is very good in good lighting. In full daylight a luminance difference between surfaces as small as 1% can be distinguished, but under poor lighting conditions surfaces with up to 10% luminance difference may be perceived as equal. Contrast is expressed as the ratio of luminance difference to the lower of the two luminances:

$$C = \frac{L_1 - L_2}{L_2} \tag{2.4}$$

Visual acuity, or sharpness of vision, depends on illuminance. Acuity (a) is measured by the smallest detail perceived, expressed as the reciprocal of the visual angle (σ, in minutes of arc) subtended at the eye by opposite extremes of the least perceptible detail:

> if σ = 2' then a = 1/2 = 0.5

or

> if σ = 3' then a = 1/3 = 0.33.

Same as with contrast sensitivity, the law of diminishing returns applies: a small increase at a low level of illuminance produces a large improvement in acuity, but a similar increase at a higher level of illuminance is barely noticeable.

Visual performance is a function of the time required to see an object, or of the number of items (e.g. characters) perceived in unit time. The time required to perform a certain visual task decreases (i.e. the performance increases) with the increase of illuminance.

The above three terms are measures of the same stimulus-response relationship. The three together give a good measure of the efficiency of the visual process, and all three reduce with age (presbyopia). Fig. 2.14 shows the variation of visual efficiency with task illuminance. The curve is a good example of the law of diminishing returns.

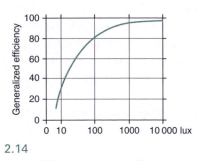

2.14

Visual efficiency curve: η vs E

2.2.3 Lighting requirements

The **adequacy** of lighting is a quantitative requirement, which depends on the visual task: the contrast, the fineness of detail and the speed at which the view changes. To set the required lighting level the risk of possible errors must be judged and balanced against the affordability of lighting. As people's visual efficiency reduces with age, it is advisable to provide better illuminance for older people. Duration of the visual task is also a factor: to avoid visual fatigue, higher levels are necessary.

Recommended or prescribed illuminance values also depend on socio-cultural, as well as economic factors. Data sheet D.2.6 gives illuminance values for various visual tasks recommended by several UK and Australian Codes. American sources distinguish nine illuminance categories (A to I), which roughly correspond to the 'visual task' categories of Data sheet D.2.6, except that the illuminance requirements are somewhat higher, especially at the higher levels (G–I). Over the last century the recommended illuminance levels have tended to increase, partly due to more efficient lamps becoming available, partly because of increased affluence and expectations. There were also differences between fully developed and developing countries, i.e. what can be afforded and what is expected. More recently these differences have reduced. As energy conservation became an important issue, some high recommendations were also reduced.

The **suitability of lighting** is a qualitative requirement and has at least four component factors:

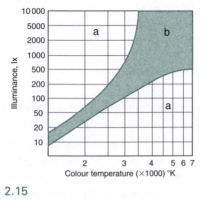

2.15
Relationship of colour temperature and illuminance: with high colour temperature high illuminance is expected. The 'a' areas are disliked.

1 Colour appearance and colour rendering. As our eyes developed over millions of years to operate under natural lighting conditions, their sensitivity corresponds to the sunlight spectrum. Some research suggests that at high levels of illuminance we expect light of a higher colour temperature (i.e. daylight) and daylight gives the norm for colour rendering, it is the best to reveal all colours. With low levels of illuminance, a light of lower colour temperature is expected and preferred (Fig. 2.15) ('warm' colours: the light of fire or candle, or an oil lamp).

2 Colour appearance of an environment is associated with mood and the expected 'atmosphere'. These are psychological and aesthetic effects. The architectural character of a space can be enhanced, but also counteracted, changed or even destroyed by lighting. For example, one does not want 1000 lx illuminance of a blue-white colour (> 10 000 °K colour temperature) in an intimate restaurant. Light can be handled purely functionally but it can be an important design element from the aesthetic viewpoint.

3 Directionality of light must suit the functional as well as the psychological requirements of a visual task. A more diffuse light is normally judged as 'more pleasant', but it will cast little or no shadows, so it may create a hazy or even eerie atmosphere. Where 3-D perception is essential, a more directional lighting is necessary, as shadows will reveal form and texture.

4 Glare should be avoided, but the extent of acceptable (desirable?) glare must suit the visual task. This is discussed in more detail in the next section.

2.2.4   Glare

Glare can be caused by a saturation effect or by excessive contrast. We can distinguish discomfort glare and disability glare, depending on the magnitude of the effect.

Saturation glare can be caused when the average luminance of the field of vision is in excess of 25 000 cd/m² (80 000 asb). This can happen on a white sandy beach (ρ = 0.9) with full sunshine (100 000 lx), giving 90 000 asb (or 28 600 cd/m²) or looking directly into a bright light source. Isolated bright white clouds, when sunlit, can reach similar luminances. This would cause *disability glare*, i.e. vision will be impaired. Some sources distinguish 'direct glare' caused by a light source itself and 'indirect glare' caused by reflective illuminated surfaces.

The eye (both the pupil and the retina) adapts to the average luminance of the visual field. Driving at night this average luminance is quite low, even when the high beam of headlights illuminates part of it. So, the retina contains a high level of visual purple and the pupil is wide open.

An oncoming car, travelling with high beam on, can cause disability ('blinding') glare as the pupil closes down to minimum in a few seconds, so only the headlights are visible, not the rest of the field. Such disability glare can normally be avoided, but discomfort glare is more of a problem.

One cause of glare is contrast, and if the luminance ratio (L_{max}/L_{av}) within a visual field is greater than about 15 (some sources suggest 10), visual efficiency will be reduced and discomfort may be experienced. When looking at a theatre stage (with low level of auditorium lighting) and a brightly lit 'Exit' sign is at the edge of my field of view, my vision is somewhat impaired, but it certainly causes discomfort and annoyance.

Viewing a computer screen when facing a window with a sunlit background is very uncomfortable. Reflected glare is caused when a lamp behind me is reflected from the computer screen, or when trying to look at a glossy photo and my anglepoise lamp gives a reflection into my eyes. These are often referred to as 'veiling reflections'. In a general office fitted with bare fluorescent lamps all over the ceiling, these may be in my visual field and cause discomfort glare.

Contrast grading is one way of reducing glare. If the luminance of the visual task on my desk is taken as 100%, its immediate surrounding should not be more than 50% and the rest of the visual field not more than 20%.

Some sources distinguish the 'field of vision' (= visual field), the area looked at when neither the head nor the eyes move (a visual angle of about 20°) and the 'field of view' (the immediate surrounding), that visible with the head fixed, but the eyes moving (a visual angle up to about 40°). The 'environment' is taken as that with the head turned but the body (the shoulders) fixed (up to 120° vertically and 180° horizontally).

Some contrast grading (below the above limits) will assist in focusing attention on the task. The most recent norms and standards (e.g. the joint BS EN ISO 29241, or the European EN 12964) tend to shift the emphasis from illuminance (lux) requirements to the control of luminance and luminance distribution. These are more relevant to electric lighting, but perhaps give a guidance for daylighting design.

The glare index concept will be discussed in Section 2.5.5, in the context of electric lighting design, together with further discussion of luminance distribution.

2.3   DAYLIGHT AND SUNLIGHT

Light outdoors is generally referred to as natural light. It has two main components: that arriving directly from the sun is referred to as *sunlight* (or 'beam sunlight'). Varying fractions of this are diffused by the atmosphere, e.g. by clouds, which is referred to as *daylight*. (Some authors refer to the latter as 'skylight', but in general usage, also adopted here, 'skylight' means a roof window.)

The term *daylight* in a loose sense is often used for both, but in technical language (also used here) it means only the diffused light arriving from the sky hemisphere.

2.3.1 Sky conditions

The available light is determined by sky conditions. The fully **overcast sky** acts as a diffuse light source, i.e. the whole sky hemisphere is a source of light. The CIE standard overcast sky has a luminance distribution (3 to 1) defined as a function of altitude angle (γ). If the zenith luminance is L_z, then at any altitude angle

$$L\gamma = \frac{L_z}{3} \times (1 + 2\sin\gamma) \qquad (2.5)$$

i.e. the zenith luminance is three times that at the horizon and it gradually increases from horizon to zenith.

The illuminance produced by an overcast sky strongly depends on the solar altitude angle (ALT) behind the clouds. In the absence of measured data it can be estimated as

$$E \approx 200 \times ALT \qquad (2.6)$$

Under **clear sky** conditions direct sunlight can give an illuminance of 100 klx (1 kilo-lux = 1000 lux), but if the sunlight itself is excluded, the sky can give 40–50 klx diffuse illuminance. With clear skies, the sky luminance is taken as uniform.

In many climates **intermediate sky** conditions occur most of the time. The average illuminance produced by such a sky (excluding direct sunlight) can be estimated as

$$E \approx 500 \times ALT \qquad (2.7)$$

Measured illuminance data are rarely available. More locations have measured solar irradiance data. From this, the illuminance can be estimated by using the luminous efficacy* values of solar radiation. This is defined as

$$\text{Luminous efficacy: } F = \frac{\text{illuminance}}{\text{irradiance}} = \frac{\text{lux}}{\text{W/m}^2} = \frac{\text{lm/m}^2}{\text{W/m}^2} = \frac{\text{lm}}{\text{W}}$$

Luminous efficacy of electric lamps varies from 10 to 200 lm/W.

In daylighting, the concept of luminous efficacy is useful when the availability of light must be estimated from solar radiation data. See Method sheet M.2.1 for the various models for estimating daylight illuminance from solar irradiance data.

For the efficacy of other light sources, see Section 2.5.1 and Table 2.3.

---

* Note that whilst *efficiency* is a non-dimensional number comparing quantities of the same dimension, *efficacy* is the term used for comparing unlike quantities, therefore its dimension must be stated

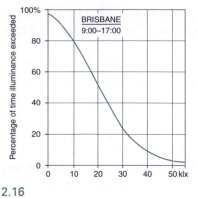

2.16
Frequency distribution of outdoor illuminance (direct sunlight excluded)

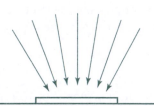
Planar illuminance

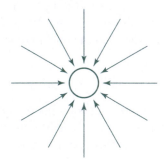
Spherical (scalar) illuminance

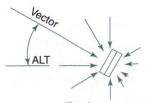
Illuminance vector

2.17
Interpretation of the vector/scalar ratio

Table 2.3 Luminous efficacies (F) of some natural light sources

Sunlight	ALT = 7.5°	F = 90 lm/W
	ALT > 25	117
	Average	100
Sky light	Clear	150
	Average	125
Global (sun + sky)		100–115
	Overcast sky	110

For the efficacy of other light sources see Section 2.5.1 and Table 2.4.

2.3.2 Daylight illuminance

Measured outdoor illuminance data are usually presented in terms of frequency of occurrence (in %), in the form of an ogive curve, such as that shown in Fig. 2.16. Measurements usually exclude direct sunlight, so the horizontal scale of this diagram is diffuse illuminance (on a horizontal surface, from an unobstructed sky) and the vertical scale is % frequency. From the example of Brisbane, it can be seen that, e.g. 30 klx is exceeded some 22% of the time (taken for the year between 9:00 and 17:00) and 10 klx would be exceeded some 80% of this time.

The above are planar illuminance data, i.e. measurements of illuminance on a plane, in this case a horizontal plane surface. This, however, does not give the full picture.

Overcast sky illuminance is diffuse, i.e. light is received at a point from all directions of the sky hemisphere. A theoretical perfectly diffuse field of light would mean a uniform spherical illuminance. A spherical light meter would measure the *mean spherical illuminance* (i.e. a scalar illuminance, E_s), whether it is uniform or not.

The *illuminance vector* is given by the largest difference between illuminances from two diametrically opposite directions ($\Delta E_{max} = E_{max} - E_{min}$). This is the magnitude of the vector and its direction is defined by a horizontal (bearing or azimuth) and a vertical (altitude or elevation) angle. The vector/scalar ratio (v/s) is a measure of directionality of light (Fig. 2.17).

$$v/s = \Delta E_{max} / E_s \qquad (2.8)$$

e.g. if the largest difference is found as $E_{max} = 200$ lx and the mean spherical illuminance is $E_s = 100$ lx, then the ratio is v/s = 200/100 = 2, but if $E_s = 400$ lx, then v/s = 200/400 = 0.5/.

In a completely uniform diffuse field $\Delta E_{max} = 0$, thus v/s is also 0.

In a monodirectional light, if the beam of light (within 1 sr) gives 800 lx, the ΔE_{max} is also 800 lx and the E_s is likely to be 800/4 = 200 lx (the 800 lx from 1 sr is averaged over the surface of the sphere, $4\pi\ r^2$, so v/s = 800 / 200 = 4). This is the maximum value possible, with a monodirectional light, so the theoretical limits for v/s ratio are 0 to 4, and in real situations values between 0.2 and 3.5 are encountered.

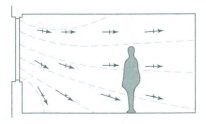

2.18
Illuminance vectors in a side-lit room

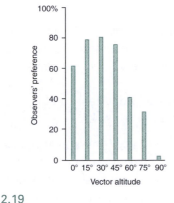

2.19
Preferences for vector altitude

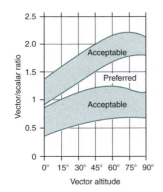

2.20
Preferred vector/scalar ratios for looking at a human face

Outdoors, under an overcast sky the illuminance vector is likely to be vertical and v/s ratios around 2.5 are found, depending on the reflectance of the ground. The light from an overcast sky entering through a window is likely to have a vector altitude of 42° (the altitude of average luminance), near the window. Further into the room it tends to become near horizontal (Fig. 2.18). If a person A faces the window, talking at B with his back to the window, A will see B only in silhouette. (This can be improved by light coloured room surfaces, with reflected light reducing the ΔE_{max}.) There is evidence that looking at a human face most people prefer it to be illuminated with a v/s ratio between 1.1 and 1.5, and a vector altitude of 15–45° (Figs 2.19 and 2.20), but a v/s ratio of up to 2.2 is acceptable with higher altitudes.

2.3.3 Luminance distribution

The entry of sunlight through a window may or may not be desirable and it depends very much on the visual task to be performed. Sunlight (solar radiation) has a strong heating effect, which may be desirable in winter, but not under warm conditions. The question of 'right to sunlight' will be discussed in Section 2.3.4, here its illumination effects are considered.

On the surface of a desk near a window, the daylight illuminance may be around 200 lux. The luminance of white paper ($\rho = 0.8$) may be some 160 asb. If a beam of sunlight reaches part of this surface, giving an illuminance of 10 klx, it will produce a luminance of some 8000 asb. The luminance ratio within the field of view will be 8000:160 = 50, which is far too much, when anything above 15 would cause glare.

The preferred luminance ratio would be:

task: surround: background = 1: 0.5: 0.2.
(mentioned in Section 2.2.4 as 100:50:20%)

The immediate response of people would be to move away or draw the blinds. But then the daylight won't be enough, so they will switch on the electric light.

For critical visual tasks, such as an artist's studio, large 'north-light' windows are preferred ('south-light' in the southern hemisphere) which would maximise diffuse light but avoid direct sunlight.

The design of fenestration is affected by conflicting requirements. Increased reliance on daylighting, as an energy conservation measure, may make a larger window desirable. This may increase the risk of glare. Even if sunlight is excluded, a view through the window of a sun-lit wall, a water surface, or a sandy beach, of sun-lit clouds or a bright sky can cause glare. Glare occurring in daylighting can be reduced by the following measures:

1 **Reduce** the luminance of the view by using low-transmittance glass ($\tau \approx$ 0.3) at least for critical (upper) parts of the window, perhaps some self-adhesive 'solar film', or by the use of blinds or curtains.
2 **Increase** the luminance of areas near the high luminance view, e.g. by having windows in other (opposite) walls to illuminate the surfaces adjacent to the window considered or by using supplementary top lighting.

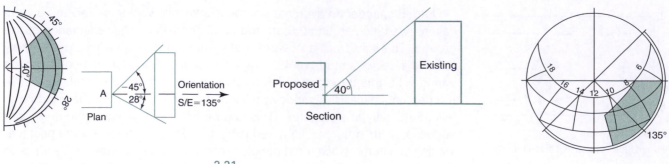

2.21
Assessment of overshadowing

3 **Increase** the luminance of the window's surrounds by using light colour surfaces and contrast grading: having high reflectance surfaces next to the window, reducing away from the window. With very large windows this measure won't work.

4 **Use** external protective devices (similar to shading devices) to block out the view of the brightest problem-area, most often the sky.

Care should be taken with the design of such devices. If the sun-lit device itself is visible (especially a white or bright metallic device), it can cause glare. If the device or a screen allows sun penetration in narrow beams, producing alternating patches of sunlight and shade, it may be worse than the unprotected window.

Quantitative treatment of glare is presented in Section 2.5.5, in the context of the design of artificial lighting.

2.3.4 Overshadowing

The thermal effects of solar radiation have been discussed in Part 1 (especially in Section 1.4.1) where the use of sun-path diagrams and the shadow angle protractor were also introduced. These can be put to use also for the control of sunlight.

In temperate climates it is desirable to admit some sunlight into habitable rooms (including schools or hospital wards), if not for physical, certainly for psychological reasons. Some codes of practice prescribe that such rooms should be able to receive sunlight for at least one hour per day for 10 months of the year (if available). This 'right to sunlight' originates from the nineteenth century, but the problem became more acute after the 1973 energy crisis when installations of various solar energy devices proliferated (and more so in recent times) and their access to solar radiation needs to be protected. This will be discussed in some detail in Part 4.

A task before starting a design would be to assess any obstructions around the site and establish the extent and duration of overshadowing. Fig. 2.21 shows a method of assessing overshadowing in a simple case.

Take point A, at the ground floor window sill level of the proposed building. Lines drawn on the plan to the edges of the obstructing existing building can be transferred to the shadow angle protractor, to delineate the horizontal

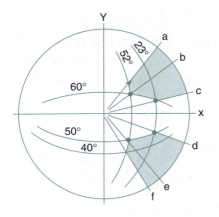

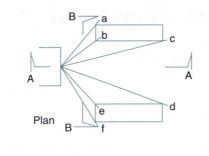

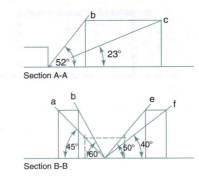

Section A-A

Section B-B

2.22
A somewhat more involved case

extent of overshadowing (in this case −45° and +28°). Then on a section, the line drawn from point A to the top edge of the existing building gives the VSA (vertical shadow angle), in this case, 40°, which is represented by the 40° arc of the protractor.

This completes the shading mask. If this is superimposed on the sun-path diagram for the location, according to orientation (in this case S/E, or 135°), the times end dates of overshadowing can be read: on midsummer day only for a few minutes at about 7:30, but on equinox dates from 6:00 to about 11:00.

Fig. 2.22 shows the same procedure for the effect of two buildings opposite, but sideways offset. Here two sections are necessary (A-A and B-B). Use the shadow angle protractor so that its centreline is in the plane of the section.

Method sheet M.2.2 presents the use of this technique for a site survey, to examine the extent of overshadowing of a given point on the site.

2.4   DESIGN METHODS

Daylight may be introduced into a building using a variety of techniques, side-lighting or top-lighting strategies. The integration of daylighting with building design can have a decisive influence on the architectural form. In daylighting design, for the positioning and sizing of apertures, there are three main issues to be considered:

- to satisfy the visual tasks (provide enough daylight);
- to create the desired 'mood' and provide visual focus;
- to integrate daylighting with the architecture.

For the first of these, to quantify daylight in buildings (or predict daylight performance from a plan), four methods will be described in this section. Some of these use luminous quantities (flux, illuminance), others are based on relative quantities: daylight factors.

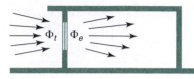

2.23

Flux entering through a window

2.4.1 Total flux method

The building (or a room in the building) is considered as a closed box, with an aperture (a window) that will admit a light flux. The illuminance on the plane of the window (E_W) must be known. If this is multiplied by the window area, the total flux entering the room is obtained (Fig. 2.23).

$$\Phi_t = E_W \times A \text{ (lm)} \tag{2.9}$$

This will, however, be reduced by three factors:

1 M, the *maintenance factor*, which allows for dirt or other deterioration of the glazing in use.
2 G, or the *glass factor*, allowing for the type of glazing, other than clear glass.
3 B, the 'bars' or framing factor, allowing for obstruction due to solid elements of the frame and sashes, that would reduce the effective area.

(See Data sheet D.2.2 for all three factors, M G B – the 1960s sports car – is a useful mnemonic.)

Thus the effective flux entering will be

$$\Phi_e = \Phi_t \times A \times M \times G \times B \text{ (lm)} \tag{2.10}$$

If this flux were to be uniformly distributed over the floor area, the illuminance would be

$$E_{av} = \Phi_e / A \tag{2.11}$$

which is not the case, but it can be taken as the average illuminance. The actual illuminance at any particular point in the room (on the work-plane) will depend on the *utilization factor* (UF) at that point. This is determined by:

1 the geometrical proportions of the room, expressed by the room index: RI

$$RI = \frac{L \times W}{(L + W) \times H} = \frac{\text{horizontal surfaces}/2}{\text{vertical surfaces}/2}$$

where L, W and H are the length, width and height of the room
2 reflectance of ceiling and wall surfaces
3 type of fenestration
4 position of the point relative to the window(s).

Such UF factors are usually presented in extensive tables. The method has been widely used in the USA, but it is suggested that its use be restricted to roof lighting, for a general illumination of the work-plane. Data sheet D.2.1 is an example of such a UF table, also giving the uniformity criteria for the main types of roof lighting.

2.4.1.1 Daylight design diagrams

Daylight design diagrams have been produced (Paix, [1962] 1982) by the Australian EBS (Experimental Building Station), based on 'design sky' outdoor horizontal illuminances, those exceeded in 90% of the time (from 5:00 to 17:00 h) (see also Fig. 2.16 above and Method sheet M.2.1). For Australian

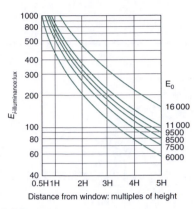

2.24

Daylight design diagram: work-plane illuminance as a function of distance from window for various levels of outdoor illuminance

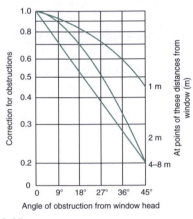

2.25

Corrections for other than infinite windows and for obstructions

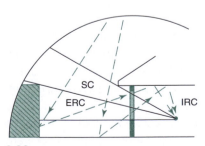

2.26

Daylight flux split into three components

cities this varies from 6000 lx (Hobart) to 16000 lx (Darwin), with other states in between (7500 for Melbourne, 8500 for Sydney, Canberra, Adelaide, 9500 for Perth and 11000 for Brisbane).

The first diagram used (Fig. 2.24) shows the work-plane illuminance as it reduces with the increase of distance from the window. This distance is expressed as a multiple of the window head height above the work-plane. The illuminance values read are valid for a horizontal strip window of infinite length. For windows of finite length and for any external obstruction, the correction factors given in the second diagram (Fig. 2.25) are to be applied.

For narrow windows			
Width/height	2	1	0.5
Correction	0.8	0.6	0.4

2.4.2 Daylight factor

It has been observed that though overcast sky illuminance may vary between quite wide limits, the ratio between illuminance at a point indoors to that outdoors remains constant. This ratio is the daylight factor (DF) expressed as a percentage.

$$DF = \frac{E_1}{E_0} \times 100. (\%) \qquad (2.12)$$

As outdoor lighting conditions are highly variable, design can only be based on the 'worst conditions' (that are judged to be 'reasonable'). This approach has the same theoretical basis as the selection of 'design outdoor temperatures' discussed in Section 1.6.1. Such 'worst conditions' would occur when the sky is overcast. In Northern Europe and North America the 15th percentile outdoor illuminance (of the daylight period, usually taken as between 9:00 and 17:00) is accepted, that would be exceeded for 85% of the time.

However, in many countries this *design sky* illuminance has been standardised as 5000 lx. Thus, for example, a 2% daylight factor would mean 5000 × 2/100 = 100 lx indoor 'design' illuminance, that is likely to be exceeded 85% of the time. For the remaining 15% of time the electric lighting can be switched on, or behavioural adjustments can be made (e.g. moving closer to the window). The adaptation mechanisms of the human eye are such that an illuminance of 1000 lx can be just as comfortable as 100 lx and – as Fig. 2.14 shows – over 100 lx there is little change in visual efficiency. Beyond any individual limit of comfort, negative control is easy, but facility for this should be provided (such as a curtain or blinds). Thus the prediction of the daylight factor becomes an important design tool.

Daylight can reach a point of the work-plane by three routes (Fig. 2.26), thus three components of the daylight factor are distinguished:

1 SC, the sky component: light from a patch of sky visible from the point considered;

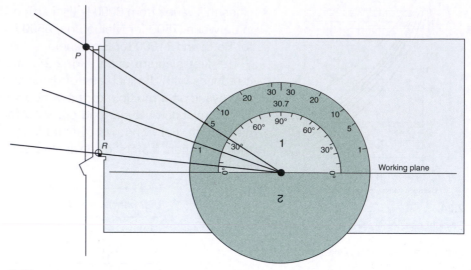

2.27
Determine initial sky component

2 ERC, the externally reflected component: light reflected by outdoor objects, e.g. other buildings;
3 IRC, the internally reflected component: any light entering the window, not reaching the work-plane directly, but only after reflection by internal surfaces, notably the ceiling.

Thus

$$DF = SC + ERC + IRC \qquad (2.13)$$

Consequently this is referred to as the *split flux method*.

For the prediction of the sky component a set of protractors have been produced by the British BRE (Longmore, 1968). Such a (circular) protractor consists of two sides: the first is to be used with a sectional drawing of the room and window (Fig. 2.27) to find the initial sky component (for an infinitely long strip-window) and the second is to be used with a plan of the room (Fig. 2.28) to get a correction factor for the window of a finite length. The set consists of 10 protractors, one of which, No. 2, for a vertical window under a CIE overcast sky is given in Data sheet D.2.3 and its reduced image is used in the following explanations, with Figs 2.27 and 2.28.

For side 1: place the protractor on the section, with its base on the work plane and its centre at the point considered. Draw two lines: to the window head (P) and sill (R). Read the values at the outer scale: in this case, 5.0 and 0.4. The difference between the two, 4.6%, is the *initial sky component*. Read the average altitude angle, in this case, 20°.

For side 2: place the protractor on the plan (Fig. 2.28) with its centre at the point considered and its base line parallel with the window plane. There are three concentric semi-circular scales, for 30°, 60° and 90° altitude angles.

Interpolate an arc for the average altitude angle (in this case 20°, between 0 and 30°). Draw radial lines from point O to the two edges of the window (M and N) and mark the points where these intersect the arc interpolated. Read

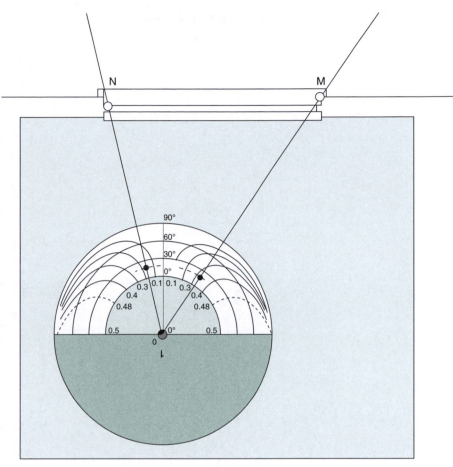

2.28
Correction factor to the sky component

the values on the inner scale, following the drooping lines: in this case, 0.32 and 0.18. As these are on either side of the centreline, the correction factor will be the sum of the two. If both were on the same side, i.e. if the point considered is outside the lines of the window width, the correction factor will be the difference between the two values. In this case, the sum is 0.5 (which is the correction factor), thus the sky component will be

$$SC = 4.6 \times 0.5 = 2.3\%$$

Other protractors are available for sloping and horizontal glazing and unglazed apertures, both for CIE and uniform skies.

If there is an obstruction outside the window, the outline of this must be established in section and the O–R line should be drawn to the top of this obstruction, rather than the window sill. The SC will be taken above this line only. The angle below this line should also be read and treated as if it were another patch of sky, but finally multiplied by the reflectance of that obstruction's surface (if not known, use $\rho = 0.2$). This will give the ERC, or externally reflected component.

The IRC can be determined by using the nomogram (given in Data sheet D.2.4) as indicated in Fig. 2.29.

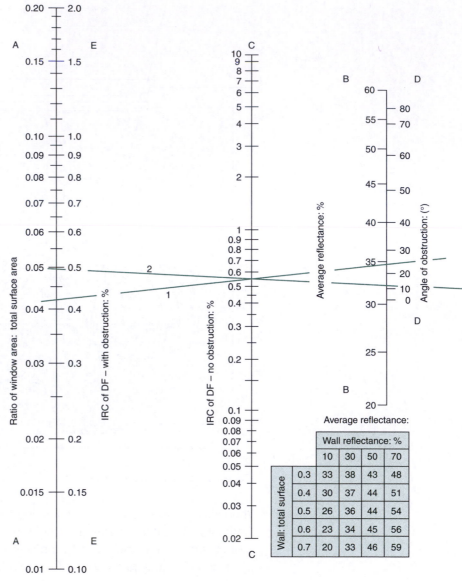

2.29
Use of the IRC nomogram (see Data sheet 2.4 for the full size version)

1 Find the ratio of window area to total surface area of the room (ceiling + floor + walls, including the window) and locate this value on scale.
2 Find the average reflectance of room surfaces, which should be the area-weighted average, but if the ceiling $\rho \approx 0.7$ and the floor $\rho \approx 0.15$, then the small Table 1 included with the nomogram can be used. First find the ratio of wall area to the total surface area (as in 1. above) and locate this value in the first column.
3 The average reflectance is then read in the column headed by the wall reflectance. Locate this $\bar{\rho}$ on scale B.
4 Lay a straight edge across these two points to find the IRC on scale C.
5 If there is an obstruction outside the window, determine the altitude angle of its top edge and locate this on scale D.

6 A straight edge laid across this point (D) and the point on C previously determined will give the IRC on scale E.

A correction factor should be applied to this IRC for the deterioration of internal decoration (D-factor), which depends on location and room usage, as given in Table 2 of Data sheet D.2.4.

EXAMPLE 2.1   INTERNALLY REFLECTED COMPONENT (IRC)

Assume a room $5 \times 4 \times 2.7$ m, with one window of 2.5×1.5 m. The total surface area is $5 \times 4 \times 2 + 2 \times (5 + 4) \times 2.7 = 88.6$ m^2. The window area is 3.75 m^2, thus the ratio is $3.75 / 88.6 = 0.042$. Mark this on scale A. The wall/total surface ratio is $48.6/88.6 = 0.549$. If $\rho_{walls} = 0.3$ (30%), from the small table the average will be 34.9% (interpolating between 34 and 36). Mark this on scale B, to define line 1 in Fig. 2.29. The intersection of this with scale C gives the IRC of 0.55%. If the altitude of obstruction is 12° (on scale D), this gives line 2 and the corrected IRC is 0.5% on scale E.

The three components can then be added (as eq. 2.13) and three further corrections should be applied to the sum: M (maintenance factor), G (glass factor) and B (bars, or framing factor), which are the same as used in the total flux method, and are given in Data sheet D.2.2.

Similar to this, the LBL Environment and Energy Technologies division uses a set of daylighting design nomograms developed by SERI as well as daylight utilisability graphs for many locations in the US.

If a grid of, say, 1 m spacing is established over a plan of the room, the daylight factor can be calculated at each of these grid-points and the contours of the daylight factor can be drawn by interpolation (Fig. 2.30). If the room is symmetrical, these can be done for half the room and mirrored for the other half. This would give an indication of the distribution of light across the whole work-plane (see also Fig. 2.35).

If greater precision is required for the determination of IRC, the BRE inter-reflection expression can be used:

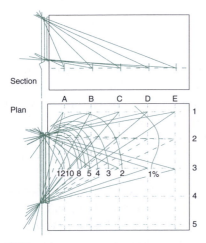

2.30

Daylight factors at grid-points and interpolation of DF contours

$$IRC = \frac{0.85.W}{A(1 - R)} \times (C.R_{fw} + 5.R_{cw}). \tag{2.14}$$

where

W = window(s) area m^2

A = total area of room surfaces (ceiling, floor, walls, including windows)

R = area weighted average reflectance (of all of A)

R_{fw} = average reflectance of floor and walls (excluding window), to window mid-level

R_{cw} = average reflectance of ceiling and walls above the mid-window level

C = coefficient to allow for external obstructions.

angle:	0°	10°	20°	30°	40°	50°	60°	70°	80°
C:	39	35	31	25	20	14	10	7	5

2.4.2.1 The pepper-pot diagram

The pepper-pot diagram is a derivative of the split flux method. The diagram itself is given in Data sheet D.2.5 and it is to be used with an internal perspective of the window and the wall it is in. This is a one-point perspective, and must be drawn to a perspective distance of 30 mm, as explained in Method sheet M.2.3.

When this is done, lay the pepper-pot diagram (a transparent copy) over the window, with its base line at the work-plane level and its centre point (the O-point) corresponding to the point considered (the view point, VP). Count the number of dots within the window area. Each dot represents 0.1% of SC. In the example shown in Method sheet M.2.3 we have 11 dots and two half dots, i.e. a total of 12, thus the SC = 1.2%.

Any external obstructions can be drawn on the perspective, within the window aperture. Any dots falling on such obstructions can be counted in the same way, but the result must be multiplied by the reflectance of that obstruction to get the ERC. For example, if we had 6 dots falling over the obstruction, that would count as 0.6%, but multiplied by an assumed reflectance of 0.3, we get an ERC of 0.18%.

The IRC must be found the same way as above, using the nomogram or the equation given above.

2.4.3 Models

The above methods are fairly easy to use with simple, conventional rooms and simple, conventional fenestration. For more complex geometries and unusual situations the most reliable way of prediction of daylighting is by the use of physical models. The model should not be too small, a scale of 1:20 is often used, and it is important that internal surface reflectances should match the realities as near as possible. If the sky component alone is to be determined, the interior of the model can be painted matt black.

Such models can be tested under outdoor conditions, if a representative overcast sky condition is available. Waiting for such conditions would interrupt any testing program, so artificial skies have been developed, which simulate overcast sky conditions, thus allow the testing to be carried out independently of the changing weather, under precisely controlled conditions.

Artificial skies may be of two types: rectangular or hemispherical. The latter can be of two types:

1 an opaque solid dome, with a diffusely reflecting internal surface, with the lighting installation below (lighting upwards) all around an annular space (Fig. 2.31);
2 a hemispherical translucent diffuser (inside of a structural dome) with the lighting installed behind it (Fig. 2.32).

In all three cases there would be a model table at the centre, with a space around it for the observers, most often with access from below. Some installations allow the selection (by switching) of a sky with uniform luminance or one with the CIE (1: 3) luminance distribution.

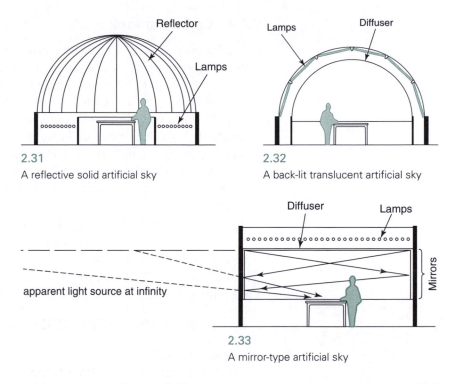

2.31
A reflective solid artificial sky

2.32
A back-lit translucent artificial sky

2.33
A mirror-type artificial sky

Many workers in the field prefer the rectangular, mirror-type artificial sky. Here all four walls would be lined with mirrors from table height up to the ceiling. This ceiling would be made of a translucent diffusing material, with the lighting installation behind it. The multiple inter-reflections between opposed mirrors would create the effect of an infinite horizon (Fig. 2.33), which is much closer to reality than domes limited to 6–8 m diameter.

The technique of model studies itself is quite simple, as long as the model is well made, its interior reflectances are realistic and light seepage through cracks and joints is prevented. Measure the 'outdoor' illuminance, usually on the top of the model, measure the illuminance 'indoors' at various points and find the daylight factor at each of these points as DF = $(E_i / E_o) \times 100$. Instruments can measure the illuminance at many points (with miniature light sensors placed at grid-points) and produce the daylight factor automatically.

Such artificial skies were developed over 50 years ago and were extensively used by research workers. Indeed, the daylight factor calculation (split flux) method discussed above has been created with the aid of such artificial skies. After the 1958 Oxford conference of the RIBA (which acknowledged the great significance of science in architectural design and education), practically all schools of architecture set up laboratories and built artificial skies.

With the rise of post-modern and deconstructivist ideologies and the predominance of formalist attitudes, most of these laboratories fell into disrepair. Only in the last decade – or so – when daylighting came to be recognised as a tool for energy conservation and a contributor to sustainability, have such laboratories been revived to regain their role. We now have measurement systems coupled with a PC, we can display the DF values at grid-points on the screen and generate the DF contours as well as converting these into illuminance (isolux) contours.

2.4.4 Computer tools

Fig. 2.35 on p. 167 is a reduced scale summary of a study examining the effect of window size, shape and position on daylight distribution. It can be seen that the height of the window determines the depth of daylight penetration, while the width influences the sideways spread of daylight. This is the result of using a very simple computer program, which employs the algorithm of the BRE 'split flux' method. Today there are a large number of computer programs, using a variety of algorithms, the most sophisticated ones based on ray-tracing techniques, which can present the results in photo-realistic internal views, with an indication of graded illuminance distribution on room surfaces.

The split flux method of daylight factor calculation is based on the assumption of an overcast sky, originally of uniform luminance, but later using the 'CIE sky' luminance distribution (as in eq. 2.5 above). It has been shown (Robledo *et al.*, 1999) that even with overcast skies (cloud cover 7–8 oktas), the zenith luminance itself changes as a function of solar altitude:

$$L_Z = 0.0803 + 10.54597\,a - 0.6364\,a^3 \text{ (in kcd/m}^2) \tag{2.15}$$

where a = tanALT.

The annual variation of L_Z (for Madrid) is shown by Fig. 2.34.

The most recent daylight prediction programs include a much more sophisticated sky model and consider not only the diffused daylight entering the room, but also beam sunlight and its internal lighting effects. The lighting would thus vary not only with the location and sky conditions, but also with the time of day.

SUPERLITE can initially calculate outdoor illuminance, then it produces indoor illuminances under different sky conditions. SUPERLINK can predict lighting energy savings.

RADIANCE is perhaps the best-known program to produce photo-realistic images representing daylight distribution and it can do this in hourly time-steps. SUPERLITE 2.0 has an integrated CAD model. In several instances daylight simulation is included in a broader design package (e.g. ECOTECT) and some are attached to existing CAD programs (e.g. LIGHTSCAPE to AUTOCAD). PERFECT LITE and LIGHTSOFT are for electric lighting design only (see also Section 1.4.1 for thermal programs).

GENELUX, and particularly DELight, are intended for early stages of the design process. The latter has an easy-to-use graphic input/output system. Several of these programs (e.g. ADELINE) have a model that can be used for both daylighting and electric lighting design (see e.g. the report by IEA/SHC Task 21 Daylighting Buildings, *Survey of Simple Design Tools*, The Fraunhofer Institute, Stuttgart).

A photo-realistic output is certainly an impressive presentation tool, but should only be used as a design tool if its workings, its algorithms and its assumptions are fully understood. Responsibility for the performance of a building lies with the building designer, and not with the authors of the program.

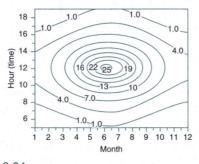

2.34

Zenith luminance isopleths in kcd/m²
Hour × month graph

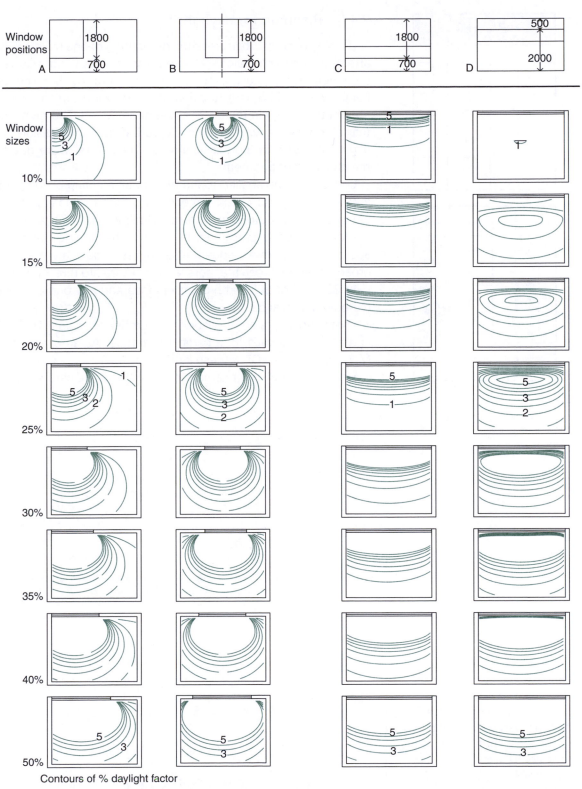

Contours of % daylight factor

2.35

A study of daylight distribution. Column A: height and left jamb fixed, width variable; B: height fixed, centreline of window is centreline of room; C: full width, sill fixed, head variable; D: full width, head fixed, sill variable. Each variant is examined with sizes 10 to 50% of wall area (after T. Yamaguchi, 1983). Originally each plan was A4 size.

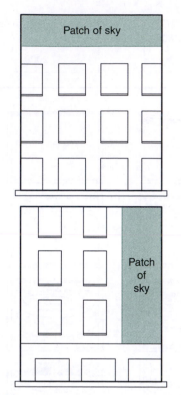

2.36
The patch of sky visible through a window: either could be acceptable

2.4.5 Planning for daylight

In densely built-up urban areas the daylighting of one building can be adversely affected by other buildings. The concept of 'right to light' emerged already in the nineteenth century, especially in relation to row housing: the permissible height was limited as a function of street width. In the second half of the twentieth century in the UK this was superseded. The rationale adopted was that a very high tower may be allowed, if the sky is visible to the side of it (Fig. 2.36). Sets of 'permissible height indicators' were devised to facilitate the checking of geometry.

One set can be applied to the front of an existing building (to the sill of the lowest window) to check a proposed building opposite, another set to the boundary or the street centreline. Outside the 'V'-shaped limits (wedges) any obstruction is permitted, but within the wedge height restrictions will apply. With a narrow wedge the height restrictions are quite stringent, with a broader wedge, these are more lenient. There are three indicators in each set, with 20°, 45° or 90° width of acceptance and any one of these can be used to show compliance.

These indicators are available in a number of scales (1:200, 1:500, 1:1250) and each set is valid for a particular latitude. As an example, Method sheet M.2.5 gives a set (D) of these indicators.

Fig. 2.37 shows an example of how these indicators are used. Both the

The existing block, from its ends to points A and B respectively receives enough light, passing by the sides of the proposed block.

The most critical point is C, half-way between A and B.

The most permissive indicator 'D' shows a permissible height of 13 m at point 'x' (measured from sill level of the ground floor at point C.

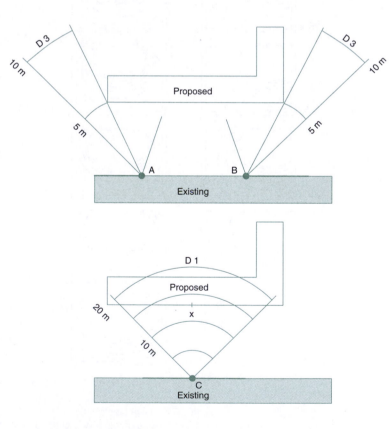

2.37
Use of permissible height indicators.

technique and the criteria behind the technique are under continued review, as it is not so much a technical, rather a socio-economic issue.

2.4.6 Control of sunlight

Solar geometry has been discussed in some detail in Section 1.4.1 and Method sheet M.1.1 gives all the necessary algorithms. Here the subject is the lighting effect of solar radiation (often referred to as *beam sunlighting*) and its control.

Climatic data, such as the hours of clear sunshine, can give an indication of the available resource, or the magnitude of the sunlight problem. Solar irradiation data could be converted to luminous quantities by using luminous efficacy values (such as discussed in Section 2.3.1 and Method sheet M.2.1).

In dominantly overcast cool climates most people would welcome sunlight, whenever it is available. Where glare or excessive contrast may be a problem, the designer must consider the situation: are the occupants free to exercise behavioural adjustments (e.g. draw the blinds or curtains, or move away from the sun-lit area of the room)? If not, what are the consequences of direct sunlight?

If it is found that sunlight must be controlled, the first question is: will the sun reach the window considered, or will it be obstructed by external objects, such as other buildings?

The techniques presented in Section 2.3.4 and Method sheet M.2.2 are useful in assessing the duration of obstruction and exposure of a selected point. When the critical time is selected, then the extent of sun penetration can be examined, assuming that weather conditions are such that there will be sunshine available. This is a purely geometrical task.

The sun's position in relation to the window is to be established first. The horizontal shadow angle (HSA) at the time in question is the azimuth difference between the sun's direction and the orientation (see Method sheet M.1.1). The solar altitude (ALT) must be projected onto a plane perpendicular to the window, to get the vertical shadow angle (VSA, as shown e.g. in Fig. 1.49 and Method sheet M.1.1). Once these two angles are known, the sun penetration, the sunlit patch on the floor or on the work-plane, can be constructed, as shown in Fig. 2.38.

A beam of solar radiation incident on a window pane may produce an irradiance of up to over 450 W/m².

This depends on geographical latitude and orientation, e.g. in equatorial latitudes, such as Nairobi, an east- or west-facing wall can receive up to 550 W/m², and a north or south wall only some 250 W/m² while at higher latitudes, such as Stockholm, an east or west wall can go up to 200 W/m² only and the south-facing one can exceed 350 W/m².

With a glass transmittance of 0.78, the above 450 W/m² would be reduced to 350 W/m². If the luminous efficacy of this is taken as 100 lm/W (as an average value), the illuminance produced will be some 35,000 lx. In such a situation the general illuminance is also increased, perhaps to 1000 lx. So the contrast is 35: 1. This is too much for comfort. The occupants must be given the option

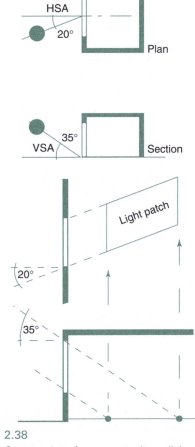

2.38
Construction of sun penetration: a light patch on the floor

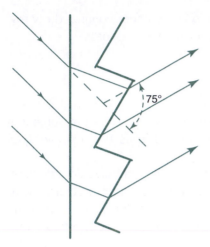

2.39
Prismatic glass for beam sunlighting with a diversion angle of 75°

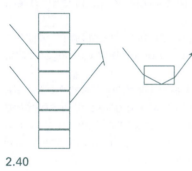

2.40
Laser grooved acrylic sheet

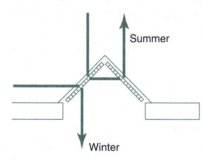

2.41
Laser-grooved roof light: at a low angle the sun is admitted, at high angle excluded

of some control, such as a curtain or blind. It is, however, likely that irradiance would be controlled for thermal reasons, preferably by some external shading devices, possibly by some adjustable mechanisms.

The use of tinted (heat absorbing or reflective) glasses may provide a remedy; they can avoid glare and reduce sunlight. The problem is that they affect diffuse light as much as beam light and that their properties are fixed, they have no selectivity in time: they perform the same way in winter as in summer, and they would reduce daylighting even when it is scarce.

A fixed control should only be used where its necessity is beyond any doubt, otherwise it may be perceived by the users as 'dictatorial'. Some architects adopt the attitude (not just in the lighting context) that they know best what is good for the user. They would argue that one visits a doctor for advice and not to tell him/her what therapy should be prescribed. Others may perceive this as professional arrogance. It is always useful to allow some degree of control to the user, be it an adjustable thermostat, an adjustable shading device or just a set of blinds.

Even automatic (motorised) louvres have been shown to be disliked by occupants of offices, as they seem to take away the freedom of choice of the users.

2.4.6.1 Beam sunlighting
Beam sunlighting is very useful in areas of the building that are not reached by daylighting through side windows. Several techniques are in use:

1 *Prismatic glass* is often used, normally for the top one-third of a window to divert the beam of sunlight (by refraction) upwards, to the ceiling, which will then diffuse it to the rear part of the room (Fig. 2.39).
2 *Laser-grooved acrylic sheets*, divided into small elements by laser cuts to some 90% of the thickness, which will serve the same purpose partly by refraction, but mainly by full internal reflection in each element (Fig. 2.40). These have a particular relevance for roof lights in low latitude climates, where the midday sun can be quite a problem. In a prismatic roof light they can completely reject high altitude (near zenith) radiation, but would admit the morning and late afternoon sunlight (Fig. 2.41).
3 *Light shelves* have been used for similar purposes for many years. In its simplest form this would be a horizontal element (an extended transom) across the window at a height of about 2.1 m, with a reflective upper surface, which directs the light up to the ceiling (Fig. 2.42). These would work well in a fairly high room (≈ 3 m). If mounted externally, they could also serve as a shading device for the lower part of the window, but it may be difficult to keep the top surface clean. The problem is less serious if mounted internally.

Many varieties of such light shelves exist. Some have a specular top surface, some are diffusing. Partially reflecting semi-transparent materials have also been used. Various clever profiles have been developed to respond to the changing solar altitude. Others are adjustable, to compensate for summer–winter difference in the sun's path. One system provides seasonal adjustment by using a flexible reflective film with a 'V'-shaped shelf (Fig. 2.43).

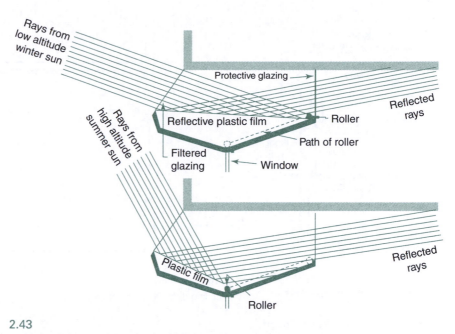

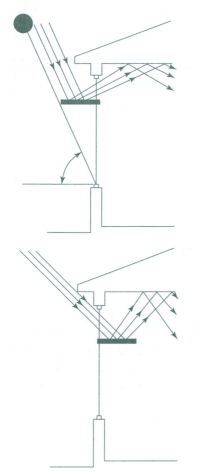

2.42
External and internal light shelves

2.43
A fully enclosed light shelf with a flexible reflective film (the 'Valra' system)

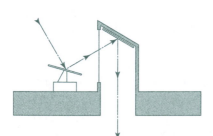

2.44
Heliostat for beam sunlighting

Beam sunlighting is also used with roof lights. Fig. 2.44 shows a heliostat (a motorised system, the mirror tracking the sun) and a fixed mirror that can direct the solar beam downwards where it may enter the room through a diffuser. Such a system serving a single-storey building (or the top floor of a multistorey building) can have an efficiency of around 50%. This means that if a solar beam of 60 klx is incident on the primary mirror of 1 m², of the 60 klm light flux some 30 klm is emitted by the ceiling diffuser, which can produce an average illuminance of 300 lx over a 100 m² area of the work plane.

A system of mirrors and 'light tubes' (or pipes, or ducts) would allow the use of such systems over several storeys (Fig. 2.45). These light tubes are made of some highly polished material, or lined with a reflective film. A light tube of an elongated oblong section can have 'tapping off' mirrors at several levels and for each of these its size is reduced.

Such a system can have an efficiency over 25% measured from light incident on the primary collector mirror to that emitted by all ceiling diffusers. This efficiency depends on the quality of the reflective surfaces and on how well the light beam is collimated. Unfortunately the system will work only when clear sunlight is available, so its success very much depends on weather conditions. One must also have a stand-by electric lighting system. However, in reasonably sunny climates, it can save operating energy and cost.

A version of light tubes is the 'anidolic ceiling' (non-imaging reflective duct). This has an upward-looking 'collector' at the outer end, a 3–4 m-long duct within the ceiling space (Fig. 2.46) and a light outlet in the ceiling, to contribute light to the rear part of the room. This can be effective also under overcast conditions, as it 'sees' the upper part of the sky, which is of a greater luminance.

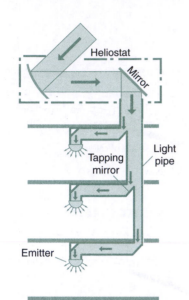

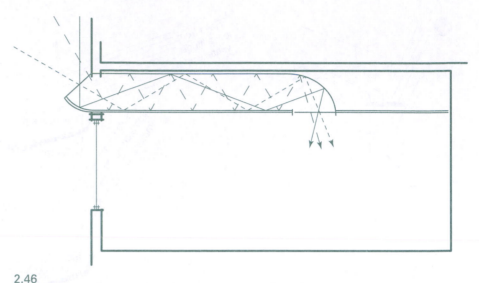

2.46

A ceiling duct: 'anidolic' ceiling

2.45

Beam sunlighting by heliostat and light pipes

2.47

A concentrator + optical fibre lighting system

The idea of using optical fibres to convey light of some concentration was suggested by a group of my students in 1975. Fig. 2.47 is reproduced from their original sketch. Since then several research teams have worked on such ideas and recently a group reported on a precision-engineered mini-dish (200 mm diameter) connected to an optical fibre conductor of 1 mm diameter, which has successfully produced a concentrated beam of 11 kilo-suns (11 000 suns!) conveyed to a diffuser at a distance of 20 m. This technique certainly has a future.

2.4.7 The daylight utilisation factor

DUF brings in the time factor for the performance analysis of daylighting/sunlighting and various control systems (Robbins, 1986). The space (room) considered is divided into control zones: the area nearest to windows is zone 1 and the one receiving least daylight/sunlight is the highest number. The analysis is carried out for each zone separately.

A design illuminance is set (E_d). The time considered is the working day, 8:00–17:00. The term duf_r is the fraction of this period when daylight can 'replace' (obviate the need for) electric lighting (Fig. 2.48), when the internal illuminance (E_i) without electric lighting is adequate ($E_i > E_d$). The fraction of time when E_i is less than adequate, but can still provide a useful contribution, 'supplementing' the electric lighting is referred to as duf_s and the daylight utilisation factor is the sum of these two:

$$DUF = duf_r + duf_s \qquad (2.16)$$

and, by definition, $duf_r + duf_s + ND = 1$, where ND is the no-daylight fraction. On the basis of this, a sophisticated control strategy and economic analysis of the benefits of daylighting can be (and has been) built up.

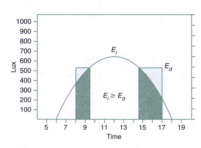

2.48

Interpretation of DUF: centre part daylight alone, dark shaded: daylight as supplement

2.5 ELECTRIC LIGHTING

To clarify the terminology: **lamp** is the source of light (bulb or globe are not technical terms). The lamp is usually inside a **luminaire** (which in the past was often referred to as a light fitting), though many lamps can be used without a luminaire, and are just fitted into a lamp holder. *Lamp holders* are the electrical connectors, into which the lamp is inserted or screwed. The generally used ones are the BC (bayonet caps) or the ES (Edison screw), as well as bi-pin plugs and sockets used for halogen lamps, but many other types are available for specialised purposes.

2.5.1 Lamps

The earliest electric light source was the carbon-arc lamp, invented in the early nineteenth century. Two carbon rod electrodes were connected to DC electricity (originally to batteries). First, they are in contact, to start the current flow, but then are pulled apart, as the gas (initially: air) is ionised and an arc of discharge develops. Various automated systems were developed to do this, but later fixed rods were introduced, and instead of the variable gap, a variable voltage was employed: a high voltage DC to start the arc, then reducing to normal operating voltage. A variable resistance was often used to control the lamp current. These produced very large quantities of light of a rather harsh nature, thus they were mostly used in open-air situations (railway stations, sports fields), or in factories. The early film industry used these for the lighting of studios as well as in early film projectors.

By the end of the nineteenth century, thousands were in use in the UK, Europe and the USA. Later tungsten electrodes replaced the carbon rods and were enclosed in a glass globe filled with argon (or some other inert gas), with a complicated control circuitry. The arc itself is of several thousand degrees temperature and the glass enclosure can be at 500°C. Argon-arc (or krypton- or xenon-arc) lamps are still used for specialised applications. Fig. 2.49 is an example of a modern xenon-arc lamp.

Modern electric lamps make use of two different processes of light generation: *thermo-luminescence* and *electro-luminescence* (e.g. gas discharge). The former is used in *incandescent* lamps. These have a thin wire (usually tungsten, or the German name: wolfram) filament, with a high resistance, which is heated by the electric current passing through it. These operate around 2700–3000°K temperature. To prevent oxidation of the filament, it is enclosed in a glass envelope, in a vacuum or partial vacuum with some small quantity of inert gas (krypton, argon, or xenon). The life expectancy of these lamps is around 1000 hours.

Most of the emission of incandescent lamps (up to 95%) is in the infra-red region, i.e. radiant heat. Their luminous efficacy is 10 to 18 lm/W.

In operation, some of the tungsten evaporates and condenses on the inside of the glass bulb, causing a slight blackening. To allow higher temperature operation (and smaller lamp size), some halogen elements (iodine, bromine) can be added. These adsorb the tungsten vapour and deposit it back on to the filament. The enclosure of these *tungsten-halogen* lamps is quartz, to withstand higher temperatures and quick changes of temperature. These are

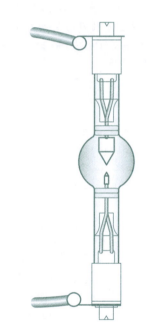

2.49
A 2 kW xenon-arc lamp: XE/D

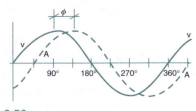

2.50

The effect of inductive load: the current is delayed

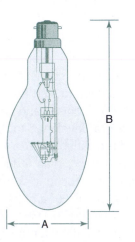

2.51

A typical mercury lamp, 160W A = 76 mm, B = 175 mm

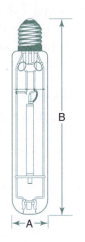

2.52

A high pressure tubular sodium lamp (SONT, 70 W) A = 71 mm, B = 154 mm

available in tubular (double-ended) and single-ended (two-pin) form, both for mains voltage (120–240 V) and low voltage (12–24 V) versions, from 20 W up to 2000 W size. Their efficacy is slightly better than the above: 16–23 lm/W.

Discharge lamps are a particular application of electroluminescence. They have no filament; light is produced by excitation of the gas or metallic vapours (mercury or sodium) contained in the lamp. The ordinary fluorescent tube is in fact an arc-lamp filled with mercury vapour. They need a device to start the discharge between the electrodes. The discharge is a chain reaction, exponentially increasing, so a device is needed to limit the current, otherwise the lamp would short the circuit. This can be a resistive ballast or an inductive load with a high impedance. If the latter is used, a power factor correction device is needed (see Fig. 2.53).

In direct current V × A = W (power is the product of current and potential). With an alternating current and an inductive load (a motor or any electromagnetic coil), this would delay the current behind the voltage changes (Fig. 2.50), so the actual useful load (W) is less than the V × A product. If the full cycle is 360°, the delay or phase angle is φ and cos φ is referred to as the power factor. Thus

$$\text{Power factor} = \cos \phi = \frac{\text{actual useful load (W)}}{\text{apparent load (V} \times \text{A)}}$$

With no phase lag φ = 0, cos φ = 1, but with a heavy inductive load, φ may be as much as 60° and the power factor can go down to 0.5. Most supply authorities set a limit of 0.9. The correction device is a capacitor connected in parallel, which accelerates the current with respect to voltage.

Mercury lamps (MB) have a very discontinuous spectrum but a high efficacy (up to 85 lm/W). The spectrum can be improved by a fluorescent coating of the inner surface of glass (MBF) lamps. A tungsten filament may improve the red end of the spectrum and serve as the current limiting device (MBT).

Fig. 2.51 shows a typical mercury lamp and Fig. 2.52 is a high pressure sodium (tubular) lamp (SONT), which gives a slightly better spectrum than the low pressure SOX lamps, which are practically monochromatic yellow. Efficacies are 90–140 lm/W.

Fig. 2.53 shows a control circuit for a fluorescent lamp, but many others are possible. Fluorescent tubes are actually low-pressure mercury lamps, emitting UV radiation. A fluorescent coating on the inside of the tube absorbs this and re-emits it at visible wavelengths.

Lamps are characterised by their electrical load (W) and by their light emission, both in quantity and quality. The quantitative measure is their light emission in lumens (the term *lamp lumens* is often used). Data sheet D.2.10 shows some typical values. The qualitative measure is their colour appearance and – more importantly – their colour rendering.

Incandescent lamps have a continuous emission spectrum and are adequately characterised by the colour temperature. This is 2700–3000°K for general service incandescent lamps, up to 3200°K for photographic or TV studio (halogen) lamps.

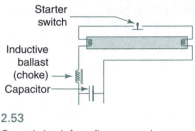

2.53

Control circuit for a fluorescent lamp

Gas discharge lamps have a discontinuous, often 'spiky' spectrum. The extreme case is the low pressure sodium lamp which has a practically mono-chromatic emission in the 580–590 nm range, which appears to be an orange/yellow colour and has the worst colour rendering properties. The emission of a discharge lamp is determined by the gas and metallic vapour used, which is mostly in the UV range, but modified by a fluorescent (phosphorous) coating on the inside of the glass enclosure. This absorbs the UV and re-emits the same energy in visible wavelengths, (depending on the phosphorous com-pound), hence the large range of lamp colours available.

Various colour rendering indices are in use, some quite complicated, but for general purposes a set of simple adjectives is quite sufficient, such as those used in Table 2.4. The CIE colour rendering index (CRI) has a scale up to 100. Table 2.5 shows how the CRI matches the five categories of tasks from the colour rendering viewpoint and Table 2.6 indicates the CRI values of several lamp types.

A recently developed application of electro-luminescence is the LED lamp. Light emitting diodes are solid state semiconductor devices (e.g. silicon alloys, indium phosphide (InP), gallium nitride (GaN) or gallium arsenide phosphide, (GaAsP)). These would have an 'electron hole' separated from electrons by (e.g.) a 'p − n junction'. When switched on, the electrons become 'excited', and recombine with the hole and, in the process, photons are emitted.

An LED device is very small, less than 1 mm^2. LEDs have been used for electronic displays, e.g. for pocket calculators, since about 1968. Later many

Table 2.4 Colour properties of tubular fluorescent lamps

Lamp name	Colour rendering	Colour appearance	CCTK	Efficacy (F) lm/W	Uses/remarks
White	Fair	Average	3400	70	Most efficient for general lighting
Plus white	Good	Average	3600	67	General lighting, good colour rendering
Warm white	Fair	Warm	3000	69	General lighting, good efficiency
Daylight (cool white)	Fair	Cool	4300	67	General lighting, to blend with daylight
Natural	Good	Average	4000	52	General lighting for shops, offices
De luxe natural	Good	Warm	3600	38	Same with red content for food shops
Kolor-rite	Excellent	Average	4000	46	Best colour rendering for general lighting
Northlight (colour matching)	Excellent	Cool	6500	42	For matching materials, colours
Artificial daylight	Excellent	Cool	6500	30	For analytical colour matching
Home-lite	Good	Warm	2600	62	To create a 'warm' atmosphere

Table 2.5 Categories of colour rendering tasks (what is needed)

	Task	CRI
1A	accurate colour matching	90–100
1B	good colour rendering	80–89
2	moderate colour rendering	60–79
3	colour rendering of little significance	40–59
4	colour rendering of no importance	20–39

Table 2.6 Colour rendering indices (CRI) of some lamp types

Lamp type	CRI
Incandescent	100
Tungsten halogen	100
Fluorescent, white (worst)	15
Fluorescent, northlight 'colour-matching' (best)	85
Sodium, high pressure (best)	70
Sodium, low pressure (worst)	0
LEDs of various types (white	70–85

2.54
A multiple LED tube and an LED downlighter

inventions made LEDs usable for VDUs (replacing the CRTs*) and also for significant light emissions, combining many LEDs in one lamp. The colour of light emitted depends on the 'band gap'. White light was initially produced by combining red, green and blue LEDs (RGB white) but later phosphorous coatings were introduced to absorb the coloured emission and re-emit it as white light (as happens also in fluorescent lamps).

Today LED lamps are available in many forms, to replace incandescent lamps (BC or ED caps) or instead of fluorescent tubes, as well as by-pin caps to suit halogen lamp luminaires. While the luminous efficacy of incandescent lamps is 14–18 lm/W, Table 2.4 shows the efficacy of fluorescent lamps: 30–70 lm/W, but LED lamps are between 70 and 100, and can be as high as 150 lm/W. They use only 10–20% of the electricity of what is used by incandescent lamps to produce the same quantity of light. Their 'carbon footprint' is also reduced by some 85%. Their life expectancy is about a hundred times greater. They are now widely used, e.g. for car indicator lights and even headlights. Numerous local authorities have introduced LED lights for street-lighting and some claim that their energy use is reduced by 80%.

It has been suggested that the rapid growth of LED production and sales signals the end of the incandescent lamp era (the 'good old light bulb') which dominated the lighting scene for some 125 years (Edison patented it in 1878). Compared to these, the CO_2 emission due to LED lighting is reduced by 85% (to 15%). Fig. 2.54 shows some examples of now available compound tubular LED lamps, and Fig. 2.55 shows them in 'bulb' form. This is a rapidly developing field and new products are expected with increasing frequency. These lamps include all the necessary control circuits.

2.5.2 Luminaires

In the simplest case, the lamp is held by a lamp holder, without any enclosure, shade or light directing device. This is the case with the internally silvered (reflector) lamps, which can be narrow beam *spotlights* or *floodlights* with a broader spread. (The *crown silvered lamps* are used with a shallow parabolic reflector as narrow-beam spotlights. See Fig. 2.56.) There is a very large variety of luminaires available and the choice is (unfortunately) often based on the 'look', the appearance of these, rather than on their lighting performance.

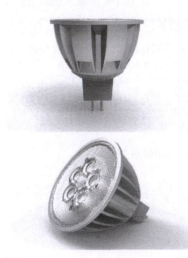

2.55
Some multiple LED lamps

* CRT = cathode ray tube; VDU = visual display unit.

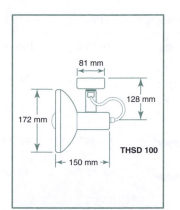

81 mm

128 mm

172 mm

THSD 100

|← 150 mm →|

2.56
A crown silvered narrow beam spotlight

Essentially there are two basic types: those with fully enclosed lamps, and those with partial enclosure or light directing device.

The most popular lamps are the 1200 mm fluorescent tubes and the largest variety of luminaires is available for these. The old 40 W/38 mm diameter tubes have largely been replaced by the 36 W/26 mm diameter ones, but they use the same bi-pin ends, have the same lumen outputs and fit the same luminaires.

Luminaires can be characterised photometrically in relation to the lumen output of the lamps they contain, by the light output ratio:

$$LOR = \frac{\text{flux output of luminaire}}{\text{flux output of lamp}(-s)} \qquad \text{expressed usually as a \%}$$

and this may be divided into upward and downward parts (divided by the horizontal plane across the centre of the lamp), e.g.

lamp output	1000 lm		100%
up	300 lm	ULOR	30%
down	500 lm	DLOR	50%
luminaire output	800 lm	LOR	80%
(absorbed in luminaire	200 lm		20%)

Alternatively, the output of the luminaire can be taken as the basis (the 100%) and the flux fractions can be defined as UFF upward and DFF downward, defining the flux fraction ratio

$$FFR = \frac{UFF}{DFF}$$

e.g   continuing the above example:

luminaire output	800 lm		100%
upward flux	300 lm	UFF	37.5%
downward flux	500 lm	DFF	62.5%

flux fraction ratio $$FFR = \frac{37.5}{62.5} = 0.6$$

(the same ratio is given by the above $$\frac{ULOR}{DLOR} = \frac{30}{50} = 0.6)$$

Fig. 2.57 shows some general descriptive terms used for luminaires and symbols used for these on plans.

A more precise definition of a lamp/luminaire combination (or a lamp acting as a luminaire) is given by the *polar curves* (or polar intensity diagrams). For luminaires of a rotational shape (symmetrical about any vertical plane laid across the axis of the luminaire), a semi-circular polar diagram is used on which the source intensity (cd) viewed from different directions (view angles) is plotted (Fig. 2.58). For elongated luminaires, two such semi-circles are put together, the left side for the cross-section and the right side showing the distribution lengthwise (along the longitudinal vertical plane) (Fig. 2.59).

For a lamp alone or for a luminaire with a specified lamp, the polar curves give the actual source intensity values. Where the same luminaire can be used with a range of different lamps (e.g. different fluorescent tubes), the

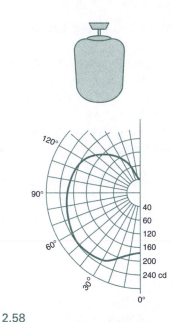

2.58

A diffuser luminaire and its polar curve

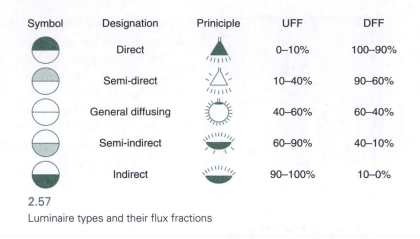

Symbol	Designation	Priniciple	UFF	DFF
	Direct		0–10%	100–90%
	Semi-direct		10–40%	90–60%
	General diffusing		40–60%	60–40%
	Semi-indirect		60–90%	40–10%
	Indirect		90–100%	10–0%

2.57

Luminaire types and their flux fractions

polar curves would give the values per 1000 lm lamp output, which then has to be adjusted for the lumen output of the lamp used. Data sheet D.2.8 shows polar curves for some typical luminaires/lamps.

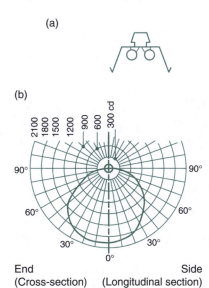

End
(Cross-section)

Side
(Longitudinal section)

2.59

An open trough luminaire and its polar curves

EXAMPLE 2.2   READING OF POLAR CURVES

From the polar curve (Fig. 2.59), the source intensity at 20° view angle is read as 1950 cd (interpolated between the 1800 and 2100 cd arcs). If a 'warm white' lamp is used which gives an output of 2700 lm, the intensity has to be adjusted as

$$I_{20} = 1950 \times \frac{2700}{1000} = 5265 \text{ cd},$$

but if it is used with a 'Kolor-rite' tube, which has an output of 1800 lm (D.2.9), then

$$I_{20} = 1950 \times \frac{1800}{1000} = 3510 \text{ cd}$$

In the past 30 years or so, a series of *compact fluorescent lamps* have become available (Fig. 2.60). These fit into ordinary BC or ES lamp holders and can now be inserted into most luminaires originally designed for incandescent lamps. Their luminous efficacy is some five times that of incandescent lamps, e.g. the same flux output is obtained from the two types.

compact fluorescent	incandescent
10 W	50 W
15 W	75 W
18 W	90 W

With these, all the control gear (starter, choke, power factor corrector) are incorporated in the base of the lamp. Lamp life is claimed to be about eight times that of incandescent lamps, some 8000 hours. The use of such compact fluorescent lamps (instead of incandescent) can result in energy savings up to 80%, thus it is an important contribution to sustainability.

2.60
Compact fluorescent lamps

2.5.3 Local lighting: point-by-point method

The quantitative design of local lighting from a single source is simply the application of the inverse square law (eq. 2.3), corrected by the cosine law for angle of incidence.

EXAMPLE 2.3   SPOTLIGHTING OF A HORIZONTAL SURFACE

For an internally silvered spotlight aimed at a point on a horizontal surface (Fig. 2.61), we read from Data sheet D.2.8 the intensity of I = 3800 cd along the axis of the lamp (0° viewing angle), and if the angle of incidence is 45°, with a distance of 3 m, we get an illuminance

$$E = \cos INC \times \frac{I}{d^2} = \cos 45° \times \frac{3800}{3^2} = 299 \text{ lx.}$$

EXAMPLE 2.4   DIFFUSE LIGHTING ON A HORIZONTAL SURFACE

An opal diffuser luminaire is mounted at 1.75 m above the work-plane, with its axis vertical, and the illuminance at 1 m to one side of the aiming point is to be found (Fig. 2.62). First, find the viewing angle:

$$\theta = \arctan \frac{1}{1.75} = 30° \text{ the geometry is such that INC} = \theta = 30°$$

and the distance is $d = \sqrt{1^2 + 1.75^2} = 2$ m
from the polar curve (Fig. 2.58), the source intensity is found as $I_{30} = 230$ cd

$$E = \cos 30 \times \frac{230}{2^2} = 50 \text{ lx.}$$

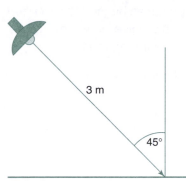

2.61
Spotlight on a horizontal surface (example 2.3)

For a linear source (of 'infinite' length), the illuminance is proportional to the distance, so instead of the inverse square law we have the inverse distance law: $E = \frac{I}{d}$.

EXAMPLE 2.5   LINEAR LAMP FOR A NOTICEBOARD

We have a noticeboard illuminated by a row of tubular lamps (battens) from a distance of 2.5 m, which is continuous beyond the edges of the board by the same length as the distance of 2.5 m (thus it can be considered as 'infinite'). The source intensity is read from Data sheet D.2.9 as 150 cd, corrected for a warm white lamp:

$$I = 150 \times \frac{3800}{1000} = 570 \text{ cd} \qquad \theta = 30°$$

at a point on the board where the angle of incidence is 30°, the illuminance will be

$$E = \cos 30 \times \frac{570}{2.5} = 197 \text{ lx.} \qquad INC = \theta.$$

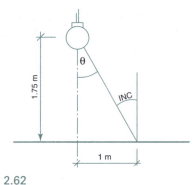

2.62
Diffuser lighting a horizontal surface (example 2.4)

If two or more lamp /luminaires contribute to the lighting of a point, the illuminance from each has to be calculated and these illuminances are simply additive. This is the basis of the *point-by-point method* of lighting design. This is quite simple and manageable for one or two lamps contributing to the

Table 2.7 Lamp power required: the Watt method

Lamp type		$W/(m^2 lx)$
Incandescent	Open enamelled reflector	0.150
	General diffusing	0.175
Mercury	Industrial reflector	0.065
Fluorescent, white	Open trough	0.040
	Enclosed diffusing	0.050
	Louvred, recessed	0.055
Fluorescent, de luxe warm white	Enclosed diffusing	0.080
	Louvred, recessed	0.090

lighting of, say, a noticeboard, but if we have a large room (e.g. an office or a classroom) with many light sources, calculations for the whole work-plane become cumbersome. However, the method can provide the algorithm for a computer program.

For general lighting a rough estimate can be produced by the *Watt method*. This is based on a table (such as Table 2.7), which gives the lamp power requirement (W) per unit floor area, per lux illuminance required.

EXAMPLE 2.6   THE WATT METHOD

Given a large general office of 120 m², from Data sheet D.2.6, the required illuminance is 400 lx. We choose fluorescent white lamps in enclosed diffuser luminaires. The total wattage of the lighting will be:

120 m² × 400 lux × 0.050 W/(m²lx) = 2400 W.

If 40W fluorescent lamps are used, we need 2400/40 = 60, and with twin-tube luminaires we need 30.

Somewhat similar is the concept of 'unit power density' (UPD) in W/m², and long tables give UPD values for different room usages (Robbins, 1996). These are in fact products of recommended illuminance and the watt factors in Table 2.7. For the case of Example 2.6, the UPD is given as 14–25 W/m², without distinguishing lamp and luminaire type.

The alternative is to use the lumen method of general lighting design.

2.5.4   The lumen method

The lumen method (or total flux method) of general lighting design is applicable where a regular array of luminaires produces a uniform lighting over the work-plane. The criterion for uniformity is that at the point of least illuminance, it is no less than 70% of the maximum. In practice, this is provided by limiting the spacing of luminaires to 1.5 times the height of luminaires from the work-plane, i.e. the mounting height (H_m).

For a given system, the total lumen output of lamps is calculated, which is referred to as the *installed flux* (Φ_i) and the *flux received* on the work-plane will be (Fig. 2.63):

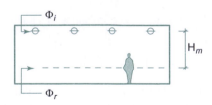

2.63

Interpretation of flux installed and flux received

$$\Phi_r = \Phi_i \times UF \times MF$$

then the illuminance is

$$E = \frac{\Phi_r}{A} \qquad (2.17)$$

where MF is the maintenance factor, to allow for the deterioration of the lamp, luminaire and room surfaces. In the absence of more accurate data, this is taken as 0.8. UF is the utilisation factor and the method hinges on finding the appropriate UF value.

The magnitude of UF depends on the following factors:

1 Properties of the luminaire: an enclosed luminaire or one with less than perfect internal reflectance will have a value much lower than an exposed lamp.
2 The DLOR (downward light output ratio) of the luminaire. Light emitted upwards will reach the work-plane only after reflection from room surfaces and some of it is absorbed in these surfaces. A larger DLOR normally means a higher UF.
3 Reflectance of room surfaces, which is more important if the DLOR is smaller, but can influence the lighting even with high DLOR values.
4 Geometrical proportions of the room, as expressed by the room index, the ratio of horizontal areas: L × W × 2 and vertical areas (L + W) × 2 × H_m, where H_m is the mounting height, from the work-plane to the luminaire (the multiplier 2 cancels out).

$$RI = \frac{L \times W}{(L+W) \times H_m} \qquad (2.18)$$

5 Direct ratio: how much of the downward emitted light reaches the work-plane directly (Fig. 2.64). This has a low value with a narrow and high room (small room index), but a high value for a wide room (large RI) and 'downlighter'-type luminaires.

Data sheet D.2.9 gives the UF values for some typical luminaires with specified DLOR, for various room reflectances and room indices. Most catalogues of luminaires would give similar tables. If an installation is to be designed, the above equation (eq. 2.17) is inverted:

- if an illuminance E is required, this is multiplied by the work-plane area to get the flux **to be received**, Φ_r;
- the type of luminaire is selected and the UF is found;
- the MF is taken as 0.8 (higher in very clean spaces, lower in dusty or dirty situations, or in the absence of regular cleaning);
- thus the flux **to be installed** will be

$$\Phi_i = \frac{\Phi_r}{UF \times MF}$$

Combining these steps we have a single expression:

$$\Phi_i = \frac{E \times A}{UF \times MF} \qquad (2.19)$$

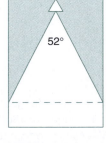

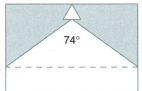

2.64
Interpretation of the direct ratio

Then we have to work back, divide the Φ_i by the output of one lamp to get the number of lamps required, decide whether single or a double lamp luminaire would be used, devise a luminaire layout (a ceiling plan) and check the spacing limits.

EXAMPLE 2.7   GENERAL LIGHTING FOR AN OFFICE

A general office space is 12 m × 9 m and 2.7 m high. The illuminance required (from Data sheet D.2.6) is 400 lx. Reflectances are: ceiling 0.7, walls 0.5. If the work-plane is at 0.8 m and ceiling-mounted luminaires are to be used, then H_m = 2.7 − 0.8 = 1.9 m, thus the room index will be:

$$RI = \frac{12 \times 9}{(12 + 9) \times 1.9} = \frac{108}{39.9} = 2.7$$

We select an enclosed plastic diffuser type luminaire, which has a DLOR of 0.5. In Data sheet D.2.9 we locate the column headed ρ ceiling 0.7 and within this the sub-heading for ρ walls 0.5. There are lines for RI 2.5 and 3, so we make a note of both UF values of 0.55 and 0.58 and interpolate:

$$\frac{0.58 - 0.55}{3 - 2.5} \times 0.2 = 0.012,$$

which is to be added to the lower value, thus

UF = 0.56 (two decimal precision is quite sufficient).

From eq. 2.14 the flux to be installed is:

$$\Phi_i = \frac{400 \times 12 \times 9}{0.56 \times 0.8} = 96\,429 \text{ lm}$$

For uniformity, the spacing limit (D.2.6) is 1.5 × H_m = 1.5 × 1.9 = 2.85 m.
   From Data sheet D.2.10 we see that 1200 mm fluorescent lamps are available from 1120 to 2800 lm output and select a medium quality for good colour rendering: for example, the Kolor-rite lamp with a flux output of 1800 lm. Of these, we may need 96 429 / 1800 = 54 lamps. We can have twin-tube luminaires, so we need 27 of these. We may have 7 rows of 4 luminaires, so the spacing may be 1.7 m in the 12 m length (0.9 m from the walls) and in the 9 m width the spacing would become 2.25 m (giving just over 1 m between ends of luminaires). Both are well within the 2.85 m limit.

Significant energy savings could be achieved with a composite lighting scheme (low level general + local) designed as demonstrated by Method sheet M.2.6.

2.5.5   Glare in artificially lit interiors

Glare, as a phenomenon affecting vision, has been discussed in Section 2.2.4. While in daylighting/sunlighting it is difficult to quantify glare (though some quantitative methods exist) and it is best to tackle the problem in qualitative terms, in electric lighting all the contributing factors are identifiable and controllable. For this, the well-developed quantitative methods will now be described. This approach is supported by the fact that under 'natural' light-

It has been argued that there is no such thing as 'artificial' light, thus this title should be 'electrically lit interiors'.

Light may not be artificial, but **lighting** certainly is, whether it is electrical or gas or using oil pressure-lamps. The term is used in contradistinction to daylighting, or 'natural' lighting.

ing conditions people seem to be more tolerant and adaptable, while in an artificially lit interior glare is more readily noticed and not willingly tolerated. A quantitative method is developed, with reasoning as follows:

1 Glare is a function of luminance ratios within the field of vision, but it is influenced by other factors:

$$g = f \frac{L_1}{L_2}$$

where L_1 is the higher luminance, of the potential glare source.

$\frac{L_1}{L_2}$ is the lower, the background luminance.

2 The coefficient f depends on several factors:
the size of the glare source, measured by the visual angle (solid angle) subtended by the source area, ω:

$$\omega = \frac{\text{area of glare source} (m^2)}{\text{square of its distance} (m^2)}$$

3 The position of the glare source, as measured by the position index (p) derived from the horizontal (ϕ) and vertical (θ) angle of displacement from the line of vision: p (ϕ,θ) so the above expression is empirically modified:

$$g = \frac{L_1^a \omega^b}{L_2 p^c}$$

and values for the three exponents suggested by various researchers are:

a = 1.6 to 2.2; b = 0.6 to 1.0; c = 1.6.

The IES (Illuminating Engineering Society) adopted the following expression for the *glare constant*:

$$g = \frac{L_1^{1.6} \omega^{0.8}}{L_2 p^{1.6}} \tag{2.20}$$

In many situations where the observers' line of vision cannot be determined, the position index (p) term can be omitted.

The 'glariness' of a given space can be expressed by the *glare index* (GI), after calculating the glare constant (g) for each potential glare source:

$$GI = 10 \times log_{10}(0.478 \times \Sigma g) \tag{2.21}$$

The probable subjective responses to situations described by this glare index are

GI = 0–10: imperceptible
GI = 10–16: perceptible
GI = 16–22: acceptable
GI = 22–28: uncomfortable
GI > 28–: intolerable

The least significant increment in GI is 3.

The acceptable level of glare depends on the visual task and on illuminance. Usually in a more exacting task, the higher illuminance would attract a stricter glare limit. The recommended limits are:

GI = 25: for most industrial tasks
GI = 22: for fine industrial tasks
GI = 19: inspection and offices
GI = 16: drawing offices and classrooms
GI = 13: sewing
GI = 10: very small instruments

Data sheet D.2.6 gives the recommended glare index limits alongside the illuminance values. Method sheet M.2.4 gives details of the calculation method.

The glare index system described above was developed in the 1950s and found general acceptance after the 1967 IES publication, Technical Report No. 10. In the USA several methods were used: the *Visual Comfort Probability* (VCP) system and the *Discomfort Glare Rating* (DGR) method. The Cornell formula is in fact quite similar to eq. 2.20 above:

$$g = \frac{L_1^{1.6} \omega^{0.8}}{L_2 + 0.07 \times \omega^{0.5} \times L_1}$$

The CIE is working to reconcile the British glare index method with the Scandinavian Einhorn formula and the American VCP system. Their current proposal for a Unified Glare Rating (UGR) system is also similar to eq. 2.20 above:

$$UGR = 8 \times \log \frac{0.25 \times L_1^2 \times \omega}{L_2 \times p^2} \tag{2.22}$$

The Australian Standard 1680 uses a luminance limiting method. Tables are given for source surface luminance limits for various situations and for lengthwise and crosswise view of the luminaires between 1 and 16 kcd/m². To avoid veiling reflections, Table 2.8 reproduces from the Standard the lowest limits for the E/L ratio:

$$\frac{E}{L} = \frac{\text{task illuminance}}{\text{source luminance}} = \frac{lx}{kcd/m^2}$$

This is, however, a luminaire selection method rather than glare evaluation.

Total avoidance of glare is not always desirable. In some situations monotony and uniformity can be relieved by a controlled amount of glare; it can create interest or 'sparkle'. Unscrupulous designers can use it to create striking psychological effects ('bedazzling' the viewer) such as an east-facing (sunlit) altar window in an otherwise dark church or the use of exposed high brightness small (tungsten-halogen) spotlights with chrome plated surfaces in a pop fashion boutique. (One academic even created a mathematical

Table 2.8 Minimum E/L ratios to limit veiling reflections

Light-coloured tasks with good contrast; only slightly glossy details, e.g. pencil on white paper, as in offices or schools	80
Light-coloured tasks with good contrast, with an overall gloss, e.g. pencil on coloured paper or tracing, reading glossy paper	160
Dark-coloured tasks with an overall gloss and light coloured tasks, with poor contrast, e.g. glossy photos, half-tone on glossy paper	800

expression – only half-jokingly – for the 'glitter quotient'.) The most extreme deliberate use of glare is in a dark night club, with glaring spot-lights, possibly with strobe lights, which produces an intoxicating, practically narcotic, effect.

To avoid the opposite effect, namely surfaces appearing 'too dark', the CIBSE* Code for Interior Lighting recommends that in offices, if work-plane illuminance is $E_w = 1$, then the walls should receive 0.3–0.7 E_w, the ceiling 0.3–0.9 E_w, the floor 0.2–0.4 E_w and the wall containing a window at least 0.6 E_w.

2.5.6 Integration/discussion

In side-lit rooms the level of daylighting rapidly drops with the increase of distance from the window. It often happens that daylighting near the window is quite sufficient, but not at the back of the room. The rear part of the room could be used for storage (e.g. filing cabinets) or visually less demanding functions (e.g. tea-making) but work areas may still be left with inadequate daylight. Probably the full electric lighting system would be switched on. The energy conservation (thus sustainability) requirement would dictate that daylighting be used whenever and as far as possible.

A simple solution is to arrange the electric lighting in rows parallel with the window wall and switch these rows on only as and when necessary (Fig. 2.66). It is rare to find side-lit spaces where daylight alone would be sufficient beyond a depth of about 2.5 times the window head height (from the work-plane). In this case there may be some permanent electric lighting at the rear of the room, hence the acronym PSALI (permanent supplementary artificial lighting of the interior).

It has been demonstrated that people prefer daylight to artificial light and they do like (perhaps even *need*) visual contact with the outside world and its continually changing lighting conditions. For all these reasons the principles of PSALI have been established as:

1 utilisation of daylight as far as practicable;
2 use of electric lighting to supplement the daylight in the interior parts of the room;
3 design of the lighting in such a way that the essentially daylit character of the room is retained.

The last of these principles sets a qualitative as well as a quantitative requirement. Warmer light (a lower colour temperature) is acceptable with low levels of illuminance. Here it should be comparable to daylight, which is of a colour temperature of 5000–6500°K. In situations where visual tasks are all important (drawing offices, laboratories) for precision work and good colour rendering, an 'artificial daylight' lamp (of 6500K) is advisable. In less critical situations a 'cool white' (of 4300°K) is acceptable.

The illuminance provided by the supplementary lighting should be comparable to the quantity of daylight available near the window, at the 2% DF

---

* Chartered Institute of Building Services Engineers.

contour. Above this, there would be no supplementary lighting, and below this, we would attempt to bring the illuminance up by artificial light input. The magnitude of this can be estimated as follows:

1 Determine the daylight zone, either as the 2% DF contour, or take the DF at 0.2 H distance from the window and multiply this by 0.1 (where H is the window head height above the work-plane).
2 Find the average DF_{av} for the rest of the room.
3 The illuminance to be added to this area is $E_{add} = 500 \times DF_{av}$.

One additional benefit of PSALI is that of correcting the illuminance vector. It has been mentioned (in Section 2.3.2) and shown (Fig. 2.18) that at some distance away from the window, the vector becomes near horizontal (whereas people's preference is for a vector altitude of at least 15–20°).

Fig. 2.65 is a reminder of the addition of vectorial quantities and it can be seen that the near-vertical light from ceiling-mounted luminaires at the back of the room would increase the vector altitude.

Fig. 2.66 shows a practical arrangement in diagrammatic terms. The electric lighting luminaires are arranged (e.g.) in five rows. At night one lamp (or line of lamps) would operate in each row. During the day, rows 1 and 2 would be switched OFF. Rows 3–5 will be switched ON. Daylight factor at 0.2 × H is 20%, 0.1 times this is 2%, which in this case is at 2 H distance. For the rest of the room, the DF_{av} is about 1%. $E_{add} = 500 \times 1 = 500$ lx. This is to be provided by three lamps, but in row 3 only two lamps are used, as here the DF is about 1.5% and to provide a smooth transition.

Commercial buildings (e.g. in the USA) use some 35–50% of the total electricity consumption for the purposes of lighting. By relying on daylighting (whenever available), up to 50% of this could be saved. The National Institute of Building Sciences (within their 'smart building' program) has introduced 'daylight-responsive' electric lighting controls, to achieve such savings. With such a reduction of electricity use, the heat output is also reduced, thus, 10–20% reduction in air conditioning cooling load also is achieved. A beautiful example of integration.

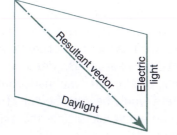

2.65

Addition of vectors (the parallelogram of vectors)

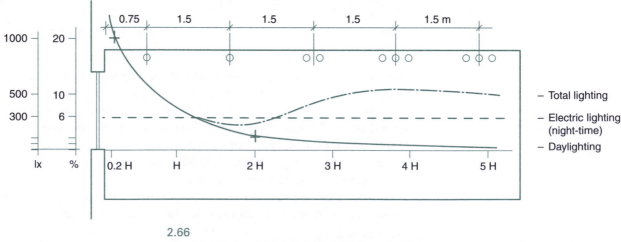

2.66

Switching arrangement in rows of luminaires, for PSALI

Integration of daylight control with the control of solar radiation input (for thermal reasons) is an important issue. This is true in cool or temperate climates where some passive solar heating system may be used (perhaps for some part of the year) which may create glary conditions, but especially so in a warm climate where the shading system is often overdesigned to exclude solar heating. The designer wants to be on 'the safe side'.

This is just as bad as inadequate shading. We may say that if daylight is reduced while heat gain is reduced, then so be it, but the room may become unduly dark and electric lighting may have to be used all day. This is not only wasting energy for lighting, but may also cause a significant addition to the thermal load. Unfortunately, the reason is the designer's lack of knowledge and skill. Sustainability would demand that the solar control be 'just right'.

If the orientation is correct and the window is facing the equator, it is easy to design a device for the right shading, making use of an automatic seasonal adjustment. With less than perfect orientation, often some degree of compromise may be necessary.

The designer has to consider a balance of benefits and disadvantages. Which is worse: having an undesirable sun penetration for some time of the year or having an overdesigned shading, thus suffering inadequate daylight for the rest of the year?

Besides lighting and solar heat gain other issues may have to be included in the balance equation, such as the view out, or the view in (privacy?), or indeed the effect of such devices on natural ventilation. The designer should be able to quantify all terms of such an equation, but experience may help to develop a sense of magnitude of these factors and may aid in making reasoned judgements in qualitative terms, without meticulous (and lengthy?) calculations in each instance.

The effect of daylight beyond the physical must not be forgotten. In some French studies it was shown that in various bird populations deprivation of daylight and sunlight led to a loss of sexual drive and reduced multiplication. Human populations are not immune from the effects of such deprivation.

Some years ago, as part of the SER (Schools Environment Research) project at the University of Michigan, Ann Arbor, USA, it was found that pupils' learning performance was much better in windowless classrooms with electric lighting than in others with windows and daylighting. The explanation offered was that pupils are not distracted by view through the windows. However, it was also found that prolonged stay in such windowless classrooms led to ill effects psychologically, possibly causing neurotic behaviour symptoms.

Attempts to explain these effects were pure speculation, but the need for daylighting, for contact with natural changes, to experience the circadian rhythm is well established.

Fortunately, this psychological need coincides with the need for energy conservation, for ecological as well as economic benefits. It is a need which must be considered when the first design ideas are formulated. Recognition of such needs led to the development of a pre-design tool, a 'forward analysis' method (as named by Otto Koenigsberger), namely the LT (Lighting and Thermal) method, which is the subject of the next section.

2.5.7 The LT method

Lighting is the second largest energy user in many buildings. In terms of percentage of total energy used, we have:

	%
hotels	9
banks	19
supermarkets	11
schools	9–12
factories	15
offices	20–50

As offices are among the largest users of lighting, often throughout the day, the LT method has been developed for office buildings (Baker & Steemers, 1995). It is not really a lighting design tool, but it gives a pre-design guidance for the energy-saving potential of daylighting (it is about the same level as the CPZ method, see Section 1.5.1, for thermal design). It is based on the assumption that daylighting can save energy used otherwise for electric lighting, but it would probably increase the thermal (including the solar) load. Hence the name: **L**ighting/**T**hermal (LT) analysis.

This is intended for office building design and it considers the 'passive zone', i.e. the area within 6 m of the external walls. A complex program has been written, that takes into account the energy (heat) flows (see Fig. 2.67) affected by the fenestration for this passive area. It will show the energy use (requirement) as a function of the window area, expressed as a 'percentage of the glazing ratio', in graphic form, such as that shown in Fig. 2.68. A series of such graphs have been produced for schools, colleges, offices and institutional buildings, for the north and south parts of the UK, for different orienta-

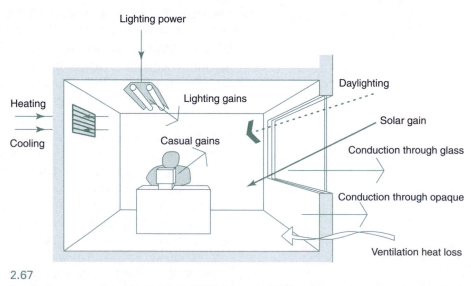

2.67
Energy flows considered in the LT model (Baker et al. 1999)

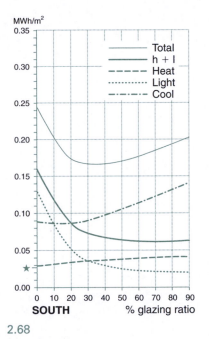

2.68

A typical LT graph

tions, for 150 to 500 lux illuminance, and various levels of internal load (from 10 to 50 W/m^2). The model is also available in spreadsheet form.

Fig. 2.68 is a typical example of such graphs for an office (for the south UK, a south-facing window and adjacent passive area, 300 lux illuminance and 15 W/m^2 internal load, casual gains). It shows that the cooling load substantially increases with the increase of glazing ratio, while the lighting and heating load decrease. The total load curve shows an optimum (in this case) around 30–40% glazing ratio. The vertical axis is in MWh/m^2 annual energy use.

Several modified versions of the LT spreadsheet have been produced, such as LTr, for refurbishment of non-domestic buildings or LTV, the model for warm climates which takes into account natural ventilation as well.

2.5.8 Lighting design strategies

For residential buildings the thermal factors dominate, lighting is not much of a problem. For offices and institutional buildings lighting and thermal design are of about the same weight. Passive thermal design and daylighting design contribute to sustainability:

- **Thermal design**: the integration of passive and active controls has been discussed in Section 1.6.5. Coordination with the NHVAC engineers is essential.
- **Lighting design**: the integration of daylighting and electric lighting has been outlined in Section 2.5.6.

The LT method gives some pre-design guidance for office buildings, valid for the stated assumptions, but even if it is not directly applicable, the thinking behind the formal method is worth considering.

DATA SHEETS AND METHOD SHEETS (LIGHT)

DATA SHEET D.2.1

Daylighting: utilisation factors for roof lights

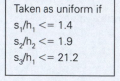

Taken as uniform if
$s_1/h_1 <= 1.4$
$s_2/h_2 <= 1.9$
$s_3/h_1 <= 21.2$

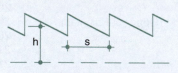

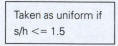

Taken as uniform if
$s/h <= 1.5$

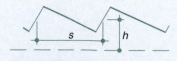

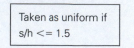

Taken as uniform if
$s/h <= 1.5$

ceiling	surface reflectances 0.7			0.5			0.3		
walls	0.5	0.3	0.1	0.5	0.3	0.1	0.5	0.3	0.1
RI	utilisation factors								
SHED ROOF									
0.6	0.34	0.30	0.27	0.34	0.30	0.27	0.30	0.27	0.27
0.8	0.40	0.39	0.36	0.40	0.39	0.36	0.39	0.36	0.35
1.0	0.45	0.423	0.41	0.44	0.42	0.41	0.42	0.41	0.38
1.25	0.50	0.47	0.46	0.50	0.47	0.45	0.47	0.45	0.44
1.5	0.52	0.49	0.47	0.51	0.49	0.47	0.49	0.46	0.46
2.0	0.57	0.55	0.53	0.56	0.53	0.52	0.53	0.52	0.51
2.5	0.59	0.56	0.55	0.59	0.56	0.55	0.55	0.52	0.52
3.0	0.62	0.60	0.59	0.62	0.59	0.58	0.59	0.58	0.56
4.0	0.64	0.63	0.61	0.64	0.63	0.61	0.61	0.60	0.60
5.0	0.68	0.65	0.65	0.66	0.65	0.63	0.63	0.62	0.62
infinite	0.76	0.76	0.76	0.74	0.74	0.74	0.73	0.73	0.71
SAW-TOOTH ROOF (VERTICAL)									
0.6	0.07	0.06	0.04	0.07	0.05	0.04	0.05	0.03	0.03
0.8	0.11	0.08	0.07	0.10	0.08	0.06	0.08	0.06	0.05
1.0	0.14	0.11	0.10	0.13	0.10	0.09	0.10	0.08	0.07
1.25	0.16	0.13	0.12	0.15	0.13	0.11	0.12	0.10	0.09
1.5	0.17	0.15	0.13	0.16	0.14	0.12	0.13	0.12	0.10
2.0	0.19	0.17	0.16	0.18	0.16	0.15	0.15	0.14	0.12
2.5	0.21	0.20	0.18	0.20	0.18	0.17	0.17	0.16	0.14
3.0	0.22	0.21	0.19	0.21	0.19	0.18	0.18	0.17	0.15
4.0	0.24	0.22	0.21	0.22	0.21	0.20	0.19	0.18	0.17
5.0	0.25	0.24	0.23	0.23	0.22	0.21	0.20	0.18	0.18
infinite	0.30	0.30	0.30	0.29	0.29	0.29	0.27	0.27	0.27
SAW-TOOTH ROOF (SLOPING)									
0.6	0.19	0.16	0.15	0.19	0.16	0.17	0.16	0.14	0.14
0.8	0.25	0.21	0.20	0.25	0.21	0.20	0.21	0.20	0.18
1.0	0.30	0.26	0.25	0.29	0.26	0.24	0.25	0.24	0.21
1.25	0.31	0.30	0.27	0.31	0.29	0.26	0.27	0.26	0.24
1.5	0.34	0.31	0.30-	0.32	0.31	0.29	0.30	0.27	0.26
2.0	0.36	0.35	0.32	0.36	0.34	0.32	0.34	0.32	0.29
2.5	0.39	0.38	0.35	0.38	0.36	0.34	0.35	0.32	0.31
3.0	0.40	0.39	0.38	0.40	0.36	0.36	0.36	0.35	0.32
4.0	0.42	0.41	0.40	0.41	0.40	0.39	0.39	0.38	0.35
5.0	0.44	0.42	0.41	0.42	0.41	0.40	0.40	0.39	0.36
infinite	0.49	0.49	0.49	0.48	0.48	0.48	0.45	0.45	0.42

Data Sheet D.2.1 (Continued)

	surface reflectances								
ceiling	0.7			0.5			0.3		
walls	0.5	0.3	0.1	0.5	0.3	0.1	0.5	0.3	0.1

MONITOR ROOF (VERTICAL)

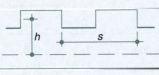

0.6	0.07	0.05	0.04	0.06	0.05	0.04	0.05	0.04	0.03
0.8	0.09	0.07	0.06	0.09	0.07	0.06	0.07	0.06	0.05
1.0	0.12	0.10	0.08	0.11	0.09	0.08	0.09	0.08	0.07
1.25	0.14	0.12	0.10	0.13	0.11	0.10	0.11	0.10	0.09
1.5	0.15	0.13	0.12	0.15	0.13	0.12	0.13	0.11	0.11
2.0	0.17	0.15	0.14	0.16	0.15	0.14	0.15	0.13	0.13
2.5	0.18	0.17	0.15	0.18	0.16	0.15	0.16	0.15	0.14
3.0	0.20	0.18	0.17	0.19	0.18	0.17	0.17	0.16	0.16
4.0	0.21	0.20	0.19	0.20	0.19	0.19	0.19	0.18	0.17
5.0	0.22	0.21	0.20	0.21	0.20	0.19	0.20	0.19	0.18
infinite	0.25	0.25	0.25	0.25	0.25	0.25	0.24	0.24	0.23

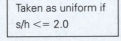

Taken as uniform if s/h <= 2.0

MONITOR ROOF (UNEQUAL VERTICAL)

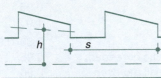

0.6	0.07	0.05	0.04	0.07	0.05	0.04	0.05	0.04	0.04
0.8	0.10	0.08	0.06	010	0.07	0.06	0.07	0.06	0.06
1.0	0.13	0.11	0.08	0.12	0.11	0.08	0.11	0.08	0.08
1.25	0.16	0.13	0.11	0.14	0.13	0.11	0.13	0.11	0.10
1.5	0.17	0.14	0.12	0.16	0.14	0.12	0.13	0.12	0.12
2.0	0.19	0.17	0.16	0.18	0.17	0.16	0.16	0.14	0.14
2.5	0.20	0.18	0.17	0.19	0.18	0.17	0.18	0.17	0.16
3.0	0.22	0.19	0.18	0.20	0.19	0.18	0.19	0.18	0.17
4.0	0.23	0.22	0.20	0.23	0.22	0.20	0.20	0.20	0.19
5.0	0.24	0.23	0.22	0.24	0.23	0.22	0.22	0.22	0.20
infinite	0.29	0.29	0.29	0.27	0.27	0.27	0.27	0.27	0.26

Taken as uniform if s/h <= 2.0

MONITOR ROOF (VERTICAL & SLOPING)

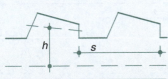

0.6	0.15	0.12	0.09	0.13	0.12	0.09	0.11	0.09	0.09
0.8	0.19	0.16	0.13	0.19	0.16	0.13	0.16	0.13	0.13
1.0	0.23	0.20	0.18	0.22	0.19	0.18	0.19	0.18	0.16
1.25	0.26	0.23	0.20	0.24	0.23	0.20	0.22	0.20	0.19
1.5	0.27	0.24	0.22	0.26	0.24	0.22	0.22	0.22	0.20
2.0	0.30	0.27	0.24	0.28	0.26	0.24	0.26	0.24	0.24
2.5	0.32	0.30	0.27	0.31	0.28	0.27	0.28	0.27	0.26
3.0	0.34	0.31	0.30	0.32	0.31	0.28	0.30	0.28	0.27
4.0	0.35	0.34	0.32	0.34	0.32	0.31	0.32	0.31	0.30
5.0	0.35	0.34	0.34	0.35	0.34	0.32	0.34	0.32	0.31
infinite	0.40	0.40	0.40	0.40	0.40	040	0.39	0.239	0.38

Taken as uniform if s/h <= 2.0

DATA SHEET D.2.2

Daylighting: correction factors

These correction factors are applicable to both the total flux method and the BRS split-flux method of daylight prediction. With the latter these should be applied to the sum of the three components (SC + ERC + IRC).

MAINTENANCE FACTORS

	location	slope	room use	
			clean	dirty
M	non-industrial area	vertical	0.9	0.8
		sloping	0.8	0.7
		horizontal	0.7	0.6
	dirty industrial area	vertical	0.8	0.7
		sloping	0.7	0.6
		horizontal	0.6	0.5

GLASS FACTORS

	clear drawn, plate or float glass		1.00
	polished wired plate glass		0.95
	wired cast glass		0.90
	rough cast or rolled glass		0.95
	cathedral glass		1.00
G	figured glasses		0.80–0.95
		arctic or reeded	0.95
		small morocco	0.90
	6 mm 'antisun'		0.85
	6 mm 'calorex'		0.55
	clear double glazing		0.85
	transparent plastic sheets		0.65–0.90

BARS or FRAMING FACTORS

generally

$$B = \frac{\text{net glass area}}{\text{overall window area}}$$

B

in the absence of precise information:

all metal windows	0.80–0.85
metal windows in wood frames	0.75
wood windows and frames	0.65–0.70

DATA SHEET D.2.3
BRS daylight factor protractor no. 2

for vertical windows, CIE overcast sky

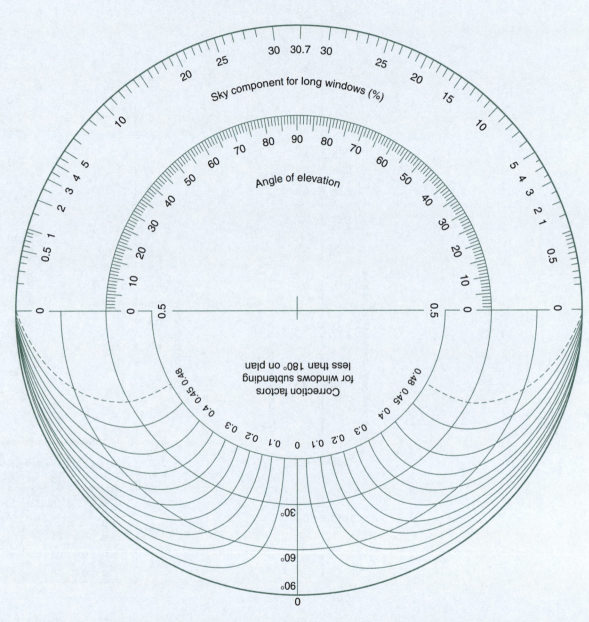

For use with section and plan of room and window
As described in Section 2.4.2, and Figs. 2.27–28

DATA SHEET D.2.4

Daylight factor: nomogram for the IRC (internally reflected component)

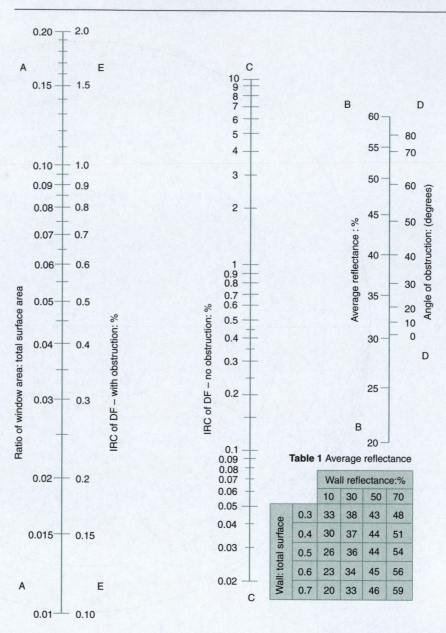

Table 1 Average reflectance

		Wall reflectance:%			
		10	30	50	70
Wall: total surface	0.3	33	38	43	48
	0.4	30	37	44	51
	0.5	26	36	44	54
	0.6	23	34	45	56
	0.7	20	33	46	59

Table 2   D-factors for deterioration of surfaces

location	room use	
	clean	dirty
clean	0.9	0.7
dirty	0.8	0.6

Use of the nomogram is explained in Section 2.4.2 and Section Fig. 2.29

DATA SHEET D.2.5

The pepper-pot diagram for daylight factor

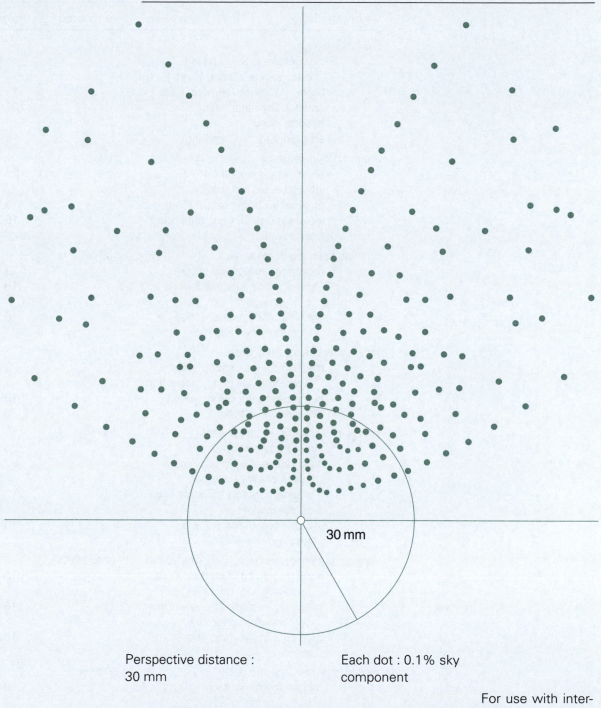

30 mm

Perspective distance :
30 mm

Each dot : 0.1% sky
component

For use with internal perespective of a window, drawn to a perspective distance of 30 mm, as per method sheet M.2.2.

The 30 mm radius circle indicates a cone of vision of 45° all around (a cone with the height of 30 mm, which is the perspective distance, and the base circle is shown).

DATA SHEET D.2.6

Recommended illuminance and limiting glare index values

visual task	illuminance	glare index limit
casual viewing	100 lx	
cloak room, locker, lavatory, bathroom, auditoria, foyer		no limit
boiler or furnace room, bulk store		28
corridor, escalator, stairs		22
hospital ward		13
art gallery (general lighting)		10
rough task, large detail	200 lx	
store, rough workshop		25
lift, kitchen, dining room		22
pharmacy, library, casual reading		19
lecture room, surgery, telephone exchange		16
ordinary task, medium detail	400 lx	
reception areas, food shop		22
general office, keyboard work, control panels		19
drawing office, dispensary, laboratory, reading		16
fairly severe task, small detail	750 lx	
mechanical workshop, fine woodwork, painting, inspection		22
computer room, dressmaking		19
needlework, art room		16
severe prolonged task, small detail	900 lx	
supermarket display		25
electronic or fine mechanical assembly veneer work		22
instrument factory, fine painting, colour inspection		19
jewel or watch factory, proof reading		16
very severe prolonged task, very small detail	up to 2000 lx	
sorting, grading of leather, cloths, hand-tailoring, engraving		19
precision instrument or electronic components assembly		16
gem cutting, gauging very small parts		10
exceptional task, minute detail	3000 lx	
minute instrument work using optical aids		10

These are general recommendations compiled from many sources. The Australian Standard AS1680, as well as the IES Code for Interior Lighting give extensive tables for general lighting and various industrial processes as well as for public and educational buildings.

DATA SHEET D.2.6 (continued)

Recommended spacing of luminaires (for uniformity of general lighting)

luminaire type	maximum	end luminaire to wall	work position next to wall
general diffusing or direct	$1.4\,H_m$	$0.75\,H_m$	$0.5\,H_m$
concentrating reflector luminaires	H_m	$0.5\,H_m$	$0.5\,H_m$
indirect, semi-indirect, (mounted 0.25–0.3 Hc below ceiling)	$1.5\,H_c$	$0.75\,H_c$	$0.5\,H_c$

(H_m mounting height, work-plane to luminaire, H_c work-plane to ceiling height)

DATA SHEET D.2.7

Recommended daylight factors

Homes and hotels	living rooms	1% over at least 8 m² and half the room depth
	bedrooms	0.5% over at least 6 m² and half the room depth
	kitchens	2% over at least 5 m² and half of the total floor area
Offices	general offices,	2%
	typing, computers	4%
Schools, colleges	assembly halls, classrooms	2%
	art rooms	4%
	laboratories (at benches)	3%
	staff offices, common rooms	1%
Hospitals	reception, waiting rooms	2%
	wards	1%
	pharmacies	3%
Surgeries	reception, waiting rooms	2%
	surgery	2%
	laboratories	3%
Sports buildings	sport halls	2%
	swimming pool, pool surface	2%
	pool surrounds	1%
Airport, coach stations	reception, customs halls	2%
	circulation areas, lounges	1%
Assembly and concert halls	auditorium and foyers	1%
	corridors	0.5%
	stairs, ramps	1%
Libraries	shelves	1%
	reading tables	1%
Museums, galleries	general	1%
	Note special conservation requirements	
Churches	body of church	1%
	pulpit, lactern, choir	1.5%
	altar, communion table	3 – 6%
	vestries	2%

DATA SHEET D.2.8

Luminaire characteristics: polar curves

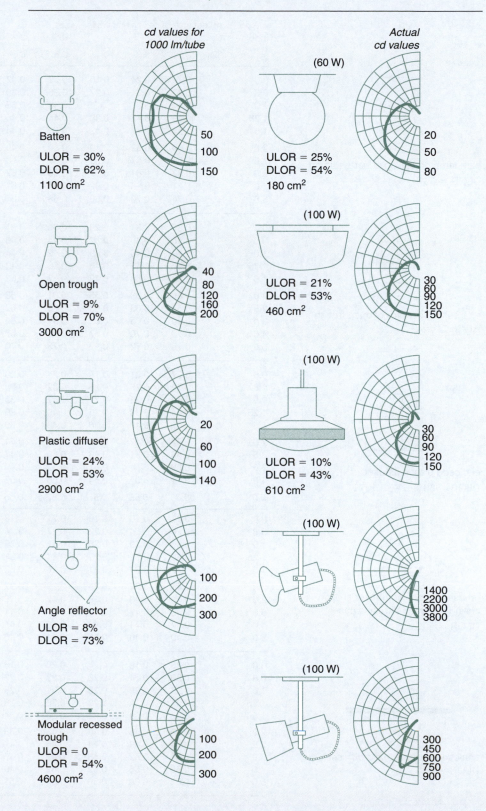

cd values for 1000 lm/tube

Actual cd values

Batten
ULOR = 30%
DLOR = 62%
1100 cm²

50
100
150

(60 W)
ULOR = 25%
DLOR = 54%
180 cm²

20
50
80

Open trough
ULOR = 9%
DLOR = 70%
3000 cm²

40
80
120
160
200

(100 W)
ULOR = 21%
DLOR = 53%
460 cm²

30
60
90
120
150

Plastic diffuser
ULOR = 24%
DLOR = 53%
2900 cm²

20
60
100
140

(100 W)
ULOR = 10%
DLOR = 43%
610 cm²

30
60
90
120
150

Angle reflector
ULOR = 8%
DLOR = 73%

100
200
300

(100 W)

1400
2200
3000
3800

Modular recessed trough
ULOR = 0
DLOR = 54%
4600 cm²

100
200
300

(100 W)

300
450
600
750
900

DATA SHEET D.2.9

Utilisation factors of typical luminaires

room index	reflectance of ceiling and walls C: 0.7			0.5			0.3		
W:	0.5	0.3	0.1	0.5	0.3	0.1	0.5	0.3	0.1
0.6	0.29	0.24	0.19	0.27	0.22	0.19	0.24	0.21	0.19
0.8	0.37	0.31	0.27	0.35	0.30	0.25	0.31	0.28	0.24
1.0	0.44	0.37	0.33	0.40	0.35	0.31	0.35	0.32	0.29
1.25	0.49	0.42	0.38	0.45	0.40	0.36	0.39	0.36	0.33
1.5	0.54	0.47	0.42	0.50	0.44	0.40	0.43	0.40	0.37
2.0	0.60	0.52	0.49	0.54	0.49	0.45	0.48	0.44	0.41
2.5	0.64	0.57	0.53	0.57	0.53	0.49	0.52	0.48	0.45
3.0	0.67	0.61	0.57	0.60	0.57	0.53	0.56	0.52	0.49
4.0	0.71	0.66	0.62	0.64	0.61	0.57	0.59	0.55	0.52
5.0	0.74	0.70	0.66	0.68	0.64	0.61	0.62	0.58	0.54

bare lamp on ceiling or batten fitting
DLOR = 65%

room index	0.5	0.3	0.1	0.5	0.3	0.1	0.5	0.3	0.1
0.6	0.36	0.31	0.28	0.35	0.31	0.28	0.35	0.31	0.28
0.8	0.45	0.40	0.37	0.44	0.40	0.37	0.44	0.40	0.37
1.0	0.49	0.45	0.40	0.49	0.44	0.40	0.48	0.43	0.40
1.25	0.55	0.49	0.46	0.53	0.49	0.45	0.52	0.48	0.45
1.5	0.58	0.54	0.49	0.57	0.53	0.49	0.55	0.52	0.49
2.0	0.64	0.59	0.55	0.61	0.58	0.55	0.60	0.56	0.54
2.5	0.68	0.63	0.60	0.65	0.62	0.59	0.64	0.61	0.58
3.0	0.70	0.65	0.62	0.67	0.64	0.61	0.65	0.63	0.61
4.0	0.73	0.70	0.67	0.70	0.67	0.65	0.67	0.66	0.64
5.0	0.75	0.72	0.69	0.73	0.70	0.67	0.70	0.68	0.67

enamelled reflector or open trough
DLOR = 75%

room index	0.5	0.3	0.1	0.5	0.3	0.1	0.5	0.3	0.1
0.6	0.27	0.21	0.18	0.24	0.20	0.18	0.22	0.19	0.17
0.8	0.34	0.29	0.26	0.32	0.28	0.25	0.29	0.26	0.24
1.0	0.40	0.35	0.31	0.37	0.33	0.30	0.33	0.30	0.28
1.25	0.44	0.39	0.35	0.40	0.36	0.33	0.36	0.33	0.31
1.5	0.47	0.42	0.38	0.43	0.39	0.36	0.38	0.35	0.33
2.0	0.52	0.47	0.44	0.47	0.44	0.41	0.41	0.39	0.37
2.5	0.55	0.51	0.48	0.50	0.47	0.44	0.44	0.42	0.40
3.0	0.58	0.54	0.51	0.52	0.49	0.47	0.47	0.45	0.43
4.0	0.61	0.57	0.54	0.55	0.52	0.50	0.49	0.47	0.45
5.0	0.63	0.59	0.57	0.57	0.55	0.53	0.51	0.49	0.47

enclosed plastic diffuser
DLOR = 50%

room index	0.5	0.3	0.1	0.5	0.3	0.1	0.5	0.3	0.1
0.6	0.21	0.18	0.16	0.21	0.18	0.16	0.20	0.18	0.16
0.8	0.28	0.24	0.22	0.27	0.24	0.22	0.26	0.24	0.22
1.0	0.32	0.29	0.26	0.31	0.28	0.26	0.30	0.28	0.26
1.25	0.35	0.32	0.29	0.34	0.31	0.29	0.32	0.30	0.28
1.5	0.37	0.34	0.31	0.36	0.33	0.31	0.34	0.32	0.30
2.0	0.41	0.37	0.35	0.39	0.37	0.34	0.38	0.36	0.34
2.5	0.43	0.40	0.38	0.42	0.39	0.37	0.40	0.38	0.37
3.0	0.45	0.42	0.40	0.44	0.41	0.40	0.42	0.40	0.39
4.0	0.47	0.44	0.43	0.46	0.44	0.42	0.44	0.42	0.41
5.0	0.49	0.46	0.45	0.47	0.46	0.44	0.46	0.44	0.43

recessed modular diffuser shallow
ceiling mounted diffusing panel
DLOR = 50%

room index	0.5	0.3	0.1	0.5	0.3	0.1	0.5	0.3	0.1
0.6	0.23	0.18	0.24	0.20	0.16	0.12	0.17	0.14	0.11
0.8	0.30	0.24	0.20	0.27	0.22	0.18	0.22	0.19	0.16
1.0	0.36	0.29	0.25	0.31	0.26	0.22	0.26	0.23	0.19
1.25	0.41	0.34	0.29	0.35	0.30	0.26	0.29	0.26	0.22
1.5	0.45	0.39	0.33	0.39	0.34	0.30	0.31	0.28	0.25
2.0	0.50	0.45	0.40	0.43	0.38	0.34	0.34	0.32	0.29
2.5	0.54	0.49	0.44	0.46	0.42	0.38	0.37	0.35	0.32
3.0	0.57	0.52	0.48	0.49	0.45	0.42	0.40	0.38	0.34
4.0	0.60	0.56	0.52	0.52	0.48	0.46	0.43	0.41	0.37
5.0	0.63	0.60	0.56	0.54	0.51	0.49	0.45	0.43	0.40

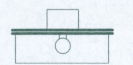

enclosed opal prismatic diffuser
DLOR = 45%

DATA SHEET D.2.10

Lamp characteristics

lamp type		wattage	ballast	lumen output
incandescent (at 240 V)	pear-shaped	25W	-	200
		40	-	325
		60	-	575
		100	-	1160
		500	-	7700
	mushroom-shaped	40	-	380
		60	-	640
		100	-	1220
sodium #	SOX (low pressure)	35	20	4200
		90	25	12500
	SON (high pressure)	70	25	5300
		250	30	24000
mercury #	MB	80	15	2700
	MBI (metal halide)	400	50	24000
	MBF (mercury fluorescent)	50	15	1800
	MBT (mercury/tungsten)	100	-	1250
fluorescent ('white')	0.6 m	20	5	1050
	0.6 m	40	8	1550
	1.2 m	40	10	2800
	1.5 m	50	20	3100
	1.5 m	80	15	4850

Note: # the smallest lamps in each type are shown. The upper limit is some 200 klm

CORRECTIONS TO THE OUTPUT OF FLUORESCENT LAMPS

lamp type	correction	lumens (1200 / 40 W)
white	1.00	2800
warm white	0.96	2700
daylight	0.95	2660
natural	0.75	2100
warmtone	0.70	1960
de luxe warm white	0.67	1950
colour 32 and 34	0.65	1820
colour matching	0.65	1820
Kolor-rite	0.65	1800
de luxe natural	0.55	1500
softone 27	0.55	1500
trucolor 37	0.55	1500
artificial daylight	0.40	1120

DATA SHEET D.2.10 (continued)

LED LAMPS
These consist of many small diodes, permitting a great variety of lamps, in the form of bulbs, downlighters or tubular lamps.
From   12 V / 6 W – 420 lm (replacing 60W incandescent)
To   240 V / 12 W – 800 lm (replacing 80W incandescent
or tubular 240 V / 22 W – 2200 lm (replacing 65 W fluorescent)

METHOD SHEET M.2.1

Daylight availability

---

1 MEASURED ILLUMINANCE DATA

The most useful format of data presentation is the frequency distribution diagram, e.g. that shown in Fig. 2.14 (diffuse only, excluding beam sunlight), or Fig. A here (global illuminance) based on long-term measurement. These are taken for the 'day-time', usually 9:00–17:00 h. The frequency of occurrence is shown against horizontal illuminance.

2 CONVERSION FROM SOLAR RADIATION DATA

This is a good way to estimate illuminance, based on the luminous efficacy of solar radiation. This efficacy (F) can vary between 90 and 150 lm/W (see Section 2.3.1 and Table 2.3). If solar altitude is higher than 10° then it is at least 100 lm/W. Rather than guessing this efficacy value, it can itself be estimated from solar altitude angle. Unfortunately the correlation equations are location-specific and also change with the seasons.

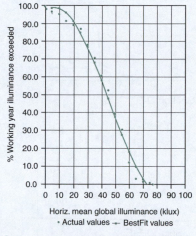

A

E.g. the global radiation efficacy for Lagos
in annual average terms

$$F = 61.3113 + 1.969176\,ALT - 0.019501\,ALT^2$$

rainy season:

$$F = 76.7868 + 1.21599\,ALT - 0.012755\,ALT^2$$

dry season:

$$F = 51.88835 + 2.347397\,ALT - 0.021422\,ALT^2$$

For Garston (UK)
the global horizontal efficacy was found to be

$$F = 104.4 + 0.18\,ALT - 0.0009\,ALT^2$$

e.g. for ALT=45°   F = 110.7

or simply   F = 106 + 0.009 ALT   e.g. for 45°   F= 106.4

where ALT is in degrees and F is lm/W

3 ESTIMATE WHERE NO MEASURED DATA EXIST

Where there are no measured data either for illuminance or for solar radiation, illuminance can be estimated from solar altitude angle. The simplest relationship was proposed by Hopkinson (1966) for Europe:

overcast sky   E = 215 × ALT lx   e.g. for 45° ALT: E = 9 675 lx
cloudy sky   E = 538 × ALT lx   E = 24 210 lx

For Japan, Nakamura and Oki (1979) found

$$E_{max} = 2 + 80 \times \sin(0.8 \times ALT)\ \text{for 45°:}\qquad E = 49\ \text{klx}$$
$$E_{min} = 15 \times \sin(1.2 \times ALT)\qquad\qquad E = 12.1\ \text{klx}$$
$$E_{av} = 0.5 + 42.5 \times \sin ALT\qquad\qquad E = 30.5\ \text{klx}$$

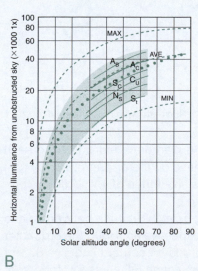

B

The graph (B) plots the results of the last four equations (and a few others) and proposes a considered average (the heavy dotted line) which can be used with reasonable confidence if there are no better data available.

METHOD SHEET M.2.2

Overshadowing: a site survey

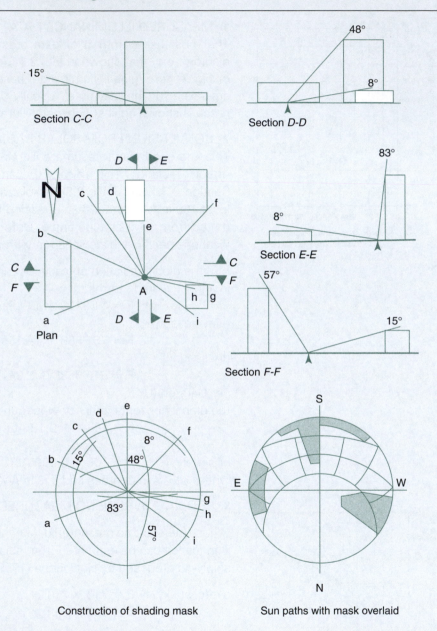

Section *C-C*

Section *D-D*

Plan

Section *E-E*

Section *F-F*

Construction of shading mask

Sun paths with mask overlaid

Point A is surrounded by three buildings. On plan draw radial lines to each corner of each building (a to i) and transfer these on the diagram below. From section C-C the top of the east building gives an altitude of 15°. With the protractor facing east, trace the 15° arc from a to b.

Section D-D shows that the south building give 48° altitude between d and e and 8° for the low block (c to f). Trace the respective arcs with the protractor facing south. Section E-E confirms the 8° altitude for corner f and give 83° for corner h. Draw the 83° arc between g and h. Section F-F gives 57° for corner h, draw the 57° arc between h and i.

METHOD SHEET M.2.3

Construction of internal perspective for the pepper-pot diagram

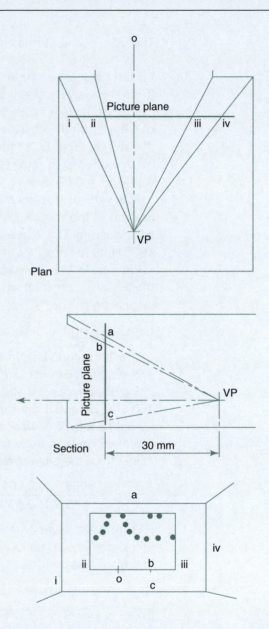

The distance between the point considered (the view-point, VP) and the picture plane must be 30 mm, irrespective of the scale of plan and section, whether the picture plane falls inside or outside (for a VP nearer to the window the picture plane will be outside).

Mark the width points (i to iv) on the plan of the picture plane, as well as the O point. Mark the height points (a to c) on the section, as well as the O point. Transfer this onto the perspective, left and right, up and down from the O point.

This is a one-point perspective, and the O-point is also the vanishing point.

METHOD SHEET M.2.4

Glare index calculation

The glare constant is (as eq.2.20) $g = \dfrac{L_1^{1.6} \times \omega^{0.8}}{L_2 \times p^{1.6}}$

L_1, the luminance of the glare source can be found as the source intensity (from the viewing direction) divided by the apparent area of the source.

E.g. we have a 40 W bare tube fluorescent lamp at a horizontal distance of 4.6 m from the observer and 1.4 m above eye level. The actual distance is $d = 4.8$ m. From D.2.7 the projected area of this lamp is 1100 cm^2, i.e. 0.11 m^2 thus the visual angle (solid angle) subtended by the lamp is $\omega = area/d^2 = 0.11/4.8^2 = 0.0048$ sr

The vertical displacement angle is $\theta = \arctan(1.4/4.6) = 17°$, i.e. with respect to the vertical axis of the luminaire the viewing direction is 73°. The polar curve in D.2.7 gives a source intensity for this direction of 125 cd for 1000 lamp lumens.

For a 40 W warm white lamp D.2.9 gives a lumen output of 2700 lm, thus the actual source intensity is $I = 125 \times 2700/1000 = 337.5$ cd and the source luminance will be

$L_1 = 337.5/0.11 = 3068$ cd/m^2

L_2, the background luminance, can be estimated from the average reflectance and average illuminance of the field of view.

E.g. if surfaces are about Munsell value 4, then (from eq.2.2) $\rho = 4 \times 3 / 100 = 0.12$, and if the illuminance is $E = 400$ lx, then the luminance will be $L_2 = 400 \times 0.12 = 48$ asb or $48/\pi = 15.2$ cd/m^2. If the lamp is directly in the line of vision ($\phi = 0$), with the vertical displacement angle of 17° the position index (from the table overpage) is 0.67.

Thus $g = \dfrac{3068^{1.6} \times 0.0047^{0.8}}{15.2 \times 0.67^{1.6}} = 661$

If there were several luminaires/lamps in the field of view the glare constant (g) of each should be found and summarised.
The glare index will be

$GI = 10 \times \log_{10}(0.478 \times \Sigma)$

in this case

$GI = 10 \times \log(0.478 \times 661) = 25$

In terms of the limiting values given in section 2.5.5, (or in D.2.6) this is acceptable for an industrial situation, but not for an office.

METHOD SHEET M.2.4 (continued)

Position indices (p)
as determined by displacement angles

Vertical displacement angles (θ) →

Horizontal displacement angle (φ)

θ ↓	0	6°	10°	17°	22°	27°	31°	35°	39°	42°	45°	50°	54°	58°	61°	68°	72°
62°	–	–	–	–	–	–	–	–	–	0.02	0.02	0.02	0.02	0.02	0.02	0.02	0.02
61°	–		–	–	0.02	0.02	0.02	0.02	0.02	0.02	0.02	0.02	0.02	0.02	0.02	0.02	0.02
58°	0.03	0.03	0.03	0.03	0.03	0.03	0.03	0.03	0.03	0.03	0.03	0.03	0.03	0.03	0.03	0.03	0.03
54°	0.04	0.04	0.04	0.04	0.04	0.04	0.04	0.04	0.04	0.04	0.04	0.04	0.04	0.04	0.04	0.03	0.03
50°	0.05	0.05	0.06	0.06	0.06	0.06	0.06	0.06	0.06	0.06	0.06	0.05	0.05	0.05	0.05	0.04	0.04
45°	0.08	0.09	0.09	0.10	0.10	0.10	0.10	0.09	0.09	0.09	0.08	0.08	0.07	0.06	0.06	0.05	0.05
42°	0.11	0.11	0.12	0.13	0.13	0.12	0.12	0.12	0.12	0.11	0.10	0.09	0.08	0.07	0.07	0.06	0.05
39°	0.14	0.15	0.16	0.16	0.16	0.16	0.15	0.15	0.14	0.13	0.12	0.11	0.09	0.08	0.08	0.6	0.06
35°	0.19	0.20	0.22	0.21	0.21	0.21	0.20	0.18	0.17	0.16	0.14	0.12	0.11	0.10	0.09	0.07	0.07
31°	0.25	0.27	0.30	0.29	0.28	0.26	0.24	0.22	0.21	0.19	0.18	0.15	0.13	0.11	0.10	0.09	0.08
27°	0.35	0.37	0.39	0.38	0.36	0.34	0.31	0.28	0.25	0.23	0.21	0.18	0.15	0.14	0.12	0.10	0.09
22°	0.48	0.53	0.53	0.51	0.49	0.44	0.39	0.35	0.31	0.28	0.25	0.21	0.18	0.16	0.14	0.11	0.10
17°	0.67	0.73	0.73	0.69	0.64	0.57	0.49	0.44	0.38	0.34	0.31	0.25	0.21	0.19	0.16	0.13	0.12
11°	0.95	1.02	0.98	0.88	0.80	0.72	0.63	0.57	0.49	0.42	0.37	0.30	0.25	0.22	0.19	0.15	0.14
6°	1.30	1.36	1.24	1.12	1.01	0.88	0.79	0.68	0.62	0.53	0.46	0.37	0.31	0.26	0.23	0.17	0.16
0°	1.87	1.73	1.56	1.36	1.20	1.06	0.93	0.80	0.72	0.64	0.57	0.46	0.38	0.33	0.28	0.20	0.17

METHOD SHEET M.2.5

Permissible height indicators

Scale 1:500

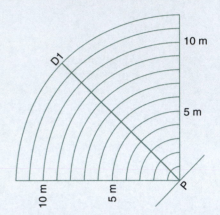

the radius of the highest arc
in each case should be

D1   46 mm
D2   53 mm
D3   79 mm

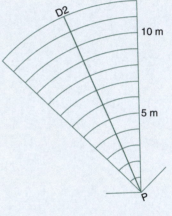

For use with the method described
in Section 2.4.5
and Fig. 2.37

For this D set the slope of the limiting
plane (within the wedges) is

D1   10°
D2   25°
D3   27.5°

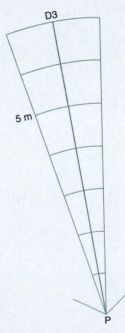

Based on MoHLG Planning bulletin no. 5,
Planning for daylight and sunlight
and *Sunlight and daylight*, DoE Welsh Office
HMSO, 1971.

May be reconstructed for a
scale of 1:200
with the following radii:

D1   116 mm
D2   133 mm
D3   198 mm

METHOD SHEET M.2.6

Comparison of two alternative lighting schemes

In some situations it may be possible to replace a high level general (electric) lighting system with a low level general lighting supplemented by local lighting where required, e.g. at individual work-stations. This would produce a reduction in electricity use, as illustrated by the following example:

Assume a library reading room of 10 m × 20 m (200 m²) and 2.9 m high, which is to accommodate 20 reading desks. Take surface reflectances as 70% for the ceiling and 50% for the walls.

If the desk height is 0.8 m and the luminaires are 0.1 m from the ceiling, the mounting height will be 2.9 − 0.8 − 0.1 = 2 m, thus the room index becomes

$$RI = \frac{10 \times 20}{(10 + 20) \times 2} = 3.33$$

Use 1.2 m fluorescent tubes in enclosed plastic diffuser luminaires,

From sheet D.2.8 (first column, interpolating for RI 3.33 between 0.58 and 0.61) the utilisation factor is UF = 0.59

Lamp output of (from D.2.9) 2800 × 0.75 (for "natural") = 2100 lm

Scheme **A**: general lighting to give work-plane illuminance of 400 lux

flux to be received	Φ_r = 10 × 20 × 400 = 80 000 lm
if maintenance factor is	M = 0.8

installed flux required $\Phi_i = \dfrac{80\,000}{0.59 \times 0.8} = 169\,492\,\text{lm}$

number of lamps required $N = \dfrac{169\,492}{2100} = 81$

installed power: 81 × (40 + 10) = 4050 W

thus power density $\dfrac{4050}{200} = $ **20.25 W/m²**

Scheme **B**: general lighting of 100 lux + local lighting to 20 desks
combining four of the above equations

$$N = \frac{10 \times 20 \times 100}{0.59 \times 0.8} / 2100 = 20 \text{ lamps}$$

installed power: 20 × (40 + 10) = 1000 W

thus power density $\dfrac{1000}{200} = $ 5 W/m²

+ 20 desk lamps Φ_i = 20 × 40 = 800W
thus power density   800 / 200 =   4 W/m²

Total power density   **9 W/m²**

which is less than half of that required with scheme A

and if we consider that the 20 desk lamps would not be used at all times, the energy advantage is much greater.

PART 3   SOUND: THE SONIC ENVIRONMENT

CONTENTS

SYMBOLS AND ABBREVIATIONS

a	absorption coefficient
f	frequency (Hz) (or interval of averaging for L_{eq})
f_c	octave band centre frequency
h	height
p	sound pressure (Pa)
r	radius
s	surface area
v	velocity
Abs	total absorption (m² open window units)
ARS	assisted resonance system
C	a constant
CRT	cathode ray tube
DIN	Deutsche Institut für Normung
I	intensity (W/m²)
L	sound level
L_{eq}	equivalent continuous sound level
M	mass, surface density (kg/m²)
MCR	multi-channel reverberation

NC	noise criteria
NNI	noise and number index
NR	noise rating
P	sound power (W)
R	response
RT	reverberation time
S	stimulus or sound source
SIL	speech interference level
SiL	sound intensity level
SpL	sound pressure level
SRI	sound reduction index
STC	sound transmission class
TL	transmission loss
TNI	traffic noise index
V	volume or volt
α	absorptance
λ	wavelength
ρ	reflectance or density
τ	transmittance

LIST OF FIGURES

LIST OF TABLES

LIST OF WORKED EXAMPLES

LIST OF EQUATIONS

3.1 PHYSICS OF SOUND

Sound is the sensation caused by a vibrating medium as it acts on the human ear. Loosely, the term is also applied to the vibration itself that causes this sensation. Acoustics (from the Greek ακουστικος) is the science of sound, of small amplitude mechanical vibrations.

A simple acoustic system consists of a source, some conveying medium and a receiver. The source is some vibrating body, which converts some other form of energy into vibration, e.g. mechanical impact on a solid body, air pressure acting on a column of air, such as in a whistle or pipe, electrical energy acting on a steel membrane or on a crystal, etc. The word *transducer* is often used for devices converting other forms of energy into sound (e.g. a loudspeaker) or vice versa (e.g. a microphone). The conveying medium may be a gas (e.g. air), which transmits the vibration in the form of longitudinal waves (alternating compressions and rarefications), or a solid body, where lateral vibrations may also be involved (e.g. a string). Fig. 3.1 illustrates the longitudinal (compression) waves and their representation by a sine curve.

In buildings we are concerned with *airborne sound* and *structure-borne sound*, the latter being transmitted by the building fabric.

3.1.1 Attributes of sound

Sounds are characterised by wavelength (λ in m) or frequency (f in Hz) and the product of the two, the velocity (v in m/s). Hz = Hertz, which, in the past, was referred to as 'cps' (cycles per second). The velocity depends on the transmitting medium. In air it is usually taken as 340 m/s, but it varies with temperature and humidity (faster in warmer, less dense air).

The relevant equations are very similar to those given for light (eq. 2.1):

$$v = f \times \lambda \tag{3.1}$$

from which

$$\lambda = \frac{340}{f} \text{ and } f = \frac{340}{\lambda}$$

The output (power, P) of a sound source is measured in W (watts). Table 3.1 gives some typical sound power values.

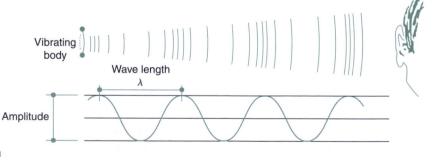

3.1
Sound waves: longitudinal (compression) waves and their sinusoidal representation

Table 3.1 Sound power of some sources

Jet airliner	10 kW (10^4 W)
Pneumatic riveter, accelerating motorcycle	1 W
50 kW (electrical) axial flow fan	0.1 W (10^{-1} W)
Large (symphonic) orchestra	0.01 W 10^{-2} W)
Food blender, coffee grinder	0.001 W 10^{-3} W)
Conversational speech	0.000 01 W (10^{-5} W)

> Note that p (lower case) denotes sound pressure, P (capital) denotes sound source power.

Frequency is perceived as pitch and the 'strength' of sound is measured either by its pressure, p (in Pa) or by its power density or intensity, I (in W/m^2). The latter is the density of energy flow rate. Sound pressure actually varies within every cycle from zero to positive peak, then through zero to a negative maximum, so what we measure is the RMS (root-mean-square) pressure.

The relationship of p and I depends on the conveying medium, but in air under 'standard conditions' (air density of ρ = 1.18 kg/m^3 and v = 340 m/s), it is usually taken as

$$p = 20\sqrt{I} \tag{3.2}$$

3.1.2 Pure tones and broad-band sound

A sound that can be described by a smooth sine curve, and is of one particular frequency, is referred to as a *pure tone sound*. This can only be generated electronically. Sounds produced by instruments always contain some harmonics.

> *The fundamental frequency itself is the first harmonic. The second harmonic is double that frequency, the third is three times that, etc; e.g. middle C has a frequency of 256 Hz. Its harmonics will be:*
>
> *2nd = 512 Hz*
> *3rd = 768 Hz*
> *4th = 1024 Hz*

Most sounds contain many frequencies and are referred to as *broad-band sounds*.

An octave extends from f to 2f frequency, e.g. from 1000 Hz to 2000 Hz. An octave band is usually designated by its centre frequency (f_c), then the limits are defined as

$$f_{lower} = f_c \times \frac{1}{\sqrt{2}} \text{ and } f_{upper} = f_c \times \sqrt{2}$$

Table 3.2 shows the standard octave band centre frequencies and the octave boundaries. If the sound is measured in each octave (or third-octave) separately (by using 'octave band or third-octave filters') then a sound spectrum can be built up, such as those shown in Fig. 3.2.

Table 3.2 Standard octaves (in Hz)

Centre		31.5		63		125		250		500		1000		2000		4000		8000	
Limits	22		44		88		177		354		707		1414		2828		5656		11 312

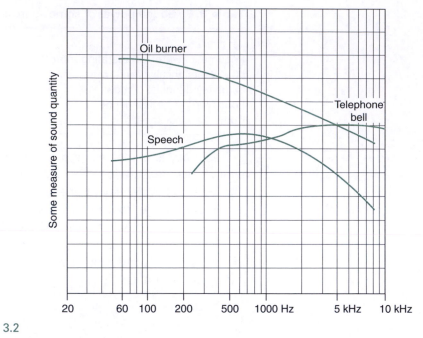

3.2
Some typical sound spectra

3.1.3 Propagation of sound

A sound field is the volume of space where vibrations emitted by a source are detectable. A *free-field* is one where the effects of boundaries are negligible, where there are no significant reflections. When a uniform point source emits a sound, this energy flow spreads in all radial directions, distributed over the surface of a sphere of increasing radius. As the surface of a sphere is $4 \pi r^2$, the sound intensity (power density) at any distance r from the source will be

$$I = \frac{P}{4\pi r^2} \ (W/m^2) \tag{3.3}$$

This is known as the inverse square law. Intensity is proportionate to the square of sound pressure, sound pressure reduces with the distance (and not with the square of distance), e.g.

if power, P = 10 W

	$I \ (W/m^2)$	$p \ (Pa)$
at 2 m	0.2	8.94
at 4 m	0.05	4.47
at 8 m	0.0125	2.236

In addition to such reduction with distance, there will be some molecular absorption of energy in air, which is hardly noticeable at low frequencies (up to about 1000 Hz) but quite substantial at high frequencies (e.g. at 8 kHz, over a 300 m distance it would be a reduction of 10^{-4} W/m²).

When a wave-front reaches an obstacle (e.g. a wall or a screen), the original pattern of waves continues above the top of this obstacle, but it will create an

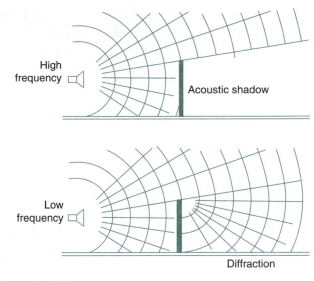

3.3

Acoustic shadow and diffraction

acoustic shadow. This may be quite clearly defined for very high frequency of sound (similar to a light shadow), but at low frequencies a diffraction occurs at the edge of the obstacle, so that edge behaves as a virtual source, as shown by Fig. 3.3.

If two sources contribute to the sound field, the intensities are additive, but for pressure the squares of the contributing pressures must be added and the result will be the square root of this sum:

$$I = I_1 + I_2$$

e.g.

$$I = 0.05 + 0.0125 = 0.0625 \text{ W/m}^2$$

But

$$p = \sqrt{p_1^2 + p_2^2} \qquad \text{e.g. } p = \sqrt{4.47^2 + 2.236^2} = 5 \text{ Pa}$$
$$\text{check: (from eq. 3.2):} \quad p = 20 \sqrt{0.0625} = 5 \text{ Pa}$$

3.1.4 Acoustic quantities

Fechner's law suggests that human response to a stimulus is logarithmic; in general terms

$$R = C \times \log S$$

where

R = response
C = a constant
S = stimulus (log is to base 10).

Intensity and pressure are measures of the stimulus. At low intensities we can distinguish quite small differences, but the ear's sensitivity reduces with higher intensities. As a first approximation of auditory response a logarithmic scale has been devised: the *sound level*.

The logarithm of the ratio I/I_0 has been named Bel (after Alexander Graham Bell), but as this is a rather large unit, its sub-multiple the decibel (dB) is used. It can be derived from intensity or from pressure:

$$\text{Sound intensity level: SiL} = 10 \times \log \frac{I}{I_0} \tag{3.4}$$

$$\text{Sound pressure level SpL} = 20 \times \log \frac{p}{p_0} \tag{3.5}$$

and the reference values have been standardised as the average threshold of audibility:

$I_0 = 1 \text{ pW/m}^2$ (pico-Watt $= 10^{-12}$W)

$p_0 = 20\mu\text{Pa}$ (micro-Pascal $= 10^{-6}$Pa)

Under standard atmospheric conditions both derivations give the same result, so in practice both may be referred to as sound level (L).

The intensities of two sounds are additive, but not the corresponding sound levels. If sound levels are given, they must be converted to intensities, these intensities can be added, then the resulting sound level must be found.

EXAMPLE 3.1   ADDING SOUND LEVELS

Two sound levels are given: L' = 90 dB, L" = 80 dB.
  The sum of the two is NOT 170 dB!
  From eq. 3.4:

$$I = 10^{-12} \times 10^{L/10}$$

Thus

$$I' = 10^{(9-12)} = 10^{-3} = 0.001$$

$$I'' = 10^{(8-12)} = 10^{-4} = 0.0001$$

$$I' + I'' = 0.0011 \text{ W/m}^2$$

$$L_{sum} = 10 \log \frac{0.0011}{10^{-12}} = 10 \log(11 \times 10^8) = 10 \times 9.04 = 90.4 \text{ dB}$$

The nomogram given in Fig. 3.4 can be used to add two sound levels:

dB difference

| 0 | 1 | 2 | 3 | 4 | 5 | 6 | 7 | 8 | 9 | 10 | 11 | 12 | 13 | 14 | 15 |

| 3 | 2.5 | 2 | 1.5 | 1 | 0.5 | 01 |

dB increment

3.4

Nomogram for adding two sound levels

Find the difference between the two levels on the upper scale and add this to the larger of the two levels given. To continue the above example: the difference is 90 − 80 = 10 dB. On the nomogram opposite the 10 dB read 0.4, so the sum will be 90 + 0.4 = 90.4.

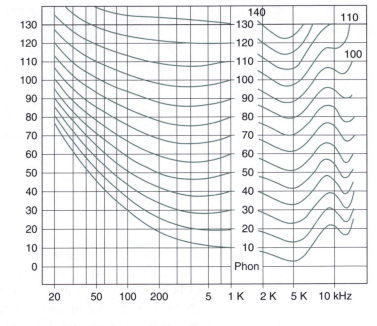

3.5

Equal loudness contours: definition of the phon scale

The next step in quantifying the auditory response recognises that the sensitivity of the ear varies with the frequency of the sound. It is most sensitive to about 4 kHz (4000 Hz). Sensitivity to various pure tone sounds has been plotted on a (logarithmic) frequency graph, giving the *equal loudness contours* for pure tone sounds (Fig. 3.5). These curves are designated by the sound level at 1 kHz and define the loudness level (phon) scale (i.e. the sound level and loudness level scales coincide at 1 kHz frequency).

For example, take the 30 phon curve. This indicates that at 1 kHz a sound level of 30 dB is perceived as of 30 phon loudness level, but 30 dB at 100 Hz would only give 10 phon while at 4 kHz it is perceived as of about 37 phon loudness level. Conversely, 40 phon loudness level is produced by (e.g.) each of the following sounds:

at 40 Hz . . .	70 dB
at 100 Hz . . .	52 dB
at 250 or 1000 Hz or 5500 Hz	40 dB
at 4000 Hz . . .	32 dB

i.e. all sounds along one of these equal loudness contours would be perceived as of the same loudness level.

A true measure of the human ear's sensitivity is thus found, after two adjustments:

1 for logarithmic response to the stimulus, which gave the sound level scale (dB);
2 for the frequency-dependence of our ear, which gave the loudness level (phon).

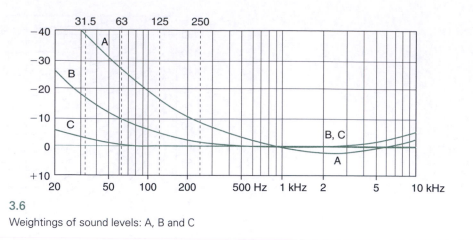

3.6
Weightings of sound levels: A, B and C

Phon cannot be measured directly, but an electronic weighting network provides an approximation. The effect of 'A' weighting is shown in Fig. 3.6. Sound levels measured with this weighting are referred to as dBA. (The German DIN Standards refer to such a weighted scale as 'instrument phon'.) Other weighting scales also exist, but of no great relevance to architecture. These dBA values are often used to describe a broad-band sound with a single figure index. However, numerous combinations of levels and frequencies may give the same dBA value, thus an accurate description of a broad-band sound can only be given by its spectrum.

3.2 HEARING

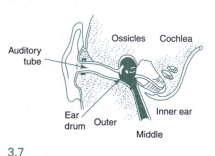

3.7
The human ear

Aural perception (from the Latin *auris* = ear) starts with the ear. Airborne sounds reach the ear-drum through the auditory tube and it will start vibrating (Fig. 3.7). This vibration is then transmitted by the ossicles (hammer, anvil and stirrup) to the inner membrane of the oval window and through this it reaches the inner ear, the cochlea. Some 25 000 hair-like endings of the auditory nerve are located in the cochlea, which selectively respond to various frequencies and generate nerve impulses, subsequently transmitted to the brain.

These impulses are interpreted by the brain, but the first selection takes place in the inner ear. The ear is thus not only a very efficient microphone but also an analyser. Most of the auditory brain functions involve pattern recognitions, filtering out what is relevant, and interpretation, based on memory, i.e. past experience.

3.2.1 The audible range

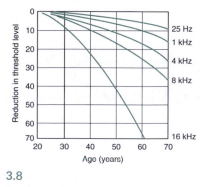

3.8
Presbycousis: loss of hearing with age

The human ear is sensitive to vibrations between 20 Hz and 16 kHz, but these limits also depend on the 'strength' of the sound. The audible range of frequencies may also be reduced (especially at high frequencies) by the listener's state of health and definitely by old age. Fig. 3.8 shows that at age 60 people can expect to have a hearing loss of 70 dB at 16 kHz, but only a loss of about 10 dB at 1 kHz.

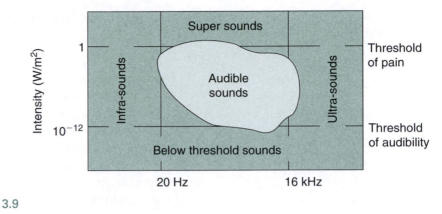

3.9

The range of audible sounds

Fig. 3.9 illustrates the range of audible sounds, both in terms of frequency and 'strength'. Strength is measured by three scales: pressure, intensity and sound level. Note that the top and bottom parts of the outline correspond to the equal loudness contours (at 0 and 120 phon). It also shows that there are vibrations below and above the limits: referred to as *infra-sounds* and *ultra-sounds* (infrasonic and ultrasonic vibrations). The bottom of the audible area is the *threshold of audibility* and the top is the *threshold of pain*. Above the latter there may be super-sounds, but there is no specific term for the below threshold sounds. (For calculation purposes, both thresholds are fixed in terms of intensity, pressure or sound level, regardless of frequency.)

If pitch is the subjective interpretation of the frequency of a sound, it clearly relates to pure tone (or near pure-tone) sounds. Complex sounds are physically determined by their spectrum, while the subjective term for the 'colouring' of a sound of a certain pitch is *timbre*. Several everyday expressions can relate to certain types of sound, e.g. Fig. 3.10 shows a pure tone, a hissing sound and a rumble. The hiss is due to the many high frequency overtones, as shown by the middle curve.

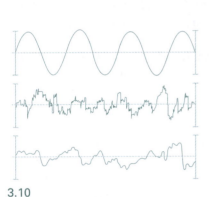

3.10

A pure tone, a hiss and a rumble (graphic level recording)

3.2.2 Noise: definition and rating

An attempted definition of noise in objective terms is 'random vibrations, showing no regular pattern'. However, noise is a subjective phenomenon, one person's enjoyable sound may be another's racket. The only meaningful definition of noise is therefore 'unwanted sound'. This is similar to the definition in telecommunications, where the *signal* is distinguished from the *noise*, which is everything else.

The term *white noise* is used for a set of vibrations which contains equal amounts of energy in all wavelengths (by analogy, white light, which includes all visible wavelengths of light). It is a common fallacy to believe that white noise would eliminate or suppress noise: it only reduces the intelligibility of such unwanted sound (if it has some information content).

Table 3.3 Limits of continued 'occupational noise' (in Hz)

Centre frequency:	63	125	250	500	1000	2000	4000	8000
Maximum level:	103	96	91	87	85	83	81	79

In broad terms the following noise effects can be distinguished:

65 dBA	Up to this level, noise or unwanted sound may create annoyance, but the result is only psychological (nervous effects). Above this level, physiological effects, such as mental and bodily fatigue may occur.
90 dBA	Many years of exposure to such noise levels would normally cause some permanent hearing loss.
100 dBA	With short periods of exposure to noise of such a level the aural acuity may be temporarily impaired (TTS = temporary threshold shift) and prolonged exposure is likely to cause irreparable damage to the auditory organs.
120 dBA	Painful.
150 dBA	Causes instantaneous loss of hearing.

In more precise terms the spectral composition of the noise must also be taken into account. As opposed to stating the above 90 dBA limit, 'safe' levels of continued occupational noise exposure can be specified for each octave-band (Table 3.3).

The level of acceptable noise depends not only on objective, physical factors, but also on subjective, psychological ones. It depends on the state of mind and expectations of the listener. In a sleeper train the monotonous noise of 65–70 dBA does not disturb, but in a quiet home for a person 'badly tuned', the ticking of an alarm clock at 25dBA can cause annoyance.

Noise may adversely affect concentration, particularly if the noise has an information content. In a work situation switching of the worker's attention from task to noise and back may take several seconds, and would affect work performance. The most obvious effect of noise is its interference with aural communication. This will be discussed in some detail in Section 3.4.1. Very loud sound (such as popular music) can have a direct psychological (almost narcotic) effect, while being only noise for others.

A pure tone sound can be described and quantified using the phon scale, but this is only possible if both its level (dB) and its frequency are known. A complex sound can be described in terms of its A-weighted sound level (dBA) but this is only a sketchy description. For a complete picture an octave band analysis (for more precision: a third-octave analysis) is necessary, which would produce its spectrum.

Fig. 3.11 shows the spectra of noises produced by some everyday sources.

A single-figure description of such broad-band noises is available in terms of their *noise rating*. A family of curves (the NR curves, Fig. 3.12) (or in the USA the very similar 'noise criteria', NC curves, which are still used there) must be laid over the noise spectrum, and the curve which just touches the spectrum at its (relatively) highest point gives the rating of that noise. Fig. 3.13 indicates that a high frequency noise has a greater effect on noise rating than one which has a dominantly low-frequency spectrum.

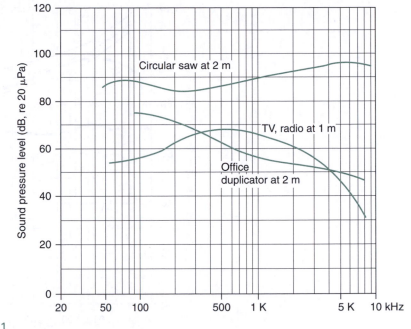

3.11

Noise spectra from some typical sources

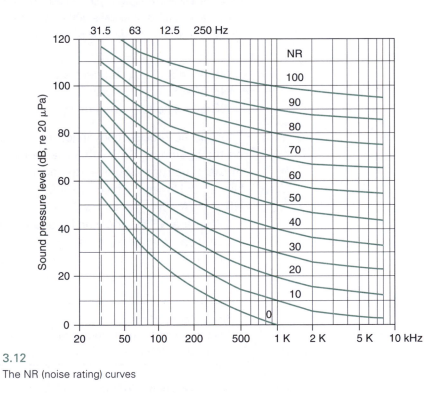

3.12

The NR (noise rating) curves

Subjective assessment of the noisiness of a given situation is closely related to its NR number. Generally people judge the situation as

| NR 20–25 | very quiet |
| NR 30–35 | quiet |

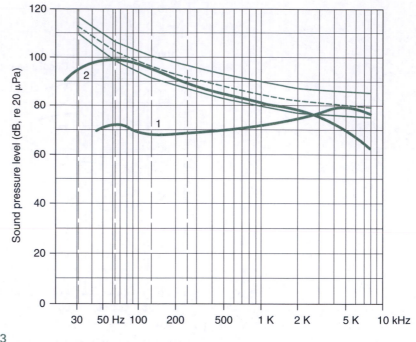

3.13

Rating of a high and a low frequency noise: NR80 and 90 curves.

1) circular saw at 16 m, touches NR85 at 5000 Hz

2) heavy road traffic, touches the same NR85 at 125 Hz

NR 40–45	moderately noisy
NR 50–55	noisy
NR 60 and over	very noisy

There is no precise conversion of NR to dBA (or vice versa) as it depends on the spectrum. While dBA is a weighted average, the NR is an upper limit of the spectrum. However, generally (and roughly) it can be taken as dBA = NR + 10. However, if a measurement is taken in dBA, it can be converted as NR = dBA – 5.

While the NR number can be used to describe the noisiness of a situation, it can also be used as a criterion to specify the acceptable noise level in a space, e.g. as a specification item given in a brief for a building design. For some common room uses, the following criteria are recommended:

Studio, concert hall	NR 15
Lecture theatre, court room, church	NR 25
Shops and stores	NR 35–50

See also Data sheet D.3.1.

The NC (noise criterion) curves have been developed in the USA for use in rating air conditioning noise (Fig. 3.14) and they are widely used to specify the tolerable limit of noise, in a way similar to the NR curves. Note that the NR curves coincide with and are calibrated by the sound pressure level at 1000 Hz and the NC at 2000 Hz. A slightly relaxed set of requirements (the NCA curves) is shown in dashed lines.

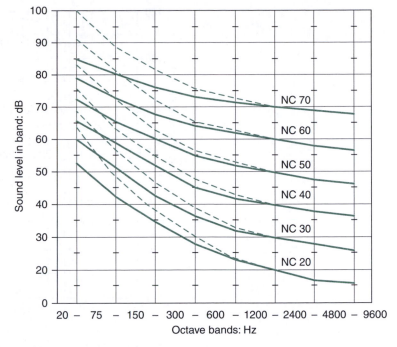

3.14
Noise Criteria (NC) curves

3.2.3 Noise spectra

In a building interior (a closed field) with many sources of little directional tendencies, with multiple reflections the sound field would be fairly uniform and either a dBA value or an NR number would give a reasonable indication of the sonic environment. Fig. 3.15 shows typical noise spectra of some indoor environments.

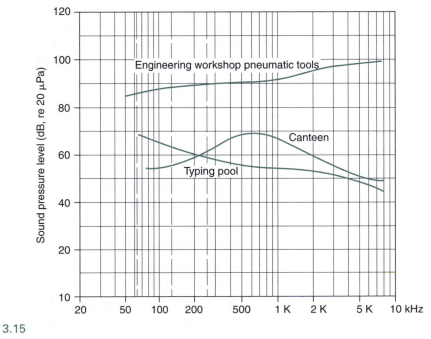

3.15
Noise spectra in some indoor environments

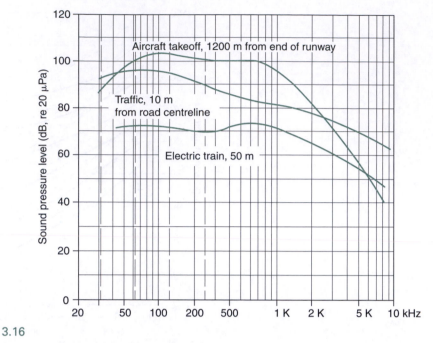

3.16
Spectra of some typical outdoor noises

Under open-air conditions, in a free field, there being no reflections, the sound decreases with distance from the source. Any measurement must relate to a specified point, i.e. distance and direction from the source or notional location of the source. For example, for traffic noise the centreline of the road is often taken as a linear source of noise. Fig. 3.16 presents the spectra of some typical outdoor noises, as measured at the stated distance from the source.

While some sources emit sound fairly uniformly in all directions, others have strong directional tendencies. In a free field such directional tendencies must be ascertained and can be depicted in the form of polar curves (somewhat similar to the luminous intensity polar curves used for the light emission of luminaires, see Section 2.5.2).

Fig. 3.17 gives two forms of representation:

1 showing dB values in different directions from the source (relative to a stated axis) at some stated distance, or
2 the relative reduction in dB at different directions from the peak value along the directional axis.

It is noticeable on the second of these, that high frequency sounds have much stronger directionality than those of low frequency (as mentioned in connection with barriers and shown in Fig. 3.3).

3.2.4 Noise climate

All the measures and all discussion so far related to an instantaneous noise condition, as it were, give only 'snapshots'. If variation in time is to be considered, we need to record the noise. A sample of such graphic recording is shown in Fig. 3.18. Such a recording is usually taken in dBA, to bring

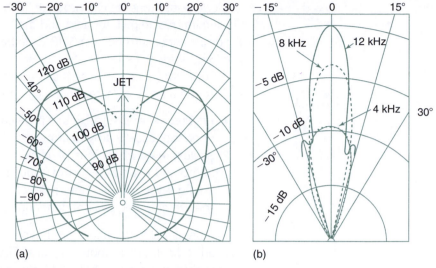

(a)   (b)

3.17

Directionality of some sources:
a) noise levels at 30 m from jet, b) relative levels from loud hailer

different frequencies to a common denominator, but this way any indication of frequency is lost. It will be useful to characterise a noise climate where the spectral composition of noise does not vary significantly (e.g. traffic noise).

Even if such a recording is maintained for only 24 hours, it will be necessary to use statistical methods to obtain any meaning from it. A frequency distribution diagram (e.g. a bell-curve) can be produced and various percentile values of the sound level calculated. Fig. 3.18 shows the following:

L_{10} the sound level exceeded 10% of time, i.e. in statistical terms the 90th percentile level, an indication of peak values.

L_{50} the 50th percentile level, which is the median value for the measurement period.

L_{90} the value exceeded 90% of the time, or the 10th percentile sound level, which can be taken as the average background sound level.

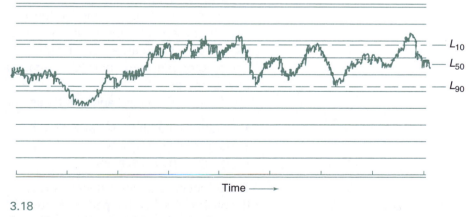

Time ⟶

3.18

A graphic sound level recording, showing L_{10}, L_{50} and L_{90}

Modern instruments can produce such analyses automatically. Both the sampling interval (e.g. 1 second) and the 'bin width' can be set (e.g. counting the number of occurrences in 5 dB wide bands, and putting the measured values in 5 dB wide 'bins').

Such statistical analyses can form the bases of various measures to describe a noise climate. These can be of two kinds:

1 *indices*, i.e. measures with a physical basis, on which other factors may be imposed, usually arrived at by social science (survey) methods;
2 *scales*, in which various physical factors affecting people's responses are combined over a period of time. Examples of these are the equivalent sound level or mean energy level, the effective perceived noise level and the weighted equivalent continuous perceived noise level.

Such noise climate scales are beyond the scope of this work, but two often used indices are introduced here. First, the *traffic noise index* (TNI) is an empirical expression of the 24-hour noise climate in a given situation, where the main contributor is road traffic. It is based on the above L_{10}, L_{50} and L_{90} values:

$$TNI = 4 (L_{10} - L_{90}) + L_{90} - 30 \qquad (3.6)$$

This has been found to give the best correlation with the nuisance effect of traffic noise. Some British legislation uses a similar derivation based on only 18 hours recording of the noise climate (excluding the 6 'quiet' hours of the night).

Several studies have shown that traffic noise is the most intrusive and most often complained about source of annoyance, but is closely followed by aircraft noise in areas around an airport. Here the influencing factor is not only the noise generated by each flight, but also the frequency or the number of flights. Thus, the *noise and number index* (NNI) has been devised, which is based on recordings between 6:00 and 18:00, where the contributing factors are the number of flights (N) and the peak noise level produced by each flight. It uses the PNdB (perceived noise level) scale and the empirical expression provides the best correlation with the disturbance effect ascertained by social survey methods.

Community noise is a generic term, which includes the above traffic and aircraft noise, but also industrial noise and 'neighbourhood noise' (from lawn mowers to parties, the neighbour's TV, construction work to air conditioning or ventilation noises) – in fact, any noise that may exist in a given environment.

Different criteria will apply as these noises affect

- people in their homes, infringing their aural privacy;
- people in work situations;
- people in public spaces.

The effect of such noise depends very much on people's expectations: those directly involved with a particular noise may hardly notice it, may even enjoy

Table 3.4 Limits of community noise inside of residences (dBA)

	Day	Night
Country areas	40	30
Suburban areas	45	35
Inner city areas	50	35

it (e.g. a football crowd or a noisy party) while others may be greatly annoyed. The great complexity of the problem makes legislative controls difficult. Consideration of other people, reasonableness and common sense would probably be a better solution than legal control. Unfortunately 'common sense' is a very rare commodity.

People in their homes would have the lowest annoyance threshold. As a general guidance, the above L_{10} (90th percentile) noise levels should not be exceeded inside any residential unit (Table 3.4).

The ISO (International Standards Organisation) already in 1971 recommended the use of a single index, L_{eq}, (equivalent continuous sound level) for measuring and rating noises in residential, industrial and traffic areas. L_{eq} is a notional sound level that would cause the same sound energy to be received (measured in dBA) as that due to the actual sound over a period of time. If the variability of a 'steady' sound is within ±4 dB, a reading of a sound level meter, set to 'slow' response, visually averaged can be taken as the L_{eq}.

Continuous recording is sampled at fixed time intervals (i). The mean sound level (Li) is taken as the arithmetic average between measurements at the end points of the interval (in dBA). The interval (f) is expressed as a percentage of the total time (T) of measurement. Then L_{eq} (or, to be precise: L_{AeqT}) will be

$$L_{eq} = 10 \log_{10} [0.01\ \Sigma\ f \times 10^{(Li/10)}] \tag{3.7}$$

as defined by ISO 1999:1990, which also makes provision for the inclusion of impulse noise effects. This has been endorsed by the EU and is also gaining popularity in the UK.

3.3 NOISE CONTROL

The basic principles of noise control (or noise abatement) are summed up in the acronym SPR, which stands for 'Source, Path and Receiver'. This gives the structure of the present section.

3.3.1 Control at source

It is far easier (and far less expensive) to control noise at or near the source than at some distance from it. Often the noise generated is an avoidable by-product of some process. Careful design can eliminate or at least reduce

(a)

this. Often a mechanical component generates a vibration (which may be below the audible range), which is transmitted, e.g. to some sheet metal component, which will vibrate, perhaps at some upper harmonics of the original frequency, and emit sound. It is the task of equipment designers to avoid vibration (e.g. by good balancing) and prevent the transmission of such vibration (e.g. by using flexible mountings or flexible connectors in a duct or pipework).

Impact noise can be reduced at the point where the impact would transmit mechanical energy into the building fabric, by e.g. a resilient lining. The most common form of this is the use of carpets with underfelt.

Airborne noise emission from a source can be reduced by some form of (possibly partial) enclosure. A complete and heavyweight enclosure would be the most effective. If it has some openings (e.g. vents), then the inside could be lined with absorbent materials to reduce the sound field. If access is needed (e.g. for an operator of some machinery), a four-sided box can be installed, with one side open, and lined with absorbents. Fig. 3.19 shows a possible partial enclosure and its sound reduction effect in directional terms.

In an industrial situation, where the noise sources are in the same space as the receivers, the American 'room criteria' (RC) curves (Fig. 3.20) may be applicable. These are similar to the NC curves (Fig. 3.14) but are extended at the low-frequency end (16 Hz), they coincide with and are calibrated by the dB level at 1000 Hz, do not extend above 4000 Hz and include the range from RC25 to RC50 only. Beyond this range the NC (or

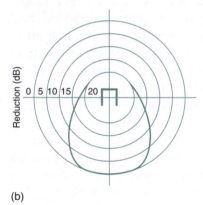

(b)

3.19

A partial enclosure for sound control and its effect on sound distribution (polar curve)

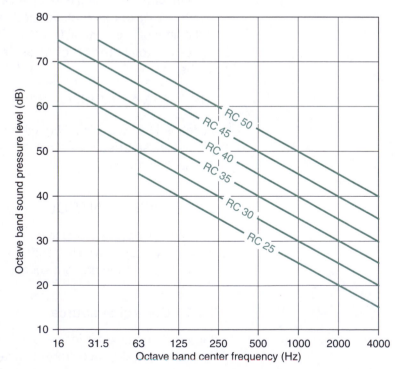

3.20

Room criteria (RC) curves

NR) curves are more applicable. For speech intelligibility RC35 should not be exceeded. Above that, the sound would have a masking effect, which may be desirable for privacy purposes. If at the low frequency end the specified curve is exceeded by more than 5 dB, it will be perceived as 'rumble', and such an excess at the high frequency end will be judged as 'hissy'.

The term 'environmental noise' is often used for noise that had escaped from its source and exists in the general environment, possibly from numerous sources, mainly from

- industry
- road traffic
- air traffic.

The reduction of industrial noise is primarily an engineering task: to make the machinery less noisy. Confinement (as Fig. 3.19) or enclosing the sources before the noise escapes into the environment may involve the building designer.

High-flying aircraft (at around 10 km) have little effect on environmental noise at ground level. The problem is more acute around airports as aircraft come low to land and even more so at take-off. Only regulatory and planning measures can have the desired effects, such as banning aircraft movements between, say, 23:00 and 5:00, by requiring aircraft to use less than maximum power (thus maximum noise) at take-off (e.g. sound level metering at the end of the runway, with penalties set if a noise limit is exceeded). Planning measures could include, in the first place, locating the airports in non-sensitive areas, e.g. on a peninsula, or where at least the main take-off path is over water or non-residential (e.g. industrial/agricultural) areas.

Planning measures can greatly reduce the noise problem, if zones of noise-producing industries are kept separate from noise-sensitive areas, e.g. residential areas. In positioning industries (and other noise sources) the directionality of the source must be taken into account, to point away from noise-sensitive zones and to be downwind from such zones. (NB: this should also be done for reasons of air pollution.) The control of community noise, as discussed in Section 3.2.4 above, is a regulatory question and very much dependent on reasonableness, a responsible attitude to noise generation and on consensus.

3.3.2 Transmission acoustics

Sound is transmitted by a medium which can vibrate: most often we are concerned with airborne sound, but it can also be transmitted by liquids or solids. Environmental noise may be ubiquitous, but identifying the paths of transmission may provide opportunities for control.

- *In a free field* sound reduces with the square of distance from the source. This means that for every doubling of distance the sound level is reduced by 6 dB. (If intensity is reduced by a factor of 4, then $L = 10 \times \log 4 = 6$

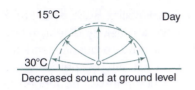

3.21

The effect of daytime temperature gradient

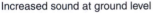

3.22

The effect of temperature inversion at night on a sound wavefront

dB.) The additional molecular absorption in air at high frequencies is shown in Data sheet D.3.2. Such molecular absorption will change the sound spectrum, by filtering out the higher frequency components (e.g. while nearby thunder has a 'clang', from a greater distance it sounds more as a rumble).

- *Ground cover*, over which the sound travels, may cause a surface friction, thus reduce the sound, which is noticeable if both source and the receiver are near ground level. Paved surfaces give no such reduction, but the effect of tall grass, shrubs and trees can be quite significant, as indicated by the table given in Data sheet D.3.2.

- *Temperature gradients* can have an effect. During the day the temperature near the ground is higher, sound travels faster, so sound in a lower layer overtakes that in higher layers, so the 'sound ray' is curved upwards: at ground level, at a given distance the sound level will be less than what it would be in air of uniform temperature (Fig. 3.21). At night, when temperature inversion occurs (the ground surface is cooled by outgoing radiation), it is the upper (warmer layers) where the sound travels faster, thus 'sound rays' are deflected downwards, reinforcing the sound near ground level (Fig. 3.22).

- *Wind* reduces sound upwind from the source and increases it downwind, not only because of the velocity effect, but due also to the distortion of the spherical wavefront. In Fig. 3.23 the arrows show the hypothetical 'sound rays' as they are deflected. The small vector diagram is an enlargement of the top of a wave-front. The result of this is that some sound, which would in still air travel upwards, is deflected and reinforces the sound at ground level.

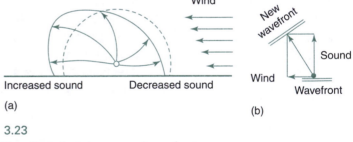

3.23

The effect of wind on a sound wavefront

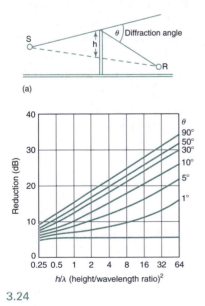

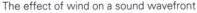

3.24

a: a noise barrier, defining h and θ

b: its sound reduction effect

Even if not 'controlled', some noises may be attenuated by barriers. *Barriers*, such as walls, screens or other objects (including buildings) create an acoustic shadow. The attenuation within this shadow depends on the frequency of the sound. While high frequency sounds behave similar to light, at low frequencies much diffraction can occur at the edge of the barrier, which will diminish the shadow effect. One method of predicting this shadow effect requires the calculation of the h/λ (height /wavelength) quotient and determination of the 'diffraction angle' (θ) belonging to the receiver's point (see Fig. 3.24a).

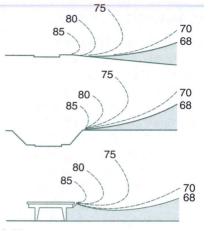

3.25

Noise contours at roads: on level, in cut and elevated (contours in dBA)

Note that the 'height' is taken only as above the straight line connecting the source with the receiver. The reduction (in dB) can then be read from the graph (Fig. 3.24b). This shows that the effect is much greater with a larger λ angle (nearer to or higher barrier) and at larger h/λ ratios (shorter wavelengths). Other methods to estimate the barrier effect are given in Method sheet M.3.2.

For any noise barrier to be effective, it should have a surface density of not less than 20 kg/m². A 10 mm thick dense concrete panel, 15 mm fibrous cement sheeting, or a 30 mm hardwood boarding would satisfy this requirement.

Noise effects from a road can be lessened by placing it either in a cutting or have an elevated road. Fig. 3.25 shows (in section) the expected noise contours adjacent to such roads.

If a large site is available, the first step would be to place the building as far away from the noise source as possible. If possible, any building should be placed outside the 68 dBA contour. The area between the buildings and the noise source could be heavily vegetated. The noise reduction effect of such 'tree-belts' is given in Data sheet D.3.2. Shaping the terrain, e.g. forming a mound or a hill, can provide a barrier effect.

In some residential developments near busy roads (e.g. motorways) certain blocks of flats have been designed to act as barrier blocks (Fig. 3.26). These would have all habitable rooms facing away from the noise source road, and have service areas on the side facing the road, with very small windows.. The best arrangement is if this block is parallel to the road. The difference in noise exposure between the two sides of such a block can be as much as 30 dBA. If the sheltered side is at an angle to the road, the reduction is less, as indicated by Fig. 3.26.

For buildings that are acoustically more critical, a full spectral analysis should be carried out. This is best illustrated by an example.

If noise at A is 80 dBA

then at B: 77 dBA
C: 65 dBA
D: 50 dBA
E: 50 dBA

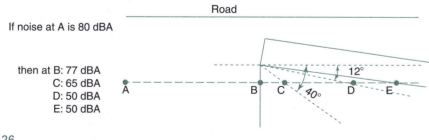

3.26

A building as barrier and its noise reduction effect

EXAMPLE 3.2   NOISE CONTROL: SPECTRAL ANALYSIS

The analysis can be carried out graphically (Fig. 3.27) or in tabulated form (Table 3.5). A lecture theatre block is to be built near a busy road. The noise spectrum at the boundary (10 m from the centreline of the road) is taken as that shown in Fig. 3.15 (line 1). The site is large enough to allow placing the building at a distance of 40 m from the road. This means two 'doublings' of the distance, i.e. a reduction of 12 dB. The reduced spectrum is line 2. The requirement is that the intruding noise should be no more than NR25 (from Data sheet D.3.1). This is drawn as line 3. The difference between lines 2 and 3 is the noise insulation requirement, and this is now plotted up from the base line (line 4). The next step is to select (e.g. from Data sheet D.3.3) a form of construction which would give the required TL values in each octave. It will be seen that for 1000 Hz and above, a 110 mm brick wall would be adequate, but the traffic noise is strong in low frequencies. The critical octave will be 125 Hz, thus a 220 mm brick must be used. The octave-band TL values of this are plotted and are given in Table 3.5.

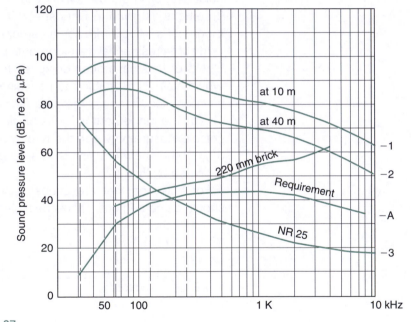

3.27
Spectral analysis for required insulation

Table 3.5   Spectral analysis in tabulated form (in Hz)

Octave band centres:	63	125	250	500	1000	2000	4000	8000
1 at 10 m from road	98	95	89	85	81	77	71	64
2 at 40 m from road	86	83	77	73	69	65	59	52
3 NR 25	55	44	35	29	25	22	20	18
4 insulation required	31	39	42	44	44	43	39	34
5 TL of 220 mm brick		41	45	48	56	58	62	

If all these measures are insufficient, then the building envelope itself must be noise insulating. If the building is at the 68 dBA contour (Fig. 3.27), the transmission loss of the envelope should be at least 20 dB, but preferably 25 or 30 dB. Data sheet D.3.3 shows that most wall elements are more than adequate. However, the weakest points are air-bricks, ventilator openings and windows. If the overall noise insulation is not enough, the most economical measures would be to improve these weak points. A single-glazed window, with TL = 22 dB, would be just about enough, but openings should be avoided.

3.3.3 Transmission in buildings

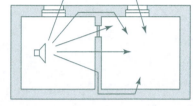

3.28

Sound transmission paths between two rooms

Building design measures would consist of having sealed buildings in the noise-affected area, with good noise insulation, which would imply the use of mechanical ventilation or air conditioning. Failing that, some partial control of noise admission is still possible. Often the problem is not so much the entry of external (environmental) noises, but, if the noise source is within the building, then its transmission from one room to another. Sound can be transmitted not only through a dividing partition, but through a number of flanking paths, as indicated by Fig. 3.28. Sound-insulating properties of a partition or dividing wall can be expressed in two ways:

1 as a sound reduction index (SRI) or transmission loss (TL) – the two terms mean the same – in units of dB;
2 as transmittance (τ), which is a coefficient of intensity (I) or rate of energy transmission.

Similar to light transmission, sound energy incident on a solid object (such as a partition) would be distributed in three ways: part of it can be reflected (ρ), part of it can be absorbed (α) and the reminder transmitted (τ). The sum of the three components is unity:

$$\rho + \alpha + \tau = 1$$

If the sound intensity on the source side is I', the transmitted (received) sound intensity will be

$$I'' = I' \times \tau$$

but if the sound level on the source side is L', then the sound level on the receiving side will be

$$L'' = L' - TL$$

thus TL $\propto$ $(1/\tau)$ (or the loss is proportionate to that NOT transmitted). Fig. 3.29 is an example of sound transmitted in two ways.

The relationship is

$$TL = 10 \log(1/\tau) = 10 \, (-\log \tau) \tag{3.8}$$

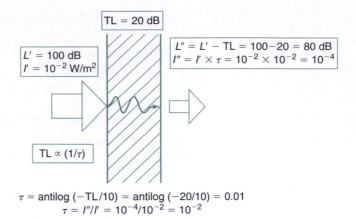

$$\tau = \text{antilog}\,(-TL/10) = \text{antilog}\,(-20/10) = 0.01$$
$$\tau = I''/I' = 10^{-4}/10^{-2} = 10^{-2}$$

3.29

An example of expressing transmission two ways

conversely

$$\tau = \frac{1}{\text{antilog}\left(\dfrac{TL}{10}\right)} = \text{antilog}\,\frac{-TL}{10} \tag{3.9}$$

The mass law states that every doubling of surface density (or unit area mass) of a partition increases the TL by 6 dB and

$$TL \approx 20\,\log M$$

where M is surface density in kg/m^2.

In practice, due to various imperfections, the increase in TL is likely to be only 5 dB for a doubling of the mass, thus $TL \approx 17\,\log M$.

Transmission is also frequency-dependent. If a molecule of a body has to vibrate faster (at higher frequency), its dampening effect will be greater. Thus the mass law also states that the TL will increase by 6 dB for every doubling of the frequency. Therefore, the TL graph as a function of frequency will show an upward slope. This TL will, however, be reduced by (a) resonance and by (b) coincidence. The first, the *resonant region*, depends on the resonant frequency of the wall. For sounds at this frequency (or its upper harmonics), the TL is greatly reduced.

The second is the *coincidence region*, which depends also on the angle of incidence of sound, as the incident wavefronts sweep the wall surface. As Fig. 3.30 indicates, (a) is likely to cause problems in buildings at low frequencies, and (b) at high frequencies. The mass law will be fully operative in the medium frequencies only. The purpose of sound insulation improvements is to push the resonance region downwards and the coincidence region upwards.

Data sheet D.3.3 gives the TL values of various building elements for different frequencies and an overall average.

Some simple empirical expressions for the average TL of solid, homogeneous elements are:

$$TL = 18\,\log M + 8 \text{ if } M > 100\ kg/m^2 \tag{3.10}$$

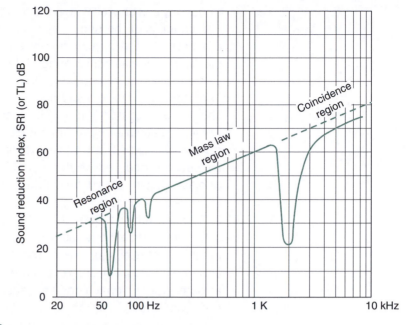

3.30

A transmission graph showing resonance and coincidence regions

and

$$TL = 14.5 M + 13 \text{ if } M < 100 \text{ kg/m}^2 \qquad (3.11)$$

or for the TL in any octave band

$$TL_f = 18 \log M + 12 \log f_c - 25$$

where f_c = octave band centre frequency.

The highest achievable TL value is 55 or 60 dB. When the TL of a partition reaches about 50 dB, the flanking transmission paths become progressively more and more dominant.

Method sheet M.3.1 shows the calculation of average TL values for a dividing element consisting of different components, e.g. a partition with a door or a wall with a window. It shows that the 'chain is as good as its weakest link', that e.g. a relatively small opening can destroy the TL of a heavy wall. For double-leaf walls or partitions (provided that the two leaves are not connected), the TL value will be some 8 dB higher than if the same mass were used in one leaf, e.g.

110 mm brickwork	TL = 45 dB
220 mm brickwork	TL = 50 dB
270 mm cavity wall	TL = 58 dB

This improvement is, however, reduced at the resonant frequency, and at this frequency the TL of the cavity wall could become less than the solid double thickness wall.

For best effects the cavity should be at least 100 mm as the resonant frequency of this cavity would be lower. With light materials the resonant frequency can be well within the audible range, so the cavity should be wider. The coupling of the two skins by a resonant sound field in the cavity can be prevented by the introduction of some porous absorbent (e.g. a glass wool blanket). This may improve the TL by some 5 dB.

A special case of double walls is a double-glazed window. Here the most important point is to avoid acoustic coupling of the two layers. The cavity should be at least 200 mm wide, otherwise the cavity resonance will be well within the audible range. Airtight closure of both leaves is important and the reveals should be lined with an absorbent material, to reduce any cavity resonance. To further reduce the probability of acoustic coupling, the two sheets of glass should be of different thickness, thus of different resonant and coincidence frequencies.

If one examines Data sheet D.3.3 it is apparent that no window would satisfy the insulating requirements, therefore there cannot be any windows in this (most exposed) wall. In many countries, building regulations prescribe airborne sound insulation requirements between different occupancies, such as party walls in terrace (row) houses and flats, as well as floors between flats or maisonettes.

Some regulations specify only the *sound transmission class* (STC) values for such separating elements, but these are no substitute for an octave band analysis. STC is a single-figure index based on measurements of the TL for each 1/3-octave band between 125 and 4000 Hz, the number given by the TL measured at 500 Hz. Tables give the limiting values for each of the 16 measurements and the sum of deviations from these should not exceed 32 dB.

Sound can be readily transmitted by an air conditioning or ventilation duct, both from the plant itself (e.g. fan-noise) or from one room to another. This can be reduced by lining the duct with an absorbent material. A 25 mm fibrous material lining could give the following reductions in dB per m length:

	125 Hz	250 Hz	500 Hz	1000 Hz	2000 Hz	4000 Hz
Bare metal	0.3	0.3	0.3	0.3	0.3	0.3
With absorbent lining	0.9	2.4	5.7	16	15	8

The Australian EBS (experimental building station) produced a 'noise control nomogram', which is shown as Fig. 3.31. The first column shows the noise source in one space and the last column shows the receiver space functions. A straight edge laid across will show in the middle column what construction would be adequate to separate the two.

3.3.3.1 Structure-borne sound insulation

Structure-borne sound insulation is a totally different problem. While airborne sound impinging on a building surface would generate some vibration in the fabric, i.e. some structure-borne sound, it would be of negligible level. Structure-borne sound is significant where it would be generated by mechanical impacts or vibration. (Impact noise is often confused with structure-borne

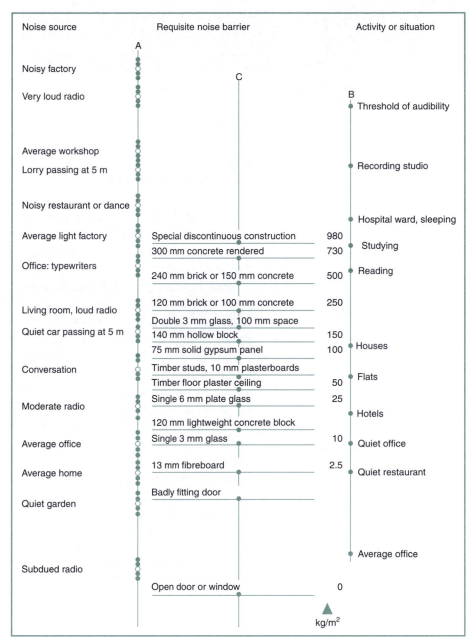

3.31
A noise control nomogram

noise, as they are strongly connected. Impact is the source, the structure transmits the noise.) Impacts are the major source of structure-borne sound, but not the only source. It can be reduced at the source by resilient surface linings (e.g. carpets), and its transmission can be prevented (or reduced) by structural discontinuity.

The most likely source of structure-borne sound is footsteps or dropping objects on a hard floor. Dropping a spoon on kitchen floor (a tiled concrete slab) can generate a noise of over 80 dB in the room below. It would be a short transient noise, quickly dying away, but can be quite disturbing.

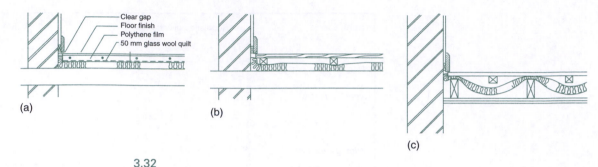

(a)　　　　　　　　　　(b)

(c)

3.32
Some 'floating floor arrangements

Fig. 3.32 shows some arrangements for 'floating floors', where a resilient layer would isolate the floor surface from the structural floor below it. Some building regulations prescribe the use of such floors between separate occupancies (e.g. flats).

Note, however, that structure-borne and airborne sound insulation are two separate matters. Fig. 3.32c may provide discontinuity, but may not give an adequate TL for airborne noise insulation. The table of TL values given in Data sheet D.3.3 relate to airborne noise transmission.

Structural discontinuity may also have a role in double layer partitions. One leaf may be rigidly connected to the floor below and above, as well as the adjoining main walls, but the second leaf should sit on flexible mountings and be isolated all around from the adjoining elements, at least by a cork strip. This would reduce the structure-borne transmission of vibrations.

As an example, take a 220 mm solid brick wall, both sides plastered, with a surface density of 440 kg/m^2. Compare the possible improvements, without changing the wall mass:

The original 220 solid brick wall	av TL = 50 dB
Two skins of 110 mm of the same	av TL = 53 dB
With a glass wool quilt in the cavity	av TL = 58 dB
Same, but one skin isolated	av Tl = 60 dB

The theoretically possible limit is a TL of about 62 dB.

3.3.4　Noise control by absorption

The task of the designer may be to reduce the noise level in the room where the noise source is. As Fig. 3.33 shows, the sound field at any point in a room consists of two components: direct and reverberant sounds. The direct component reduces with the distance from the source, but the reverberant component (all possible reflections and interreflections) is taken as homogeneous throughout the room, and is dependent on room surfaces.

As mentioned in Section 3.3.2, sound incident on a surface can be reflected, absorbed or transmitted, thus reflectance + absorptance + transmittance: $\rho + \alpha + \tau = 1$. From the point of view of a room where the sound is gener-

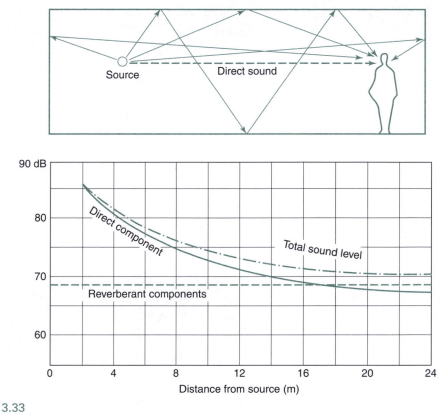

3.33

Direct and reverberant sound in a room

ated and considered, the *absorption coefficient* (a) is **all that is not reflected**. Thus, a = 1 − ρ, or a = α + τ. Indeed the unit of absorption is the 'open window unit' which does not reflect any sound (a = 1), and it is measured in m². The total absorption (Abs) in a room is the sum of all surface elements area(s) × absorption coefficient (a) of the materials and products.

$$Abs = \Sigma \ (s \times a) \tag{3.12}$$

Data sheet D.3.5 lists the absorption coefficients of numerous surfacing elements and proprietary products. It is this total absorption that determines the reverberant component. If the absorption is doubled, the reflected power is reduced by half, which means a reduction of 3 dB in sound level (as 10 log ½ = −3).

In a room which has poor absorption (all hard surfaces), it may not be too difficult to increase the absorption by a factor of 8 (three doublings or 2^3), which would give a reduction of 9 dB. However, if the room already has highly absorbent surfaces, it may be quite difficult (and expensive) to produce even one doubling.

For most room surfaces, if transmittance (τ) is negligible:

a = α

where α is the actual absorptance, and 'a' is the absorption coefficient (all that is not reflected).

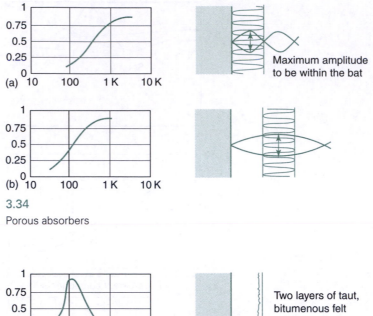

(a)

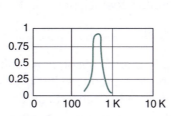

(b)

3.34
Porous absorbers

Maximum amplitude
to be within the bat

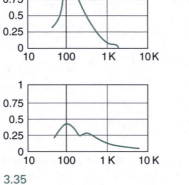

Two layers of taut,
bitumenous felt

10 mm plywood

3.35
Membrane absorbers

3.36
A cavity resonator absorber

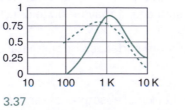

Perforated hardboard
glass fibre bat behind

3.37
Perforated panel absorber

There are four basic types of absorbers, the absorption being due to different processes:

1   *Porous absorbers*, such as mineral wool, glass wool, fibreboard or plastic foams which have an open cell structure (Fig. 3.34a). Vibrations are converted to heat by the friction of vibrating air molecules and the cell walls. These are most effective for high frequency (short wave) sounds. If the thickness (b) is less than quarter wavelength (b $<$ λ/4), they have little effect. If such a sheet is fixed at some distance from a solid surface (Fig. 3.34b), it will have almost the same effect as a thicker absorber. It will be most effective for sounds with a ¼ wavelength equal to the distance from the solid surface to the centre of the absorber. In this case the maximum amplitude of both the incident and the reflected wave would occur within the porous material.

2   *Membrane absorbers* may be flexible sheets stretched over supports, or rigid panels mounted at some distance from a solid wall. Conversion to heat would occur due to the rapid flexing of the membrane and repeated compression of the air behind it. These will be most effective at their resonant frequency, which depends on the surface density of the membrane, the width of the enclosed space and on the fixing and stiffness of the membrane or panel. Most such absorbers are effective in the low frequency range (Fig. 3.35).

3   *Cavity (Helmholz) resonators* are air containers with narrow necks (Fig. 3.36). The air in the cavity has a spring-like effect at the particular resonant frequency of the enclosed air volume. These have very high absorption coefficients in a very narrow frequency band. Large pottery jars built into stone walls with their opening flush with the wall surface are the original examples from Greek amphitheatres.

4   *Perforated panel absorbers* combine all three of the above mechanisms (Fig. 3.37). The panel itself may be plywood, hardboard, plasterboard or metal and many act primarily as a membrane absorber. The perforations, holes or slots with the air space behind them act as multiple cavity resonators, improved by some porous absorber. Most of the broad-spectrum commercially available 'acoustic materials' (e.g. ceiling tiles) fall into this category.

There are several misconceptions prevalent in this context. Many people confuse absorption with insulation, probably because some materials are used for both purposes. *Fibrous materials* (glass- or mineral wool) are good for thermal insulation but useless for noise insulation. Air vibrations would penetrate these like a sieve. If it is possible to blow air through them, sound will travel through them with very little loss. They may be good absorbers if mounted on a solid backing, reducing reflections. For noise insulation, that is for stopping noise going through a wall or partition, mass is the best answer.

The case is different with *porous materials*. For thermal insulation the best ones have a closed pore structure, such as polystyrene, but these would be useless for acoustic absorption, where an open pore structure is best.

Similar materials, e.g. a glass fibre quilt, can be used to reduce impact noise transmission, e.g. for supporting a floating floor. Here it is not any absorbent

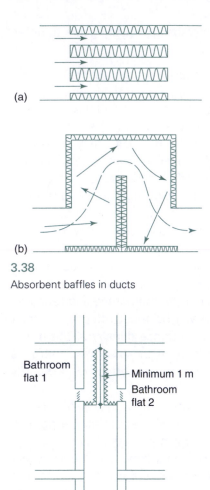

3.38

Absorbent baffles in ducts

3.39

Absorbent baffle between bathrooms

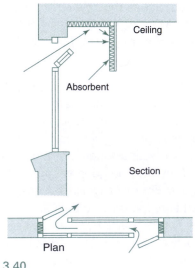

3.40

A: an absorbent pelmet
B: a ventilating window

property which would be used, it is only providing a resilient support for a 'floating floor', to break the rigid connection and thus the path of structure-borne sound transmission.

Another instance which may cause confusion is the use of absorbent materials in the cavity of a double layer construction. Here the mechanism of transmission is that as the source-side skin vibrates, it sets up a sound field within the cavity, which will in turn cause vibrations in the second skin. This is referred to as 'acoustic coupling' of the two skins. Placing some absorbent in the cavity would reduce the intensity of the sound field, thus reducing the effect on the second skin. The overall effect is an improved TL.

Absorbers can be applied to reduce sound going through openings, which must be kept open for ventilation purposes. The most common example of this is the 'silencer' of car exhaust pipes. In air conditioning a 'silencer' is fitted in after the fan, to absorb aerodynamic noise created by the fan (Fig. 3.38a). If a ventilation duct serves two bathrooms, an absorbent section is provided to stop sounds going across, to ensure aural privacy (Fig. 3.39).

A ventilator opening in a window would admit noise: this can be reduced by an absorbent lined pelmet or baffles (Fig. 3.40). This will not be 'noise insulation', only a reduction of noise penetration by absorption.

In hot climates, where the window is kept open for natural ventilation, an absorbent lining on the soffit of a canopy or on the ceiling near the window would produce some reduction in the transmitted noise (Fig. 3.41). Even louvres used in windows to allow ventilation can have such absorbent lining (Fig. 3.42). Rarely would even the best of such absorbent openings produce a reduction in sound level more than about 6 dB.

Absorption has a role in reducing the noise level in a given space where the noise source is (as discussed above), but its role is most important in designing for room acoustics, which will be discussed in Section 3.4.

3.3.5 Vibrations

Sound itself is vibration between 20 Hz and 16 kHz, but there are also subsonic and supersonic vibrations (infra- and ultra-sounds), as indicated by Fig. 3.9. Generally the term 'vibration' is used for the subsonic range.

In buildings, vibration may be caused by mechanical equipment, such as air conditioning fans, compressors, pumps or lift machinery. Vibration itself is rarely perceived, but as it is transmitted by the building fabric, it may cause vibration of some components at upper harmonic frequencies, which are audible. Such resonance of e.g. lightweight partitions or suspended ceilings can be quite disconcerting. The problem is somewhat similar to structure-borne noise control. The best solution is to tackle the problem at or near the source.

Source vibration should be limited. Table 3.6 lists such recommended limits of vibration displacement (peak-to-peak) of some (noise source) equipment types.

Any unavoidable vibration should be isolated, e.g. by placing the machinery on flexible mountings and have flexible connections (e.g. to ducts). Many different isolators are commercially available, but the choice should be left to specialists. Fig. 3.43 shows the principles of some solutions.

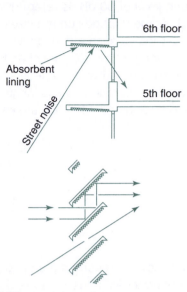

Absorbent lining

Street noise

6th floor

5th floor

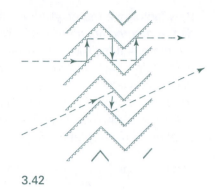

3.42
Absorbent louvres (plan views)

3.41
Absorbent lining of soffit and absorbent louvres

Table 3.6 Equipment vibration limits

Equipment	Peak-to-peak	mm
Pumps	1800 RPM	0.05
	3600 RPM	0.025
Centrifugal compressors		0.025
Fans	under 600 RPM	0.1
	600–1000 RPM	0.075
	1000–2000 RPM	0.05
	Over 2000 RPM	0.025

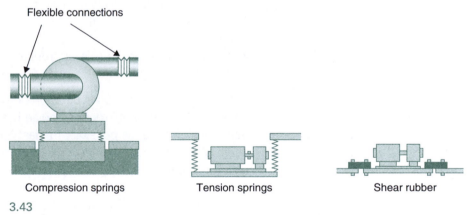

Flexible connections

Compression springs   Tension springs   Shear rubber

3.43
Main types of flexible mountings

3.4 ROOM ACOUSTICS

In a room when a sound source is switched on and it operates at a steady level, the intensity of the sound field increases (the room – as it were – is being filled with sound) until the energy absorption rate equals the energy input rate. At that point, equilibrium would exist and the sound field would be steady.

When the source is switched off, the reverberant sound field would persist for a little time as it gradually decays. The time taken for the sound field to drop

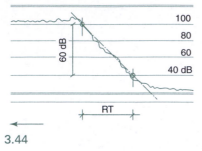

3.44

Chart recording of reverberation time

by a factor of a million (10^6), i.e. a drop in sound level of 60 dB, is referred to as the *reverberation time* (RT). The length of this time depends on the size of the room and the room surfaces. A little energy is lost at each reflection. With hard surfaces it will take more reflections, thus a longer time for the sound to decay. In a larger room the sound travels a longer time between reflections, there are fewer reflections in unit time, thus the reverberation time is longer.

A simple empirical expression was proposed by Sabine (1922) (for the calculation of reverberation time:

$$RT = 0.16 \times \frac{V}{Abs} \text{ (in seconds)} \tag{3.13}$$

where

V = volume of room (m³)
Abs = total absorption in room (m²)

Fig. 3.44 shows a paper strip on which the sound level is recorded graphically against time, referred to as the 'decay curve' that defines the RT.

3.4.1 Requirements

A room, where listening to some sound is an important function, is said to have 'good acoustics' if the following conditions are satisfied:

1 Any background noise is low enough and the wanted sound is loud enough for it to be audible, intelligible, enjoyable and free of disturbance.
2 The sound field is well diffused, free of deaf spots and loud zones.
3 There are no echoes, flutter echoes, standing waves or other acoustic distortions.
4 The reverberation time is appropriate for the purpose (see Fig. 3.50 on p. 250) and well balanced across the audible frequencies.

The first of these is the consideration of the receiver. The individual's space is taken as the 'receiving' room. If noise has been tackled at the source and in transmission as far as possible, the last line of defence is the receiving room itself. Massive construction for its enclosure can minimise airborne transmission. Structure-borne noise and vibrations can be eliminated by discontinuous construction.

The ultimate form of this is the 'floating room', used for acoustic laboratories or other extremely noise-sensitive rooms. An example of this is shown in Fig. 3.45. It is a room-within-a-room, where the inner shell is not in rigid contact with the outer building structure, even the floor sits on flexible mountings.

Such construction was used for the old BBC studios in Portland Place in London, to isolate these from the vibration and structure-borne sound of the Tube, running immediately below it. In the Royal Festival Hall the whole auditorium sits on flexible rubber pads and has a dual wall structure, following the principles indicated by Fig. 3.45. Some BRE laboratories at Garston, Watford, follow this method and will be discussed in Section 3.4.4.3 below.

The other requirements will be discussed in the sections following.

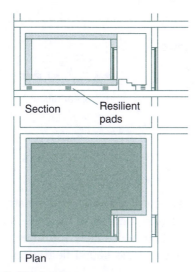

Section   Resilient pads

Plan

3.45

A fully isolated 'floating room' construction

In spaces where voice communication (listening to speech) is important, the noise limits can be set in terms of *speech interference level* (SIL). As for human speech the most important frequencies are 500, 1000 and 2000 Hz, this has been defined as

$$SIL = (L_{500} + L_{1000} + L_{2000}) / 3 \qquad (3.14)$$

i.e. the arithmetic average of the three octave band sound levels.

Comparing this with Fig. 3.12, it can be seen that the NR curves are in fact a straight line from 500 to 2000 Hz, thus they coincide with the SIL. The SIL is a sub-set of the NR curves. Frequencies below 500 and above 2000 Hz are less important for speech intelligibility.

3.4.2 Room size and shape

Up to about 300 m³ room volume a single voice can be heard without difficulty and without any special treatment of room surfaces. Echoes are unlikely to occur, but if one room dimension is less than the half wavelength of the lowest audible frequency (some 8.5 m), standing waves can develop between parallel opposing (reflective) surfaces. This causes room resonance, i.e. an increase in loudness and reverberation time for the particular frequency.

As the room size increases from 300 to 30 000 m³, the need for reinforcement of the sound for the further part of the audience also increases. Geometrical acoustics helps determine room surfaces for directed reflections. If a single voice is to be intelligible, an amplification system may be necessary in rooms larger than about 8000 m³. In larger auditoria standing waves are unlikely, but echoes can occur. Good diffusion and correct RT will be critical. Fig. 3.50 shows the recommended RT values for speech and music, as a function of room volume.

In normal speech, 6 to 10 syllables are pronounced per second, which – on average – corresponds to 0.13 second per syllable. The same sound may arrive at a listener first by a direct path and after a reflection again, with a time delay. If this delay is less than 0.035 s (35 milliseconds), the second arrival will not be distinguishable from the first, it will reinforce it. If the delay is more than about half the time per syllable (0.06–0.07 s), it will be perceived as a repetition of the same sound, i.e. an *echo*.

A delay between the two limits (0.035 and 0.07 s) may give a blurring effect. Fig. 3.46 shows the decay curve with a distinct echo and one with a *flutter-echo*. The latter may be experienced in interconnected rooms or a room with a (large) alcove, but also (at particular frequencies) between opposing parallel surfaces.

In 0.06 second, sound would travel some 20 m. If there is a difference in path length between the direct and reflected sound, an echo will be perceived. Fig. 3.47 shows some situations where an echo could occur. This could be avoided by checking room geometry both in plan and in section, to find any situation where a path-length difference over 20 m could occur and using highly absorbent materials for surfaces which could produce such unwanted reflections. A special case is the *corner echo*, in rectangular corners, where the sound may be reflected, returned parallel with the original. These can be avoided if there are no rectangular corners, if the wall and a 1–2 m strip of the ceiling are lined with absorbents.

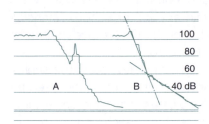

A: Echo
B: Flutter echo (double slope, due to interconnected rooms, or an alcove)

3.46

An echo and a flutter echo

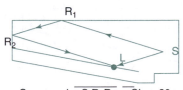

Corner echo $\overline{S R_1 R_2} > SL + 20$ m

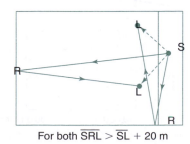

For both $\overline{SRL} > \overline{SL} + 20$ m

3.47

Situations where echo could occur

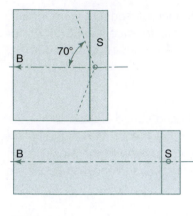

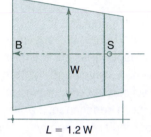

$L = 1.2\,W$

3.48

Basic issues for shape of auditoria

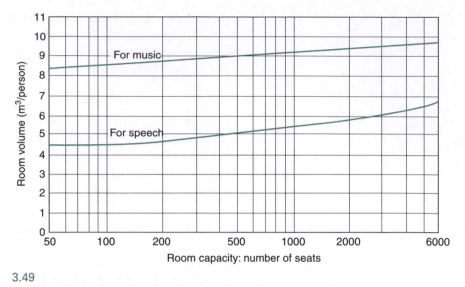

3.49

Minimum volume of auditoria for music and speech

The most likely source of problem in an auditorium is the rear wall, which should be as absorbent as possible. To avoid any flutter echo or standing waves, the side walls should not be parallel, they should be divergent by at least 2.5–3° relative to the longitudinal axis (Fig. 3.48).

For reasons of economy and for the best non-amplified sound the auditorium should be as small as possible, but a lower limit is set by the need for some reverberation. The graph of Fig. 3.49 indicates the minimum volume of auditoria (as a function of number of seats) for speech and for music. The room can be made larger than indicated, at the expense of using more absorbent materials.

The best sound is received in the 'near field' where the direct sound dominates over any reflections. This suggests that the distance between the

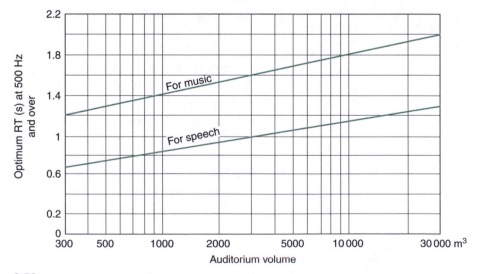

3.50

Recommended reverberation time (RT) for speech and music

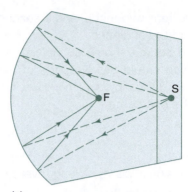

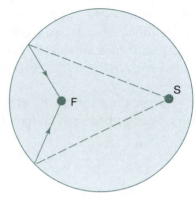

(a)

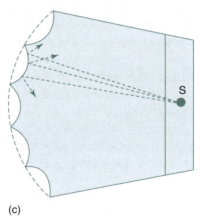

(b)

(c)

3.51

Concave shapes: risk of focussing and uneven sound field: breaking up rear wall into convex elements may help

speaker (or sound source) should be as small as possible: a short, wide room is better than the same area in an elongated form. Intelligibility is reduced beyond about 70° from the direction the speaker is facing, and this sets a limit to width. The length should be between 1.2 and 2 times the width of the room. A trapezoidal plan may have several advantages (see Fig. 3.48). Fig. 3.51 shows other shapes.

Geometrical or optical acoustics (using light beam and reflection analogies) can help to solve many acoustic problems. The designer's aim is to get most of the sound emitted by the source to the audience directly and evenly. Fig. 3.52 indicates that in a lecture room with a flat floor the audience would receive sound from within a (vertical) angle of 17° from the source. Putting the speaker on a dais can increase this to some 30° and a raked floor to 40° and more. The floor slope should be at least 8°, but in lecture theatres (especially if demonstrations are to be visible), 15° is justifiable. Method sheet M.3.4 gives the setting out technique for what is referred to as the 'progressive rake'.

Serious distortions can be caused by the focussing effect of concave room surfaces. A dome or a circular room can create a very uneven sound field, but a room with a curved rear wall is also liable to cause such a focussing effect. Fig. 3.51 indicates these, but also shows that (in the latter case) the rear wall can be broken up into convex segments to diffuse the sound. In many auditoria (such as the Royal Albert Hall in London), the solution was to suspend discs of various sizes (double convex 'flying saucers') from the ceiling at many points, to disperse and diffuse the sound.

If preference is for direct sound, the second best is the 'first reflections', i.e. for the receiving sound to be reflected only once (before it dissipates into the general reverberant field), which would reinforce any direct sound received. Fig. 3.53 indicates how part of the ceiling can be used to direct such reflections to the rear part of the audience, or how a *sounding board* can be positioned above the source for the same purpose. Progressive reinforcement is

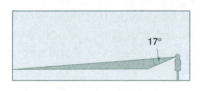

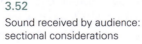

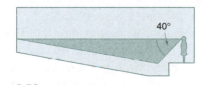

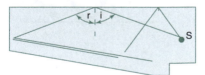

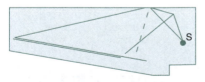

3.52

Sound received by audience: sectional considerations

3.53

Sound reinforcement by reflections
S = speaker or source

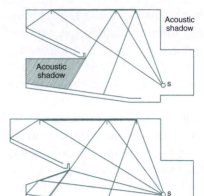

3.54

Acoustic shadow caused by a balcony and a way to avoid it

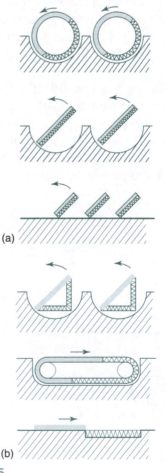

3.55

Systems to provide variable absorption

also possible: one sounding board serving the rear two-thirds, and a second sounding board directed at the rear one-third of the audience.

From any part of the auditorium the sound source should be visible, but acoustic shadows also must be avoided which would deprive parts of the audience of reflected sound reinforcement. Fig. 3.54 shows such a case, the shading effect of a balcony and how it could be overcome.

3.4.3 Room surfaces

For listening to speech the most important criterion is *clarity*. A long reverberation time gives a booming effect, it would reduce clarity. Hence for speech a short reverberation time is desirable. For music, *fullness of tone* is a main criterion. This requires a longer RT. Fig. 3.50 gave the desirable RT for speech and large orchestral music. For chamber music or multipurpose halls the RT should be between the two limits. For music, the given times are valid for 500 Hz and above. The given times should be multiplied by 1.15 for 250 Hz and by 1.5 for 125 Hz.

As shown by eq. 3.13, the RT depends on room volume and on the total absorption. If the volume is given, the required total absorption can be found by inverting the same equation:

$$Abs = (0.16 \times V) / RT \tag{3.15}$$

A large part of the Abs will be the sum of the products of each component surface area multiplied by its absorption coefficient (a). Another significant part may be what is referred to as 'room contents', which includes at least people and seats, but (at high frequencies) also room air. Data sheets D.3.4 and D.3.5 give the absorption coefficients of many materials as well as the total absorption values of some room contents.

Method sheet M.3.2 shows a worked example of reverberation time calculation for the design of room finishes. Note that values averaged for all frequencies are to be avoided, and the calculations should be carried out for at least three frequencies (at two octave distances). A number of simple computer programs are available to carry out such calculations, which may involve numerous trial-and-error loops and may be quite lengthy if done manually.

It is not too difficult to achieve the desired RT for a particular room use and assumed occupation. If the room is to be used for different purposes or if it is to work well for different occupancy rates, some variable absorbers may have to be used. It is customary to design an auditorium for between 2/3 and 3/4 of the seats occupied. To compensate for the absence of human bodies, the underside of tilting seats is made absorbent, but this cannot match the absorption of a human body.

With a lesser occupancy, the RT will be longer, and with a full house it may be shorter than the ideal. To compensate for this, a range of different surfaces of variable absorption can be provided. In the simplest case this can be just drawing a (heavy) curtain over a reflecting wall surface, but rotating or reversible panels can also be used, such as those shown in Fig. 3.55. Some electrical systems to serve the same purpose will be discussed in Section 3.4.4.

3.4.3.1 Acoustic quality

Achieving acoustic quality can be quite elusive. It can happen that all four requirements listed in Section 3.4.1 appear to have been satisfied and the acoustic qualities of the room are still unsatisfactory. It is relatively easy to provide for good listening conditions for speech, but to ensure full enjoyment of music is not an easy task. Many 'acoustic experts' have burnt their fingers. Some, even today, suggest that good acoustics is an 'act of God'. Beyond the four requirements discussed above, it is difficult even to define what constitutes good acoustics. An attempt should be made at least to define some of the terms used.

- *Definition* means that the full timbre of each instrument is heard clearly, so that each would be individually distinguishable and also that successive notes can be distinguished even in a fast passage (up to 15 notes per second). The term *clarity* is often used with the same meaning.
- *Blend* is not the opposite of definition, although it implies that a whole orchestra is perceived as a homogeneous source and the sound is not fragmentary.
- *Balance* is the correct loudness ratio, as perceived at any point in the auditorium, both between different frequencies and between different parts of the orchestra. It implies that the room will not selectively influence the sound.
- *Fullness of tone* is the term used synonymously with warmth, full body, sonority or resonance. It is absent if an instrument is played under open air conditions. It is the perception of the whole range of harmonics, but also the persistence of these harmonics for a few milliseconds. What the room does to the orchestra is similar to what the body of the violin does to the vibrations of the string.

In auditorium design very often too much emphasis is placed on the calculation of reverberation time. This can be calculated quite accurately and in a clear-cut way. This is important, but it is not the only criterion. The location of absorbent and reflective surfaces is at least as important. If one side is more reflective than the other, the sound diffusion will suffer and even our binaural location sense may be deceived, and may come into conflict with the visual. This may be most disconcerting for the audience at the rear of the hall, where the reflected sound may dominate over the direct one.

For example, large glazed areas on one side can cause a distortion of the spectrum. Glass is highly reflective for high frequency sounds, but it may absorb up to 30% of low frequency components, acting as a panel absorber. People at the back may lose the bass component.

Generally it is better to use absorbers in relatively small areas, alternating with reflective surfaces. In historical auditoria good diffusion was achieved, (often perhaps inadvertently) by the highly ornamented and sculptured surfaces. In some modern auditoria, with large plain surfaces, an uneven and ill-balanced sound field has been produced.

There are now great expectations that electrical/electronic measures can be relied on to compensate for the lack of good room acoustics. I am yet to be convinced about this.

3.4.4 Electroacoustics

The trend in cinema design is to rely increasingly on the electrical sound system: in the room itself to provide as much absorption as possible (to get the shortest possible reverberation time), as all resonance, reverberation and other acoustic effects can be produced electronically and included in the sound track. This arrangement is probably where electroacoustics started.

Three items are normally discussed under this heading:

- sound reinforcement systems
- acoustic correction systems
- acoustic measurements.

The first two will be discussed in this section in some detail, but the third one only briefly, as is sufficient for architectural purposes.

3.4.4.1 Sound reinforcement

Sound reinforcement is definitely necessary in auditoria seating more than 1500 people ($\approx$ 8500 m^3), but it is desirable for rooms seating more than 300 people ($\approx$ 1500 m^3). If the room has less than perfect acoustic qualities, or an intruding noise is louder than the recommended NR (e.g. in Data sheet D.3.1), then these limits will be much lower.

A reinforcement system has three main requirements:

1 It is to provide an adequate sound level uniformly over the whole auditorium, so that there are no 'deaf spots' or loud areas.
2 It must not add any noticeable noise.
3 It should preserve the characteristics of the original sound, both in frequency composition and localisation.

Such a system consists of three main parts:

- a microphone
- an amplifier
- loudspeaker(s).

These may be connected by 'hard wiring' or may rely on high frequency radio transmitter/receivers.

Ribbon or *moving coil microphones* are based on electrodynamic effects, and use a permanent magnet, which needs no polarising potential; their output is fairly large, thus they do not need a preamplifier. Disadvantages: they are rather bulky and their frequency response is limited. They are rarely used these days.

Condenser microphones are widely used; they have a good flat response across all audible frequencies and over a wide range of sound levels. Their electrical output is small, therefore they need a preamplifier, as well as a static polarising charge of some 100 V.

Crystal microphones rely on the piezoelectric effect. They can be quite small and need a preamplifier. They are less vulnerable than the former ones and they can be placed in a liquid (to serve as a hydrophone).

Table 3.7 Electrical speaker power requirements (W/100 persons)

Venue	For speech	For music	For dance music
High reverberation rooms	0.5	1	2
Low reverberation rooms	1.0	2	3
Open air	5.0	2	3

There are many different solutions for a microphone assembly, with different directionality characteristics. For sound measurement omnidirectional (spherical) microphones are used, but these are not wanted in an auditorium, as they pick up the sound of loudspeakers and may generate a feedback effect: a howling, screaming noise. Directionally selective microphones are much preferred.

Amplifiers are not our subject, but it should be remembered that an oversized amplifier used at partial capacity gives a much better sound than a less powerful one stretched to its limits.

The average sound power in a medium sized room, without sound reinforcement, due to one human voice is some 3×10^{-6} W, but a loud voice can reach 3×10^{-3} (0.003) W. The electrical-to-acoustic power conversion efficiency of loudspeakers is 0.03 to 0.05. To match a loud voice the speaker power would need to be $P = \frac{0.003}{0.03} = 0.1$ W. A safety factor of 10 to 30 is usually applied to compensate for distribution deficiencies and to avoid using the speaker near its limits. Table 3.7 gives suggested electrical power for speakers, in terms of W per 100 person audience.

Ordinary box-mounted speakers tend to distribute low frequency sound almost spherically, but they have strong directional properties for higher frequencies (Fig. 3.56). 'Column speakers', i.e. 6 to 10 individual speakers mounted in a line, produce strong directionality in the plane they share (normally vertical), while their sideways distribution is the same as of a single speaker (Fig. 3.57). Emission of the top and bottom speakers 'constrains' the emission of the intermediate ones. This is an obvious advantage (and saving of energy) in open air situations or in large halls.

Two basic types of speaker systems can be distinguished:

1 high level (central) system, which consists of a few speakers (possibly columns), located near the dais or stage, near the original source, aimed at the audience to give an even coverage;
2 low level (distributed) system, which uses many small output speakers, distributed over the whole auditorium (usually ceiling-mounted).

The former is less expensive, readily adjustable and has the advantage that the amplified sound comes from the same direction as the original. It can be disastrous in large, non-acoustic spaces, such as a railway concourse or older airport terminals, where announcements are just unintelligible.

The design of low-level systems in auditoria relies on the *Haas effect*. This is the interesting phenomenon that the location (direction) of a source is perceived as the origin of the first sound that reaches the listener. If the same sound arrives with a delay of 10–30 ms (milliseconds), the total sound energy

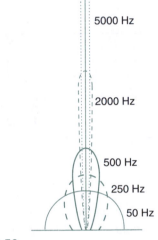

3.56
Directionality of a speaker for different frequencies

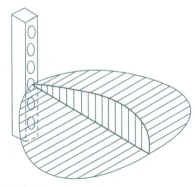

3.57
A column of speakers constrains the distribution vertically, but not horizontally

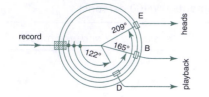

3.58

A rotating magnetic disc time delay system

is perceived as if it were coming from the direction of the first. This happens even if the second sound is much stronger than the first.

Deliberate time delays in the past were created by a rotating magnetic disc (Fig. 3.58) with one recording head and several pickup heads, where the angular distance provided the time delay. This is now done electronically. The output of each speaker in such a system should be small enough to avoid interference.

EXAMPLE 3.3   THE HAAS EFFECT

The Haas effect is made use of by the system shown in principle in Fig. 3.59 (a diagrammatic longitudinal section of an auditorium). There are three rows of low level (low power) speakers. If the distance to a listener at C (the A–C distance) is 40 m, the sound travel time will be 0.12 s and if the distance from the loudspeaker at B (the B–C distance) is 7 m, the travel time will be 0.02 s, so the time difference is 0.1 s. The delay system must provide this plus the intended delay of, say, 0.015 s, a total of 0.115 s (115 ms).

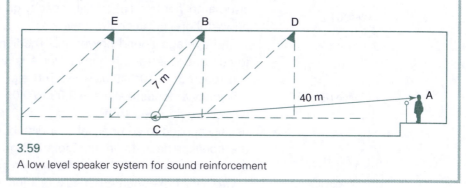

3.59

A low level speaker system for sound reinforcement

The principle is similar to that of PSALI (Section 2.5.6), i.e. to supplement daylighting so that it is hardly noticeable, the daylit character of the room is maintained. Here the sound reinforcement is provided in such a way that the audience is unaware of it.

For public address (and background music systems, if you must have one), the low level system is the only satisfactory solution. In auditoria another advantage of such a system is that the contribution of low power speakers to the reverberant field is imperceptible.

3.4.4.2 Acoustic corrective systems

Acoustic corrective systems have been designed to improve the acoustics of some concert halls. The first such system developed for the Royal Festival Hall in London was euphemistically referred to as an *assisted resonance system* (ARS). This consists of 172 separate channels tuned to very narrow (4 Hz) frequency bands from 20 to 700 Hz (above 700 Hz the room resonance was satisfactory), each consisting of the following components:

- a condenser microphone in a resonant box or tube (with a very narrow frequency response);
- a preamplifier with gain control and delay mechanism and filters to elimi-nate any harmonics picked up by the microphone in the resonator (a reso-nator responds to a particular frequency but also to its upper harmonics);

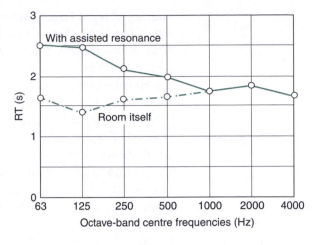

3.60
Reverberation time in the Royal Festival Hall with and without the ARS operating

- a 20 W amplifier;
- a speaker of 250–300 mm diameter.

A complex switchboard allows the low frequency resonance to be adjusted and balanced. The hall itself, with its short RT for low frequencies, was very good for speech intelligibility, but not for large orchestral music. For example, in the 125 Hz octave, the room RT is 1.4s, with the ARS it can be increased to 2.5s. Fig. 3.60 shows the spectral variation of the RT in the Royal Festival Hall itself and with the ARS operating.

Multi-channel reverberation (another acronym: MCR) systems are now commercially available and often included in the original design of auditoria (and not as 'correction') to produce variable acoustic properties, e.g. for multipurpose halls.

Another kind of 'correction' is the design and use of *masking noise systems*. These have been developed and are used mainly in large 'landscaped' offices. Sounds with information content are much more disturbing than a steady hum. A masking noise can suppress the intelligibility of sounds received, but also gives the assurance of aural privacy for people talking who don't want to be overheard. 'White noise' has been used for such purposes, but it has been found that a broad-band sound is more effectively masked by a lower frequency noise. Hence the latest trend is to use a 'pink noise' of a continuous spectrum with a slope of 3 dB per octave (by analogy: pink light: with continuous spectrum, but slightly biased towards longer wavelengths: i.e. a faint red).

In many practical situations, ventilation or air conditioning diffusers are deliberately designed to give a noise of 45 dB at around 1000 Hz, to give a masking effect, but most often masking noise is produced by a generator-amplifier-speaker system.

3.4.4.3 *Acoustic measurements*
Acoustic measurements are based on a sound level meter, using a condenser microphone. It has a built-in RMS rectifier and a read-out device. It usually has a range selector working in 10 dB increments. The second digit is given by a

voltmeter. Most have a set of switchable weighting circuits (the 'C' weighting is practically linear, see Fig. 3.6). Many have an attached octave band filter (more precise measurements use third-octave filters). The output of such meters may be recorded, graphically, on magnetic tape or electronically. Statistical analysers may produce various noise climate indices, such as those mentioned in Section 3.2.4.

Meters and filters coupled with a CRT can produce a real-time spectrogram. Graphic recorders can be used to produce paper versions of the same. Graphic level recorders can be used to measure reverberation time, using either a pistol shot for broad-band measurements or a noise generator with a filter set, producing octave band noise with a 'no-noise' (clean break) switch for cut-off. The latter would produce a decay curve for each octave in sequence (usually 8 octaves). This would give the spectral RT values, such as those shown in Fig. 3.60.

There are two types of acoustic laboratories used for testing the properties of materials, elements or products:

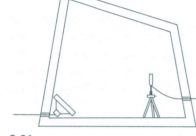

3.61
A large reverberant room for absorbent testing

- *Reverberant rooms* are used to test the absorption properties of material samples for random incidence, including frequency-dependent absorption coefficients. These must be fairly large compared to the wavelength of the lowest frequency sound used, e.g., the wavelength of a 125 Hz sound is 2.72 m and this would need a room of 180 m³. The room must have hard, reflective surfaces; it must be of an irregular shape and include convex, diffusing surfaces, to generate a homogeneous sound field (Fig. 3.61). Here the RT would be measured (both for the empty room and with the absorbent sample present) and from this the absorption of a sample can be found.
- *Transmission test facilities* consist usually of three rooms. These are of very heavy and discontinuous construction, to eliminate flanking transmissions. Two rooms are side-by-side, with a dividing wall of heavy construction, which has an aperture, into which the element to be tested is fitted. Sound generated in the 'source room' is measured in the receiving room, thus the TL (transmission loss), or SRI (sound reduction index) can be established. A third room is often above the receiving room, and the dividing floor has an aperture, into which a floor test sample can be fitted (Fig. 3.62). The

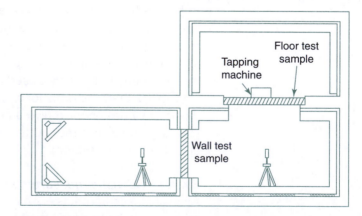

3.62
Sound transmission test rooms

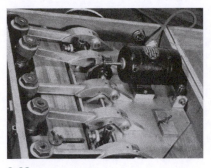

3.63
A standard tapping machine

noise source will be loudspeakers for airborne transmission and a standard tapping machine (Fig. 3.63) to test impact noise transmission.

3.4.5 Integration/discussion

The analytical treatment of heat, light and sound and their relationship to humans, pursued above, is only an approach. All three sets of physical influences affect one and the same person. As Gestalt psychology has it, the totality of the experience is what counts. Component effects must be studied to gain an understanding, but *'the whole is more than the sum of its parts'*. The psychological effects and subconscious cross-channel connections are only rarely identifiable, but do exist. A few examples will serve as illustration:

1 If a room has strong and harsh electric lighting, then a noise will be perceived as louder than the same noise in a room with lower illuminance provided by 'warm' (e.g. incandescent) lights.
2 In a hot climate a well-shaded dimly lit room will be perceived as cooler than another at the same temperature but brightly lit.
3 A low level of illuminance is relaxing, but work demands higher levels: low illuminance in a work place is soporific.

Even motivation, attitude and personal relationships can influence the perception and response.

- A professor carrying out a thermal comfort survey in an African country received unbelievable questionnaire responses and on further inquiry found that the subjects (his students) were guessing what answers he would expect, as they liked him and wanted to please him.
- The classic example is the *Hawthorn effect* found by Elton Mayo in 1927 at the Hawthorne Works of the Western Electric Company in Cicero in Illinois. Production line workers interpreted environmental improvements as 'care' and 'being looked after', and this affected productivity more than an increase in wages. In another factory, with poor work relations the same improvements had the opposite effect. The study showed that the effects of environmental changes were mediated by individual attitudes and group processes.

Skinner and the Behaviourist School through their experiments with rats may have identified numerous simple stimulus–reaction relationships, but as Sommer (1969) observed, rigorous laboratory experiments are no substitutes for studies of important relationships under natural conditions and field studies. These are, however, meaningless if the observer does not understand the processes involved. He suggests leaving the single variable laboratory experiments to physics and chemistry. The designer's work is closer to the life-sciences (hence *bioclimatic* architecture) and we would profit more from systematic observation.

DATA SHEETS AND METHOD SHEETS (SOUND)

DATA SHEETS

METHOD SHEETS

DATA SHEET D.3.1

Noise rating (NR) and speech interference level (SIL)

ROOM USAGE		max NR
broadcasting and recording studios		15
concert halls		15
theatres, intimate		20
theatres, large		25
music rooms		20–25
TV studios		20–25
churches		25
law courts		25
lecture theatres without amplification		25
cinemas		25
classrooms		30
hospital wards or operating theatres		30
hospital day rooms or treatment rooms		35
restaurants, intimate		35
restaurants, large		45
shops, sophisticated		35
department stores		40
supermarkets		45
shops, general		50
banks		50
offices:	executive	20
	conference room (max.50 pers.)	25
	private offices	30
	reception rooms	30
	conference room (max.15 pers.)	35
	general office	40–45
	keyboard operators, printers	50–55
dwellings		25–35
	living area	30
	bedrooms	25
hotels	preferable	25
	acceptable	35

SPEECH INTERFERENCE LEVEL LIMITS

LISTENING DISTANCE	max. SIL (dB)
0.2 m	69
0.4 m	63
0.6 m	59
1.0 m	54
2.0 m	48
3.0 m	45
4.0 m	42

ADJUSTMENTS:	
for female voice	−5 dB
for raised voice	+ 6 dB
for very loud voice	+12 dB
for shouting	+18 dB

DATA SHEET D.3.2

Attenuation by ground cover and absorption in air

ATTENUATION in dB per 100 m DISTANCE

ground cover	125	250	500	1000	2000	4000 Hz
thin grass, 0.1–0.2 m	0.5	0.5	1	3	3	3
thick grass, 0.4–0.5 m	0.5	0.5	0.5	12	14	15
evergreen trees	7	11	14	17	19	20
deciduous trees	2	4	6	9	12	16

ABSORPTION IN AIR in dB per 100 m DISTANCE

climatic conditions		1000	2000	4000	8000 Hz
21°C	40 % RH	0.3	1.3	3.3	13
	60 % RH	0.3	0.6	1.6	8
	80 % RH	0.3	0.6	1.6	5
2 °C	40 % RH	1	3.3	5	8
	60 % RH	0.6	1.6	5	13
	80 % RH	0	0.3	3.3	8

DATA SHEET D.3.3

Transmission loss (dB) of some constructions

		average	125	250	500	1000	2000	4000 Hz
			octave centre frequencies					
WALLS								
1	110 mm brick, plastered	45	34	36	41	51	58	62
2	150 mm concrete	47	29	39	45	52	60	67
3	220 mm brick, plastered	50	41	45	48	56	58	62
4	330 mm brick, plastered	52	44	43	49	57	63	65
5	130 mm hollow concrete blocks	46	36	37	44	51	55	62
6	75 mm studs, 12 mm plaster boards	40	26	33	39	46	50	50
7	75 mm studs, 6 mm ply both sides	24	16	18	26	28	37	33
8	do. but staggered separate studs & ply	26	14	20	28	33	40	30
FLOORS								
9	T&G boarding, plasterboard ceiling	34	18	25	37	39	45	45
10	do. but boards floating on glass wool	42	25	33	38	45	56	61
11	do. but 75 mm rock wool on ceiling	39	29	34	39	41	50	50
12	as 10 + 75 mm rock wool on ceiling	43	27	35	44	48	56	61
13	as 10 + 50 mm sand pugging	49	36	42	47	52	60	64
14	125 mm reinforced concrete slab	45	35	36	41	49	58	64
15	as 14 + floating screed	50	38	43	48	54	61	65
16	150 hollow pot slab + T&G boards	43	36	38	39	47	54	55
WINDOWS								
17	single glazed, normal	22	17	21	25	26	23	26
18	double 4 mm glass, 200 absorb. reveals	39	30	35	43	46	47	37
19	do. but 10 mm glass panes	44	31	38	43	49	53	63
PARTITIONS								
20	two sheets 10 mm ply, 38 mm cavity		20	25	23	43	47	
21	do. + 10 kg/m^2 lead on inside faces		25	31	38	57	62	
22	do. but also fibreglass absorber in cavity		29	42	49	59	63	
23	studs, 10 mm plasterboard both sides		16	35	38	48	52	37
24	do. + 13 mm fibreglass under plasterboard		22	39	46	56	61	50
25	do. but staggered independent frames		34	40	53	59	57	58

DATA SHEET D.3.3 (continued)

		octave centre frequencies					
	average	*125*	*250*	*500*	*1000*	*2000*	*4000 Hz*
PARTITIONS							
26 75 mm studs, 2 × (5 mm hardboard)		12	21	25	40	46	48
27 do. but 2 × (13 mm softboard)		15	25	37	51	51	51
28 100mm studs, 2 × (5 mm hardboard)		9	19	28	39	51	60
29 do. but 2 × (6mm hardboard)		13	30	32	38	41	44
30 200 mm hollow concrete blocks		35	35	40	47	54	60
31 100 mm precast concrete panel		36	39	45	51	57	65
32 110 mm brick (2 × 12 render, 50 × 12 battens, 12 softboard with bonded 6 mm hardboard)		35	43	54	65	73	80
DOORS							
33 50 mm solid timber, normally hung	18	12	15	20	22	176	24
34 do. but airtight gaskets	22	15	18	21	26	25	28
35 50 mm hollow core, normally hung	15						
36 do. but airtight gaskets	20						
37 double 50 mm solid timber, airtight gaskets, absorbent space (lobby)	45						
SHEETS							
38 50 mm glass wool slab (26 kg/m²)	30	27	23	27	34	39	41
39 corrugated fibre.cement (34 kg/m²)	34	33	31	33	33	42	39
40 25 mm plasterboard (2 × 12.5 laminated)	30	24	29	31	32	30	34
41 50 mm plasterboard (4 × 12.5 laminated)	37	28	32	34	40	38	49

DATA SHEET D.3.4

Absorption coefficients (a) of materials and components

	octave centre frequency		
	125	500	2000 Hz
BUILDING MATERIALS			
boarded underside of pitched roof	0.15	0.1	0.1
boarding on 20 mm battens on solid wall	0.3	0.1	0.1
exposed brickwork	0.05	0.02	0.05
clinker concrete exposed	0.2	0.6	0.5
concrete or tooled stone	0.02	0.02	0.05
floor: cork, lino, vinyl tiles, wood blocks (parquetry)	0.02	0.05	0.1
25 mm cork tiles on solid backing	0.05	0.2	0.6
13 mm softboard on solid backing	0.05	0.15	0.3
same but painted	0.05	0.1	0.1
13 mm softboard on 25 mm battens on solid wall	0.3	0.3	0.3
same but painted	0.3	0.15	0.1
floor: hard tiles or cement screed	0.03	0.03	0.05
glass in windows, 4 mm	0.3	0.1	0.05
same but 6 mm in large panes	0.1	0.04	0.02
glass or glazed ceramic wall tiles, marble	0.01	0.01	0.02
plastering on solid backing (gypsum or lime)	0.03	0.02	0.04
plaster on lath, air space, solid backing	0.3	0.1	0.04
plaster or plasterboard ceiling, large air space	0.2	0.1	0.04
plywood or hardboard on battens, solid backing	0.3	0.15	0.1
same but porous absorbent in air space	0.4	0.15	0.1
exposed water surface (pools)	0.01	0.01	0.02
timber boarding on joists or battens	0.15	0.1	0.1
COMMON ABSORBERS			
25 mm sprayed fibres on solid backing	0.15	0.5	0.7
carpet, e.g. Axminster, thin pile	0.05	0.1	0.45
same, medium pile	0.05	0.15	0.45
same, thick pile	0.1	0.25	0.65
carpet, heavy, on thick underlay	0.1	0.65	0.65
curtain, medium fabric, against solid backing	0.05	0.15	0.25
same but in loose folds	0.05	0.35	0.5
25 mm glass wool on solid backing, open mesh cover	0.15	0.7	0.9
same with 5% perforated hardboard cover	0.1	0.85	0.35
same with 10% perforated or 20% slotted cover	0.15	0.75	0.75
50 mm glass wool on solid backing, open mesh cover	0.35	0.9	0.95
same with 10% perforated or 20% slotted hardboard cover	0.4	0.9	0.75
3 mm h'b'd, bit felt backing on 50 mm air space on solid wall	0.9	0.25	0.1
two layers bituminous felt on 250 mm air space, solid backing	0.5	0.2	0.1
25 mm polystyrene slab on 50 mm air space	0.1	0.55	0.1
50 mm polyurethane foam on solid backing	0.25	0.85	0.9
25 mm wood wool slabs on solid backing	0.1	0.4	0.6
same but on 25 mm battens	0.15	0.6	0.6
same but plastered, mineral wool in cavity	0.5	0.2	0.1

DATA SHEET D.3.4 (continued)

	octave centre frequency		
	125	*500*	*2000 Hz*
PROPRIETARY ABSORBERS			
6 mm fibrous cement sheet on battens	0.23	0.5	0.2
Burgess perforated metal tiles, 38 mm glass wool	0.15	0.7	0.8
Caneite, 20 mm softboard tiles on solid wall	0.15	0.45	0.8
Celotex 13 mm perforated tiles on solid wall	0.1	0.4	0.45
same but on 25 mm battens	0.1	0.45	0.4

DATA SHEET D.3.5

Absorption coefficients (a) continued and Abs of room contents

	octave centre frequency		
	125	*500*	*2000 Hz*
PROPRIETARY ABSORBERS (cont'd)			
same but 32 mm thick, on 25 mm battens	0.25	0.85	0.55
Echostop perforated plaster tiles, 22 mm mineral wool	0.45	0.8	0.65
Euphone glass wool quilt, 25 mm on 25 mm battens	0.3	0.85	0.85
same but 38 mm in wire netting	0.5	0.9	0.9
fibreglass 25 mm, resin bonded mat on 25 mm battens	0.1	0.55	0.75
same but 50 mm tick on 50 mm battens	0.2	0.7	0.75
fibreglass, 25 mm tiles on solid wall	0.1	0.6	0.6
Frenger perforated metal panel 20 mm glass wool	0.2	0.65	0.35
Gypklith 25 mm wood wool tiles on 25 mm battens	0.1	0,.6	0.6
Gyproc 10 mm perforated plasterboard on 50 mm battens	0.1	0.4	0.15
Gyproc slotted plaster tiles on 50 mm battens	0.05	0.25	0.15
same with 25 mm fibreglass backing	0.15	0.8	0.25
Paxfelt fibrous cement, 25 mm on 25 mm battens	0	0.55	0.7
Paxtile, perforated f.c. sheet, 13 mm on 50 mm battens	0.2	0.5	0.75
Perfonit. perforated wood fibre tile, 25 mm air space	0.2	0.7	0.75
Semtex 25 mm resin board on 25 mm battens	0.2	0.5	0.3
Stramit 50 mm strawboard on 50 mm battens	0.25	0.35	0.45
Thermacoust wood wool slab, 50 mm on solid wall	0.2	0.8	0.75
Tyrolean Callumix plaster, 13 mm on solid wall	0.05	0.15	0.35
same but 20 mm	0.1	0.2	0.45
Unitex, perforated wood fibre tile, 13 mm	0.2	0.6	0.65
same but 20 mm thick	0.25	0.65	0.8
W Callum muslin covered felt on solid wall	0	0.75	0.7
W Callum perforated metal + 75 mm rock wool in calico	0.4	0.2	0.15

ROOM CONTENTS absorption (Abs) in m² open window units

	octave centre frequency		
	125	*500*	*2000 Hz*
air (per m³)	0	0	0.007
audience in upholstered seats (per person)	0.186	0.4765	0.51
audience in wooden or padded seats (per person)	0.158	0.4	9.436
seat, unoccupied, upholstered	0.121	0.279	0.316
seat, unoccupied, wooden, padded or canvas	0.075	0.149	0.177
orchestral player with instrument (average)	0.37	1.07	1.21

Note:			
the floor absorption should be reduced , if 'shaded' by seats (its effectiveness is reduced) by	20%	40%	60%

DATA SHEET D.3.6

Sound insulation of floors

Insulation for airborne sound is given in terms of TL (transmission loss), same as for walls (e.g. as in D.3.3). Impact noise insulation is measured as the sound level transmitted when impact is generated by a standard tapping machine. Only two grades are distinguished (in the UK) as indicated by Fig. 3.64 (the ISO standard is shown for comparison).

concrete slab[+], floating screed	>48	gr.l
concrete slab, floating wood raft	>48	gr.l
heavy* concrete slab, soft finish	>48	gr.l
concrete slab, suspended ceiling	>48	gr.l
concrete, lightweight screed, soft finish	>48	gr.l
concrete trough beam, floating screed, plasterboard ceiling	>48	gr.l or II
wood joists, floating raft, sand pugging	>48	gr.l
concrete, hard finish	45	gr.II
same, plus suspended ceiling	48	worse than gr.II
concrete, soft finish	45	gr.l
concrete, hard finish, lightweight screed	48	worse than gr.II
heavy* concrete, hard finish	48	worse than gr.II
concrete, hard finish	42	worse than gr.II
concrete, hard finish, suspended ceiling	45	worse than gr.II
concrete, timber finish	48	worse than gr.II
steel beam, timber floor, soft finish with suspended ceiling	48	gr.l
wood joists, wood floor, plasterboard c.	35	worse than gr.II
wood joists, wood floor, lath & plaster c.	40 – 45	worse than gr.II
same with sand pugging	45 – 48	gr.II
steel joists, precast concr.units, lightweight screed, soft finish, suspended c.	49	gr.l

*heavy: >365 kg/m^2, +normal: >220 kg/m^2,

A standard tapping machine

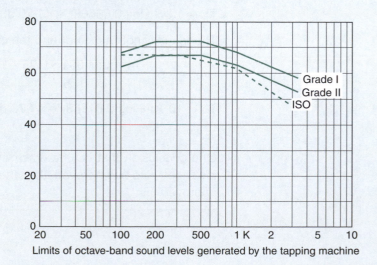

Limits of octave-band sound levels generated by the tapping machine

METHOD SHEET M.3.1

Averaging of TL for different wall areas

1

A wall of 15 m² consists of 14 m² of 220 mm brickwork (TL = 50 dB) and a 1 m² single glazed window (TL = 22 dB). What is the average TL?

The TL values must first be converted to transmittances (τ), the area-weighted average transmittance found and converted back to TL.

from eq. 3.8: $\quad \tau = \text{antilog} \dfrac{-TL}{10}$

for brick wall: $\quad \tau_b = \text{antilog} \dfrac{-50}{10} = 0.00001$

for window: $\quad \tau_w = \text{antilog} \dfrac{-22}{10} = 0.00631$

average $\tau = \dfrac{14 \times 0.00001 + 1 \times 0.00631}{15} = 0.00043$

from eq. 3.7: $\quad TL = 10 \times (-\log \tau)$

$\quad\quad\quad\quad\quad TL = 10 \times (3.367) = \textbf{33.67 dB}$

The window has a dominant influence, even if it is only 1 m².

2

If we have the same wall, but with an unglazed opening of 1 m², the result is even more striking:

$\tau_b = 0.00001 \quad$ as above
$\tau_o = 1 \quad\quad\quad$ by definition

average $\tau = \dfrac{14 \times 0.00001 + 1 \times 1}{15} = \dfrac{1.00014}{15} = 0.06668$

$TL = 10 \times (\text{-log } 0.06668) = 11.76 \text{ dB}$

The result is not much better if the opening is only 0.25 m²:

average $\tau = \dfrac{14 \times 0.00001 + 0.25 \times 1}{15} = \dfrac{0.2514}{15} = 0.01668$

$TL = 10 \times (-\log 0.01668) = \textbf{17.78 dB}$

One conclusion that can be drawn from these examples is that if the noise insulation is to be improved, then the component with the least TL should be improved first.

METHOD SHEET M.3.2

Traffic noise reduction by a barrier

One method of finding the noise reduction effect of a barrier is given in Section 3.3.3. An alternative uses a 'u' term to find the noise reduction effect.

1

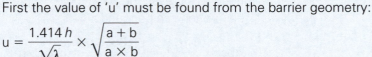

First the value of 'u' must be found from the barrier geometry:

$$u = \frac{1.414\,h}{\sqrt{\lambda}} \times \sqrt{\frac{a+b}{a \times b}}$$

then locate this value on the X-axis and read the reduction on the Y-axis.

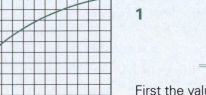

2

Both the above method and that given in Section 3.3.3 are wavelength-specific. A third method is applicable for traffic noise and will give the reduction in dBA of the L_{10}(18-h) noise

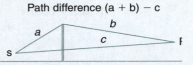

Path difference $(a + b) - c$

First find the sound path length difference from the barrier geometry, then locate this value on the X-axis and read the traffic noise reduction on the Y-axis. The value found is valid for a very long barrier. For barriers of a finite length, the following correction is applicable.

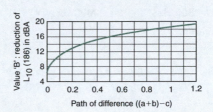

3

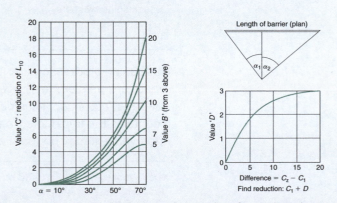

Find the angle α_1 $(= \alpha_1 + \alpha_2)$ at the receiver point, from the plan and locate this on the X-axis of main graph 3. Select the curve corresponding to the reduction from an infinite barrier (from above). Read the 'C' value. Repeat for a_2 and get the difference between the two C-values. Locate this on the X-axis of graph 4. From the curve read the value 'D' on the Y-axis and add this to the larger C-value to get the corrected traffic noise reduction effect in dBA.

METHOD SHEET M.3.3

Calculation of reverberation time

A simple rectangular lecture room is to be designed to seat 120 people. Fig. 3.49 suggests a volume of 4.5 m³/pers, which would give 540 m³. If 2.7 m height is chosen, this gives a floor area of 200 m². For ease of access this is increased to 240 m². Take the floor dimensions as 20 × 12 m. Thus the volume is 20 × 12 × 2.7 m = 648 m³.

The desirable reverberation time is suggested by Fig. 3.50 for this room volume as **0.8 s**. As the room is used for listening to speech, there is no need to increase the RT at lower frequencies. Inverting eq. 3.11 the required absorption can be found :

$$\text{Abs} = \frac{0.16\,V}{RT} = \frac{0.16 \times 648}{0.8} = 129.6 \text{ m}^2$$

The total absorption given in the room is calculated in a tabulated format. Absorption coefficients are obtained from D.3.4 and the absorption of room contents from D.3.5. Assume that the room is 2/3 occupied.

		125 Hz		500 Hz		2000 Hz	
		Abs		Abs		Abs	
Room contents:							
persons on hard seats	80	0.158	12.64	0.4	32	0.436	34.88
seats unoccupied	40	0.075	3	0.149	5.96	0.177	7.8
air	648 m³	–		0.007			4.54
Surfaces:		a	Abs	a	Abs	a	Abs
walls, brick, plastered	168 m²	0.02	3.36	0.02	3.36	0.04	6.72
doors	4.8 m²	0.3	1.44	0.1	0.48	0.1	0.48
ceiling, plasterboard	240 m²	0.2	48	0.1	24	0.04	9.6
floor vinyl on concrete	240 m²	0.05	12	0.05	12	0.1	24
- less shading by seats		20%	−2.4	40%	−4.8	60%	−14.4
totals			78.04		73		72.9

As the required absorption for all frequencies is 129.6 m², some improvements are needed, fairly evenly across all frequencies. The rear wall should not be reflective, so it can be lined with an absorbent. Its area is 32.4 m², but it contains the two doors, so the net area is 32.4 − 4.8 = 27.6 m². The second improvement may be to lay carpet on the floor:

		125 Hz		500 Hz		2000 Hz	
wood wool slabs	27.6 m²	0.15		0.6		0.6	
- less original		−0.02		−0.02		−0.04	
		0.13	3.59	0.58	16.01	0.56	15.46
carpeting	240 m²	0.1	24	0.25	60	0.33	80
- less shading by seats		20%	−4.8	40%	−24	60%	−48
- less original			−9.6		−7.2		−9.6
new totals			91.23		117.81		110.76

METHOD SHEET M.3.3 (continued)

Both these absorbers when introduced are more effective in the high frequencies, so the absorption is now rather unbalanced. Some improvement is
still needed at the higher frequencies, but much more at the 125 Hz band. A
part of the ceiling may be replaced by a felt-backed hardboard panel absorber.
This may tip the balance the other way, so the final adjustment is made by
hanging a curtain over some of the wall, that is more effective at the high
end .

		125 Hz		**500 Hz**		**2000 Hz**	
hardboard panel	50 m²	0.9		0.25		0.1	
- less original ceiling		−0.2		−0.10		−0.04	
		0.7	35	0.15	7.5	0.06	3
curtain, loose	32 m²	0.05		0.15		0.5	
- less original wall		−0.02		−0.02		−0.04	
		0.03	0.96	0.13	4.16	0.46	14.72
new totals			127.19		129.47		127.48

check RT = 0.16 V/A = 103.68/A :   0.81 s   0.8 s   0.81 s ∴ O K

METHOD SHEET M.3.4

Progressive rake and principles of optical acoustics

The purpose of raked seating is to ensure uninterrupted sight-lines of the speaker (or e.g. the bottom of a projection screen) for all members of the audience. At the same time the rake should not be more than necessary.

On a longitudinal section of the auditorium locate the F (focus) point, usually 0.8–1 m above stage level. Locate a vertical line representing the first row of seating and draw such vertical lines at distances corresponding to row spacing, for each row of seats in the auditorium.

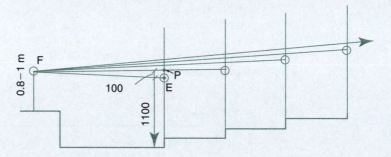

Mark the notional eye-level (point E) for the front row at 1100 mm above the floor.

Mark a point P at 100 mm above E. Draw a line from the F point to this P and extend it to the second row. Its intersection with the vertical will give the second E point. Repeat this for the second to the third row, and for all rows. This will locate the eye-level for each row, and for each eye level measure 1100 mm down, to determine the floor level for that row.

In an auditorium with a flat floor (where the source and listeners are at about the same level) the setting out of a ceiling reflector is quite easy. For example, if it is decided that the rear half of the listeners should receive reinforcement reflected from the ceiling, take the distance between the source and the furthest listener, and halve that distance to locate the edge of the sounding board furthest from the stage. Repeat for the mid-point, and the halving of that distance will give the edge of the sounding board nearest to the stage. The horizontal ceiling between the two points should be treated as a sounding board.

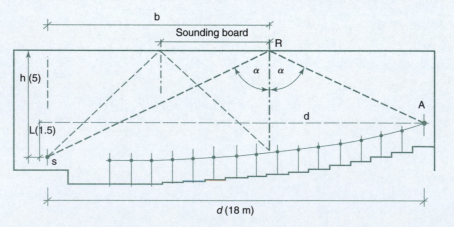

METHOD SHEET M.3.4 (continued)

With raked seating there are two possibilities:

1 The distance between the source and the rear seating row can be halved to mark the edge of the sounding board. As the 'sound ray' incident on the board and that reflected are not symmetrical, the angle between the two should be halved and the sounding board must be at right angles to this halving line. The sounding board will have to be slightly tilted.

2 If the sounding board is to be kept horizontal, then the position of the edge of the sounding board furthest from the stage (the reflection point R) can be found as follows:

   • the horizontal distance between the speaker (S) and the rear row of the audience (A) is d
   • the level difference between A and S is L
   • the ceiling height from point S is h
   • the horizontal distance between S and R is b
   • then b can be determined as we have two triangles, where the angle of incidence and angle of reflection at the point R must be the same, say, α, then
   $\tan(\alpha) = b/h = (d-b)/(h-L)$
   d, h and L are known; say, d = 18 m, h = 5 m and L = 1.5 m

   then b is to be determined
   b/5 = (18-b)/(5 - 1.5), from which 3.5 b = 5(18−b) = 90 − 5 b
   8.5 b = 90, thus b = 90/8.5 = 10.6 m

Repeat the same for the edge of the sounding board nearest to the stage.

PART 4 RESOURCES

CONTENTS

SYMBOLS AND ABBREVIATIONS

c	velocity of light
df	diversity factor
v	velocity
A	area, ampere
AC	alternating current
BCA	building code of Australia
BMAS	building materials assessment system
BRE	Building Research Establishment
BREDEM	BRE domestic energy model
BREEAM	BRE environmental assessment method
C	coulomb or capital energy
CHAPS	combined heat and power solar (system)
CHP	combined heat and power
CoP	coefficient of performance
CSIRO	Commonwealth Scientific and Industrial Research Organisation
DC	direct current

DG	distributed generation
DHW	domestic hot water
DSM	demand side management
E	energy
ETC	evacuated tubular collector
EU	European Union
GPO	general purpose outlet
HDR	hot dry rock
IEA	International Energy Agency
LCA	life cycle analysis (or assessment)
LCC	life cycle cost
LDC	less developed country
LEED	leadership in energy and environmental design
M	mass
MEC	model energy code (USA)
MRET	mandatory renewable energy target

SYMBOLS AND ABBREVIATIONS (Continued)

NatHERS	nationwide house energy rating scheme (Australia)	SSM	supply side management
NFFO	non-fossil fuel obligation	STE	solar thermal electric
NHER	national home energy rating (UK)	TETD	total equivalent temperature difference
NREL	National Renewable Energy Lab (Colorado)	UNCED	UN Conference on Environment and Development
O	operational energy	UNEP	UN Environment Program
OTE	ocean thermal electric	V	volt
OTTV	overall thermal transfer value	VAWT	vertical axis wind turbine
P	power		
PER	process energy requirement	Ω	(omega) ohm, resistance (electrical)
PV	photovoltaic	ϕ	(phi) phase angle
SEDA	sustainable development authority (of NSW)		

LIST OF FIGURES

LIST OF TABLES

4.1 WATER AND WASTES

Water is one of our most precious resources. It seems to be most abundant, but very little is actually available for use. The Earth as a whole has some 1338 million km^3 (1338 EL) water, but most of this (97%) is salt water, forming all the seas and oceans. The remaining 3%, 40.14 EL (exa-litre), is fresh water. Of this:

L = litre
kL = m^3
ML = 1000 m^3
GL = 10^9 L = 1000 ML = 10^6 m^3
TL = 10^{12} L = 10^9 m^3 = km^3
PL = 10^{15} L = 10^{12} m^3
EL = 10^{18} L = 10^{15} m^3 = 10^6 km^3

%	EL	Is in the form of
68.7	27.571	Ice (ice caps, glaciers)
30.1	12.082	Ground water (in aquifers)
0.3	0.120	Surface water
0.9	0.361	Minerals or in the atmosphere as vapour

Of the 0.120 EL or 120 PL surface water

%	PL	Is found in
87	104.4	Lakes
11	13.2	Swamps or wetlands
2	2.4	Rivers

4.1.1 Water

The human body requires a minimum of 1 L of water per day for its proper functioning. The usual amount of intake is some 2 L/day, in the form of food and drink.* The per capita daily water consumption for all uses (Table 4.1) in a large city can be as much as 2000 L (2 kL = 2 m^3). How is the remaining 1998 L used? The answer is that (in developed countries) it is used mostly by industry and commerce, but also for some other purposes (on average):

	%
Residential buildings	44
Industry	22
Commerce	18
Health facilities	5
Parks and streets	7
Urban fringe agriculture	4

However, these proportions are highly variable, e.g. in a large town with little or no industry, residential buildings may use up to 56% of the total, while in a city with heavy industries the residential use may be only 12%.

In residential buildings alone the per capita use can exceed 800 L/day, although this can also vary between 300 and 900 L/day and it is largely determined by user attitudes.

---

* Some health fads recommend 3 L/day.

Table 4.1 Per capita (national average) water use

Location	Litres per person per day
Africa	10–40
South America, Asia	50–100
France	130–250
Germany, Austria	250–350
Canada, Japan	400–600
Australia	500–800
USA	800–1600

This domestic consumption approximately divides as:

	%
Ablutions and sanitation	36
Cooking, washing up, laundry	23
Household gardens	41

Obviously there are large variations with the type of accommodation unit (a house with a garden, or a high-rise apartment block) and where there is a garden, also with the climate. In a dry climate more is used for gardening. A domestic swimming pool can lose 5–10 mm of water per day by evaporation, depending on the weather (more on a dry, hot and windy day), which on a 30 m^2 pool may add up to 150 to 300 L/day. This may be reduced by using a removable floating pool cover (similar to a bubble-wrap).

A bath may take more than 100 L of water, while a shower only 30–40 L. A single toilet flush takes between 7 and 25 L of water. In some cities of Australia severe water restrictions were introduced (due to the unprecedented drought): the limit was set as 140 L/(pers. day), above which penalty rates apply. The actually consumed water is less than 1% of the total public water supply.

The commercial use is made up of components such as

Offices	120 L/pers. day
Hotels	1500 L/room. day
Restaurants	10 L/meal served
Laundry	40 L/kg of washing

The largest single user of water is agriculture. It has been estimated that it takes some 4000 L of water to produce 1 kg of maize and some 2500 L to grow the grain for a loaf of bread.* To produce one person's daily food would take some 33 m^3 of water. The production of one single egg would require

---

* This is not as bad as it sounds: one ha (hectare) of land may produce 2000 kg of maize, thus it would require 4000 × 2000 L, i.e. 8000 m^3 of water. However, in an average rainfall area (1 m/y) one ha would receive 10000 m^3 of rain in a year, which would be enough (unless it is a dry climate) if it falls at the right time and the run-off is minimal.

about 1000 L of water. Industrial usage can be unexpectedly large, e.g. it takes 300 m^3 of water to produce a tonne of steel, to produce a car takes 75–150 m^3 of water. Power stations use over 500 m^3 of water while burning 1 tonne of coal. To refine 1 L of crude oil takes 44 L of water. To produce 1 L of biofuel requires between 1000 and 4000 L of water.

Water usage is rapidly increasing. In OECD countries this growth is only 18% per annum, but in developing countries (starting from a very low base) it exceeds 50% in a year. However, there are still some 2.6 billion (2.6 $\times$ 10^9) people across the world without adequate water supply and sanitation.

4.1.1.1 Sources

All our fresh water is the product of solar energy. It causes evaporation, largely from ocean surfaces, and starts the hydrological cycle. Vapour-laden air and clouds are carried by winds (which themselves are produced by differential solar heating). Precipitation (rain, snow) will also occur over land areas. Some of this may run off and form streams and rivers, some may be retained by the soil, some may percolate into porous subsoil strata. We may tap any of these sources, but all this water comes from precipitation.

Dry land areas of earth receive (on average) about 1000 mm rainfall per year, but this may vary between some 200 mm (e.g. in North Africa) and 2600 mm (in western parts of India and Central America). It also varies from year to year. It is so variable that an annual variation of $\pm$ 20% is considered as steady and highly reliable. Some desert areas may receive rain once in 10 years.

Gaining water can take many forms, from collecting roof water in tanks to large dams collecting run-off from their catchment area. Near-surface ground water may be obtained through shallow wells. Deeper water-bearing strata (e.g. in artesian basins) may be tapped by bore-holes. Natural springs may be made use of. Rivers can provide water by surface pumping, by wells near the flow-bed or by construction of dams to form water reservoirs. Dams take up large areas, which may be valuable agricultural land, and they may have strong environmental effects (often positive ones), they may also silt up over the years, thus reducing the storage volume. Whatever the source, the problems are both the quantity and the quality of such supply.

River valley authorities or other water resources management bodies may exercise strict control over both the allocation and use of the available water and over the possible sources of water pollution. In some instances the whole catchment area of a water reservoir is controlled. It is a continuing struggle both to preserve the quality and to justly divide the water available among potential users. Water used for agricultural irrigation is a huge quantity and the right to use it is often disputed.

Whatever the source, potable water (for human consumption) must satisfy the following criteria:

- It must be clear, free of any suspended clay or silt. Many natural sources provide *turbid* water. Turbidity can be controlled by filtering.
- It must be without taste or odour. Taste and smell are caused by foreign matter, which should not be present in the water.

- It must not contain chemicals in dangerous or harmful quantities. Maximum permissible levels (in ppm i.e. parts per million) are established for many possible substances. Frequent analysis should ensure that these limits are not exceeded.
- It must be free of bacteria and other micro-organisms. Minute quantities of some are tolerable, but these should be checked by frequent counts. The most common one is the *bacillus coli*, which causes *enterocolitis*. A count of 100/mL is the acceptable limit.

Waterworks are usually operated by local authorities or water boards, being consortia of several such authorities. Waterworks include pumping, filtering and water treatment facilities. This may include *flocculation*, which is an often used filtering method in many industrial processes. Aluminium sulphate ('alum') is added to the water, in the form of flakes. Suspended particles, turbidity, colouring, even some solutes are removed adhering to the alum. A froth is formed, which may be skimmed off. Any residue is filtered off. Sand filters can remove solid particles down to about 0.1 mm size. As most bacteria adhere to the surface of such particles, these will also be removed. Bacteria on their own are about 1 μm in size, and cannot be removed by filtering. If such bacteria are found after filtering, the water must be disinfected, most often by adding chlorine of 1 ppm (1 g/m^3). At the draw-off points chlorine should not exceed 0.2 ppm, as this could add an undesirable taste. Ozone treatment is equally effective, it is without taste or harmful effects, but it is expensive.

In the absence of rivers, lakes or adequate ground water the last resort is desalination of seawater or brackish water. Table 4.2 lists the major users of this technology. Most of these plants operate using a reverse osmosis process. If a semi-permeable membrane separates two solutions of different concentrations, the solvent will pass through the membrane until the concentrations equalise.

If an external pressure is applied to the higher concentration solution, reverse osmosis will occur. A modern plant will use some 6 kWh of electricity to produce 1 m^3 (1 kL) of desalinated water from seawater. The disposal of the highly concentrated residue is a separate problem to be solved in each case.

Table 4.2 Countries of major desalination capacity (m^3/day)

Saudi Arabia	5 600 194	Hong Kong	183 079
United States	2 799 000	Oman	180 621
United Arab Emirates	2 134 233	Kazakhstan	167 379
Kuwait	1 284 327	Malta	145 031
Libya	638 377	Singapore	133 695
Japan	637 900	Russia	116 140
Spain	492 824	India	115 509
Iran	423 427	Mexico	105 146
Bahrain	282 955	Egypt	102 051
Korea	265 957	Israel	90 378
Algeria	190 837	Australia	82 129

Long-distance pipelines are designed for continuous flow from the source to local service reservoirs. The function of these is to even out the fluctuations of demand. In some countries (e.g. in the UK), many authorities 'pass the buck' to even out the flow in the local pipework: any residential unit is allowed only one 13 mm pipe connection and one tap on this service in the kitchen, all other outlets must be served from a high level storage tank or cistern to serve as a buffer. At peak times these may be almost emptied and will be refilled only slowly, through a float-valve.

4.1.1.2 Water supply

In buildings the water supply must be available for the following purposes:

- domestic: drinking, cooking, toilet flushing, as well as both hot and cold supply for baths, showers, basins, kitchen washing up and laundering;
- fire fighting: automatic sprinklers and hydrants (for use by the fire brigade) and hose reels (for occupants' use);
- commercial: restaurant kitchens, some service counters, toilets and washrooms;
- environmental plant: air washing and humidification, evaporative cooling and heat transport (including cooling towers);
- external: garden hoses and sprinklers, car washing, etc.;
- manufacturing: process cooling and industrial process water for a multitude of purposes.

The design and installation of the water system (at the domestic scale) are often left to the licensed plumber, to serve all fittings indicated by the architectural plans. In larger buildings a consulting engineer may do this work. It is, however, the architect's task to show what fittings are to be installed and where. A few small points are worth remembering:

1 Grouping all the 'wet' areas together would reduce both the water and the drainage pipework necessary.
2 It is both wasteful and irritating if, when opening a hot tap, one has to wait for the hot water to arrive after discharging the cold water content of the 'dead leg' pipe. This is wasting much water, but also energy. After a short use of the hot water the dead leg pipe is full of hot water and will lose its heat in a short time, even if the pipe is insulated. In a residential unit it is the kitchen where a small amount of hot water is used quite frequently, it is therefore advisable to have the H/W system near the kitchen.
3 In a hotel or hostel type building a whole series of draw-off points may be served by a hot water loop. The hot water is slowly circulating (a small pump may be used) and it is available as soon as a tap is opened. The piping in this case should have a good insulation. Even then some heat may be lost, but much water would be saved. This has been mentioned in Section 1.6.2 (hot water supply) and shown in Fig. 1.109.
4 In buildings of more than one or two storeys it is useful to have a tank full of 'fire reserve' water at the highest level. In many places this is a statutory

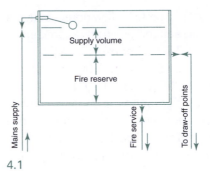

4.1

Combined supply header and fire reserve tank

requirement. Where service water storage is also a requirement, the two can be combined by using the piping arrangement shown in Fig. 4.1.

5 Up to the middle of the twentieth century the piping was often installed on the outside of the building (often such piping was an afterthought or a later addition in 'modernisation'). Even in London's relatively mild winters this often led to the freezing of water in the pipe and – as water expands as it freezes – this often caused cracks in the pipes and consequent leakages. Today all pipes are located internally, but it is useful not to 'bury' pipes in the building fabric, but place them in service ducts or make them accessible by other means (e.g. using removable cover plates). Plumbing repairs may cause consequential damage much more costly than the plumbing repair itself. Even the best pipework is unlikely to be trouble-free for more than some 30 years, while even the cheap and flimsy buildings would have a life expectancy of at least three times that.

4.1.2 Wastes

Our civilisation, particularly our towns and cities, produce a huge amount of waste. This includes solid, liquid and gaseous wastes and the following examines these in turn.

4.1.2.1 Gaseous wastes

Today gaseous wastes mostly consist of motor vehicle emissions and the discharge of power stations and heavy industry. In the past it consisted mostly of visible smoke, mainly fly ash, soot and (with internal combustion engines) some metallic particles: lead, mercury, cadmium. The thousands of smoking chimneys of residential districts, the chimney stacks of industries and railway steam engines were the prime causes of air pollution, especially of the London fogs (smogs) and the sooty, grimy blackness of the industrial cities of the eighteenth and nineteenth centuries.

The UK 'Clean Air Act' of 1956, the 1963 Act of the same name in the USA (and similar legislation in many other countries) radically changed the situation. Fuels were changed, (e.g. 'smokeless fuels'), new technologies were introduced, controlling agencies were established by governments and emissions were drastically reduced. Catalytic after-burners reduced motor vehicle emissions and power stations started building super-tall chimney stacks (up to 300 m). The latter helped the local atmosphere, but produced long distance effects, such as the sulphuric rains in Scandinavia caused by the tall chimney emissions of power stations in the north of England.

It is interesting to note how our understanding and our reactions change. In the 1950s all blocks of flats in Sydney had to have an incinerator (!), to reduce domestic solid wastes, unaware of (or disregarding) the gaseous emissions and air pollution effects. Now, these are banned and the air is much cleaner, at the expense of increased solid waste disposal problems. Today buildings emit very little (if any) gaseous wastes, but emissions are only shifted: electricity consumption in buildings is responsible for huge amounts of CO_2, NO_x (sodium oxides) and SO_x (sulphurous oxides) emissions at the generating plant.

Much can be done to reduce such emissions. The use of various catalysts (platinum, aluminium) over the last decade has reduced gas turbine emissions of sulphur, nitrogen and carbon monoxide from 25 to 2 ppm.

Global warming is an atmospheric phenomenon, caused by the 'greenhouse effect', as introduced in Section 1.3.2 and Fig. 1.36. Its main cause is the increase in atmospheric CO_2 and some other greenhouse gases (see Data sheet D.4.1). In buildings, CO_2 emissions are caused by gas, liquid and solid fuel appliances, or indirectly, by the use of electricity. The CO_2 emission rate of buildings is often shown as a 'carbon footprint', sometimes given per unit floor area, $CO_2/(m^2.y)$.

A useful rule of thumb is that every kWh consumed is responsible for 1 kg of CO_2 emission. Actually, it depends on how the electricity is generated. Table 4.7 on p. 301 shows that it varies from brown coal at 1.23 kg/kWh, down to 0.26 kg/kWh with gas-fired co-generation. Data on CO_2 emissions are few and far between (and are unreliable) but can be estimated as a function of energy use. In buildings the most effective way of reducing CO_2 emission is to reduce energy consumption.

Agriculture, notably the cattle industry (intestinal methane production or 'enteric fermentat' of cows) is the greatest producer of methane, but large amounts are produced by garbage dumps or landfills. Methane emissions in the USA alone are equivalent to 600 million tonnes of CO_2. Methane can be a valuable fuel, as described in the following section. Methane persists in the atmosphere for 10–15 years. The present concentration is approaching 1.8 ppm.

4.1.2.2 *Liquid wastes*

Liquid wastes from buildings are largely the product of our sanitary arrangements. Since the nineteenth century our disposal systems, both sanitary fittings and the supporting pipework, have improved tremendously. Up to the 1950s the *two-pipe system* was generally used, separating the waste water pipes (the discharge of baths, showers, basins, kitchen sinks and laundry tubs) and the 'soil' pipes (servicing WC pans, urinals and slop hoppers). Subsequently the *one-pipe system* took over and the installations were greatly simplified. At one stage 100 mm pipe was required for soil and 50 mm for waste pipes, today 90 mm and 38 mm, respectively, are in common use.

Today, at least at the domestic scale, it is taken as desirable (and beginning to be adopted) to separate the 'grey water', what was earlier referred to as 'waste water' and to make use of it, for flushing the toilet, watering the garden, or hosing down the driveway. This would obviously need a storage tank and separate pipework. The 'black water', the effluent discharged by soil fittings, must be connected to the public sewerage system to be treated at 'sewage farms'. In less densely built-up areas, or for isolated houses, this effluent may be treated on the site, in septic tanks.

These domestic-scale septic tanks and the public sewage treatment plants are based on the same principles. Fig. 4.2 shows the section and plan of a domestic septic tank. The first chamber is just a holding tank, sometimes referred to as the liquefying chamber, where *anaerobic bacteria* decompose organic matter (consuming some 30% of organic solids), which constitutes

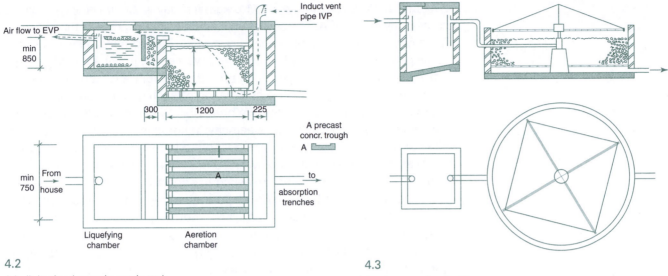

4.2

A built-in-situ domestic septic tank

4.3

A rotary aeration facility

the *primary treatment*. Methane (CH_4) and CO_2 are produced and must be vented to the atmosphere. A slightly modified set-up may allow the methane to be collected and used as a fuel (see Section 4.3.3.1), under biomass conversion. In some large-scale sewage treatment plants, the methane collected is used to generate electricity in the MW order of magnitude. One plant in Sydney operates a methane-based CHP system, producing 3 MW electricity and 3 MW of thermal energy. Many such (and larger) systems are operating world-wide. In small-scale systems, India is the leader.

Secondary treatment is provided in the aeration chamber which (in this case) is a series of trays allowing the effluent to be sprinkled over a gravel (or crushed rock) bed, where on the surface of gravel particles *aerobic bacteria* breed. These will consume a further 60% of organic matter. Good ventilation of this chamber must be ensured. An alternative to this chamber (for larger systems) is an open, circular gravel bed with a slowly rotating spraying system (Fig. 4.3) to distribute the effluent from the anaerobic tank.

The effluent at this stage is rich in phosphates and nitrates: a good fertiliser. It may be used for watering, but it must not be allowed to enter natural waterways, as it may cause algae blooming. These have a large BOD (biochemical oxygen demand), deoxygenate the water, which may thus no longer be able to support aquatic life and may become abiotic.

A *tertiary treatment* of sewage (a more complicated process and not practicable at the scale of an individual house) may remove phosphates and nitrates and produce a marketable fertiliser. The solid residue (sludge) of the primary and secondary treatment may be dried and incinerated. The ashes left may be used for land fill ('concentration and confinement') or loaded on barges and dumped at sea ('dilution and dispersal').

4.1.2.3 Solid wastes

Solid wastes (refuse, garbage or trash) are normally collected by special trucks (using a variety of mechanised systems). The average waste produced is about 1 kg/pers. day in the UK, 1.5 kg/pers. day in Australia and up to 2.5 kg/pers. day in the USA. The collection, handling and disposal of this are quite a problem. Garbage tips have been created in disused excavations, quarries or clay pits, filled, compacted and covered with earth. In flat areas quite large garbage hills have been created, covered with earth and landscaped. However, we are running out of space for the creation of such garbage dumps.

Large-scale incinerator plants have been built, some of which can be used to generate steam and drive an electricity generation system. Local authorities (and their contractors) are quite desperate in trying to reduce the bulk of such wastes. Various levels of recycling arrangements have been introduced. At the simplest level residents are asked to separate the recyclable and non-recyclable wastes (the latter would be further sorted at the garbage processing stations), in other cases paper, glass, metals and plastics are collected separately (putting the onus of sorting on the householders), and directed to various recycling plants. The paper recycling industries are now quite significant, but only a few plants are commercially successful. Most require some public assistance, at least to get started. It is now driven by the users: more and more people are using recycled paper.

The possibility of collecting methane gas generated in garbage dumps is mentioned in Section 4.3.3.1 (methane gas as biomass conversion). The disposal of toxic industrial waste is quite a problem, but beyond the scope of this work. Collection of solid wastes within a building project must be considered at the design stage. In the simplest case (of a suburban house) it may not be more than providing a location for the garbage bin (often the 'wheely bin'), which would be emptied (e.g. once a week) by the local authority's or contractor's garbage truck.

A **garbage chute** is often provided in a block of flats, if not serving every kitchen, at least one hopper at each floor level (Fig. 4.4). The hopper should have a sealed self-closing door. As this is opened, another flap should close off the chute. The chute must be round, of at least 375 mm diameter (450 if serving more than 10 storeys), with a smooth inside surface (e.g. precast concrete or glazed vitrified clay elements). The space between the circular chute and the surrounding rectangular walls is often filled with a weak concrete mix, to help with sound insulation. The wall separating the chute from a habitable room must have a mass of at least 600 kg/m² (340 mm brick or 250 mm concrete), but for any other adjoining room 110 mm brick is adequate. This would lead to a central collection point (e.g. at the basement), to feed into a large container. The bottom of the chute should have a sliding shutter, to close it off while the container is being emptied or replaced.

In the UK, a cylindrical, 1–3 m³ container is normally used, mounted on castors. In Australia, a cube shaped steel container of about 1.5 m³ is often used, referred to as an 'industrial bin'. This must be accessible for the special collecting truck. The local authority operating this truck must be consulted regarding the special requirements. The form of collection for commercial and industrial waste is dependent on the communal disposal system, but must be considered at the design stage.

Under-sink **waste grinders** became quite popular some years ago. In the USA some 50% of households have one; much less so in the UK (6%) and

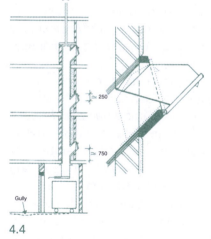

4.4
A refuse chute and its hopper door

even less in Australia. The sink outlet must be 90–100 mm diameter, but the normal 38 mm waste pipe connection is adequate. These have a 500–1500 W electric motor, and a range of safety features. They can grind normal kitchen waste (which is about 15% of all refuse) to particles less than 2 mm, but cannot accept any metals, glass, plastic, fibrous material or string. They use water at the rate of 0.12 L/s while operating, or a daily average of 7 L/person served. Larger units are available for use in hospitals or restaurant kitchens, which need 100 mm pipes, connected to the soil drains.

They are now out of fashion, because of the noise, the electricity and water use and the limited usefulness, and they tend to overload the sewage treatment plants.

The **Garcey system** is independent of the drainage. A 100 mm outlet would lead to a container (taking some 50% of the domestic waste). When this is full, its content is flushed through a 100 mm pipe (not more than 1 m length) into a 150 mm stack, leading to a collection chamber (tank) in the basement, which also collects waste water. This is emptied at set intervals by a tanker, which is fitted with a ram that squeezes out the surplus water, discharging it into the drainage system (Fig. 4.5).

Several kinds of pneumatic or hydraulic waste disposal systems have been tested and some are available on the market, such as:

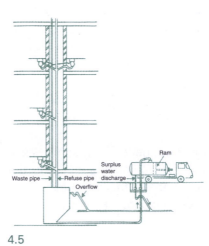

4.5
The Garcey system of waste disposal

- **Floating container system**. Wastes are compressed to about one-third of the original volume and forced into waterproof containers of 150 mm diameter and 400 mm length.. When full, they are sealed and flushed down the soil drains (which need to be increased in size). At the collection point (of the estate or the neighbourhood), the containers can be removed from the effluent by a simple mechanism and emptied. Final disposal is the same as any conventional method.
- **A crude pneumatic transport system**. *Centralsug* was developed in Sweden. A chute collects the refuse in the bottom 3 m, or so. At set intervals (e.g. twice a day) the plate-valve opens, the refuse drops into a 600 mm horizontal transporter pipe, where it is carried by a high velocity (25–28 m/s) air stream to a collection point, where it is dropped into a hopper of an incinerator. The turbo extractors of the transporter pipe operate continuously during the day, the plate valves of the connecting branches opening in turn. Suitable for large-scale high density housing developments.
- **The slurry transport system.** This uses a grinder at every input point, breaking down refuse (including glass and metals) into fine particles. Water is added and a pump after the grinder pushes the slurry along a 50 mm pipe into a 100 mm main. The entry of every branch is fitted with a non-return valve. The individual pumps provide the motive force along the mains. Public pumping is introduced after about 1 km. This is marketed and available in the USA. The grinder-pumping machinery is rather bulky for a domestic kitchen, so the system is mostly used for commercial and industrial situations,
- **A pulverised transport system**. Garbage chutes feed into a grinder-pulveriser, where the refuse is broken down into some 10 mm particles, which are then blown along a 75 mm pipe a short distance and deposited.

At set time intervals a valve opens and the refuse is admitted into a 225 mm transport pipe, where high velocity air (suction) takes it to a collection point, at about 1 km away. Here it is transferred into a positive pressure pipe, which blows it to the treatment plant, possibly several km away. The final treatment may be incineration or composting.

A comparative study a few years ago considered capital as well as operating costs, including final disposal and comparing it with the current manual collection method. It produced the following results:

Current practice: weekly manual collection method	1
Floating container system	1.41
General use of under-sink grinders	1.59
Crude pneumatic transport system	1.62
Slurry transport system	1.88
Pulverised pneumatic transport system	2.88

The study, however, did not consider any indirect benefits: in some cases obviating the need for garbage trucks, reduction of traffic and fuel use or the elimination of the noise nuisance resulting from the manual collection (e.g. banging of bins while emptied), or the improved hygiene.

4.2 ENERGY

Energy is the potential for performing work and it is measured in the same unit: J (joule). Energy flow rate is measured with the unit W (watt), which is the flow of 1 J per 1 second (J/s). Watt also measures the ability to carry out work (J) in unit time (s), i.e. power. As energy and work have the same unit (J), so power and energy flow rate have the same physical dimension, thus the same unit (W).

An accepted energy unit is the Wh (watt-hour), i.e. the energy that would flow if the rate of 1 W were maintained for 1 hour. As there are 3600 seconds in an hour, 1 Wh = 3600 J or 1 kWh = 3600 kJ = 3.6 MJ. Table 4.3 lists the prefixes used with any SI unit, both sub-multiples and multiples.

A number of other energy units are still in use (some powerful specialised users refuse to adopt the SI), but in this work all these are converted to SI

Table 4.3 Multiple and sub-multiple prefixes for SI units

Sub-multiples				Multiples			
deci	d	10^{-1}	0.1	deca	da	10	10
centi	c	10^{-2}	0.01	hecto	h	10^2	100
milli	m	10^{-3}	0.001	kilo	k	10^3	1000
micro	m	10^{-6}	0.000001	mega	M	10^6	1 000 000
nano	n	10^{-9}	0.000 000 001	giga	G	10^9	1 000 000 000
pico	p	10^{-12}	0.000 000 000 001	tera	T	10^{12}	1 000 000 000 000
femto	f	10^{-15}		peta	P	10^{15}	1 000 000 000 000 000
atto	A	10^{-18}		exa	E	10^{18}	

Table 4.4 Some obsolete energy units still in use

Barrel of oil	brl[1]	6×10^9 J	6 GJ	1663 kWh
Giga-barrel (of oil	Gbrl	6×10^9 GJ	6 EJ	1663 TWh
Tonne oil equivalent	TOE	4.1868×10^{10}J	41.868 GJ	11630 kWh
Megatonne oil equivalent	Mtoe	4.1868×10^{16}J	41.868 PJ	11.63×10^9 kWh
Tonne of coal equivalent	TCE		29 GJ[2]	8056 kWh
Kilo-calorie	kcal		4.1848 kJ	1.16 kWh
British thermal unit	Btu		1.055 kJ	0.293 kWh
Calorie (gramme-calorie)	Cal		4.1848 J	1.16Wh

Notes:
1 Strictly speaking, a barrel is a volumetric unit (= 159 L) but taking the density of oil as 0.899 kg/L it will be 143 kg (or 0.143 TOE) and its calorific value as 11.63 kWh/kg thus 1 barrel will correspond to $143 \times 11.63 = 1663$ kWh.
2 Some sources use 26 GJ (7222 kWh): it depends on the quality of coal taken as the basis (IEA (International Energy Agency, Statistics, 2002), which, however, use Mtoe as the basic unit.

units, to achieve comparability and allow a sense of magnitude of numbers to develop. Some conversion factors are given in Table 4.4.

4.2.1 Forms of energy

Energy cannot be created or destroyed (except in sub-atomic processes), but it can be converted from one form to another. Some often encountered forms of energy are reviewed in the present section.

Heat, as a form of energy has been discussed at length in Part 1.

Mechanical energy can take two main forms:

Kinetic energy is possessed by a body in motion and it is proportionate to the mass of the body (M) and to the square of its velocity (v):

$$E_k = \tfrac{1}{2} M v^2$$

An everyday example of such kinetic energy often made use of is the wind. If the density of air is taken as 1.2 kg/m³ and thus the mass flow rate is

$$M = A \times 1.2 \, v \; (m^2 \times kg/m^3 \times m/s = kg/s)$$

then the power of wind over a swept area A is

$$P_k = \tfrac{1}{2} \times A \times 1.2 \, v \times v^2 = \tfrac{1}{2} A \, 1.2 \times v^3$$
$$(kg/s \times (m/s)^2) = kg.m^2/s^3 = W)$$

therefore, it is said that the power of wind is proportionate to velocity cubed.

Potential energy (or positional energy) is possessed by a body which would be free to fall over a vertical distance (height, h), i.e. height relative to a reference level

$$E_p = M \, g \, h$$

where g is the gravitational acceleration, 9.81 m/s²

$$(kg \times m/s^2 \times m = kg.m^2/s^2 = J)$$

An example of such potential energy in everyday use is water in an elevated dam, e.g. with a level difference of 100 m 1 m³ (1 kL) of water would have the potential energy

$$E_p = 1000 \times 9.81 \times 100 = 981\,000\ J = 981\ kJ$$

and if this 1 m³ water flowed in 1 s, it would have a power of 981 kW.

Chemical energy is also a relative quantity. Chemical bonding of molecules represents a certain amount of stored energy that was needed to produce that compound from its basic constituents. Chemical operations requiring energy (heat) input are termed *endothermic* and those that release energy are *exothermic*. Fuels are compounds with high chemical energy content that can be released by combustion (an exothermic process). Some heat input may be required to start the process (ignition) but then the process is self-sustaining. The energy that could thus be released is the *calorific value* of that fuel, measured in Wh/m³ or Wh/kg. From the viewpoint of energetics (the science of energy), fuels are referred to as *energy carriers*.

Electrical energy. The presence of free electrons in a body represents a charge, an electric potential. These tend to flow from a higher potential zone to a lower one. The unit of electric charge is the coulomb (C). The rate of electricity flow (current) is the ampere (amp, A):

$$A = C\,/\,s \qquad conversely \qquad C = A \times s$$

A potential difference or electromotive force (EMF) of 1 volt (V) exists between two points when the passing of 1 coulomb constitutes 1 J

$$V = J\,/\,C$$

Electric current will flow through a body if its material has free or dislocatable electrons. Metals are the best conductors (silver, copper, aluminium), which have only one electron in the outermost electron skin of the atom. In gases or liquids, electricity may flow in the form of charged particles, ions.

Even the best conductors have some resistance to electron flow. The unit of this is the ohm (Ω), the resistance that allows the flow (current) of one ampere driven by 1 volt.

$$\Omega = V\,/\,A \quad conversely \quad A = V\,/\,\Omega$$

The rate of energy flow in the current (or electric power) is the watt (W)

$$W = V \times A$$

a unit which is used for all kinds of energy flow.

The above is valid for direct current (DC), i.e. when the current flows in one direction. Alternating current (AC) is produced by rotating generators, where the resulting polarity is reversed 50 times per second, i.e. at the frequency of 50 Hertz (in most countries, except in the USA, where it is 60 Hz). With AC, the above relationship is influenced by the type of load connected to the circuit. It is true for a purely resistive load, such as an incandescent lamp or a resistance heater. Here the variations of the current are synchronous with the voltage variations (Fig. 4.6a). With an inductive load, such as a motor or any appliance incorporating an electromagnetic coil, the current is delayed with

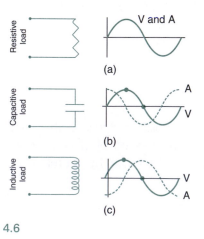

4.6

Resistive, capacitive and inductive loads end their effect on current respect to the voltage variations (Fig. 4.6c). If one complete cycle is 360°, the delay is measured by the phase angle ɸ and the actual power will be

$$W = V \times A \times \cos \phi$$

The term cos ɸ is referred to as *power factor*. If the phase lag is 90°, then cos 90° being 0 (zero), there will be no current flowing. This delay can be corrected by introducing a capacitor, which has the opposite effect (Fig. 4.6b). This has been discussed in relation to electric discharge lamps in Section 2.5.1. For this reason the power of alternating current is referred to as VA or kVA (rather than W or kW).

4.2.2 Energy sources

From the eighteenth century onwards **coal** was the most important energy source, it can be said that our industrial civilisation has been built on coal. Oil production started in the early twentieth century and with the introduction of the internal combustion engine was used in cars, trucks, aeroplanes but also in stationary applications its use has rapidly grown. By 1966 oil production exceeded coal (in energy terms) and by 2012 gas exceeded coal.

Fig. 4.7 shows the world's energy supply by source and Fig. 4.8 by region. Fig. 4.9 indicates the growth of primary energy supply since 1970, by form of fuel expressed in Mtoe (megatonnes oil equivalent):

1 Mtoe = 11.63 TWh

It is worth noting that energy production over that period more than doubled and that in the last year there was a sharp drop in the nuclear contribution. Both this and Fig. 4.7 above indicate that oil has become the largest component.

Oil is our most important fuel, not just because it is the largest single source of energy, but also because it is practically the only transport fuel (as

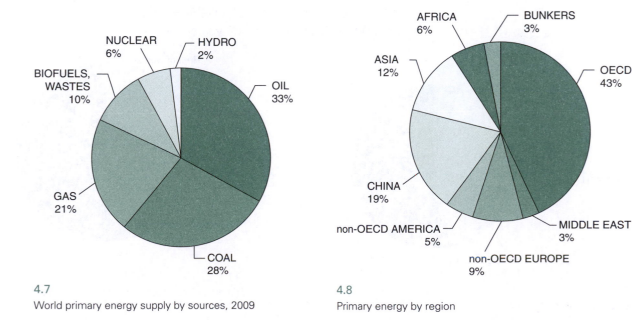

4.7
World primary energy supply by sources, 2009

4.8
Primary energy by region

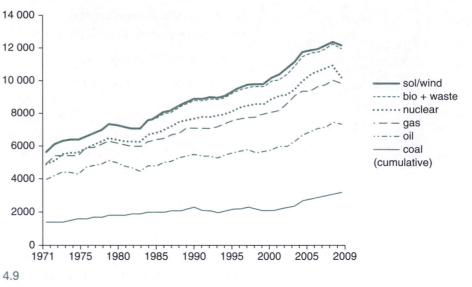

4.9

World energy production 1971–2009, by sources. Total 12150 Mtoe (the graph is cumulative, i.e. the top curve is the sum of all six)

well as the basic source material of the petro-chemical industry, especially for plastics products).

Oil production by regions is shown in Fig. 4.10, and Fig. 4.11 is an estimate of oil reserves, also by region.

The present consumption of energy in the form of oil is 128×10^9 kWh (11 Mt, megatonnes) in a day (!) and 46.7×10^{12} kWh = (**4015 Mt**) in a year. The oil stock of the Earth is estimated as

$$1600 \times 10^{12} \text{ kWh} = (\textbf{139 000 Mt}) \text{ (Fig. 4.11)}$$

Dividing the annual consumption into the reserve stock gives the 'static index', here:

$$1600 \times 10^{12} \text{ kWh}/46.7 \times 10^{12} \text{ kWh/y} = 34.6 \text{ years or}$$
$$139 000 \text{ Mt}/4011 \text{ Mt/y} = 34.6 \text{ years}$$

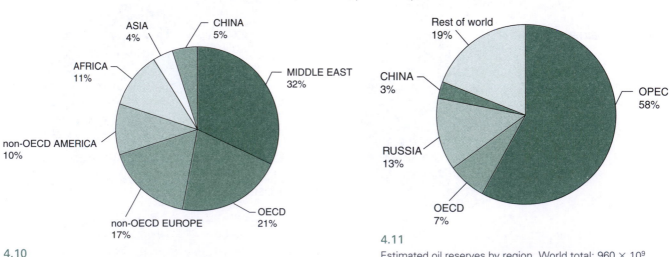

4.10
Oil production by region, 2011

4.11
Estimated oil reserves by region. World total: 960×10^9 barrels = 139 000 Mt = 1600×10^{12} kWh

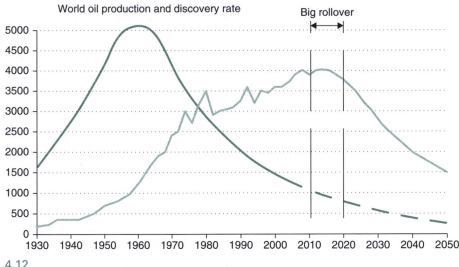

World oil production and discovery rate

Big rollover

4.12

History (to 2012) and forecast (after 2012) of world oil production in Mt (megatonnes) (the forecast is a composite of six different studies) and heavy solid line: annual rate of discovery

which means that if the present rate of consumption is continued, the stock would be exhausted in a little over 34 years. This is unlikely to happen. As supplies diminish, oil prices will increase. On the one hand, this will reduce consumption and, on the other, it will make competitive the renewable energy alternatives (some of which are at present still too expensive).

The 'roll-over period' (Fig. 4.12) from a buyer's market to a seller's market, according to the IEA, has started now and will take about a decade. After about 2022 there will be a rapidly diminishing production.

A similar 'roll-over' for coal is predicted for the middle of the twenty-second century. The even greater worry is that coal and oil are not only our primary energy sources, but also the raw materials for many of our chemical industries. The most worrying fact is that the rate of discovering new oil reserves is rapidly decreasing: from a peak of 5294 Mt/y (58×10^9 barrels) in 1965 to 1416 Mt/y (12×10^9 barrels) in 2002 (also shown in Fig. 4.12).

Consideration of energy sources would not be complete without mentioning some recent developments: recovery of coal seam gas and extraction of oil from certain types of shale. The latter is already making significant contributions to the US economy, the former is causing severe tension between farmers and gas producers in several areas of Australia, not just the legal 'trespassing' on the surface, but the extraction technology badly affects the aquifers.

The only other practical sources are nuclear and renewable energy. The latter will be the subject of Section 4.3, the former is briefly discussed here.

Nuclear energy is in fact a very primitive use of a tiny part of fissionable materials converted to thermal energy to produce heat, to generate steam and drive an ordinary steam turbine.

When certain fissionable atoms, such as uranium, U235, are split as a result of bombardment by neutrons, the total mass of fission products is slightly less than the mass of the original atom (by about 0.1%). The lost mass is converted into energy, according to Einstein's expression

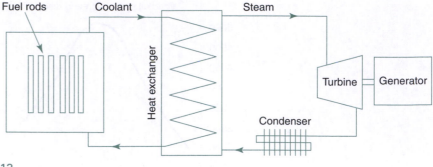

4.13

System diagram of a nuclear power station

$E = M \times c^2$ (where M is mass in kg and c is the velocity of light: 3×10^8 m/s).

For 1 kg of U_{235} $E = 0.001 \times (3 \times 10^8)^2$ J $= 9 \times 10^{13}$ J.

Some neutrons are also released which will split other atoms, thus a chain reaction is produced. The neutrons are slowed down and the process is controlled by the insertion of carbon (in the form of graphite) rods between the fuel rods.

The energy released is in the form of heat and it is removed by a coolant. The circulating coolant will give off its heat through a heat exchanger to water, generate steam, which will drive the turbine. A schematic diagram of the system is shown in Fig. 4.13.

There are many different types of nuclear reactors and they all produce radioactive waste material. The disposal of this has not yet been satisfactorily solved. Huge amounts of such wastes are in 'temporary' storage: some of this remains radioactive for hundreds of years.

There are over 430 nuclear-generating plants operating in more than 30 countries; 57% of these are pressurised water reactors (PWR), 22% are boiling water reactors (BWR) and some 8% are gas cooled reactors (GCR).

Nuclear energy is less than 9% of the national total primary energy consumption in both the UK and the USA. This would correspond to over 18% of electricity produced in the UK and some 20% in the USA. According to the IEA statistics, Lithuania is the country most heavily relying on nuclear energy for electricity generation (76% – an inheritance from the Soviet era), closely followed by France (75%), Belgium is next with some 51%. In terms of national energy consumption these are quite small percentages. France is the largest producer of nuclear electricity, with a capacity over 60 GW. The 2005 statistics show that nuclear power stations contribute 15.8% of the world's electricity production and some 6% of total energy use (Fig. 4.7).

Some 125 nuclear plants have closed down for reasons of various failures but their dismantling is delayed because of problems of radioactivity: only 17 (6300 MW) have been decommissioned. Many countries (e.g. Germany) have decided not to build any further nuclear plants and to progressively phase out existing ones. This decision was strongly supported by the economic argument. If the cost of generating electricity from ready-made fuel rods is taken

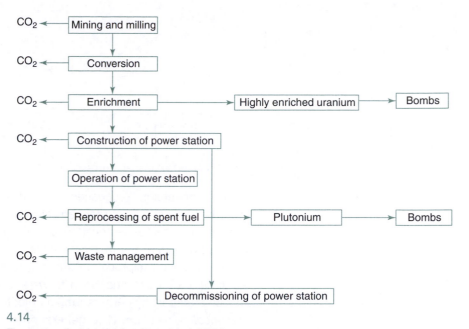

4.14

The nuclear fuel cycle (after Diesendorf, 2007)

into account, it may be competitive, but if the mining of uranium, its refinement, yellow cake production and fuel rod manufacture are taken into account, as well as the cost of handling and storage of nuclear wastes for many years, then nuclear generation becomes the most costly alternative, both in monetary terms and in terms of energy use before and after the active, generating phase. The forecast is that by 2030 only some 220 reactors will remain in operation.

Nuclear power is promoted by some as 'sustainable', saying that it is the only substantial source of electricity generation without any CO_2 emission. This may be true for the power station itself, but it is erroneous if the whole process is considered. Fig. 4.14 shows that there are CO_2 emissions every step of the way. It also indicates the potential tap-off points for military purposes.

4.2.3 Energy conversion

The most important energy conversion process on Earth is photosynthesis, which converts some substances by the electromagnetic radiation of the sun into plant material. Photosynthesis by plants and algae is the basis of the food chain for all animals: herbivorous, carnivorous and the biggest carnivores: humans.

Fig. 4.15 is a very simple and schematic representation of the food chain, but it is sufficient to demonstrate that the material content of living beings may be recycled (dashed line), but energy only flows in one direction: 'downhill' (solid line), from high energy electromagnetic (solar) radiation to very low grade heat produced by decomposers and is ultimately dissipated, re-radiated by the Earth into general space. This photochemical conversion produces all the biomass (wood and plant material) and had, over the geological time scale, produced all our fossil fuels. The thermal effects of solar radiation drive the terrestrial climate system, cause winds and the hydrological cycle, which we may tap and utilise.

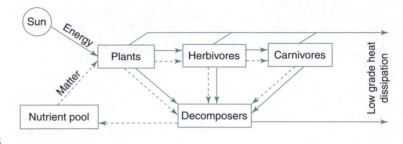

4.15
Flow of energy and matter in ecosystems

The conversion processes we make use of are chemical-to-thermal, thermal-to-mechanical, mechanical-to-mechanical (e.g. pressure to rotation) and mechanical-to-electrical. Fire is the oldest form of *chemical-to-thermal* conversion, but all our thermal engines are based on this, either by generating steam to drive reciprocating engines or turbines, or by internal combustion engines of various kinds. Such *thermal-to-mechanical* conversions drive most of our transport system as well as electricity production, via *mechanical-to-electrical* conversion. (The generation of electricity involves a triple conversion: chemical-thermal-mechanical-electrical.)

Numerous other conversion processes are made use of on a smaller scale (but some of these are of an increasing importance). Solar cells convert *radiant-to-electrical* energy by photovoltaic processes. Thermoelectric cells convert *heat-to-electricity* directly. Dry cell batteries and fuel cells convert *chemical-to-electrical* energy.

Electricity is by far the most convenient form of energy, which can be used for any and all of our everyday purposes. Motors of various kinds can produce mechanical energy and work. Electric lamps can produce light. Electricity drives our communications systems and our computers. Without electricity all our cities would come to a standstill (as demonstrated by the sequel to some recent major natural disasters) – modern life is just unthinkable without electricity. Electricity can even be used to produce other energy carriers, notably gaseous or liquid fuels, by *electrical-to-chemical* energy conversion, e.g. hydrogen generation by electrolysis.

Electricity is generated primarily by thermal power stations: steam turbines driving the generators. Hydro-electricity generation is significant in some countries where the geography ensures large amounts of water is available at high elevations (with large level differences) to drive water turbines (positional-mechanical-electrical energy conversion). Electrical conversion processes are of a very high efficiency, but the generation of electricity, the conversion of other forms into mechanical work, is very inefficient. Table 4.5 presents a summary of various conversion efficiencies. The overall efficiency from chemical (fuel) to electrical energy is often taken as 0.33, assuming that 1 unit of electricity requires the input of three units of primary energy (although it can vary from 0.36 down to 0.28).

Most electricity is produced in the form of AC, as the voltage of this can easily be converted up or down by transformers. Fig. 4.16 shows the principles of three-phase generation, in this case a 240/415 V supply (phase-to-phase 415 V, phase to neutral 240 V). For the transmission of three-phase supply

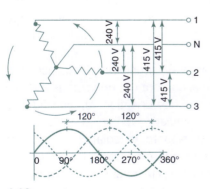

4.16
Generation of 3-phase electricity supply

Table 4.5 Conversion efficiencies of various processes

Conversion	Device	Efficiency, η
Chemical-to-heat	Open fireplace	0.30
	Coal-fired boiler, manual feed	0.60
	Coal-fired boiler, automatic	0.70
	Oil-fired boiler	0.70
	Gas-fired boiler	0.75
Heat-to-mechanical	Steam piston engines	0.05–0.20
	Steam turbines	0.20–0.50
Chemical-to-mechanical	Petrol engines	0.20–0.28
	Diesel engines	0.32–0.38
	Gas turbines	0.30–0.35
Electrical	AC generator	0.97
	AC motor	0.92
	Transformer	0.98
	Lead-acid battery (input-output)	0.75
	Electric heating	0.99

four conductors are required. If the load is well balanced between phases, the neutral can be quite small and sometimes it is omitted (connected to earth). Normally (at the consumer end) for a single-phase supply two conductors are used: one phase and a neutral. For small supplies over long distances sometimes a SWER (single-wire-earth-return) system is relied on.

The necessary cable size is determined by the current to be carried. If the current is too large for a given conductor, it will be heated, causing a loss of power. To transmit a given power with a high voltage, the current will be smaller, thus a smaller cable can be used. Therefore a higher voltage is used for long distance transmission. The normal supply voltage in the UK and Australia is 240 V, in the USA 110 V. In continental Europe 220 V is most frequent and in Japan 100 V is the most usual supply. The local distribution network is usually at 5000 V, or 11 kV (11 000 V). The primary distribution network in the UK operates at 132 kV, but the national grid uses 275 kV. For long-distance transmission (in the 'supergrid') 400 kV is used. In Australia for long-distance transmission 132 kV, 275 kV and 330 kV lines are used, some still operate at 66 kV and some new lines use 500 kV.

The cost of electricity shows wide differences across the world. In rural and remote areas it is usually more expensive. Prices often include a fixed charge for the availability and charges for the actual consumption. Some suppliers encourage electricity use by a reducing tariff. In other instances a flat rate is charged up to a set limit, beyond which a penalty rate applies (to encourage conservation). Table 4.6 compares average supply prices in some countries for residential and industrial use (in large urban areas). Such pricing is very often dictated by political, rather than economic factors.

Recently some governments have introduced a form of tax for CO_2 emissions (leading on to 'carbon trading'). Others were whipping up an almost hysterical reaction, blaming this 'carbon tax' for electricity price increases. Some electricity supply authorities or companies responded by showing that of the consumers' payments, 9% is due to these carbon charges, 20% is the

Table 4.6 Average cost of electricity in various countries (in ¢/kWh)

Country	Residential	Industrial
Denmark	46	13
Italy	34	34
Ireland	32	21
Japan	29	20
Belgium	29	18
Portugal	28	26
Spain	26	12
UK	26	16
Finland	21	12
Switzerland	20	12
France	20	13
Australia	19	9
New Zealand	19	9
USA	15	9
South Korea	10	8

Source: IEA (2009).

generating cost, 20% is the retail costs (service and funding of renewables) and 51% is the cost of 'poles and wires', that is transmission and distribution.

4.2.3.1 Cogeneration

Cogeneration, also referred to as combined heat and power (CHP), is based on the second law of thermodynamics, namely that the production of mechanical work from heat is an inherently low efficiency process and that the thermal energy must flow from a source to a sink and only part of this flow can be converted into work.

Electricity generation by heat engines is only some 33% efficient. The remaining 67% is waste heat, in the past, dissipated into the environment: the atmosphere or water bodies. Depending on the situation, on the local heat demand, up to 75% of the available heat (i.e. 50% of the fuel energy) can be utilised, resulting in up to 80% overall efficiency. Table 4.7 summarises the efficiencies and CO_2 emissions of various generating systems.

Table 4.7 Efficiency and emissions of generating systems

	Fuel type	Overall efficiency (%)	CO_2 emission kg/kWh
Conventional	Thermal: brown coal	29	1.23
	Thermal: black coal	35	0.93
	Thermal: natural gas	38	0.49
	Gas turbine (330 MWe)	48	0.39
Cogeneration	Gas (40 MWe)	72	0.29
	Gas (120 MWe)	77	0.26

Note: MWe is megawatt, electrical.

Source: Australian Cogen Association, paper 4.

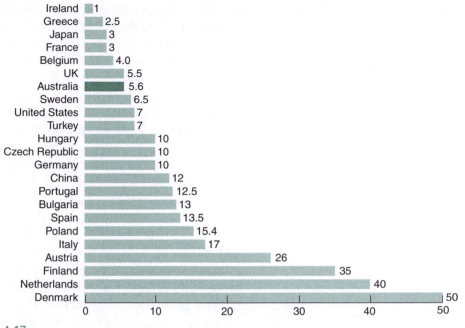

4.17

Cogeneration as % of total electricity production in some countries (International Cogen Alliance, 2000)

Until recently only large-scale systems have proved to be economical, but in the last few years several small-scale units have been introduced. There is an LPG gas-operated unit, the size of a bar-refrigerator, which can provide 3.7 kW of electricity and heat at the rate of 8 kW. It is referred to as a GPS, or general power system.* In some countries cogeneration is already a very substantial part of the total electricity production, e.g. in Denmark it reached 50% (Fig. 4.17). In the UK over 150 CHP plants contribute about 5% of the national total electricity production. In Australia some 130 plants exist, with an aggregate output of 1500 MW (most of these are in the 1–10 MW range) and a similar capacity is now being installed.

A small, domestic-scale CHAPS (Combined Heat And Power Solar) system has been developed at the ANU (Australian National University) for domestic use. It has two shallow parabolic mirrors (2 m² each) with a double-axis tracking system and a row of PV cells at the focal line, which are water-cooled by pumped circulation. This contributes hot water to a DHW system and generates electricity. The output of PV cells would be drastically reduced at elevated temperatures, this system avoids such overheating. The peak output of the system is 700 W.

4.2.3.2 Fuel cells

Fuel cells were first constructed around the middle of the nineteenth century, but it is only recently that they have become practical sources of electricity and are increasingly being used. A fuel cell is essentially a device that

---

* Not to be mistaken for 'Global Positioning System'.

converts the chemical energy of some fuel directly into electricity. In principle it is similar to the dry-cell battery, but while in the latter the finite quantity of ingredients are built in, here the fuel and oxygen are supplied continuously. Fuel cells have been used in spacecraft, with liquid hydrogen and oxygen input, using platinum electrodes. In terrestrial applications methanol, petroleum products, natural gas and LPG can serve as fuel, as well as hydrogen, relying on air as oxidant.

The US Federal Energy Management Program (FEMP) describes fuel cells as having two electrodes and an electrolyte. Fuel is fed to the anode (+) and air is fed to the cathode (-). In the presence of a catalyst, electrons and protons are separated, the former taken through an external circuit back to the electrolyte, to the cathode, to reform H, which then re-combines with O, to form H_2O. Several types of fuel cells are in development: PEM (polymer electrolyte membrane or proton exchange membrane), DMFC (direct methanol fuel cells) or AFC (alkaline fuel cells).

Today various fuel cells are commercially available in sizes from 1 kW to some 200 kW. Some are suitable for cogeneration, i.e. the heat produced can also be utilised. Such CHP fuel cell systems have achieved over 70% efficiency. In most modern fuel cells the electrodes are porous metal or carbon structures and some form of catalyst is used. Recently the Australian CSIRO (Commonwealth Scientific and Industrial Research Organisation) has developed a ceramic fuel cell using natural gas as fuel. Cars powered by fuel-cell-operated electric motors are still at the prototype stage and large-scale production is expected in a few years' time.

Fuel cell information is available on www.energylocate.com. One of the most significant developers of fuel cells is the Connecticut Center for Hydrogen Fuel Cell Coalition, www.chfcc.org.

Major international conferences have been held on fuel cells in London (2010) and in Berlin (2012). Sub-topics at such conferences usually are:

1 fuel cells in transportation, hybrids, auxiliary power units;
2 commercial/industrial, large stationary fuel cells;
3 residential and small portable fuel cells;
4 consumer electronics and micro-fuel cells;
5 fuels for fuel cell applications.

4.3 RENEWABLE ENERGY

The term includes all energy sources which are not of a finite stock, but which are continually available. This would include solar and wind energy and hydro-electric systems, as well as others, such as geothermal or tidal energy, biomass and methane generation. Table 4.8 shows the contribution of renewable sources to the world energy use.

Another way to gauge the contribution of renewable energy technologies is by comparing installed capacities. According to the IEA report,* the total

---

* International Energy Agency, *Global Status Report* (GSR) (2012).

Table 4.8 The share of renewables 2009 data

Total primary energy supply (12717 Mtoe)		*147.9 × 10¹² kWh*	*16.7%*
of which renewable sources contribute		24.7 × 10¹² kWh	
Of this	Hydro (including geothermal, ocean)	5.24 × 10¹² kWh	21.2%
	Biomass (inc. bio-diesel, ethanol)	1.38	5.6%
	Solar (hot water, PV, csp)	0.371	1.5%
	Wind (aerogenerators)	0.766	3.1%
	Combustibles (firewood, wastes)	16.943	68.6%
		24.7 × 10¹² kWh	100%

renewable energy installed capacity (excluding hydro) is 390 GW (390 × 10⁹ kW), divided between the renewable technologies as:

	GW
Wind	240
Solar PV	70
Biomass	70
Geo- and solar thermal	10
Total	390

The top seven countries are:

	Country	*GW*
	China	70
	USA	68
	Germany	61
	Spain	28
	Italy	22
	India	20
	Japan	11
Total		280
Rest of the world		110
Total installed capacity		390

Over the last nine years the growth rate was 6.5% p.a. in the USA, but over 30% in the EU countries and China. Photovoltaics (PV) is the fastest-growing technology. The price of this dropped by 50% in 2011, while that of wind generators dropped by 10%.

The most important sources of renewable energy are the sun and wind, but all (except geothermal) are derived from solar energy. Figure 4.18 attempts to summarise the technologies and purposes of using solar energy in direct or indirect form.

4.3.1 Solar energy

Solar radiation is the driving force of all terrestrial energy systems. Indeed, all plant material and living body matter, all oil, gas and coal in fact constitute

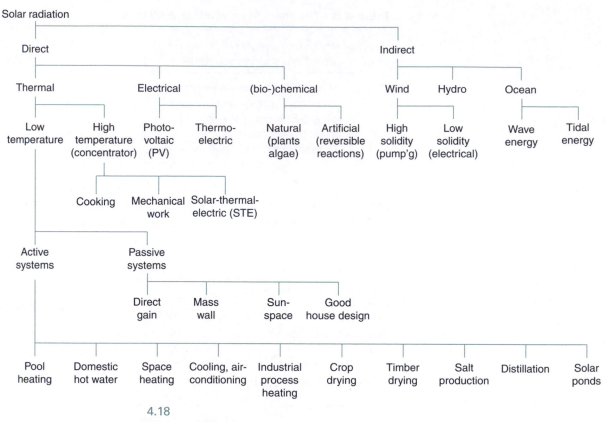

4.18

Taxonomy of solar energy systems

accumulated solar energy. Here the present day use of solar energy is to be discussed. Figure 4.18 summarises the various technologies and purposes of solar energy utilisation. Indirect uses, such as wind, hydro and ocean energy, will be discussed later, after a brief review of direct forms of utilisation.

Three main conversion processes can be distinguished: thermal, electrical and chemical (including bio-chemical). The last one of these includes natural processes, i.e. the growth of plants and algae (also referred to as biomass production), as well as artificial reversible chemical reactions. For conversion into electricity the two main routes are photovoltaic and thermo-electric devices. The direct thermal applications include the most diverse systems. It is useful to distinguish low temperature applications and concentrating devices producing high temperatures. The latter would include various solar cookers, concentrators to produce mechanical work and solar-thermal-electric (STE) systems. A sub-category of the last one is the Concentrating Solar Power (CSP) sytems.

4.3.1.1 Low temperature thermal systems

Within this category we distinguish *active* and *passive* systems. There is no sharp division, but the following boundaries have been proposed according to system CoP (coefficient of performance):

- passive system if CoP > 50
- hybrid system if 20 < CoP < 50
- active system if CoP < 20.

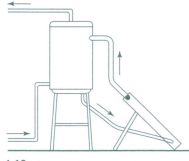

4.19

A thermosiphon solar water heater

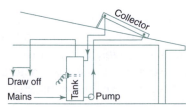

4.20

A pumped solar hot water system

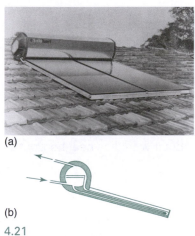

(a)

(b)

4.21

A close-coupled solar water heater (see also Section 1.6.2)

where

$$\text{CoP} = \frac{\text{energy of solar origin delivered}}{\text{parasitic energy used}}$$

and parasitic energy is that used by pumps, fans and controls to drive the system.

The simplest conversion system is the flat plate collector, which can be used for low temperature (<100°C) thermal purposes: water heating or air heating. This is a metal panel (usually copper) with some waterways (either a tube-grid or channels formed between two sheets) or air ducts, with a black surface (in better products a selective surface: high α_{solar} but low $\alpha_{<100°C}$), insulated backing and a glass cover (see Method sheet M.4.2 for collector performance calculations). If the water tank is mounted higher than the collector, a thermosiphon circulation will develop (Fig. 4.19), the tank of water will be heated. If the collectors are on the roof and the tank at floor level, a small pump must be relied on to circulate the water (Fig. 4.20) and this may be referred to as a hybrid system.

Most systems would have an electric immersion auxiliary heater, for use during inclement weather. Close-coupled systems have a horizontal cylindrical tank at the top edge of the collector panel (Fig. 4.21). Many different systems are available, classified according to pressure, circulating system and the form of auxiliary heater.

The use of such solar water heaters is mandatory for DHW (domestic hot water) systems in some countries (e.g. Israel), encouraged by tax rebates (e.g. in the USA) or attract a government subsidy of about 30% of the cost (e.g. in Australia). It is suggested that such support is necessary to restore the 'level playing field', otherwise distorted by the many hidden supports conventional energy systems receive from governments. In many countries the manufacture of solar water heaters is a well-established thriving industry.

Clearly, the thermosiphon DHW system is 'passive', but solar DHW systems have an auxiliary (booster) heater, which is still responsible for significant greenhouse gas emissions, as shown in Table 4.9.

While DHW systems may use 2 to 6 m² flat plate collectors, collector arrays of an order of magnitude greater may be used for space heating or industrial process heating purposes. These are bound to use pumps, both in the collection and heat delivery circuits, thus are in the category of 'active systems'. Fig. 4.22 is the system diagram of a domestic space heating installation. The emitter may be either a panel radiator, or a fan-coil unit or an embedded coil

Table 4.9 Greenhouse gas emissions due to DHW systems (tonne/year)

	Warm climate	Cool climate
Solar, with gas booster	0.3	0.5
'Five star' gas heater	1.3	1.6
'Two star' gas heater	1.6	
Solar, electric booster	1.2	1.9
Electric	4.8	

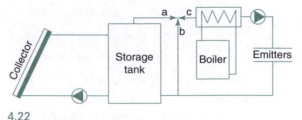

4.22
A solar space heating system with an auxiliary boiler.

floor warming system. This last one is particularly successful as it can operate with quite low water temperatures, using the large surface of the floor as the emitter. The collector efficiency is much better at lower temperatures. The auxiliary heater may be gas- or oil-fired or an electric immersion heater, or even an old-fashioned fireplace with a back-boiler.

In climates where there may be a risk of freezing of the water in the collector panels or pipework, a 'drain-down' system is often used, emptying the collectors for frost-risk periods, e.g. overnight. Alternatively some ethylene glycol may be added to the recirculating water. Because of the toxic nature of this compound, any connection to the DHW system must be through a double-wall heat exchanger.

Fig. 4.23 shows a solar air conditioning system based on an absorption type (LiBr/H_2O: lithium bromide/water) chiller system. The principles of absorption chillers have been discussed in Section 1.6.3.2 (and Fig.1.117), where an ammonia/water system was described. Here H_2O is the refrigerant and LiBr is the absorbent.

For best performance, the tilt angle of solar collectors should be the same as the latitude (this would receive the most beam radiation, while a lesser tilt would receive more of the diffuse radiation), but may be biased for the dominant need: steeper for winter heating and flatter for summer cooling. The orientation should be due south (northern hemisphere) and due north (southern hemisphere). Local climatic conditions may influence this, e.g. if foggy mornings are usual, the orientation should be slightly to the west. In equatorial locations the seasonal variations should dictate the tilt angle, but it would be near-horizontal.

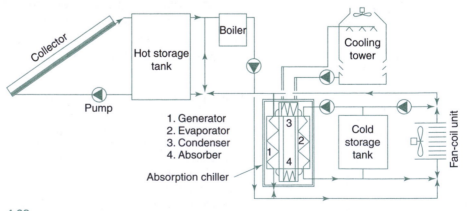

4.23
A solar-powered air conditioning system

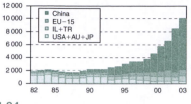

4.24

Flat plate solar collector production of the world, 1982–2003 (in MW$_{thermal}$)

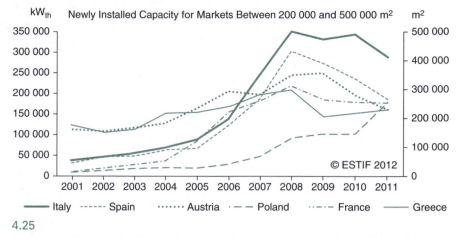

4.25

Growth of solar-thermal collectors installed each year in some countries to 2011 in kW$_{thermal}$ per 1000 of population

The use of flat plate solar-thermal collectors is the most widespread, especially for domestic hot water supply. In most places these are now competitive with electric heaters. Fig. 4.24 shows the growth of production of such collectors to 2003 in terms of rated MW (thermal) output, and Fig. 4.25 is a graph of annual growth of installations in some countries in terms of kWh$_{th}$, or m². In 2006 the EU collector output reached 2.1 GW$_{th}$, bringing the total installed capacity to 13.5 GW$_{th}$ and by 2009 this exceeded 22 GW$_{th}$. Table 4.10 shows the total installed capacity of such collectors (in kW$_{thermal}$) as well as in terms of per capita (kW$_{th}$/1000 persons or W$_{th}$/pers).

Solar collectors may use air as the heat transport fluid and fans to drive the circulation instead of pumps. Such solar air systems are often used for space heating (one advantage is that there is no risk of freezing overnight), but also for many industrial purposes, such as crop drying or timber drying. A crushed rock (or pebble) bed can be used as heat storage. Fig. 4.26 shows a solar air heating system and its ductwork.

Air heater flat plate collector panels can also be used for industrial purposes, such as crop or timber drying.

Table 4.10 Total installed capacity of flat plate thermal collectors, 2011

	kW$_{th}$	W$_{th}$/pers
Germany	8 896 300	108.5
Austria	2 517 812	301.3
Italy	1 404 361	23.4
Spain	1 262 516	27.5
Greece	2 851 940	253.3
France	1 371 370	21.2
Switzerland	538 095	69.9
Portugal	345 338	32.5
Poland	356 902	9.4
UK	332 514	5.4
Cyprus	514 640	645.8
Denmark	330 946	60.0
EU total	22 137 251	43.56

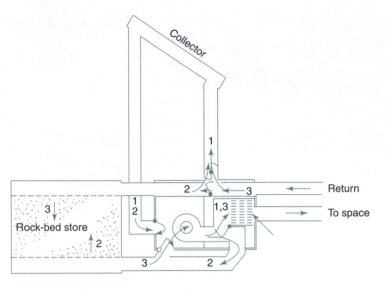

4.26

A solar air-heating system
1 collector to space circuit (possibly auxiliary heater)
2 collector to rock-bed heat storage
3 storage - (possibly auxiliary heater) - to space
The double outline indicates a prefabricated unit: the fan, auxiliary
heater and all dampers.

4.27

A large array of ETCs (evacuated tubular
collectors)

4.28

An evacuated tubular collector (ETC) with
sealed heat pipe absorbers.

A relatively recent development is the use of evacuated tubular collectors (ETCs). These employ a glass tube of 75–100 mm diameter, which houses a copper strip absorber. The selective surface of this reduces radiant losses and the vacuum in the tube largely eliminates convective heat loss, thus quite high temperatures and high efficiencies can be achieved (Fig. 4.27).

An advanced version of this uses a sealed *heat pipe* enclosed in a vacuum glass tube. This contains a small amount of heat transfer fluid. When heated by the sun, this evaporates and shoots up the top end, which is inserted into a header pipe, where the heat is transferred into the circulating water. The condensed fluid gravitates back to the lower part of the pipe. This is an extremely efficient automatic heat transfer system (Fig. 4.28).

The heating of swimming pools may use huge quantities of energy and because only low temperature heat is required, the use of electricity or gas for this purpose is considered by many as downright 'immoral'. An inexpensive (low efficiency) solar heating system will do the job quite well. Often an unglazed collector, consisting of black HDP (high density polyethylene) strips with multiple water-ways will do the job. Ordinary PVC pipes are used as headers and the pool filter pump could drive the circulation.

It has been shown that in Australia salt production uses more solar energy than all other applications put together: this involves the evaporation of sea-water from shallow ponds, with the salt being left behind and scraped up with heavy machinery.

Fig. 4.29 shows a range of passive systems used in buildings. This type of systematic categorisation was fashionable 20 years ago. Now these can be

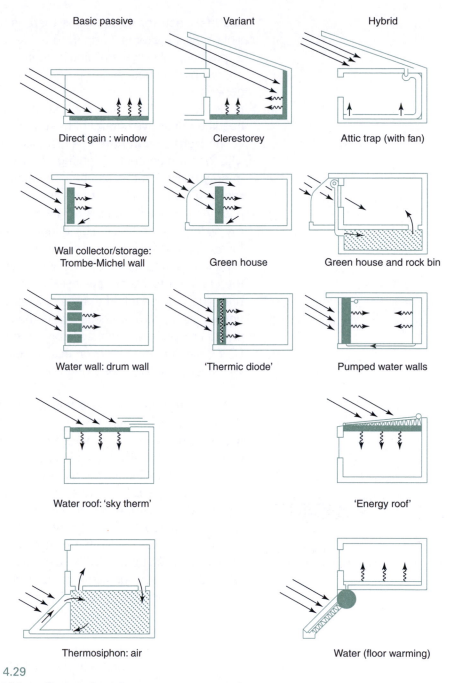

4.29

Main types of passive solar systems

• The direct gain window and clerestory is not more than a correctly oriented window and some mass in the floor or wall to absorb and store the solar heat.

• The Trombe-Michel wall and solar greenhouse have been discussed in section 1.5.1.1.

• The drum wall uses water in drums as the heat storage. The thermic diode circulates water by thermosiphon from the outer collector to the inner storage tank in a clockwise direction; a non-return valve at the top stops reverse circulation.

• The skytherm roof is some 200 mm of water in bags; winter: covered by insulating panels at night, exposed to solar input during the day; summer: exposed at night to dissipate heat by radiation to the sky, covered during the day to provide a cool ceiling.

• The thermosiphon air system uses a rock bed heat storage. The water system has a pumped emitter circuit to warm the floor.

used (at best) for guidance, as there is a practically limitless variety of possible similar systems. Furthermore, we consider that the distinction between a 'passive solar system' and a thermally well designed building is almost impossible. All houses are potential solar collectors, their success or failure depends on the design. Indeed some of these systems were discussed in Section 1.5.1.1 in the context of thermal design of buildings, under the heading of passive control of heat flows.

The **right to sunlight** was discussed in Section 2.3.4 (and Method sheet M.2.2) in the context of lighting of buildings. From the point-of-view of solar energy utilisation this can become a serious problem in legal and economic terms. To put it simply: if I invest in a solar system (whether it is active or passive or PV) and later my neighbour builds a tall block that will overshadow my collectors, do I have some legal protection? The issue is acute in urban (even suburban) situations, especially for small-scale, domestic installations.

Several states (e.g. New Mexico) have introduced legislation, modelled on the old 'right to water' law, essentially the first user establishing the right to the source. Soon it had to be repealed, as it led to unreasonable (even vexatious) claims, e.g., a cheap home-made collector mounted at ground level would prevent my neighbour from erecting any substantial building. Knowles (1977) did important work on this, developing the concept of 'solar envelope', which led to solar access legislation (e.g. in California, see Thayer, 1981).

4.3.1.2 High temperature thermal systems

The best flat plate collectors can heat water (or air) to over 90°C, but much higher temperatures can be produced by concentrating collectors. These all use some mirror, either as a single curvature parabolic trough or as a double curvature 'dish'. The former has a linear focus, the latter a point (or near-point) focus. These usually operate at 500–800°C temperatures and can produce superheated steam. Areas of several hectares may be covered by such collectors for the purposes of electricity generation. These are often referred to by the generic term STE or solar-thermal-electricity systems. Fig. 4.30 is a diagram of a field of parabolic troughs with a central boiler/turbine house (see also Fig. 4.34). Often the abbreviation/acronym for such systems is CST (concentrating solar-thermal). A particular type CST system is referred to as the 'power tower', which has a large field of individually steerable heliostat mirrors, all focussed on a central receiver mounted on top of a tower (Fig. 4.31). Large-scale prototypes of both the power tower and a field of parabolic troughs have been built both in California and for the EU in Spain and feed electricity into the grid (Figs 4.32, 4.33 and 4.34). CST generators are all high temperature systems.

Cautious, conservative governments tend to brush aside solar and wind power as incapable of providing 'base load' power. The fact is that CST plants in the order of hundreds of MW are in operation and a GW size plant is at the planning stage. It is seriously suggested that even the most industrialised countries could eliminate coal-fired power generation, by such solar systems, without resorting to nuclear power.

The largest power-tower system is under construction (with the support of US DoE) at Ivanpah, San Bernardino, California, with a projected output of 370 MW, occupying an area of almost 1500 ha (almost 4 km × 4 km) (Fig. 4.35).

4.30

A field of parabolic troughs connected to a central boiler/generator house

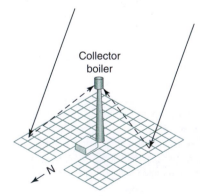

4.31

A 'power tower' system: a field of mirrors with a central tower-mounted boiler and the generator house

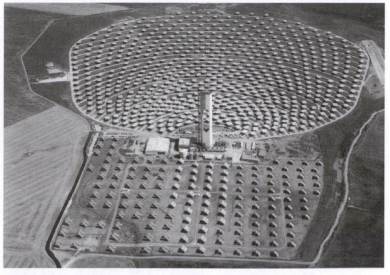

4.32
A 11 MW power-tower system in Spain (near Seville) with a 115 m high tower

4.33
A 'big dish' concentrator with point-focus

4.34
A large scale concentrating trough system, with linear focus

It is a major contribution towards the goal of producing 33% of California's electricity by 2020.

The first major solar power-tower project was 'Solar One' in the Mojave Desert, of 10 MW capacity, later upgraded to 'Solar Two' – now out of commission. Some other major operating CSP installations are

Parabolic troughs	MW	Power towers	MW
Mojave Desert, California	354	Indiantown, Florida	75
Solnova, Sanlucar, Spain	150	PS20, Seville, Spain	20
Andasol, Guadix, Spain (Fig. 4.36)	150	Gemasolar, Fuentes	20
Extersol, Torre de Miguel, Spain	100	PS10, Seville (Fig. 4.32)	11
Nevada Solar One, Boulder, Nevada	64	Sierra, Lancaster, USA	5

4.35
Image of the Ivanpah, St Bernardino CSP project (under construction)

4.36
The Andasol CSP 150 MW plant in Spain

The Andasol plant (Fig. 4.36) is innovative in that it involves heat storage in molten salt of over 1000 MWh_t which is enough for 7.5 hours of full load operation of the turbines. This allows the storage of surplus heat during peak sunshine periods, for use at night.

The world's largest power tower system of 2000 MW is said to be under construction in China, in the Mongolian Desert.

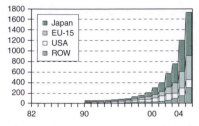

4.37

The world's PV cell production in MWp
to 2006

4.3.1.3 Photovoltaic (PV) systems

PV cells are used for direct conversion of solar radiation into electricity, relying on some semiconductor. The most widely used ones are silicon cells, which may be single crystal (grown as a cylinder and sliced into thin wafers), poly-crystalline or amorphous silicon. Single crystal cells in commercial production exceeded 24% conversion efficiency (but the theoretical limit is 40%)

Fig. 4.37 shows the growth of annual PV module production of the world since 1976 (the three main producer countries + the rest of the world, ROW). The cost of such modules moved in the opposite direction: in 1973 it was about US$ 120 per Wp, that was when we started talking about 'terrestrial applications' of PV, and now it is around $2–3 per Wp. (The size of PV instal-lations is usually given in terms of their rated peak power (watt, peak, Wp), under standard irradiance, and their cost is expressed in $/Wp.)

Polycrystalline cells, with their 15–19% efficiencies, are much less expen-sive. These have been used in large arrays, mounted on a framework at ground level, but recently the building-integrated (mostly roof-top) PV systems have become widely used (Fig. 4.38). Thin film PV is even less expensive (and less efficient), but only recently installed in larger quantities.

Several governments have large-scale programs. Germany launched its 'thousand solar roofs program' some 10 years ago and a follow-up 100 000 solar roofs program is in progress. The USA launched its 'million solar roofs' program (although that includes flat-plate thermal collectors).

Australia gives a direct subsidy of $5 per Wp (peak watt) to any domestic-scale PV installation. The most effective inducement is the guaranteed buy-back price, with grid-connected small systems, paid by the electricity supplier (subsidised by the government) for any electricity fed back into the grid. This is based on two-way metering. As a result of such policies, the domestic PV capacity installed in Australia in the last two years is over 100 MW. This is all connected to the grid, so that the grid is used as storage. The target to be reached in 2020 is 20% of electricity generation by renewable sources.

4.38

A 1.6 MW PV system for Google's HQ in San Rafael, CA : a roof over a parking area

Of all renewable energy systems PV is the fastest growing, it has overtaken wind generation only in 2011. Some of the major installations are:

Name	Country	MW
Westlands Solar Park	USA	2700
Ordos Solar Project	China	2000
Calzadilla de los Barros	Spain	400
Charanka Park, Gujerat	India	214
Golmud Solar Park	China	200
Mildura, CPV plant	Australia	185
Neuhardenberg	Germany	145
Toul-Rosiers Solar Park	France	115

While silicon solar PV cells dominate the present-day market, many other semiconductors produce a photovoltaic effect and have been used experimentally, e.g. gallium arsenite (GaAs), cadmium sulphide (CdS), cadmium telluride (CdTe), germanium (Ge), or selenium (Se). There are also some promising developments in other directions. Titanium oxide (TiO_2) cells, using an organo-metallic dye, are said to be much cheaper and produce an output higher than the Si cells, especially at low levels of irradiance, thus they can be used also for indoor purposes.

Photovoltaics can also be used with concentrating devices, such as Fresnel lenses or mirrors. The heliostat parabolic dish of the CS500 CPV system consists of 112 curved mirrors giving a 500-times concentration at the focal point. The heat-resistant GaAs PV cells are water-cooled. Each unit produces 32 kW electricity. A small installation near Alice Springs in central Australia consists of six such units, producing 192 kW, which is enough for it to be used in the small village of Hermannsburg. At Bridgewater in Victoria, a plant uses eight similar (improved) units and produces 500 kW (Fig. 4.39).

4.39
The Bridgewater CPV installation

4.40
Crown Plaza hotel in Alice Springs

These systems (as well as the 'big dish', Fig. 4.33) have double-axis tracking, which means that the collector always faces the sun, ensuring maximum possible solar input. A simpler solution is the single-axis tracking: elongated oblong-shaped PV panels are mounted on a fixed axle which is tilted by an angle equal to the latitude, and rotate from east to west, from sunrise to sunset (then reset for the next day). A major plant (180 MW) at Moree in Australia, now under construction, will use this system. It is still unclear whether the benefits of this system will compensate for the expense of the mechanical system of tracking, with associated energy use and maintenance.

Flat plate PV systems are highly competitive. There are now e.g. over 1 million grid-connected domestic scale roof-top PV systems of 2 – 5 kW capacity in Australia. There are numerous larger scale systems, such as that at a hotel in Alice Springs (Fig. 4.40) and the largest single installation is at the University of Queensland (Fig. 4.41): a 1.2 MW roof-top PV system of over 5000 panels, totalling 8200 m^2 (Fig. 4.41). Measured results indicate that this gives 5% of the peak load and 3% of the total electricity use, saving the University $6.5 million per annum.

It is thought that the world's total PV installations are around 35 000 MWp and this number is rapidly growing. For comparison, the largest nuclear power station is of 7900 MW and the Three Gorges hydroelectric plant in China will have 22,500 MW installed capacity.

4.3.2   Wind energy

This seems to be at present the most competitive of the renewable alternatives and the most widely used (perhaps with the exception of domestic solar water heaters). From 2000 to 2006 the world's total installed capacity quadrupled and since then it has trebled. Apart from the traditional windmills, and

4.41
The University of Queensland roof-top PV system

slow-moving devices with large 'sails' (e.g. in Crete and in the Netherlands, but used already in China and Babylon over 2000 years ago), two types of wind devices have been used for well over a hundred years, those with horizontal axis and those with vertical axis.

In the horizontal axis types we have high solidity rotors (Fig. 4.42), (i.e. the frontal view of the rotor is almost all solid) used primarily for water pumping and the low solidity (propeller) type, used for electricity generation (Fig. 4.43). In the vertical axis type we have the high solidity Savonius rotor (Fig. 4.45) and the low solidity rotors, developed by Darreius, also referred to as 'egg-beaters'

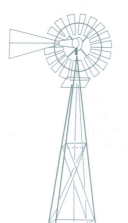

4.42
A high solidity pumping windmill

4.43
Propeller-type wind generators (aerogenerators)

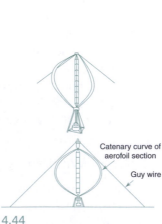

Catenary curve of aerofoil section

Guy wire

4.44
The Darreius rotor

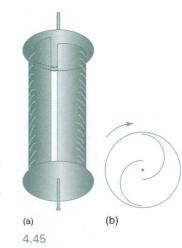

(a)   (b)

4.45
The Savonius rotor

(Fig. 4.44). Up to the 1970s most propeller-generators were of the order of 1–2 kW and since then this type became the most developed into large units, 500 kW to 1.5 MW sizes. The largest one so far is the Nordex N80 unit, with a rated output of 2.5 MW and a rotor radius of 80 m, which is the same as the wing-span of the A380 airbus. The Boeing 747's is 64 m and the new 777 is 60 m.

A 5 MW wind turbine (Beatrice) has been installed in the deep waters of Moray Firth, N/E Scotland, as part of an EU project. The largest off-shore wind farms are in Denmark, producing almost 30% of the country's electricity supply. The installed wind-generating capacity in the world has increased from less than 1 MW in 1980 to almost 203 000 MW (203 GW) in 2011 (see Fig. 4.46 and Table 4.11). The electrical energy produced has grown from 1 GWh to 375 TWh (10^{15} Wh) per annum (Fig. 4.47). Fig 4.46 shows the annually installed wind-generating capacity since 1996 in the five largest user countries and Fig. 4.48 shows the world totals up to 2011.

In the UK in 2001 there were operating wind generators with a total output of 422 MW_e, current and planned projects were to bring this up to over 6000 MW_e capacity. This has already been exceeded: 6470 MW. The UK target was that by 2010 renewables should contribute 10% of the total electricity production (which has not been achieved, only 4.2%, see Table 4.8).

The world's total installed wind-generating capacity reached 75 GW in 2006 and by 2011 it is almost 203 GW. An increasing proportion of this consists of off-shore wind-farms, much favoured as over the water surface the wind is much less turbulent than over the land. WindForce10 (an international alliance) set the target for 2020: 20% of all electricity produced should be by wind generators (which is so far only exceeded by Denmark). The Australian target is very conservative: only 2%, though the Federal Senate voted to increase the MRET (Mandatory Renewable Electricity Target) to 5% by 2020, the government is still undecided.

As with photovoltaics and solar-thermal-electric systems, the large-scale developments are paralleled by small, domestic-scale wind generators. A multitude of these can compete with the few very large systems. Recently a new VAWT (vertical axis wind turbine) became available, which is suitable for roof mounting; a low solidity device, serving the individual consumer. It is available in 1.2–2 kW outputs, with 0.8 m–1.5 m diameter and with suitable current-conditioning, it may be used as a grid-connected device. (A stand-alone system would need back-up storage batteries to ensure availability of power when there is no wind.) These are so far nowhere near as successful as small-scale PV installations.

The 'world's largest' wind farm operates at King Mountain, near McCamey, Texas, which consists of 160 turbines, each of 1.3 MW capacity, a total of over 200 MW. Apparently Texas legislation requires that 1.5% of electricity be produced from renewable sources by 2013, rising to 3% by 2019.

There seems to be a much smaller, but significant market for small wind turbines. The above VAWT is a good example, but three others should be mentioned:

1 'Air 403" of Southwest Windpower of the USA, 400 W, 1.15 m. diameter, with three narrow blades;

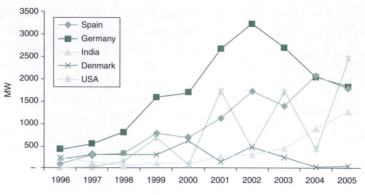

4.46
Annual rate of wind turbine installation in five countries

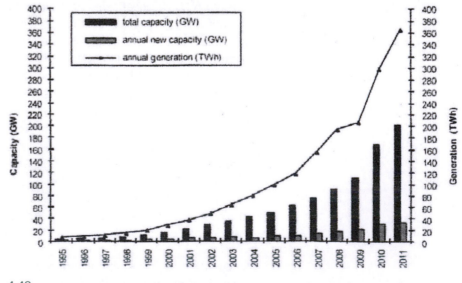

4.47
A large scale wind farm with 1 MW turbines

4.48
Annual installations, accumulated capacity and electricity supply by wind generators

Table 4.11 Installed wind-generating capacity and as % of electricity supply, 2005 and 2011 (in MW)

	2005	%	2011	%
Germany	18445	6	29075	7.6
Spain	10027	16.4	21673	16.3
USA	9181	2.3	46916	2.9
India	4253		16084	
Denmark	3087	21.9	3952	28.6
Italy	1713	2.6	6878	3.0
UK	1336	2.6	6470	4.2
China	1264	1.2	62364	1.6
The Netherlands	1221	4.2	2368	4.2
Japan	1159	0.4	2501	0.5
EU total			96000	6.3
Global total			202976	

2 'Rutland 913' of Marlec, UK, 90 W, 0.9 m diameter, with six blades;

3 'Enflo Systems 0060/05' of Switzerland, 500 W, a 5-bladed rotor of 0.6 m diameter, within a 0.8 m diameter tubular diffuser.

All three are rated with a 12.5 m/s wind speed and all three can be grid-connected with a suitable inverter and power conditioner.

From the architectural (or building) point of view, fixed flat-plate PV devices are of the greatest interest, as these can be incorporated in the building design as surfacing elements (mainly for roofs). Large wind turbines are beyond the scope of an individual building design, but small-scale aerogenerators, such as the above, can be considered even at domestic-scale buildings.

At the global level, in terms of total installed capacity wind generators dominate, but in terms of annual growth rate, for the first time in 2011, wind generators (21.4%) were exceeded by photovoltaic installations (46.7%). In the last few years PV prices have dropped by 50%, while wind generators only by 10%.

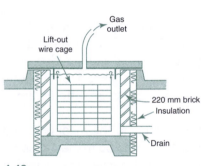

4.49
A methane generator for solid input

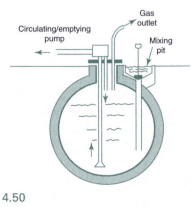

4.50
A methane generator for liquid input

4.3.3 Other renewables

The growing of trees is biomass production and burning of such wood is the most ancient form of biomass energy conversion. The burning of bagass (sugar cane residue) is the same process, to generate steam and produce electricity. Many other conversion techniques are available.

4.3.3.1 Methane gas

Methane gas (CH_4) generation can be considered as biomass conversion. Essentially this is the anaerobic digestion of farm by-products, e.g. straw and manure. The *carbon-nitrogen ratio* of the feedstock is important. Too much carbon (plant matter) will produce much CO_2 and little CH_4 (Figs 4.49 and 4.50). Some manure will help to restore the C/N ratio to the optimal 25 to 35. The methane generated is easily stored (e.g. in gasometers) and can be used in burners.

Large-scale use is possible in sewage treatment plants, where enough methane may be generated and collected to produce steam, to drive turbines and generate electricity in the order of tens of MW. In the UK the installed methane-based electricity generating capacity is some 13.4 MW.

A recent development is the capture and use of methane generated in waste dumps. The dump, when full, can be covered by a polythene film, before the usual layer of earth is put on. Significant amounts of gas may be collected over many years and used for electricity generation.

These systems have the added benefit of reducing the greenhouse effect. Methane is a greenhouse gas with an effect twenty-one times as great as CO_2 (partly because it persists much longer in the atmosphere). It would be produced anyway and dissipated into the atmosphere. If it is oxidised (burnt) it is reduced to water and some CO_2, so the use of methane should be encouraged..

4.3.3.2 Energy crops

Agriculture can produce many plants (biomass) which then can be converted into practically useable forms of energy. A significant success story is the production of ethanol (alcohol) from sugar-cane in Brazil. Cars have been manufactured that use ethanol instead of petrol (gasoline), but it has been shown that any car can use up to 30% ethanol mixed with the petrol fuel. It may have a slightly lower calorific value than petrol, but it has better ignition properties, so the consumption is about the same as of pure petrol. In the USA corn is used for ethanol production to such an extent that shortage of corn became a concern. Sorghum (Indian millet) and miscanthus (elephant grass) are also used for ethanol production.

In ethanol production from sugar-cane Brazil is by far the leader. In Australia ethanol production may be saviour of the sugar-cane industry, when there is a glut of sugar supply on the world markets. Car manufacturers and the petroleum lobby mounted a scare campaign (the risk of engine corrosion) against ethanol, but a mix of 10% is now accepted. Ethanol has a long history: in the 1920s and 1930s in Europe almost every petrol station offered a mix marketed as 'Motalco' (motor-alcohol).

Bio-diesel is another liquid fuel produced from biomass. The most favoured product is rape-seed oil, but many other vegetable oils can be treated to serve as diesel fuel. In some countries producing crops for conversion to fuel is such a profitable business that agricultural food production started to suffer. A new phrase created for this activity is 'growing fuel'. Fig. 4.51 indicates the various sources of biomass, the conversion processes and the final products and uses of biomass conversion.

4.3.3.3 Sea and earth

Sea and earth energy sources are also available and systems for their utilisation are in various stages of development.

Ocean energy may be utilised by a number of techniques. Tidal flow can be made to drive turbines and such systems are feasible in geographically favourable locations, where the tidal variations are large. If a barrage is constructed, e.g. across a river estuary, both the incoming and the outgoing tide can be made use of.

Numerous ingenious mechanical solutions have been proposed to make use of **wave energy**. No doubt that the energy available in waves is huge, but

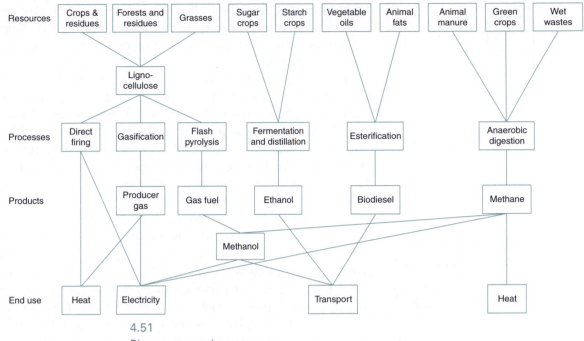

4.51

Biomass conversion processes

none of these systems is a clear winner yet and very few large-scale installations are in operation.

Ocean-thermal energy (OTE) represents a completely different approach. It makes use of the temperature differences between deep water layers (several thousand metres) and the surface layers. It is a low-grade energy, but the quantities are huge. Attempts are made to drive various heat engines with this, relatively small, temperature difference.

Geothermal energy is the heat of the interior of the Earth. It can be made use of in several ways. Surface utilisation is possible at hot springs or geysers. The first geothermal power plant was set up in Italy, in 1913, with a capacity of 250 kW. Plants of increasing size have since been constructed (mostly after the Second World War) in many countries, as summarised in Table 4.12. Notable examples are Rotorua in New Zealand and

Table 4.12 Summary of geothermal electricity production, 2005

Country	Installed MW_e	Annual output GWh/year
USA	2534	17840
Philippines	1930	9253
Mexico	953	6282
Indonesia	797	6085
Italy	791	5340
Japan	535	3467
New Zealand	435	2774
Iceland	202	1483
Costa Rica	163	1145
El Salvador	151	967
Kenya	129	1088

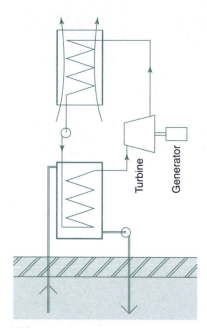

4.52
Principles of an HDR plant

Yellowstone in Wyoming, USA. The world's 'most efficient' geothermal system is said to be in Indonesia at Darajat (near the Mt Kendang volcano, in Central Java), producing 81 MW of electricity. A second similar unit is under construction.

In Australia the heat of deep layers is recovered through bore-holes delivering hot water or by the 'hot-dry rock' (HDR) technology: pumping water down a bore-hole and recovering hot water at quite high temperatures (Fig. 4.52). A 13 MW unit is in operation in the Cooper Basin and a 100 MW plant is in preparation. Here at a depth of 3.5 km, solid granite is found at over 250°C temperature. Each of these methods may produce steam to drive turbines, or (below boiling point temperatures) to drive some form of heat engines, such as 'screw-expanders' using an organic fluid.

Low-grade geothermal energy can also be made use of. The temperature of the earth at a depth of 2–3 m is practically constant all year round, at about the annual mean air temperature of the location (or slightly warmer). A pipe coil buried at this depth can produce warm water at about this temperature. A similar method saves earth-works: by drilling a large number of bore-holes and placing a U-pipe in each, to serve the same purpose, to act as a heat source. A heat pump (see Section 1.6.1.1 and Fig. 1.98) can be used to step up the temperature to a level useful for space heating (at least 30°C). This system is sometimes referred to as an 'active earth-coupled system', or an 'earth-source heat pump' system. Some versions of such installations can also serve as a heat sink, when the heat pump is used in reverse, as a cooling technique.

Over the last 30 years renewable (mainly solar and wind) electricity generation has experienced very high growth rates, albeit from a very low base in 1971 (practically nil in 1970). This is summarised in Table 4.13. The EU has proposed a binding target of 20% of the total energy consumption (not just electricity) to be obtained from renewable resources by 2020.

Table 4.13 **Growth of renewable electricity production (as % of national total generation)**

Region	2000	2030	
		Extrapolation	With new initiatives
USA and Canada	2	7	11.5
Europe	3	11	25
Japan, Australia and New Zealand	2	5	7.5

4.3.4 Energy storage

This is a major issue with most renewable energy systems, because of the mismatch in timing of supply availability and the demand. The storage requirements may be short-term (e.g. the 24-hour cycle) or long-term (inter-seasonal). Much work has been devoted to the latter, especially in cold winter climates (e.g. Scandinavia) to store heat collected in the summer to be available in the winter. Such storage must be inexpensive. Underground heat storage in either man-made containers or in natural formations, even in the aquifer, seems to be the most promising solution.

Energy can be stored by pumping water up to an elevated reservoir, to be used to drive a turbine when needed. Producing compressed air is an alternative, which can drive a turbine or a reciprocating engine for recovery of energy. Kinetic energy storage is provided by large flywheels, accelerated as an input and driving a generator as recovery. Low grade heat can be stored in the building fabric, often without any extra cost, in elements which are provided for other purposes, such as a concrete floor slab or various masonry walls. It is up to the architect or designer to realise this potential as and when needed.

Short-term storage of low temperature heat is well developed in storage-type hot water systems or block (unit) heaters for space heating. Electricity produced by PV or wind generators can be stored in rechargeable batteries, but these are expensive and their useful life is limited (maximum 10 years). Much research effort is devoted to alternative battery systems, but the (improved) lead-acid batteries are still the most reliable. If the generators (PV or aerogenerators) are connected to the grid, the grid itself will take on the role of energy storage.

Many countries now regulate the status of grid-connected 'small producers' of electricity. The local electricity supply company (or authority) must buy the electricity offered by such a small producer. This may be a house owner who has some PV devices on the roof or a small aerogenerator in the backyard. It may be a company owning an office block or some industry that has similar devices, or even a farmer who has a micro-hydro generator on his property. Two-way metering is installed. The electricity company may pay the generator only the wholesale price, but charge the normal retail rate for what is consumed. However, in most cases the price is the same both ways. By government action (and subsidy) the buy-back rate may even be higher than the supply rate, to act as an incentive.

Electricity suppliers make the distinction between base-load and variable load. The former is the lowest load that must be satisfied at any time and must be reliably available. In case of a small area of similar users (e.g. a residential suburb) all users work on the same time pattern. In a larger area many different users may be included (e.g. commercial, industrial) the load is more diversified. The term *diversity factor* (df) means the ratio of the total connected load to the actually occurring maximum simultaneous load. If all connected load is switched on at the same time, the diversity factor is 1 (one). In all other cases it is greater than 1.

$$df = \frac{\text{total connected load}}{\text{max. actual load}}$$

The reciprocal of this is the 'demand factor' which is always less than or equal to 1.

The same concepts can be applied to the supply side.

Conventional coal-fired steam turbine generation is suitable for the base-load. Often, when the demand drops, some turbines could be stopped, but this is rarely done, as it takes a long time to re-start such a turbine. If it is kept operating, it is referred to as 'spinning reserve', that is economically undesirable.

Demand side management attempts to shift some load to the off-peak period. An example of this is the storage-type water heaters, controlled by a time-switch. A more up-to-date version of this is the 'interruptible supply', where a pulse-switch in the consumer meter-box is activated by a high frequency signal (pulse) sent out through the power wiring. This gives a great flexibility to the supplier, so the electricity is sold at a reduced rate (e.g. for 15¢ /kWh instead of the 'normal' 23¢).

An interesting new development is the introduction of 'time-of day metering', made possible by the new electronic meters. The reduced cost of off-peak electricity is well established. Now the day may be divided into several time bands, each band attracting a different rate. Very high price will apply at periods of peak demand. This is very much in favour of PV system owners in hot, clear-sky climates. The peak demand is due to air conditioning, occurring at the hottest part of the day, usually in the early afternoon hours. But this is also the time of peak production by the individual PV system and the power fed back to the grid will attract a similarly high price.

Supply-side management may involve the use of some gas-turbine generators, which have a short start-up time, thus allowing a degree of responsiveness. Another possibility is the connection of grids over long distances in the east–west direction, thus spanning different time-zones (e.g. the France–England connection under the English Channel), which greatly improves the diversity factor. Another possibility is the diversification of 'small-scale producers' or renewable energy plants, such as wind and solar power plants, as the output variations of these are well staggered. However, if large numbers of small-scale producers rely on the grid as 'storage' or renewable energy power plants are connected to a grid, this may cause problems to the supplier. Much research and development work is in progress relating to the integration of diverse power plants connected to a grid with variable demand. If all else fails, some form of energy storage will have to be relied on, such as the molten salt storage system used at the Andasol CSP plant (Section 4.3.1.2).

4.3.4.1 Reversible chemical reactions
Reversible chemical reactions are some of the most promising technologies for the long-term storage of high grade energy. Ammonia (NH_3) is one of the candidates. With high temperature input it can be split into nitrogen and hydrogen (thermal dissociation), the two gases are separately stored and may be made to recombine (in the presence of some catalyst) at will, which is a highly exothermic process.

Electricity (DC) may be used to split water into H and O. That hydrogen can be stored or piped to where needed and it can be used in internal combustion engines or in fuel cells to produce electricity. Indeed, the 'hydrogen economy' is one of the most promising technologies for the future. Hydrogen is a very good energy carrier and it can be used as input for fuel cells and thus converted directly into electricity.

The only emission from these processes is H_2O, i.e. some water vapour. The 'hydrogen economy' is feasible (and desirable) only if the electricity used

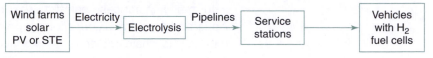

4.53
Renewable hydrogen production

for electrolysis is generated from renewable resources. Fig. 4.53 shows that hydrogen can be generated using renewable energy and it is the most useful energy carrier (and storage) which produces no greenhouse gas emissions.

Professor Bockris of Adelaide 30 years ago visualised large areas of the Australian desert used for PV-based devices, producing DC current, to be used for electrolysis of water to produce hydrogen that can be piped to the major cities. Problems to be solved were then identified as hydrogen embrittlement of steel (pipes or tanks) and the explosive nature of hydrogen. The former has been solved by various coatings (e.g. epoxy) of the inside of tanks or pipes and it can safely be stored in the form of metal hydrides, or stored and transported in liquefied form under a pressure of 200–300 kPa. Hydrogen is particularly attractive for aircraft fuel, as its energy content per unit mass is much higher than that of liquid fuels (see Table 4.21 in Section 4.5.4.2).

Recently the NREL (National Renewable Energy Laboratory, Colorado) started a project to use wind-generated DC electricity to produce hydrogen, and use this either as fuel for internal combustion engines or in fuel cells for direct production of electricity.

A number of other reversible chemical and electro-chemical reactions have been or are being examined, tested and developed.

4.3.4.2 Phase change materials

Phase change materials, in addition to any sensible heat change, can make use of their latent heat of phase change. The latent heat that was necessary for an upward change will be released during the corresponding downward change.

The simplest application is in ice storage: making ice by a compression chiller using cheap off-peak electricity, which requires the extraction of heat (some 335 kJ/kg) and using this ice for air conditioning (cooling) during the day, giving a cooling effect again of some 335 kJ/kg (93 Wh/kg). Here the phase change ('transition') temperature is 0°C. Table 4.14 lists some materials with transition temperatures that are possibly useful in building applications.

Table 4.14 Some phase change materials (salt hydrates) for latent heat storage

		Transition temperature °C	Latent heat of reaction Wh/kg
$CaCl_2.6\,H_2O$	calcium chloride	29–39	48
$Na_2CO_3.10\,H_2O$	sodium carbonate	32–36	74
$Na_2HPO_4.12H_2O$	sodium phosphate	36	73
$Ca(NO_3)_2.4\,H_2O$	calcium nitrate	40–42	58
$Na_2SO_4.10\,H_2O$	sodium sulphate (Glauber's salt)	32	67

In many instances, paraffin wax has been used for thermal storage. Apparently the transition (melting point) temperature of this can be set by cutting the chain molecule to the appropriate length. Such phase change materials are often used in conjunction with passive solar heating systems.

The most effective way of storing large quantities of high temperature heat is by molten salts (phase change) as e.g. in the Andasol CSP plant (over 1000 MWh_{th}).

Solar ponds are storage/collector devices at the lower end of the scale, producing/storing low-grade heat. These are large area, inexpensive solar collectors. When a pond of water is heated, the warmest water comes to the surface (being lighter) and rapidly dissipates its heat by convection and evaporation, then it sinks. An undesirable thermosiphon circulation develops. This can be prevented by using very salty water for a bottom layer and a fresh water upper layer. The salty water, even at near boiling-point temperatures, is heavier than the fresh water and remains at the bottom.

Water can be circulated through a pipe coil and the heat thus recovered can be used to drive some heat engine, a screw expander, possibly even a turbine, where the working fluid may be some low boiling-point organic liquid.

4.3.5 Summary

A major report on renewables by IEA (quoted in Table 4.8) shows the shares of various sources contributing to final energy consumption as:

	%
Fossil fuels	80
Renewables	16.7
Nuclear	2.7
Total	100

Of the 16.7% 'modern' renewables, solar, wind, bio-fuels and hydro constitute 10.2%. This is used as

		%
Biomass, solar, geothermal	As heat	4.9
	For electricity generation	1.1
	Biofuels	0.7
Hydropower		3.5

The annual growth rate (in 2011) is perhaps of more interest:

	%
Solar PV	74
Solar-thermal power	35
Solar heating and hot water	27
Wind power	20
Bio-diesel	16

It is interesting to note that in the 5-year period of 2006–2011 bio-diesel production grew by 27% and ethanol production by 17%, but the latter was actually reduced in 2011 by 0.5%. Market forces seem to have an increasing influence besides government actions.

4.4 ENERGY USE

4.4.1 Energy use in general

According to the *UN Statistical Yearbook* (2003) the energy production of the world in the six major forms of supply was (and is estimated as will be) as shown in Table 4.15 (converted from Mtoe into kWh).

The terms *primary* and *secondary* are often used in relation to energy. Coal, oil and natural gas and many renewables are primary sources. Any of these can be used to generate electricity, which is a secondary form of energy. It is usual to consider that in conventional coal-fired electricity generation one unit of electricity (secondary energy) is equivalent to three units of primary energy. If coal gasification is the source of gas supply, this will also be considered as secondary energy. In gas, and particularly electricity systems it should be noted where the quantity is measured, at the generating plant or at the final point-of-use.

If, at the national scale, the main energy use categories are taken as industry, transport and buildings, in terms of primary energy the values shown in Table 4.16 are obtained. It is clear that climate and geography are major influences. In Australia, the climate is mild, so building energy use is relatively less, but there are large distances between cities and towns, so much energy is used for transportation. In the UK, much of the building stock is old and thermally inadequate, hence the large use of energy in buildings, but the country is relatively small, compared to the population, so travel distances are not very large. Furthermore, in the UK, same as in Germany and France, railways take much of the transport requirements, and these are much more energy-efficient than road transport (see Data sheet D.4.1).

Table 4.15 World energy supply (in 10^{12} kWh) (last columns as predicted in 1999)

	1973	2000	2005	2010	2020
Coal	17.49	27.22	33.65	32.73	38.90
Oil	33.49	43.04	46.55	53.21	63.68
Gas	11.39	24.43	27.53	31.58	41.14
Nuclear	0.62	7.86	8.37	8.07	7.23
Hydro	1.29	2.63	2.93	3.32	3.96
Renewables	7.87	13.33	13.95	15.30	17.21
Total	72.14	118.51	132.98	144.21*	172.12

* Note that the 2010 predicted quantities have been superseded: 147.9, see Table 4.8.

Table 4.16 Energy use in some countries by main categories (as % of total)

	Buildings	Transport	Industry	Source
Australia	25%	30%	45%	
France	37	21	42	
				UN Statistical Yearbook 1992
Canada	37	24	39	
U S A	39	27	34	
Germany	41	17	42	
U K	43	21	36	
World 1973	39.8#	22.9	37.3	IEA Energy
2000	42.4#	25.9	31.7	Stats. 2002
2009	36.7	32.5	30.8	Stats.2009

Note: # includes the small quantities of the 'other sectors' category.

4.4.2 ENERGY USE IN BUILDINGS

A building, *per se*, does not need any energy. Conceptually, the need is for buildings to provide suitable conditions for the occupants and their processes. Whether this requires the use of some energy supply is a different question. We should rely on passive thermal controls provided by a well-designed house (as far as possible), rather than energy-based HVAC installations, or on daylighting rather than artificial lighting (at least for some of the time).

Three reasons can be suggested for preferring passive controls:

1 **economic**: the operation of active controls costs money; passive controls are more economical, even if their capital cost is somewhat higher (which is not necessarily the case);
2 **environmental**: active controls use energy; reduced (or avoided) active controls lead to energy conservation, thus conservation of resources and reduction of emissions;
3 **aesthetic**: a building designed to suit the given local climate is more likely to be in sympathy with its environment in formal terms than the ubiquitous glass box or globally copied fashionable forms.

The extent of reducing active controls depends on the climate and on local factors, but relies very much on the designer's skill and on the user. Some degree and form of energy import will be necessary.

Energy can be supplied to buildings in the form of solid fuels (coal, coke, but also firewood), liquid fuels (kerosene, paraffin heating oil), gas or electricity.

Gas was the main source of energy for lighting in the nineteenth century, but for this purpose electricity is used almost exclusively in all industrialised countries. Piped 'town gas' (or coal gas) supply for lighting and cooking (to a lesser extent for heating) was available in most sizeable towns. In many places, as natural gas supplies became available, the old appliances (burners) had to be converted as this has a much higher calorific value:

33.5–44.7 MJ/m^3 * (normally 37–39 MJ/m^3) as compared to town gas: 14–20 MJ/m^3. The price of gas was reduced and its use for space heating increased from the 1960s onwards. With the ready availability of piped natural gas, large boilers are used with gas burners and CHP installations (e.g. gas turbine-generators with district heating) are gaining ground.

Liquid fuel is still used in small portable appliances for heating and cooking, but also with piped supply. Often, in a housing development a central storage tank is installed (usually underground) which will be kept filled by an oil company. From this a piped supply is provided to each house or apartment, where it is metered and paid for by the occupants like any other public service. In large buildings (or complexes, such as hospitals) there may be a central oil-fired boiler which supplies hot water for direct use or for space heating as well as steam e.g. for sterilisers. There will have to be provisions for oil storage. This may provide an opportunity for cogeneration, CHP installations (see Section 4.2.3.1).

Solid fuel was practically the only fuel for space heating in the nineteenth century. It was inefficient, messy, dirty and inconvenient and has been quickly replaced in domestic applications as other fuels became available. In the 1950s solid fuel was still used in some large buildings or central boilers of large estates (in district heating schemes) or in industry. It required facilities for handling, for storage, for moving it from storage to the boilers as well as for the removal and disposal of combustion products (ashes). The use of coal for transportation (steam locomotives) and for residential purposes has disappeared almost everywhere, but it is still used in industry and it is the main primary source of energy for electricity generation. Here huge quantities of coal are handled, by a system completely mechanised, but the disposal of ashes still remains a problem. Many attempts have been made to reuse it (e.g. as aggregate for lightweight concrete, or as concrete blocks), but this is a minute portion of the total ash production.

Coal-fired power stations are the greatest emitters of CO_2 and other forms of atmospheric pollution. The overall efficiency of coal-to-electricity conversion is about 0.33, so using 1 kWh or electricity means the consumption of 3 kWh of chemical energy (which means some 0.36 kg of best coal), the burning of which releases about 1 kg of CO_2 (slightly more for brown coals and lignite).

Electricity (a secondary energy form) is a very convenient form of energy carrier at the final points of use. It is clean, it is available at the flick of a switch, its conversion efficiency is high for most purposes and the large range of electric appliances available makes its use addictive. We tend to take it for granted and squander it in a prodigal manner.

The energy needs of buildings are increasingly supplied by electricity. For example, in Australia, over half of all *electricity generated* is used in buildings (27.6% in residential and 23.1% in commercial buildings), industry is the second largest user of electricity (46.4%), with very little used in agriculture

---

* International Energy Agency, *Global Status Report* (GSR) (2012)..

(1.6%) and in transport (1.4%). Unfortunately IEA global statistics distinguish only three categories of electricity users:

	1973 (%)	2009 (%)
Industry	53.4	40.2
Transport	2.4	1.6
Other	44.2	58.2

Buildings are included in the 'other' category, but are the largest part of that, as agriculture and public services are only minor users. This seems to indicate that the Australian figure of 50.7% must be very near the global average. The contribution of electricity to total energy use is increasing: 9.4% in 1973, 17.7% in 2010 (almost doubled). Oil comes second in terms of quantity used, but its share is actually decreasing: 48.1% in 1973 to 41.2% in 2010.

The following sections will consider electrical and gas supply installations in buildings.

4.4.2.1 Electrical installations

The local electricity distribution network operates usually at 5 or 11 kV potential. This is normally a 4-wire supply (three phases + neutral, as in Fig. 4.17). Some large consumers may purchase the supply at this voltage and have their own transformers to reduce it to the standard voltage (240/415 V or 220/360 V or 110/180 V). In residential areas the supply authority (or company) would have transformers and supply the standard voltage to each customer. While the high voltage distribution uses overhead cables (on poles or pylons) almost everywhere (except in high density CBD areas), the low voltage supply cables are increasingly placed underground.

A house would normally be connected to a single phase supply (one of the three phases plus neutral), with a 2-core cable: 'live' and neutral. The *balancing of loads* between the phases is done by the supplier (e.g. two or three houses on phase 1, two or three others on phase 2, etc.). A block of flats may be connected to a three-phase supply (a 4-core cable: three cores for the three phases plus a smaller one for the neutral) and the balancing is done within the building, between the flats. In a well-balanced system the neutral will carry very little current, possibly none at all.

In a block of flats in the past a *sub-main* was taken to each flat or unit and each of these was treated as an individual consumer, similar to a house. The trend now is to have all the meters together, e.g. in an electrical switch-room, near the main entrance to the block and run the supply cables separately to each flat, where each would have a *consumer unit* inside the flat, branching out into several circuits, each through a circuit breaker. The common uses ('landlord supply', such as staircase or foyer lighting, lifts, pumps, etc.) would be metered separately and paid for by the 'body corporate' (in home units) or the building owner/manager (in rental apartments).

In houses, the connection is made to the meter panel (in a meter box accessible from the outside) followed by a consumer unit, which may be inside. Electricity meters measure the voltage and the current and display

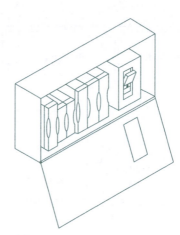

(a)

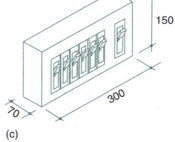

(b)

(c)

4.54

A fuse-board consumer unit and one with circuit breakers

the product of the two in kWh. Older meters have a series of rotating clock-hands, 0–9, for each digit of the cumulative consumption (very confusing, as some turn clockwise, some anticlockwise, as interlocking gears consecutively divide the rotation by 10). More modern ones have up to six disks with numbers on the outside, such as the odometer in cars or combination locks on briefcases, but the latest development is the use of a digital (liquid crystal) display.

In the past the consumer unit included a series of fuses (rewirable or cartridge type), which would melt (burn out) in the case of the current exceeding a set limit. Nowadays automatic circuit breakers are used almost exclusively (Fig. 4.54). There is usually one main circuit breaker for the whole supply, then the wiring splits into several circuits, say, two lighting and two power-point circuits, each with its own circuit breaker. The stove and the H/W system would have their own separate circuits. Circuit breakers are labelled according to the current they permit before cutting out, such as 5, 8, 15, 20 or 30 A (amperes).

While circuit breakers protect the installation against overload (which could cause fire), earthing (or 'grounding' in North America) is used as a safety device to protect the user (shock protection). If the insulation is faulty and the conductor becomes exposed or the metal body of the appliance becomes 'live' and touched by the user, a current will flow through the route of least resistance.

The earth wire, connected to metal parts is usually a multi-strand copper conductor, uninsulated, leading to an electrode buried in the ground. This has (we hope) a lesser resistance than the human body, so it takes the bulk of the current, unless the human body is well 'earthed', e.g. bare feet on a wet floor. In this case, the 240 V supply may produce a lethal current through the body.

Earth leakage circuit breakers are increasingly used, which would be tripped as soon as there is any current going through the earth wire or if the current in the active wire differs from the neutral.

Wiring within a house (or apartment) is usually in double-insulated 3-core PVC cables. The live or active conductor and the neutral are insulated separately and with a bare copper wire for earthing added, the whole is covered by a PVC sheathing. These are often referred to as TPS (thermoplastic sheathed) cables. In exposed flexible cables the earth wire is also insulated. The colour of the insulated cores is now standardised, but some old cables of different colour are still in use, as shown in Table 4.17.

While these cables can run freely in a framed/sheeted wall or floor and can be embedded in a concrete slab, it is better practice to install conduits (with a draw-wire) which would allow re-wiring, should the need arise.

Table 4.17   **Standard colours of electrical cables (insulated cores)**

Conductor	Standard colour	Old colour
Phase (line, active, live)	Brown	Red
Neutral	Blue	Black
Earth (bare or)	Green + yellow stripes	Green

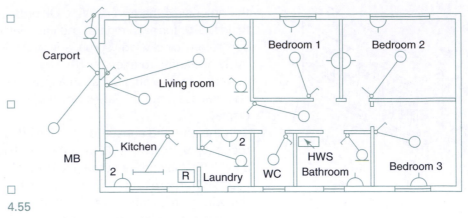

4.55
An electrical plan: location of lamps, switches, etc.

Luminaire (ceiling)	
Wall mounted luminaire	
Luminaire with switch	
Fluorescent luminaire	
Same, twin-tube	
Switches, 1, 2, 3-pole	
Two-way switch	
Socket outlet	
Switched socket outlet	

An appliance
eg: HWS hot water service
R electric range (cooker)
EF exhaust fan
AC air conditioner

Boards
eg: MB meter board
MSB main switchboard
DSB distribution board
CP control panel

Dimmer switch
Telephone outlet (wall)
Telephone floor outlet
Electric bell

4.56
Electrical location symbols

In a larger project an electrical consultant would design the system, in a single house this is usually left to the licensed electrician, but in both cases the architect/designer would set the 'human interface', the location of switches, light points, GPOs (general purpose outlets = power points) and any fixed appliances (e.g. cookers or H/W cylinders).

The requirements can be shown on a plan, which is not a circuit diagram (such as Fig. 4.55) using the standard electrical symbols (Fig. 4.56). The architect (in consultation with the client) would normally select the luminaires. It is important to consider the luminous characteristics of these (light distribution, surface luminance thus risk of glare, size of lamps to be used, see Part 2, Section 2.5) and not to select them purely on the basis of 'looks'.

4.4.2.2 Gas supply installations

Where piped gas supply is not available, gas can be purchased in bottles or cylinders. These must be located outside and a pipe must be carried to the points of use. Bottled gas is often used for cooking and has been used for refrigerators (to drive absorption cooling machines). For larger users, e.g. space heating, gas would be adopted only if piped reticulation is available.

From the gas mains a *service pipe* would connect to the meter (Fig. 4.57) and then the pipe may branch out to e.g. the cooker, the H/W system and the

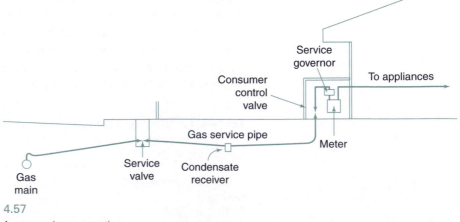

4.57
A gas service connection

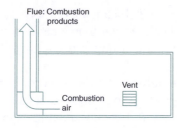

(a)

(b)

4.58

Possible flue arrangements for gas heaters

central heating boiler. These boilers are available now in a form which looks like a slightly fat radiator panel and can be installed in any habitable room.

A larger H/W system or central heating boiler must have a flue (Fig. 4.58). Boilers may be located next to an external wall and have a *balanced flue* (e.g. Fig. 1.97 which shows a gas-fired convector unit.) At one stage it was very popular to install gas burners into old open fireplaces, even in the form of artificial 'logs', to imitate a wood fire or glowing artificial embers to look like a coal fire, perhaps including a flickering light. These may well be 'mood elements' (for some) but are very inefficient heating devices.

The main concern with gas installations is the risk of gas leakage. Any small amount of gas leaking out would form an explosive mix with air and could be triggered by a small spark, e.g. from an electric light switch, or even a thermostat. An argument against the use of gas, citing the many catastrophic gas explosions and fires that regularly occur, is usually countered by referring to the equally (if not more) numerous fire disasters caused by electrical faults.

The morale of this discussion is that there are risks involved with any form of energy system, gas or electric or even with open solid fuel fireplaces; the house may be burnt down in a fire started by a candle – all the designer, the supplier and the installer can do is *risk minimisation*. Instructions for use should be supplied with any such system, various safety devices are installed, but there is no substitute for reason and common sense, the ultimate responsibility should be with the user.

4.4.3 Energy conservation

The term refers to the conservation of conventional, non-renewable energy sources and many would prefer the term *rational use of energy* applied to all forms of energy.

The aim of energy conservation can be achieved by:

* reducing the energy requirement;
* substituting renewable energy wherever possible.

Energy use in buildings is determined by four sets of decisions:

1 **setting of environmental standards**: attempts at conservation do not mean a 'lowering' of standards, but the setting of reasonable standards, e.g. not setting the thermostat at 25°C for winter, when 22°C would be adequate, and not cooling the building to 22°C in the summer, when 27°C may be quite comfortable, i.e. rely on the adaptability model of thermal comfort (see Section 1.2.4). Similarly in lighting: an illuminance of 800 lx would require twice as much energy as 400 lx, and the 400 lx may be quite adequate for most office-type tasks.
2 **building form and fabric**: the effect of these has been discussed quite extensively in Part 1 (Heat).
3 **environmental control installations**: in this area we have to rely on engineering advice to a large extent, but often the architect can influence design decisions and achieve greater efficiencies, avoid the wastage of

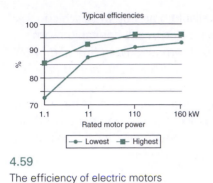

4.59

The efficiency of electric motors

energy (e.g. use more efficient motors, Fig. 4.59). Examples of this may be the choice of compact fluorescent or LED lamps rather than incandescent, or making sure that the air conditioning condenser unit is not exposed to solar heat input.

4 **choice of energy source, including renewables**: the decision for these often rests with the client and it may be based on economic considerations. These will be discussed in Section 4.5.6, but the architect should consider the possibilities, examine the feasibility of a chosen technique and advise the client accordingly.

A possible list of energy conservation measures has been suggested at a recent conference:

Building	Installations
Daylighting	Controls of HVAC systems
Shading	Energy-efficient HVAC
Natural ventilation	Economiser cycle
Insulation	Exhaust air heat recovery
Thermal mass	Energy-efficient lamps
Solar air (pre-)heating	Reduced duct leakage
Improved windows	Photovoltaics
Air infiltration control	Solar water heating
Passive solar heating	Solar/wind generators

The list is by no means comprehensive, but it includes most of the main measures. A few additional issues are mentioned below, that the architect may keep in mind and advise the client or may remind the consulting engineer.

The efficiency of electric motors varies between quite broad limits, especially for smaller motors (72–96%), as shown in Fig. 4.59. If energy is to be conserved, the use of high efficiency motors should be a requirement. Their initial cost may be slightly higher, but in terms of LCC (life cycle cost) analysis they are quite superior.

In an electricity supply system it is not only the overall load and consumption that is critical, but also its timing. The generation of peak-time electricity is far more expensive than the supply of base load. As the system must be capable of satisfying the peak demand (even if that occurs only for a short period), a lot of generating capacity lies idle most of the time. It can take up to 12 hours to start up a steam turbine generator set, thus there is no point in stopping them during off-peak periods. They are often referred to as *spinning reserve*.

Demand-side management (DSM) is aimed at levelling out the load, especially by various pricing strategies, such as:

- off-peak tariff, much cheaper than normal, for purposes not time-dependent, such as storage-type domestic hot water system or storage-type 'block' heaters or indeed 'ice storage' systems for air conditioning (see below);
- interruptible supply: the supplier can send out a high frequency signal through the supply cables to trigger a switch in the consumer's meter box, which can cut off (or switch back) non-essential circuits at peak periods;

- two-part tariffs, where the consumer pays a flat rate for all electricity used (energy rate) but also pays according to the peak load reached during the billing period (power rate). In some cases, where such metering and registering of peak power are not available, there may be a charge according to 'total connected load'.
- the latest development is digital metering, which allows the use of 'time-of-day' tariffs: higher prices at peak periods, lower prices in the off-peak 'troughs', perhaps in several steps.

A single consumer may have at least two meters, one for the 'normal' consumption (lighting and power points) and one for a 'special tariff' for off-peak domestic hot water and space heating (block or unit heaters) or for interruptible supply. In office and commercial buildings a large tank of water may be frozen overnight, using cheap off-peak electricity and the following day the melting of this ice (an endothermic process) would provide chilled water for the air conditioning system (i.e. making use of the phase change heat of water/ice).

Attempts to level out energy use rate at the individual consumer level were made in the 1960s and 1970s, by the so-called *load shedding* systems. All electric loads in the house would be ranked into an order of priority and grouped into separate circuits. A maximum load would be set and when that was reached, the lowest priority load would be 'shed', i.e. that circuit switched off. Such systems are now available in an electronic version, named IHG (Intelligent Home Gateway).

Demand side management (DSM) may reduce the total demand, but certainly shave off the peaks, to obviate the need to build new generating plants. For example, California saved the construction of a 1000 MW plant by DSM measures, such as technical advice to consumers, funding of feasibility studies, subsidising or even direct funding of more efficient equipment, such as compact fluorescent, or the latest LED lamps. Electricity suppliers also encourage the use of energy-efficient appliances, those rated at least at 4-stars. Fig 4.60 shows such an energy rating label, issued by an authorised testing institution.

Supply side management (SSM) systems include various arrangements to utilise surplus capacity at off-peak times (e.g. by large buffer storage systems) and make use of this at peak periods, such as:

- pump-back systems, which can be used where the grid has some hydro-electric generation components: surplus capacity can be used to pump back from a lower level (small) reservoir up to the main reservoir, to be used to drive the turbines at peak periods;
- other storage devices, which include batteries, reversible chemical reactions (e.g. ammonia dissociation), phase change latent heat of various salts, compressed air, flywheels and superconducting magnetic energy storage (SMES);
- distributed generation (DG), which means the incorporation into the grid of a multitude of small-scale generators, from micro-hydro or wind turbines to building-mounted PV systems. This is often considered as using the grid as storage, which is feasible because of the favourable diversity factors (see Section 4.3.4 above), of the many small generators (e.g. wind is usually strongest when there is little or no solar radiation).

4.60

An energy rating label for a refrigerator (standard AS/NZs 44742)

Table 4.18 The relationship of energy use and greenhouse gas emissions (% of national totals)

End-use	Energy consumption (%)	Greenhouse emissions (%)
Buildings	46	54
Defence establishments	37	40
Transport	15	5
Other	2	1

Source: WOGER: Whole Government Energy Report, Canberra (2002).

Energy conservation and substitution of renewable energy resources are imperative not only because of the finite availability of oil and coal, but also because of the atmospheric pollution, primarily CO_2 emissions due to their use. The magnitude of greenhouse gas emissions is not directly proportional to energy use, but certainly energy use is responsible for most greenhouse gas emissions. This can be well illustrated by statistics from the Australian Government, shown in Table 4.18 as a percentage of all energy use and emissions by government properties and activities.

Several governments have set up a 'carbon trading' scheme, as agreed in the Kyoto Protocol (1997). Those responsible for significant CO_2 emissions must buy 'carbon credits' or EUAs (EU Allowances). The EU ETS (Emissions Trading Scheme is the most successful (see Data sheet D4.1). CERs (Certified Emission Reduction) are issued as tradeable credits. The rate in 2009 was $26 per tonne of CO_2, but it fluctuates as the market develops. In 2006 the total volume of trade was $21 billion ($10^9$), growing to $31 billion the next year and to $126 billion by 2008. The trade is international, as envisaged at Kyoto.

4.4.4 Energy rating of buildings

This began in the early 1980s. Several authorities in many countries realised that building byelaws are not enough to achieve a reduction in energy use. California introduced a building energy code already in 1978 and it set a pattern for a two-pronged approach: *prescriptive* or *performance-based* regulations. The former would prescribe in detail many attributes of the proposed building and its components (such as thermal insulation) while the latter would compare the predicted energy use with the 'energy entitlement' (per unit floor area) for different building types and a number of climate zones. An applicant for a building permit may elect to comply with the prescriptive part or else they must prove, by using an approved computer simulation program (such as those discussed in Section 1.4.4.2) that the proposed building will not exceed its annual energy entitlement.

4.4.4.1 *The USA*

The Department of Energy (DOE) was created by President Carter in 1977 and since then it has grown into a huge unwieldy organisation, dealing with all energy-related issues (from nuclear, oil and electrical to renewables) and conservation. Its EERE (Energy Efficiency and Renewable Energy) division is the one most relevant to the present discussion. They administer a series of Acts, such as the ECPA (Energy Conservation and Production Act, 1978), the NAECA (National Appliance Energy Conservation Act, 1987) and the EPAct (Energy Policy Act, 1992).

EERE created a series of 'programs', such as the FEMP (Federal Energy Management Program) and the BECP (Building Energy Codes Program). This sets compulsory regulations for federal government buildings as well as various 'model energy codes' (MEC) for state governments (including fire, gas, plumbing, etc. codes). Almost each state is different, but many have adopted the MEC as the basis of regulations.

The MEC also allows three routes to compliance:

1 following the prescriptive package;
2 the trade-off approach;
3 the software approach.

Jointly with the Environmental Protection Agency they created from 1995 onwards the 'Energy Star' standards, primarily for domestic appliances, versions of which have since been adopted in the EU, Canada, Australia, New Zealand, Japan and Taiwan. Buildings are rated on a scale of 1 to 100, and those rated 75 or over qualify for the 'Energy Star' (Fig. 4.61). The ICC (International Code Council) was created in 2000 and produced the IECC (International Energy Conservation Code). The primary tool for rating is the program DOE2, which is also the simulation engine of the eQUEST design tool (James Hirsh Associates, California).* These are 'public domain' programs, but the latter is only available in I-P (inch-pound) units (the SI does not seem to have reached California). An alternative is to use the EnergyPlus program.

The IECC is referenced at many levels: it regulates the building envelope as well as HVAC (heating, ventilation and air conditioning), SWH (service water heating) and lighting installations. It is called 'international', but it appears to be a US code. It references ASHRAE and IES (Illuminating Engineering Society) standards and divides America into 38 climate zones.

A survey of the international scene identified some 30 similar rating schemes in operation, most of them in various states of the USA. A few are reviewed in the following.

4.4.4.2   The EU

The European Parliament and the Council issued 'Directive' 2002/91/EC for Energy Performance of Buildings (EPBD) in 2002. This requires the energy certification of buildings and may be based on an energy audit of existing buildings or on a computer simulation of a planned building. Member states must set standards for the energy efficiency of new buildings, including the setting of targets and prescribing the energy use prediction methods. The elements to be accounted for in calculations must include those listed in Annex 1 as:

4.61

The 'Energy Star' symbol

---

* Available from http://www.doe2.com and http://www.EnergyDesignResources.com.

1 thermal characteristics of the building fabric, including air-tightness;
2 heating system and hot water supply, including their insulation;
3 air conditioning installations;
4 ventilation;
5 built-in lighting installation;
6 position and orientation in relation to the given climate;
7 passive solar systems and solar protection;
8 natural ventilation and daylighting;
9 indoor climatic conditions, including the designed indoor climate.

The energy use targets should be revised every 5 years, in the light of techno-logical developments. The general target was set as reducing energy use by 20% by 2020 as well as 20% contribution by renewable sources.

4.4.4.3 Germany

The Bauhaus University in Weimar proposed a 'building passport', a signifi-cant part of which is the energy rating. This was adopted by an EU Directive: from 2006 onwards any building from Finland to Portugal, when sold or rented, must have such a passport. In Germany this is administered by the DENA (*Deutsche Energie-Agentur*) and an '*Energiepass*' was introduced for houses and residences (Fig. 4.62). Householders can obtain the services of an authorised person to carry out an energy audit and issue such a pass. The crucial part of this is the annual energy consumption expressed in kWh/m²y. Older, unimproved houses would be in the 400–550 kWh/m²y range, new houses should not exceed 100 kWh/m²y, but should preferably be in the range of 30–60 kWh/m²y. (Compare these values with those given in Data sheet D.4.2.) On the basis of this (and a qualitative assessment of sustain-ability), the house would be awarded an 'efficiency class' on a scale from A to I (A being the best).

Such a rating is also influenced by the life expectancy of the building. This may range from 25 years in Japan, 50 years in the USA and 75 years in the UK. This energy pass becomes an important piece of information for the owner or a prospective buyer or tenant. It would also influence the price.

4.62

. . . and what's yours using per square metre?

4.4.4.4 Denmark

A system similar to the above has been in operation since 1997, with the name '*Energiemærke*'. It must be available at every point of sale of the house, but for larger buildings the rating must be carried out annually, based on actual records of energy use.

4.4.4.5 The UK

Based on the BREDEM method, (see Section 1.4.4.2), the Open University developed the MKECI (Milton Keynes Energy Cost Index) and a modified version of this is NHER (National Home Energy Rating) system, which is the basis of the computer program *Home Rater*. NHER is owned by NES (National Energy Services). The rating scale extends from 0 to 20. Most existing dwell-ings in the UK would rate between 4.5 and 5.5 of this scale. A rating of 10 would be achieved by (e.g.) a gas heated, semi-detached, masonry house that complies with part L1 of the Building Regulations. A rating of 20 would be achieved with zero emissions of CO_2 and zero operational energy use.

Three methods can be used to satisfy such regulations:

1 the elemental method: each envelope element is to achieve the prescribed U-values and window sizes are limited to 22.5% of the floor area;
2 the 'target U-value' method: a weighted average U-value is prescribed and calculations must show that it is achieved; provisions against thermal bridging and infiltration control must be demonstrated;
3 the energy rating method, which includes ventilation/infiltration as well as SWH (service water heating).

The U-value requirement is fairly stringent: a maximum of 0.25 W/m²K is allowed for the roof and 0.35 W/m²K for walls (compare these with the values given in Table 1.5).

The Building Regulations document L1 can be satisfied by using 'accredited construction details' (e.g. U-values, the prescriptive part) or by using a SAP (Standard Assessment Procedure) performance rating. NHER is more comprehensive than SAP; it takes into account local climate and environment, its effect on energy use, space and water heating, as well as cooking, lighting and appliances. SAP has a scale of 0 to 100+. A rating of 92 would put the building into the 'A'-band. SAP uses a standard climate (East Pennines), standard occupancy and use-pattern, thus it rates the building itself, while NHER gives a more realistic prediction of energy use that can be expected in the given location, with the actual use pattern.

4.4.4.6 France

In France, the QUALITEL rating scheme is based on a qualitative assessment but also relies on energy use prediction. Rating must be disclosed (in the advertisement) for any property offered for sale or rental. Rating can be done and a certificate (*étiquette énergie*) is issued by an authorised person, by a survey and using what appears to be a spreadsheet program. RT2012 (*Réglementation Thermique*) sets the categories for energy consumption and CO_2 emissions:

Band	kWh/m²y	kg CO_2/m²y
A	< 5	< 5
B	51–90	6–10
C	91–150	11–20
D	151–230	21–35
E	231–330	36–55
F	331–450	56–80
G	> 451	>80

A good rating (*l'eco-prêt à taux zêro*) attracts tax credits and for energy-related building improvements 'eco-loans' are available.

4.4.4.7 Portugal

In Portugal, the Regulations on the thermal behaviour of building envelopes (RCCTE) are a combination of prescriptive building regulations and an energy rating. The maximum allowable energy use is set and the building data can be fed into a spreadsheet that would predict the expected energy use (by no means a full-scale simulation). If this is below the set limit, a certificate is issued and a rating is given on a scale of fair/good/excellent. The implementation of this system is at present voluntary, but it is intended to become compulsory in the future.

4.4.4.8 Australia

The first rating scheme was released in 1986, as the FSDR (Five Star Design Rating) scheme. Its 'simulation engine' was the CSIRO thermal response and energy simulation program CHEETAH. This was further developed and officially adopted in 1993 as NatHERS (Nationwide House Energy Rating Scheme). Several authorities require that such a rating be carried out and disclosed if and when the house is put on the market (e.g. based on the Trade Descriptions Act). A similar disclosure requirement relates to commercial buildings, as a BEEC (Building Energy Efficiency Certificate) must be presented.

Some concern was expressed that simulation-based ratings may be valid for a 'sealed box' building (in cool climates), but not for the tropics, where houses are used in a completely open, cross-ventilated mode. Thus AccuRate was produced by CSIRO by 2000, which includes a cross-ventilation routine. It was intended for use in the hot-humid climates of Northern Australia relying on the apparent cooling effect of air movement produced by cross-ventilation or ceiling fans. Since then NatHERS has become the framework for rating, using various programs for the necessary calculations. Three such programs are now accredited: FirstRate, BERS (Building Energy Rating Scheme) and AccuRate. The new version of the latter, 'AccuRate Sustainability', is broadened to include CO_2 emissions, water use and lighting. BERSpro is a package produced by Solar Logic, it is very user-friendly and it is fully accredited. FirstRate is a program produced for the state of Victoria.

The federal ('commonwealth') body, the ABCB (Australian Building Codes Board) formulated energy-related modification to the BCA (Building Code of Australia). This may be adopted, or possibly modified, by state governments. For any new house design the ACT, SA, Qld and Vic set the requirement at 6 stars, the NT and Tas at 5 stars (on a scale of 0 to 10 stars), and NSW requires a BSIX (Building Sustainability Index) certificate. Ten stars would imply zero energy requirement. Energy use is expressed in terms of MJ/m^2y.

The BCA (Building Code of Australia, pt. 3.12) distinguishes eight climatic zones, from the hot-humid North, to the 'alpine' zones of the cool-temperate Tasmania and the south/east mountainous area (of NSW and Victoria). NatHERS uses over 60 zones, which are selected by postcode. The stated 'performance requirements' are qualitative only, which can be satisfied by either following the deemed-to-satisfy provisions ('acceptable construction') or by 'alternative solutions' which are shown to be equivalent to the former, either by a recognised computer program or by 'expert opinion'.

Generally the BCA requirements for acceptable construction are fairly timid (see Table 1.5). The stated aim is not to achieve 'best practice' but only to eliminate 'worst practice'. A gradual progressive tightening of requirements is envisaged. An interesting point is that for roofs in the northern zones, downward heat flow is taken as critical, while upward heat flow (loss) is controlled in the south.

4.4.4.9 New Zealand

The regulatory system is similar to that of Australia, only the terminology is different. The three methods distinguished are: the Schedule method, the Calculation method and the Modelling method. The last of these requires the use of a building thermal response and energy use simulation program. The insulation requirements are not as stringent as in the UK: even in the coldest of the three climatic zones distinguished, the prescribed value is R2.5 for roofs and R1.9 for walls, which corresponds to U-values of 0.4 and 0.52 respectively.

4.4.5 Other methods

An alternative to simulation is a *point-scoring method*, where even the non-professional person can answer a series of (mostly multiple-choice) questions about the house and each answer results in a certain number of points. The number of points awarded for each building attribute has been determined by an extensive simulation-based parametric study. Categories are set in terms of the number of points achieved, in order to award a number of stars (see e.g. Data sheet D.4.2). Several states (both in Australia and in the USA) employ such methods and the Danish *Positive List Method* is similar.

Some building control authorities (especially in South-East Asia) use the OTTV (overall thermal transfer value) concept to prescribe the thermal characteristics of the building envelope. This can be considered as an average U-value for the whole of the building envelope, including solar radiation effects. Its calculation is based on the following equation (the sum of three components: envelope gain, window conduction and window solar gain, divided by the total area):

$$\text{OTTV} = \frac{A_w U_w TD_{eq} + A_f U_f DT + A_f SC \times SF}{A_t}$$

where

A = area of each element
A_t = total envelope area
U = U-value of each element
TD_{eq} = equivalent temperature difference
DT = $T_o - T_i$ (averages)
SC = shading coefficient
SF = solar factor (W/m^2).

and the subscripts

w = walls
f = fenestration (windows).

The calculation of the TD_{eq} is quite involved (it makes an allowance for solar input). It is a derivative of the TETD/TA (total equivalent temperature differential) method (ASHRAE, 1972), where TA indicates time-averaging. The method heavily relies on tables presenting empirical (simplified) values and is falling into disrepute. Furthermore, the SF concept is no longer in use (see Section 1.4.1.3).

4.5 SUSTAINABILITY ISSUES

4.5.1 Historical background

Environmental degradation was already the main concern of the Stockholm UNEP conference in 1972. Barbara Ward and Rene Dubos (1972) well summarised the situation in their book: *Only One Earth*. In the following year the OPEC oil embargo brought home the realisation of the finite nature of our fossil fuel supplies. The three main problem areas identified were:

* population explosion
* resource depletion
* environmental degradation.

Already in 1973 the RIBA (under the then president Alex Gordon) initiated the LL/LF/LE (long life, loose fit, low energy) movement. The philosophical basis of this was that it would be ecologically beneficial to erect buildings which last, which are designed in a way to remain adaptable for changed uses and which use little energy in their operation. The term 'sustainability' did not exist then, but it was a program for sustainable architecture.

The extreme view was that any 'development' would harm the environment, but it was recognised that the LDCs (less developed countries) do have the right to develop, as the ideal of equity demands it. The argument was resolved by accepting the necessity for development, as long as it is sustainable. The Brundtland Report (UN, 1987) introduced the term and gave the definition as:

Sustainable development is development that meets the needs of the present without compromising the ability of future generations to meet their own needs.

The latter point has been called 'inter-generational equity'.

In 1987, the Montreal Protocol agreed on the phasing out of organo-fluorides, which are affecting the ozone layer and as a consequence admit more UV irradiation (while also contributing to the greenhouse effect). The Intergovernmental Panel on Climate Change (IPCC) reported in 1990 and firmly established that the climate is changing and that this is largely anthropogenic, caused by the emission of greenhouse gases by humanity.

The 'Earth Summit' in 1992 by UNCED (United Nations Conference on Environment and Development) considered environmental degradation together with resource depletion and broadened the discourse in Agenda 21 and with the 'Rio Declaration' laid down the principles of sustainable development.

Equity for all humanity is one of the aims of Agenda 21 (referring to the new century), but inter-generational equity is perhaps even more important.

The UN Framework Convention on Climate Change (UNFCCC) called a meeting in Kyoto, to consider climate change and emission control, which reached a very watered-down agreement in 1997: the reduction of 1990 level of CO_2 emissions by 5% by 2012. Some 170 countries ratified the agreement by December 2008, with the notable absence of the greatest emitters: the USA, China and India. It took a change of government in Australia to ratify it in 2008.

Architecture joined the movement by the *Declaration of Interdependence for a Sustainable Future* at the Chicago Congress of the IUA in 1993. Many national bodies and institutions of architecture have adopted this declaration and produced energy and environmental policies. Such declarations and policy statements are fine words only, but even if not immediately effective, they do have a significance: they imply a commitment which individuals must recognise at the risk of being 'politically incorrect', they must pay at least lip-service to these and with frequent repetitions they do become the accepted norm. Even if an individual fails to act accordingly, at least he/she will have a guilty conscience about it.

The follow-up conference in Copenhagen (2009) did not get beyond statements of intentions. Subsequent UN conferences, at Doha (2012) and in Durban (2013), did not get much further than extending the Kyoto Protocol.

4.5.2 Philosophical basis

Some authors (e.g. Radford & Williamson, 2002) argue that the notion of sustainability (thus sustainable architecture) is a social construct, that it implies an action plan, therefore it must have an ethical basis. A good rational materialist would suggest that this is back-to-front: the physical need for survival must dictate a new ethics, an environmental or ecological ethics. In Marxist terms: the rest of it is 'superstructure'. In Maslow's hierarchy of human needs (see box in Section 1.2.2), the physical/biological needs are at the top.

Some studio/design teachers argue that teaching environmental (or architectural) science has no place on architecture courses, or at best it is a side-issue. The counter-argument is that environmental/architectural science deals with questions of survival, while they talk about the icing on the cake. They are fiddling while Rome is burning. They do not realise the urgency of fire-fighting.

Ethical systems may be based on some (alleged) 'divine' proclamation or pronouncement (e.g. the ten commandments of Moses) or some speculatively derived notion of duty (such as Kant's *categorical imperative*), or some other set of values shared by the group, by a professional body or by society as a whole. Most such differing ethical systems are built on shifting sand. In both the World Wars of the twentieth century both sides fought in the name of the same Christian God, or today the Shiites and Sunnis fight in the name of the same Allah.

Conflicts arise not just between different nations, different social systems, different religions (or other irrational belief-systems) but also within a liberal democratic society, e.g. between different interest-groups. This is a question of horizon. Individual survival and well-being depend on societal survival. The survival of societies depends on the existence of our global eco-system. It is suggested that, if humanity is to survive, our behaviour must be governed by a globally-based environmental ethics.

Over four decades ago humanity's survival was recognised to be threatened by the three trends mentioned above (in Section 4.5.1). Within the third of these, environmental degradation, global warming became the dominant threat. Local environmental problems are important, but must be seen in the context of the global problem, the problem of survival.

This concern for humanity's survival has been accused of being 'anthropocentric', implying that this is 'species-ism', just as bad as racism, that it is our duty and obligation to protect nature, the fauna and flora. Terms like 'duty and obligation' imply some external dictate or command. There is no need to postulate any such a dictate. We can unashamedly profess to be anthropocentric, while realising that we are part of a global system and the preservation of that system, of bio-diversity, of the natural environment is in our selfishly perceived best interest.

This environmental ethics dictates that our behaviour, our actions must serve, and certainly not harm, the sustainability of our habitat. It is thus a very pragmatic and rational ethics.

4.5.3   Social implications

Fig. 4.63, as proposed by Meadows and Meadows (1972), indicates that the vast majority of people are primarily concerned with the here and now (vertical spatial scale, horizontal time scale), partly because they have to struggle to survive to the next day, but partly also because of a very limited vision and understanding. Few people have a broader horizon and a longer-term view. Even those who have a global perspective and look at the distant future must think of the next minute and the next step, most of the time. However, that next step should be governed by the global view.

'Globalisation' is a highly controversial issue. It is an unavoidable necessity, but its meaning must be clarified. Is it the 'Workers-of-the-world unite!' slogan of the 'dictatorship of the proletariat'? Or does it mean the unrestrained global market of multinational corporations? Globalisation, as it happens today, is in fact extremely short-sighted. Its driving force is the individual, or small group (shareholders') interest, short-term profit. This may be acceptable, if it is within the framework set by far-sighted governments which represent the people. Acceptable, as long as it is realised that there are measures of value other than money. Acceptable, as long as these do not conflict with the global interest of humanity's survival and with the aim of 'the greatest happiness of the greatest numbers' (Hutcheson, 1725).

Dictatorships are often envied for being able to produce quick and significant results, changes without procrastination, but lasting and beneficial changes can only be based on consensus. It has been said that democracy is a luxury, which a large part of the world can ill-afford. It is painfully difficult to achieve such a consensus and international cooperation is even more difficult, as shown by the Kyoto Protocol (1997). After more than ten years it still has not been ratified by the world's largest producers of CO_2 (the USA and China).

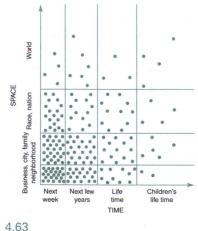

4.63

Human horizons

However, there is no other way. Globalisation, in the sense of democracy with international cooperation, is the only possible way to avoid global destruction. The role of a national government is to ensure the well-being of its people without harming others, in harmony with the global eco-system. Anything else would be suicidal.

There are millions of conflicting interests, and interest groups at work. These can be resolved and channelled in the direction of the global interest by information, education, enlightenment. There are encouraging signs. Information is influencing public opinion and politicians depend on the public opinion. In this context, is it possible to enlighten and influence our own profession?

4.5.4   What can architects do?

Buildings and their associated uses are responsible for a large part of the environmental load caused by humanity:

- 46% of all energy consumption;
- 54% of all atmospheric emissions;
- 30% of all raw materials used;
- 44% of water usage;
- 25% of solid wastes;
- 20% of liquid wastes.

All these can be strongly influenced by architects and designers.

The main practical question is how the above noble ideas can be translated into actions at the level of everyday reality. Design may be constrained by clients and regulatory authorities. However, architects work at many levels and may influence the development process. Architects may be employed by client organisations. As facility managers they may influence the client on building needs. They may be involved in site selection and feasibility studies. They may assist in formulating the brief, which may involve a series of background studies concerning organisational and social aspects, as well as ergonomics and environmental requirements.

The process from briefing to design is an iterative one. The architect may ask for clarification of the brief and may influence the client by giving expert advice. The conceptual design is often separated from the detailed design of the fabric and contract documentation. It may even be done by a different architect or firm of architects. Supervision of the building work and contract management is a distinctly separate task. Even if the whole process is carried out by one firm, different individuals may specialise in certain tasks.

Many building companies employ their own architects. Many architects specialise in interior design for shops, for shop front design or office interior 'fit-out'. Some become writers, critics, journalists, educators or theoreticians. Architects may work for local authorities and may have an influence on town planning and urban design, or may have various regulatory tasks. They may have a role in the building approval process, which is not just a yes/no task, it may involve negotiations with the designer and developer to modify the proposal in the interest of the 'public good'.

At each of these levels, environmental and energy issues are involved and must be considered. Early decisions may have unforeseen consequences: they may preclude later, environmentally sound decisions. Every action may have environmental consequences. Environmental and sustainability issues are survival issues, thus must have top priority and a decisive role. 'Minor' compromises should be avoided as these may add up and render a project completely unsustainable. Among the many roles the architect can play, the one central task is the design of buildings. Design dominates the architectural ethos. However, design is much more than just the 'looks' of the product, originality or fashion.

Sustainability, how the building works, how it uses resources can be considered under four headings: *site, energy, materials and wastes*, and these are the subject of the following sub-sections.

4.5.4.1 Site

Land is precious and not only in monetary terms. All building activity disturbs the land, the site. Such disturbance ought to be minimised. Undisturbed land, supporting an intact ecology, is particularly valuable. If possible, its use should be avoided. This could be a step in preserving bio-diversity. The use of already disturbed, possibly derelict land would be preferable. Rehabilitation of disturbed or neglected land is desirable.

Buildings should fit their environment: if possible, large scale earthworks should be avoided. If earthworks are unavoidable, the top soil, which is a valuable living system, should be preserved, stored and used in landscaping. All possible steps should be taken to prevent soil erosion, to promote land and soil conservation and, wherever possible, improvement.

Site selection also has planning implications. There is a dichotomy and argument:

- on the one hand, there is the lobby of builders and developers aiming to get land re-zoned for residential development, for subdivision. They claim that the unavailability of land is the reason for high land prices and the housing shortage.
- on the other hand, planners generally agree that higher residential densities are desirable, to reduce commuting distances and generally reduce all travel needs (thus making feasible a good public transport system), to reduce the cost of piped and wired public services, but also to preserve unspoilt (or agricultural) land and prevent urban sprawl.

The latter argument is more in sympathy with the ideal of sustainability.

Architects may have an influence in this argument, but may also devise solutions to make high density living more acceptable, even desirable.

4.5.4.2 Energy

Energy is used in buildings at two levels:

1 *Operational energy*, (O), annually used for heating, cooling, ventilation, lighting and servicing the building. This was discussed in Section 4.4 above and, indeed, throughout this book.

2 *Capital energy*, (C), or energy embodied in the materials and building processes. It is interesting to note that in the early 1970s, when building energy analysis was in its infancy, the C/O ratio was around 5, i.e. the building would use as much energy in 5 years as was necessary to produce its materials and construct it. For a very poorly constructed building the ratio was as little as 2.5 (i.e. 2.5 years). Recent analyses show ratios of 30 to 40. One study even concluded that it was 50.

The reason for this is two-fold: buildings have been improved and such improvements have increased the capital energy (embodied energy), e.g. thermal insulation, but also many plastics and metal products. At the same time better buildings have resulted in a reduced operational energy consumption. In the 1970s efforts were focused on reducing this operational energy use. Now the major concern has shifted and attempts are made to reduce the embodied energy.

The embodied energy, or to be precise: the 'process energy requirement' (PER) of some materials is shown in Table 4.19.

Table 4.19 The process energy requirement of some building materials in kWh/kg

air dried sawn hardwood	0.14
stabilised earth	0.19
concrete blocks	0.39
precast tilt-up concrete	0.52
in situ cast concrete	0.47
precast steam-cured concrete	0.55
kiln-dried sawn hardwood	0.56
clay bricks	0.69
gypsum plaster	0.80
kiln-dried softwood	0.94
autoclaved aerated concrete	1.00
plasterboard	1.22
cement	5.60
fibrous cement	2.11
granite slabs	1.64
wood particle board	2.22
plywood	2.89
glued-laminated timber	3.05
medium density fibreboard	3.14
glass	3.53
hardboard	6.69
mild steel	9.44
galvanised mild steel	10.55
acrylic paint	17.08
zinc	14.17
PVC	22.22
plastics in general	25.00
copper	27.78
synthetic rubber	30.56
aluminium	47.00

There are large differences in published data regarding the embodied energy of materials, partly due to local differences in the industrial processes, but partly also due to the different calculation methods. For example, some results published in India show cement as 1.86 kWh/kg (rather than the above 5.6) and PVC as 44 kWh/kg (instead of the above 22.22). The same source, instead of the above shown 9.44 kWh/kg for mild steel, distinguishes rods: 7.83, RSJs: 11.9 and RHS 18.14 kWh/kg. In broad terms two methods of calculation can be distinguished:

1 the *analytical method* follows the processes from gaining the raw material through various stages of manufacture and transportation to the installation in the final product: the building, and adds up all the energy used;
2 the *statistical method* examines the particular industry of a country, a state, or a region, attempts to establish the total energy use by that industry as well as its total output; dividing the latter into the former gives the embodied energy per unit mass (or other production unit).

The best data are likely to be the integration of results of the two methods.

Table 4.20 is based on a number of different sources and it groups building materials into three broad categories: low, medium and high energy materials. Differences between the two tables are a good illustration of this point. Table 4.19 is more detailed but note that the numbers (two decimals) imply an accuracy which is unlikely to exist.

If an existing building is to be improved, the first step is to determine the operational energy use, to carry out an energy audit. This should also follow a dual approach:

1 List all the energy user installations, equipment or appliances, establish their energy use rating (W) and the duration of use (h) to obtain an energy use figure (Wh or kWh). The time-base is normally one year.

Table 4.20 Embodied energy of some building materials

low	sand, gravel	0.01
< 1 kWh/kg	wood	0.1
	concrete	0.2
	sand-lime brickwork	0.4
	lightweight concrete	0.5
	medium plasterboard	1.0
1–10 kWh/kg	brickwork	1.2
	lime	1.5
	cement	2.2
	mineral wool	3.9
	glass	6.0
	porcelain	6.1
high	plastics	10
> 10 kWh/kg	steel	10
	lead	14
	zinc	15
	copper	16
	aluminium	56

Table 4.21 Calorific values of some fuels

Fuel	Energy value	Unit
Light (gas-) oil	10.6	kWh/L
Heavy fuel oil (Class G)	11.7	
Natural gas	10.6	
Propane	12.9	
Butane	12.8	
Coal	7.5–8.3	kWh/kg
Brown coal	4.5–6.3	
Coke	7.9	
Methane	15.4	
Hydrogen	34.2	

2 Summarise all the energy 'imports', electricity and gas bills, any solid or liquid fuel used. For comparability all these should be converted into kWh unit. For this the conversion factors (calorific values) given in Table 4.21 can be used.

Results of the two approaches should be identical; if not, then they should be examined and reconciled. Approach (1) should be revealing: it shows the items that are unreasonably high in energy consumption and should be improved.

Some authors distinguish three types of energy audits: preliminary, targeted and comprehensive. A *preliminary audit* involves a walk-through inspection, including the collection of energy bills; it is quick, it can be used as a feasibility study for a more detailed audit. A *targeted audit* may result from the preliminary study, if it identified some significant shortcomings or a selected system, e.g. the lighting installation or the boiler system. It would produce recommendations for upgrading or improvements.

A *comprehensive audit* is the most time-consuming and thorough (but also most expensive) exercise. It would involve tracing the energy flows and may involve extensive measurements. Such an energy audit will also be the basis of an energy management programme. Many countries have standards for the methodology of energy audits (e.g. AS.2725, or BS EN 16247-1, in response to the EU Directive and ISO 50 001:2011 or the US DOE accredited energy auditor system).

4.5.4.3 Materials

Selection of materials must be influenced by this embodied energy, but also by a number of other issues affecting sustainability of their use. A typical evaluation system (BMAS = building materials assessment system) uses 14 criteria, as shown in Table 4.22. When using such a table to evaluate a material, a score of 0 to 5 is awarded against each criterion, rating its environmental impact. Thus, 0 is no impact, 5 is much impact. 'Help' tables are available to assist such scoring. Then each score is squared (to get a better resolution) and the weighting factors (shown in Table 4.22) are applied to each score.

Table 4.22 BMAS: Building Materials Assessment System

Group	Criteria	Weighting	GRP
origin	1 damage to the environment in the extraction of raw material	3	
	2 extent of damage relative to the amount of material produced	2	
	3 abundance of source or renewability of material	4	
	4 recycled content	3	12
manufacture	5 solid and liquid wastes in manufacture and production	3	
	6 air pollution in manufacture and production	4	
	7 embodied energy (energy used for its production)	5	12
construction	8 energy used for transportation to the site	3	
	9 energy used on site for assembly and erection	1	
	10 on site waste, incl. packaging	2	6
in use	11 maintenance required during life cycle	3	
	12 environmental effects during life cycle (e.g. toxic emissions)	3	6
demolition	13 energy use in and effects of demolition at end of life cycle	2	
	14 recyclability of demolished material	4	6

The sum of the 14 squared and weighted scores is the 'ecological factor' (EF) of the material. This is not claimed to be more than a qualitative guidance figure. The scoring can be biased and the weighting factors have been established by seeking an 'expert consensus'. However, this is the most comprehensive system for judging building materials from the sustainability viewpoint.

It is worth noting that the criteria are strongly interconnected, e.g. though timber has low embodied energy, it will have a low eco-rating only if it comes from renewable resources, i.e. if it is plantation timber. If it comes from 'original growth' forests, produced by a clean-felling method, possibly causing soil erosion, its EF will be quite high.

A simpler method developed by Lawson (1996) gives an 'environmental rating' of various building products on a straightforward 5-point scale:

1: poor, 2: fair, 3: good, 4: very good, and 5: excellent

See also Data sheet D.4.3.

4.5.4.4   Wastes

Wastes have been considered in some detail in Section 4.1.2 above and it is apparent from that discussion that architects can have a strong influence on how wastes are disposed of.

In addition, attempts should be made to retain as much stormwater on the site as possible: through the collection and storage of roof water, using soft ground surfaces rather than paving to promote percolation, these encourage the soaking of water into the soil (and replenish the ground water reserve). Reducing the run-off would also help soil conservation, preventing erosion.

4.5.5 Complex rating systems

Many building energy rating systems are in use world-wide, but recently these have been extended to incorporate 'greenhouse rating' and other environmental issues. Greenhouse gas emission is an important measure of sustainability, but it can only be estimated. Energy use can be calculated with reasonable accuracy, and it is often used to calculate CO_2 emissions. It is suggested that at the building level the following conversion factors can be used for various forms of energy consumed:

	kg/kWh
electricity (average)	0.72
solid fuel (coal, coke)	0.34
fuel oil (paraffin, kerosene)	0.29
gas (natural)	0.21

Many building sustainability rating systems have been devised in various countries, but there is no sign of consensus emerging as yet.

In the USA, the LEED (Leadership in Energy and Environmental Design) rating system has been created by USGBC (US Green Building Council) and is in operation. It is also available through Vikipedia.

The Swedish *EcoEffect* rating method is based on a life cycle analysis (LCA). It considers energy use, materials use, indoor and outdoor environment. The various effects are weighted by using a complicated 'analytical hierarchic process'. It is emphasised that the single figure index produced hides the causes and problems, therefore it must be supplemented by 'environmental profiles', stating the criteria and weightings used.

The UK point-scoring ('credits' awarded) BREEAM* (Building Research Establishment Environmental Assessment Method) is broad, but relies on very qualitative judgements. Energy use and CO_2 emissions are quantified. Assessors are licensed by the BRE.

The European CRISP (Construction and City Related Sustainability Indicators) network includes 24 organisations of 16 countries. It is based on the work of CIB (Commission Internationale du Bâtiment), notably their project CIBW 082. It is aimed at creating a standardised terminology, methodology, measures of sustainability and a data-base.

---

* Not to be mistaken for BREDEM (BRE Domestic Energy Model), see Section 1.4.4.2.

In Australia, the ABERS (Australian Building Environmental Rating Scheme) has recently been introduced. This considers existing buildings, measured data), energy, water, wastes and emissions, indoor environment and awards 1 to 6 stars. Existing buildings would score, on average, 2.5 stars.

One state government body, SEDA (Sustainable Development Authority of NSW) uses a Building Greenhouse Rating (BGR) system for commercial buildings, awarding 1 to 5 stars for poor to exceptionally good buildings. This (similar to ABERS) would distinguish common services and tenants' energy use and WBR (Whole Building Rating). Its major component is energy use, but it includes greenhouse gas emissions, at least in qualitative terms. Star ratings are based on the following criteria:

- 1 star: POOR: *Poor energy management or outdated systems*. The building is consuming a lot of unnecessary energy. There are cost-effective changes that could be implemented to improve energy consumption, cut operating costs and reduce greenhouse emissions.
- 2 stars: GOOD: *Average building performance*. The building has some elements of energy efficiency in place and reflects the current market average. There is still scope for cost-effective improvements and minor changes may improve on energy and operating costs.
- 3 stars: VERY GOOD: *Current market best practice*. The building offers very good systems and management practices and reflects an awareness of the financial and environmental benefits of optimising energy use.
- 4 stars: EXCELLENT: *Strong performance*. Excellent energy performance due to design and management practices or high efficiency systems and equipment or low greenhouse-intensive fuel supply.
- 5 stars: EXCEPTIONAL: *Best building performance*. The building is as good as it can be due to integrated design, operation, management and fuel choice.

The assessment of CO_2 emissions is an important contributor to Building Greenhouse Rating and in some cases limits for rating are given directly in terms of CO_2/m^2, without reference to energy use.

Table 4.23 gives a summary of such numerical limits of CO_2 emissions in terms of CO_2/m^2 on the basis of which the star ratings would be awarded for office buildings. This is very much a function of climate and, as an indication, values for three states are shown: Darwin, Northern Territory (a hot-humid climate), Brisbane, Queensland (a warm-humid, temperate climate), and Melbourne, Victoria (a cool-temperate climate).

Table 4.23 Limits of CO_2 emission for greenhouse gas rating in $kg.CO_2/(m^2y)$

	Darwin					Brisbane					Melbourne				
stars max:	1	2	3	4	5	1	2	3	4	5	1	2	3	4	5
base bldg	148	124	101	77	53	215	181	146	112	77	225	194	163	132	101
tenancy	116	96	76	56	36	172	142	112	82	53	160	137	115	92	70
whole bldg.	264	220	177	133	89	387	323	259	194	130	385	331	278	224	171

One popular measure of sustainability is the 'ecological footprint'. Originally conceived as a method to compare the sustainability of different populations, or of the lifestyle of individuals. It is rather a measure of the ecological load an object (a project, an establishment, a suburb or indeed a city) would impose on the environment, related to the area of agricultural land that would be required to supply all materials used and energy consumed by that object (Wackernagel *et al.*, 1995).

There are many methods of calculating it and there is no consensus. There are almost as many critics of the whole concept as there are users of it. At best, it can assist the qualitative comparison of objects not too dissimilar. It may be used as an educational tool. Several self-assessment methods are available on the web. One exercise suggests that a city, such as Sydney, would need an area 27 times its actual area. The footprint of an individual is assessed in terms of his/her food, shelter, transport and goods/services use. A reasonably frugal person would have an ecological footprint of some 7 ha, but some may go as high as 30 ha.

4.5.6 Economics

Ecology and economics are often made out to be in opposition to each other. It is worth noting that both words come from the Greek οικοσ (oikos), meaning house, habitat or household. The -*logy* ending means *study of. . .* while the -*nomy* ending implies the *law of. . .*, so, ecology is the study of and economy is the laws of our house or housekeeping. Perhaps two sides of the same coin?

There are many instances when both point in the same direction, e.g. when a slightly increased capital cost would result in substantial savings in running cost. It may be easy to convince a rationally minded client when designing his/her own house to spend a little extra money, say, on insulation, which will then reduce the heating costs.

Problems may arise when a developer is producing a building for immediate sale, who has no interest in reducing the operating costs. It should be pointed out that buyers now also have a critical attitude and can gauge the added value of an environmentally sound or 'sustainable' building. There is also a prestige value added to such buildings. However, if the architect is acting as an advisor to the buyer, he or she must be able to ascertain whether the building is really good and 'sustainable' or only claims to be so. Indeed, the various energy rating systems (discussed in Section 4.4.4) may give an indication of the quality of the house considered.

Assessment of investment proposals is usually based on a cost/benefit analysis, comparing the investment cost with the longer-term benefit. Its outcome very much depends on the chosen 'accounting horizon', the useful life assumed and the limitation of indirect costs and externalities taken into account. Often the crude or simple pay-back period is used in economic analysis or investment decisions. Decisions should be based on information and, when buying a house, its energy demand is an important piece of information. Hence the various 'disclosure' requirements are as important as a 'list of contents' when buying a pre-packaged food item.

More sophisticated methods take into account the 'cost of money', i.e. how much interest would need to be paid if the sum to be invested were to be borrowed, or the interest the invested money would earn otherwise. Such a comparison can be done using a discounted cash-flow technique, to find the *present worth* of future savings, to compare it with the capital investment. Both the interest ('discount') rate and any inflation rate must be considered. Method sheet M.4.1 presents the details of this method.

An alternative to present worth calculations is the LCA or life cycle cost analysis. This may include not only the direct cost comparison, but also the maintenance cost of the alternatives and their life expectancy. Very often the appearance, the perceived quality, the prestige value of the alternatives, the expected future re-sale value must also be taken into account.

The architect, whether a decision-maker or advisor, should also be fully aware of locally applicable and current subsidies, incentive schemes, or tax benefits which may be applicable to one of the alternatives but not the other.

The economic argument should not necessarily be dominant. The Property Council (formerly BOMA, the Building Owners and Managers Association) of Australia found that only 9% of those surveyed believe that environmental and energy issues are irrelevant to their business, and for the others the main reasons for implementing environmental and energy management policies are

	%
Community relations	39
Competitiveness	24
Market opportunities	23
Shareholder pressure	5
It is irrelevant	9

On the other hand, tenants are keen to have better lighting and thermal conditions (for increased productivity) and to reduce energy consumption (thus operating costs).

Some 39% of those surveyed believe that community relations and social issues are important for policy-making. Indeed, Schumacher already in 1973 gave the sub-title '*A study of economics as if people mattered*' to his book, *Small is Beautiful*.

The financial balance of such cost/benefit comparisons is often referred to as the 'bottom line'. Recently a new term has been introduced: the 'triple bottom line'. This means an assessment of *social value* and *eco-efficiency* in addition to the conventional economic/financial balance (Fig. 4.64).

Australian energy flows, 2008–09
units: petajoules

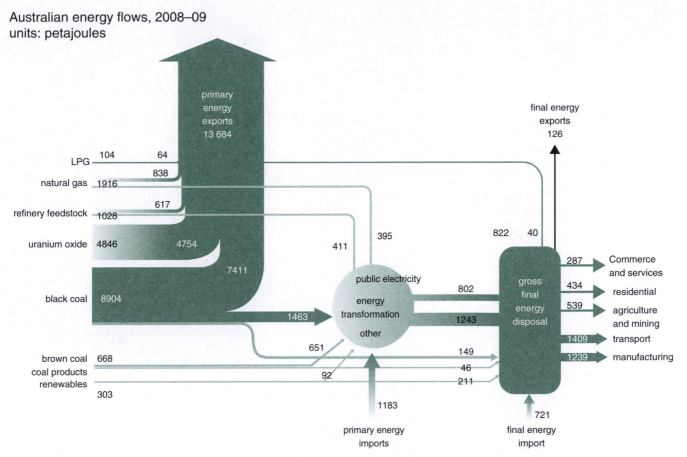

4.64

A good example of showing energy flows in the national economy
(a Sankey diagram)

DATA SHEETS AND METHOD SHEETS (RESOURCES)

DATA SHEETS

METHOD SHEETS

DATA SHEET D.4.1

Energy intensity of transportation and CO_2 emissions

Passenger transport

Air	1.2–1.6 kWh
Car, highway	0.6–0.7
Car, urban	1.4–1.6
Motorcycle	0.5–0.8
Bus, highway	0.08–0.3
Bus, urban	0.6–0.8
Tram, light rail	0.05–0.2

Goods transport

Light commercial (vans)	0.6–1.5 kWh
Medium trucks (3–5 tonnes)	1.3
Heavy trucks (long distance)	0.5–0.8
Railway trains	0.1–0.2
Shipping	0.1–0.15

measured in kWh per person-km (p.km) or per tonne-km (t.km)

CO_2 emissions due to energy use

form of supply	CO_2 kg/kWh
Electricity (average)*	0.72
Solid fuel	0.34
Oil	0.29
Gas	0.21

Global warming potential of gases

CO_2	1
Methane (CH_4)	21
Nitrous oxide	290
CFC11	1500
CFC12	4500

The EU Carbon trading system (re. Section 4.4.3, p. 333)

The EU operates a 'cap and trade' system. Factories, electricity generating stations and other major polluters are given a 'cap' – the maximum of permitted emissions. Within this they receive 'emission allowances' (EUA). These are tradable. Each year they have to surrender EUAs equal to their total emissions. If they save energy and reduce their emissions, they can sell their surplus EUAs. If they exceed their allocated caps, they have to produce EUAs to cover that excess. Otherwise they have to pay heavy fines. The caps allocated are reviewed (reduced) annually

The system operates in 30 countries (27 members + Iceland, Norway and Lichtenstein).

---

* For details see Table 4.7: function of mode of generation

DATA SHEET D.4.2

Annual energy intensity in kWh/(m²y) for various building types*

Schools	nursery	370–430
	primary, no pool	180–240
	primary, with pool	230–310
	secondary, no pool	190–240
	secondary, with pool	250–310
	secondary, with sports centre	250–280
	special, non-residential	250–340
	special, residential	380–500
	colleges	230–280
	universities	325–355
Hospitality	restaurants	410–430
	pubs	340–470
	fast-food outlets	1450–1750
	motorway service areas	880–1200
	hotel, small	240–330
	hotel, medium size	310–420
	hotel, large	290–420
Shops	department stores	520–620
	non-food shops	280–320
	small food shops, general	510–580
	small fruit & vegetable shops	400–450
	variety stores	720–830
	supermarkets	1070–1270
	supermarket with bakery	1130–1350
	banks	180–240
Offices	small, < 2000 m², naturally ventilated	200–250
	large, > 2000 m², naturally ventilated	230–290
	small, < 2000 m², air conditioned	220–310
	large, > 2000 m², air conditioned	250–419
	computer rooms	340–480
Sports	sports centre, no pool	200–340
	sports centre, with pool	570–840
	swimming pool	1050–1390
Public bldgs.	library	200–280
	museum, art gallery	220–310
	theatre	600–900
	cinema	650–780

* 'fair performance range', after CIBSE

Star-band limits for the Australian NatHERS rating scheme
number of stars awarded up to these limits in kWh/(m²y)

stars:	1	2	3	4	5
Darwin	242	94	133	117	103
Brisbane	80	44	33	25	17
Sydney	130	91	58	40	30
Melbourne	119	94	78	64	51
Hobart	205	129	110	86	60

Compare these with the German limits of 30–60 kWh/(m²y) for new houses, as described in Section 4.4.4.

DATA SHEET D.4.3

Environmental rating of some materials (on a 5-point scale)

(by Lawson, 1996)

The 5-point rating scale is:
1: poor, 2: fair, 3: good, 4: very good and 5: excellent

Any material or product is to be rated for
seven categories or attributes, as shown below
(18 materials presented, but the method can be used for any other material).

	Raw material availability	Environmental impact	Embodied energy	Product life span	Freedom from maintenance	Product re-use potential	Material recyclability
plantation-grown sawn softwood	4	4	4	3	2	2	1
hardwood from native forests	2	2	5	4	3	4	1
wood fibre hardboard	4	4	2	3	2	1	3
medium density fibreboard (MDF)	5	4	3	3	3	3	2
particleboard (chipboard)	5	4	3	3	3	1	4
plywood	4	4	3	4	3	3	1
glued laminated timber	4	4	4	4	3	4	2
plastics (synthetic polymers)	3	2	3	4	4	1	3
stabilised earth (cement or bitumen)	4	5	4	3	3	1	5
building stone (sawn)	3	2	3	4	4	4	3
clay bricks	4	3	4	5	5	2	3
cement-concrete products	3	3	4	5	5	1	3
fibrous cement (pine fibre)	4	4	3	5	5	1	1
glass	3	3	3	5	4	3	4
steel	4	3	3	4	3	3	5
aluminium	4	1	1	5	4	2	5
copper	2	1	2	5	5	1	5
lead and zinc	2	1	2	5	5	1	5

No attempt should be made to add up these numbers.
The rating is purely qualitative and in the original no numbering is used.
It is simply a convenience or short-hand to identify the qualitative rating.

METHOD SHEET M.4.1

'Present worth' and the discounted cash-flow method

1) The question is which would I prefer: to get $100 now, or $150 in three years' time? Or in more formal terms: what is the *present worth* of $150 payable in 3 years? This can be assessed by using the compound interest expression in reverse:

an amount invested at **p**resent (P) at an annual **i**nterest rate (i) for a number of years (y) will increase to an **a**mount (A) equal to the invested amount plus the compound interest earned:

$$A = P + (1 + i)^y \qquad (1)$$

from which P can be expressed as

$$P = A \times (1 + i)^{-y} \qquad (2)$$

where P is referred to as the present worth of an amount A payable (or saved) in y years

> For example, if i = 6%
> the increased sum is
> A = 100 × (1 + 0.06)³ = 119.10
>   119.1 < 150
> the present worth of $150 is
> P = 150 × (1 + 0.06)⁻³ = 125.94
>   125.94 > 100
> Both suggest that the $150 in 3 years' time is better

2) If we have a regular annual sum (B, benefit) saved (or payable) annually, the present worth of this will be

$$P = B\frac{(1 + i)^y - 1}{i(1 + i)^y} = B\frac{1 - (1 + i)^{-y}}{i} \qquad (3)$$

the latter part of this expression is referred to as the *present worth factor*

$$F = \frac{1 - (1 + i)^{-y}}{i} \qquad (4)$$

> For example, I want to buy a solar water heater. Price: $2300, less $500 government subsidy, thus net C = $1800. This would save me annually $235 in electricity. My criterion is that it should pay for itself in 10 years (amortisation period).
> Total saving: S = 235 × 10 = 2350 thus S > C, 2350 > 1800, it is OK.
> However, at an interest rate of 8%, i = 0.08 the present worth factor would be
> $$F = \frac{1 - 1.08^{-10}}{0.08} = 6.71$$
> thus the saving is
> S = 235 × 6.71 = 1576
> thus S < C, 1576 < 1800, it is not OK

3) If a capital investment (C) results in an annual benefit (B) then the *simple pay-back period* is the number of years when the accumulated benefits become equal to the investment:

$$C = B \times y, \text{ from which } y \text{ can be expressed as } y = C / B \qquad (5)$$

Total savings:

$S = B \times F$ where and F is found from eq.4
The investment is worthwhile if S > C

4) In an inflationary climate the anticipated rate of annual inflation (r) must be taken into account. Eq. 4 will become

$$F' = \frac{1}{i - r}\left[1 - \left(\frac{1 + r}{1 + i}\right)^y\right] \qquad (6)$$

> If the annual inflation is taken into account, and the rate is rate is r = 0.04
> $$F' = \frac{1}{0.04}\left[1 - \left(\frac{1.04}{1.08}\right)^{10}\right] = 7.85$$
> S = 235 × 7.85 = 1844.75
> thus S > C, 1844.75 > 1800, it is OK (marginally)

but if inflation will cause the annual benefit, B, (or operating cost) itself also to increase, then

$$F'' = \frac{1 + r}{i - r}\left[1 - \left(\frac{1 + r}{1 + i}\right)^y\right] \qquad (7)$$

> if the inflationary increase of the annual benefit is also taken into account then
> $$F'' = \frac{1.04}{0.04}\left[1 - \left(\frac{1.04}{1.08}\right)^{10}\right] = 8.17$$
> S = 235 × 8.17 = 1920
> thus S > C, 1920 > 1800, it is OK the investment is well worth it

METHOD SHEET M.4.2

Performance of flat plate solar collectors

If the operation of any system is to be understood, the following three steps are suggested:

1 describe the system
2 identify the mechanisms involved in its operation
3 analyse the operation in order to construct a model of the system.

The flat plate solar water heater collector is used as an example.

1) The collector consists of an absorber plate (usually of copper), with a black surface and thermally coupled waterways (pipes); insulation to the back and edges, with a transparent cover ((usually glass) and some sort of casing.

2) The incident solar radiation is absorbed by the plate, which is thus heated and the heat is transferred to the fluid circulating in the pipes. The insulation of back and edges prevents (reduces) heat loss and the glass cover prevents convective losses from the absorber.

3) G is the global solar irradiance (W/m²)

$Qs = A.G$ is the solar heat input (W) if A is the collector aperture area

      $A.G.\tau$ is the radiation transmitted by the glass of τ transmittance

      $A.G\,\tau\alpha$ is the heat absorbed by the plate of α absorptance

$Qin = A\,G\,F\,\tau\,\alpha$ is the heat transmitted into the fluid (F = heat removal factor)

If mr is the mass flow rate of the fluid (kg/s) and the fluid temperature increase from inlet to outlet is $T_{out} - T_{in}$, then the useful heat produced is

$Quse = mr\,(T_{out} - T_{in})\,c_p$

      where c_p is the specific heat of the fluid; for water $c_p = 4187$ J/kg.K
      (1.16 Wh/kg.K)
      dimensionally: kg/s × K × J/kg.K, by cancellations: J/s = W

The collector efficiency will be

$$\eta = \frac{Quse}{Qin} = \frac{mr(T_{out} - T_{in})\,c_p}{A\,G}$$

Analytically: the heat input into the fluid is reduced by losses caused by the temperature difference between fluid Tf and outdoor air temperature Ta. Logically the mean fluid temperature should be taken, as $Tf = (T_{in} + T_{out})/2$, then the loss would be $U'(Tf - Ta)$, but as T_{out} (thus Tf) are unknown the difference can be taken as $\Delta T = (T_{in} - Ta)$, and the loss will be modified by F, thus $Qloss = F\,A\,U'\,\Delta T$

The useful collection will be

$Quse = A\,G\,F\,(\tau\,\alpha) - F\,A\,U'\,\Delta T = A\,F\,[G\,(\tau\,\alpha) - U'\,\Delta T]$

For a particular collector η can be determined by testing. The main determinant of η is the term $\Delta T/G$

    If many test points (values of η) are plotted as a function of $\Delta T/G$, a linear function can be fitted, in the form of y = a – b x, here

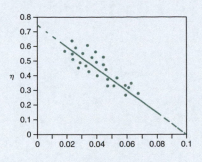

Efficiency as a function of ΔT/G data points and regression:

here: $\eta = 0.75 - 7.5\ (\Delta T/G)$

METHOD SHEET M.4.2 (continued)

$$\eta = F - B\ (\Delta T/G)$$

where F is the *no-loss efficiency*, when U' = 0, (the Y-axis intercept) and B is the slope coefficient (U')

when $\eta = 0$, i.e. $F = B\ (\Delta T/G)$

we get the *stagnation temperature* (the X-axis intercept)

The 'collector constants' F and B can thus be determined by testing and can then be used in simulation of collector performance under any conditions of temperature and irradiance.

The performance is improved if:

- τ is increased
- α_{solar} is increased while $\varepsilon_{<100°C}$ is reduced ('low-e' selective surface)
- U' is reduced (lower temperature reduces the ΔT, improves collection efficiency.

FURTHER READING

HEAT

Banham, R (1969): *Architecture of the well-tempered environment*. The Architectural Press, London.

Bedford, T (1936): *Warmth factor in comfort at work*. Med. Res. Council, Report 76. HMSO, London.

Diesendorf, M (2007): *Greenhouse solutions with sustainable energy*. University of NSW Press, Sydney.

Drysdale, J W ([1952] 1975): *Designing houses for Australian climates*. Bulletin 6, CEBS, Sydney (Commonwealth Experimental Building Station).

Egan, M D (1975): *Concepts in thermal comfort*. Prentice-Hall, Englewood Cliffs, New Jersey.

Evans, M N (1980): *Housing, climate and comfort*. The Architectural Press, London.

Fanger, P O (1970): *Thermal comfort*. Danish Technical Press, Copenhagen.

Flohn, H G. (1969): *Climate and weather* trans. Walden, D E. Weidenfeld & Nicholson, London.

Gagge, A P, Gonzalez, R R & Nishi, Y (1974): Physiological and physical factors governing man's thermal comfort and heat tolerance. *Build International*, 7: 305–331.

Geiger, R (1957): *The climate near the ground*. Harvard University Press, Cambridge, MA.

Givoni, B (1969): *Man, climate and architecture*. Van Nostrand Reinhold, New York.

Givoni, B (1994): *Passive and low energy cooling of buildings*. Van Nostrand Reinhold, New York.

Griffiths, I (1990): *Thermal comfort studies in buildings with passive solar features*. Report to EC. ENS35090. UK.

Houghten, F C & Yagloglou, C P (1923): Determination of comfort zone, *Trans. Am. Soc. Heat. Vent. Engs.* 29: 361.

Houghton, J T *et al.* (eds) (1990): *Climate change: The IPCC Scientific Assessment.* Cambridge University Press, Cambridge.

Humphreys, M (1978): Outdoor temperatures and comfort indoors. *Bldg. Res & Practice* 6(2): 92–105.

Hutcheson, F (1725): *An inquiry into the original of our ideas of beauty and virtue.* Treatise 2, 3: 8.

Koenigsberger, O H, Ingersoll, T G, Mayhew, A & Szokolay, S V (1973): *Manual of tropical housing and building: pt.1: Climatic design.* Longman, London.

Muncey, R W R (1979): *Heat transfer calculations for buildings.* Applied Science Publishers, London.

Nicol, F & Roaf, S (1996): Pioneering new indoor temperature standards: the Pakistan project. *Energy and Buildings*, 23: 169–174.

Olgyay, V (1963): *Design with climate: Bioclimatic approach to architectural regionalism.* Princeton University Press, Princeton, NJ.

Saini, B S (1973): *Building environment: An illustrated analysis of problems in hot dry lands.* Angus and Robertson, Sydney.

Threlkeld, J L (1970): *Thermal environmental engineering.* Prentice-Hall, Englewood Cliffs, NJ.

Vernon, H M & Warner, C G (1932): The influence of humidity of the air on capacity of work at high temperatures, *J. of Hygiene, Camb.* 32: 431.

Watson, D & Labbs, J (1983): *Climatic design.* McGraw-Hill, New York.

Yagloglou, C P (1927): The comfort zone for man. *Journal of Industrial Hygiene* 9: 251.

LIGHT

Baker, N & Steemers, K (1999): *Daylight design of buildings.* James & James, London.

Hopkinson, R G, Petherbridge, P & Longmore, J (1966): *Daylighting.* Heinemann, London.

Prichard, M D W (1969): *Lighting.* Longman. London.

Robledo, L *et al.* (1999): Natural light and daylighting research at the School of Architecture, Madrid, in Szokolay, S V (ed.) *Sustaining the Future.* (2 vols) PLEA'99 conference.

Yamaguchi, T. (1983): Windows for passive buildings and daylighting. PhD thesis, University of Queensland.

SOUND

Lawrence, A (1970): *Architectural acoustics*. Elsevier Applied Science, London.

Lang, Marshall (2006): *Architectural acoustics*. Elsevier Applied Science, Amsterdam.

Moore, J E (1961): *Design for good acoustics*. Architectural Press, London.

Moore, J E (1966): *Design for noise reduction*. Architectural Press, London.

Rodda, M (1967): *Noise and society*. Oliver & Boyd. Edinburgh.

Smith, B J (1971): *Acoustics*. Longman, London.

RESOURCES

Allsop, B (1972): *Ecological morality*. Frederick Muller, London.

Anluk, D et al. (1995): *The handbook of sustainable building*. James & James, London.

Beggs, C (2002): *Energy management, supply and conservation*. Butterworth Heinemann, Oxford.

Bockris, J O'M (1974): *The solar hydrogen alternative*. Architectural Press, London.

Burt, W *et al*. (1969): *Windows and environment*. Pilkington/McCorquondale, Newton-le-Willows.

Bayles, M D (1989): *Professional ethics*. Wadsworth, Belmont, CA.

Clarke, J A (2001): *Energy simulation in building design*. Adam Hilger, Bristol.

Edwards, B (1998): *Sustainable architecture, European directives and building design*. Architectural Press, Oxford.

Farmer, J (1999): *Green shift*. Architectural Press, Oxford.

Gunn, A S & Vesilind, P A (1986): *Environmental ethics for engineers*. Lewis Publishers, Chelsea, Michigan.

Mackenzie, D (1991): *Green design: design for the environment*. Laurence King, London.

Meadows, D H & Meadows, D L (1972): *The limits to growth*. Club of Rome, Potomac Associates/Earth Island Ltd, London.

Roaf, S & Hancock, M (eds) (1992): *Energy efficient building: a design guide*. Blackwell, Oxford.

Smith, P F & Pitts, A (1997): *Concepts in practice: energy, building for the third millennium*. Batsford, London.

UN World Commission on Environment and Development (1987): *Our common future* (The Brundtland Report). Oxford University Press, Oxford.

Ward, B & Dubos, R (1972): *Only one earth: the care and maintenance of a small planet*. Penguin, Harmondsworth.

GENERAL

Baird, G (2010): *Sustainable buildings in practice*. Routledge, London.

Brophy, V & Lewis, J O (2011): *A green Vitruvius: principles and practice of sustainable architectural design*. Earthscan, London.

Cowan, H J (ed.) (1991): *Handbook of architectural technology*. Van Nostrand Reinhold, New York.

Duffie, J A & Beckman, W A (1980): *Solar engineering of thermal processes*. John Wiley, New York.

Johnson, S *et al.* (1993): *Greener buildings, environmental impact of property*. Macmillan, Basingstoke.

Papanek, V (1995): *The green imperative: ecology and ethics in design and architecture*. Thames & Hudson, London.

Roaf, S, Fuentes, M, & Thomas, S (2001): *Ecohouse: a design guide*. Architectural Press, Oxford.

Schumacher, E F ([1973] 1988): *Small is beautiful: a study of economics as if people mattered*. Abacus/Penguin, London.

Senosiain, J (2003): *Bio-Architecture*. Elsevier/Architectural Press, Oxford.

Slessor, C (1997): *Eco-Tech: sustainable architecture and high technology*. Thames and Hudson, London.

Smith, P (2001): *Architecture in a climate of change*. Architectural Press, Oxford.

Szokolay S V (ed.) (1999): Sustaining the future: energy – ecology – architecture. *Proc. PLEA'99 Conf. PLEA/ Dept.of Architecture*. Uni.of Queensland. Brisbane

Vale, B & Vale, R (1991): *Green architecture: design for a sustainable future*. Thames & Hudson, London.

BIBLIOGRAPHY

INTRODUCTION

Banham, R (1969): *Architecture of the well-tempered environment.* Architectural Press, London.

Beggs, C (2002): *Energy management, supply and conservation.* Butterworth Heinemann, Oxford.

Brophy, V & Lewis, J O (2011): *A green Vitruvius: principles and practice of sustainable architectural design.* Earthscan, London.

Farmer, J (1999): *Green shift.* Architectural Press, Oxford.

Olgyay, V (1963): *Design with climate: bioclimatic approach to architectural regionalism.* Princeton University Press, Princeton, NJ.

Roaf, S, Fuentes, M, & Thomas, S (2001): *Ecohouse: a design guide.* Architectural Press, Oxford.

Smith, P (2001): *Architecture in a climate of change.* Architectural Press, Oxford.

Vale, B & Vale, R (1991): *Green architecture: design for a sustainable future.* Thames & Hudson, London.

HEAT

ASHRAE (1997): *ASHRAE Handbook of Fundamentals.* American Society of Heating, Refrigerating and Air-Conditioning Engineers, Inc., Atlanta, GA.

Atkinson, G A (1954): Tropical architecture and building standards. *Proc. 1953 Conf. on Tropical Architecture.* Architectural Association, London.

Auliciems, A (1981): Towards a psycho-physiological model of thermal perception. *Int. J. of Biometeorology* 25: 109–122.

Australia Bureau of Meteorology (1988): *Climatic averages, Australia,* Bureau of Meteorology, Canberra.

Bedford, T (1936): *Warmth factor in comfort at work*. Med. Res. Council, Report 76. HMSO, London.

CIBSE (1999): *Guide A: environmental design*. Chartered Institute of Building Services Engineers, The Yale Press.

Danter, E (1960): Periodic heat flow characteristics of simple walls and roofs. *J. IHVE*, July: 136–146.

DeDear, R J, Brager, G & Cooper, D (1997): *Developing an adaptive model of thermal comfort and preference*. Final report, ASHRAE RP-884, Macquarie University.

Du Bois, D & Du Bois, E F (1916): A formula to estimate approximate (body) surface area if weight and height are known. *Archives of Internal Medicine*, 17: 863–871.

Gagge, A P, Fobelets, A P & Berglund, L G (1986): A standard predictive index of human response to the thermal env. *ASHRAE Trans*. 92(2): 709–731.

Gagge, A P, Gonzalez, R R & Nishi, Y (1974): Physiological and physical factors governing man's thermal comfort and heat tolerance. *Build International*, 7: 305–331.

Griffiths, I (1990): *Thermal comfort studies in buildings with passive solar features*. Report to EC. ENS35090. UK.

Hong, T, Chou, S K and Bong, T Y (2000): Building simulation: an overview of developments and information sources. *Building & Environment*, 35: 347–361.

Humphreys, M (1978): Outdoor temperatures and comfort indoors. *Bldg. Res & Practice* 6(2): 92–105.

Köppen, W & Geiger, R (1936): *Handbuch der Klimatologie*, Borntrager, Berlin.

Maslow, A H (1948): Higher and lower needs. *J of Psychology*, 25: 433–436.

Milbank, N O & Harrington-Lynn, J (1974): *Thermal response and the admittance procedure*. BRE. CP 61/74, Building Research Establishment, Garston.

Nicol, F & Roaf, S (1996): Pioneering new indoor temperature standards: the Pakistan project. *Energy and Buildings*, 23: 169–174.

Olgyay, V (1953): *Bioclimatic approach to architecture*. Bldg. Res. Adv. Board, Conf. Report No.5. National Research Council, Washington, DC.

Petherbridge, P (1974): *Limiting the temperatures in naturally ventilated buildings in warm climates*. BRE, CP 7/74, Building Research Establishment, Garston.

Phillips, R O (1948): *Sunshine and shade in Australia*. TS 23, also Bulletin 8, 1963, CEBS, Sydney, Commonwealth Experimental Building Station, Sydney.

Szokolay S V (1980): *Environmental science handbook for architects*. Longman/Construction Press, Lancaster.

Szokolay, S V (1995): *Thermal design of buildings*. RAIA, Red Hill, ACT.

Thayer, R L (1981): *Solar access: it's the law*. Institute of Government Affairs, Institute of Ecology, University of California, Davis, Env. Quality series 34.

LIGHT

Baker, N & Steemers, K (1995): *The LT method*. RIBA/Martin Centre, Cambridge.

I.E.S. (The Illuminating Engineering Society) (1967): *Evaluation of discomfort glare: the glare index system*. Technical Report No. 10. The Society. London.

Longmore, J (1968): *BRS daylight protractors*. Bldg. Res. Station, HMSO, London.

Paix, D ([1962] 1982): *The design of buildings for daylighting*. Bulletin No. 7, Experimental Building Station, AGPS, Canberra.

Robbins, C L (1986): *Daylighting, design and analysis*. Van Nostrand Reinhold, New York.

SOUND

Humphreys, H R & Melluish, D J (1971): *Sound insulation in buildings*. HMSO, London.

Parkin, P H & Humphreys, H R (1958): *Acoustics, noise and buildings*. Faber & Faber, London.

Sabine, W C (1922): *Collected papers*. Harvard University Press, Cambridge, MA.

Smith, B J (1971): *Acoustics*. Longmans. London.

Sommer, R (1969): *Personal space: the behavioural basis of design*. Prentice-Hall, Englewood Cliffs, NJ.

RESOURCES

Berge, B (2001): *Ecology of building materials*. Architectural Press, Oxford.

Boyle, G (ed.) (1996): *Renewable energy; power for a sustainable future*. The Open University, with Oxford University Press, Oxford.

Diesendorf, M (2007): *Greenhouse solutions with sustainable energy*. University of NSW Press, Sydney.

Hutcheson, F (1725): *An inquiry into the original of our ideas of beauty and virtue*. Treatise 2, 3: 8.

Keating, M (1993) *Agenda for change: a plain language version of Agenda 21 and other Rio agreements*, Centre for Our Common Future, Geneva.

Knowles, R I (1977): Solar energy, building and the law. *J. of Architectural Education*, Feb.

Lawson, B L (1996): *Building materials, energy and the environment*. RAIA, Canberra.

Meadows, D H & Meadows, D L (1972): *The limits to growth*. Club of Rome, Potomac Associates/Earth Island Ltd, London.

Radford, A & Williamson, T (2002): What is sustainable architecture? in *Proc. ANZAScA 2002 conf*. ANZ Arch. Science Assoc., Deakin University Geelong.

Sommer, R (1969): *Personal space: the behavioural basis of design*. Prentice-Hall, Englewood Cliffs, NJ.

Steele, J (1997): *Sustainable architecture: principles, paradigms and case studies*. McGraw-Hill, New York.

Szokolay, S V (1992): *Architecture and climate change*. RAIA, Red Hill, Canberra.

Thayer, R L (1981): *Solar access: it's the law*. Institute of Government Affairs, Institute of Ecology, University of California, Davis, Env. Quality series 34.

UN World Commission on Environment and Development (1987): *Our common future*. (The Brundtland Report). Oxford University Press, Oxford.

Wackernagel, M, Rees, W E & Testernal, P (1997): *Our ecological footprint: human impact on the Earth*. New Society Publishers, Vancouver.

INDEX